MILITANT AND TRIUMPHANT

Cardinal William Henry O'Connell
Photo: Archives, Archdiocese of Boston

Militant and Triumphant

William Henry O'Connell and the Catholic Church in Boston, 1859–1944

James M. O'Toole

UNIVERSITY OF NOTRE DAME PRESS
NOTRE DAME   LONDON

Library of Congress Cataloging-in-Publication Data

O'Toole, James M.
    Militant and triumphant : William Henry O'Connell and the Catholic
church in Boston, 1859–1944 / James M. O'Toole.
        p.   cm.
    Includes bibliographical references and index.
    ISBN 0-268-01393-4
    1. O'Connell, William, 1859–1944. 2. Catholic Church–
–Massachusetts—Boston—Bishops—Biography. 3. Catholic Church–
–Massachusetts—Boston—History. 4. Boston (Mass.)—Church history.
    I. Title.
BX4705.03086 1992
282'.092—dc20   91-50570
[B]   CIP

Manufactured in the United States of America

CONTENTS

ACKNOWLEDGMENTS

CARDINAL O'CONNELL AND I have known each other for many years now. In getting to know him, I have come to know and appreciate many other people as well, people whose assistance made it possible to complete this work. A brief word of thanks to some of them is not sufficient repayment, but I hope they will accept my gratitude for their advice and help.

I must begin with the archivists and librarians who preserve, organize, and make available the original sources on which this or any other work of history must be based. Foremost among them for me are the successive staff members of the Archives of the Archdiocese of Boston. Over the years, Timothy Meagher, Philip Eppard, Ronald Patkus, and Phyllis Danehy put up with my constant visits and phone calls. They indulged my inclination to talk about O'Connell at the least provocation. They performed their archival duties with solid professionalism and good grace, making theirs the most pleasant place I have ever conducted research—or ever expect to. The curators of other collections have likewise left me in their debt: Sister Felicitas Powers, R.S.M., former Archivist of the Archdiocese of Baltimore; Father John Bowen, S.S., of the Sulpician Archives Baltimore; Monsignor Charles Burns and Claudio de Domenicis of the Vatican Archives; and Father Laurence McGrath, Librarian of Saint John's Seminary, Brighton.

A number of friends have read portions, drafts, and earlier versions of this work, and their suggestions improved it immeasurably. Since some of it started life as a doctoral dissertation, I must express appreciation for the direction and encouragement of Professor Thomas O'Connor and Father James Hennesey, S.J. Thomas Brown gave sage advice on how to convert a thesis into a book to a cocky young colleague who thought he did not have to worry about that. Father William Wolkovich-Valkavičius shared with me his prodigious knowledge about Catholic ethnic groups and saved me from many embarrassments.

Let me acknowledge a few final debts. Michael T. K. Sullivan provided access to certain materials still in the possession and in the memory of the O'Connell family. Besides that help, his greatest gift to me was his insistence that his great-granduncle's story be told fairly and fully. James J. Connolly, my research assistant at the University of Massachusetts-Boston, read forty years of the *Pilot* and carried out other unexciting but necessary tasks with energy and care: that he still spoke to me after such treatment is a testament to his own good character. Lois Beattie and Barbara McLaughlin typed (or "input," as we must now say) portions of the manuscript: neither one developed much affection for the cardinal, I am afraid, but I am glad they chose not to take that out on the author. Finally, I end as I should have begun: by thanking my parents, George A. O'Toole and Mildred B. O'Toole, for their love and support, for their never nagging me to find a "real" job, and for providing the sure and loving anchor of my life.

INTRODUCTION

In the fall of 1927 Cardinal William Henry O'Connell, the Roman Catholic archbishop of Boston, filled his leisure moments by reading history. "While my position has forced me, if I may say so, to have more to do with making history than with writing it," he would later remark with a characteristic sense of himself, "I have always been delighted to read it and to meditate upon it. . . . Certainly, history is, for sheer human interest, the most fascinating of studies." Organized Catholicism in the United States was not yet 150 years old, and for a person such as O'Connell, who was approaching his seventieth birthday, some combination of scholarly study and personal memory was sufficient to span the entire historical phenomenon. In particular during that unusually mild autumn, O'Connell was reading a two-volume biography of Bishop John England written by Father Peter Guilday of the Catholic University of America, the premier Catholic historian of his generation.[1]

England, the first bishop of Charleston, South Carolina, had been a controversial figure in his own time, and he remained so almost a century later. An Irish immigrant who had embraced the American republican spirit in the era of Andrew Jackson's common man, England had sought to adapt his ancient church to its New World surroundings, even permitting the active participation of the laity. These policies had brought him opposition and contention, much of it from other members of the hierarchy. Cardinal O'Connell, like the earlier bishop no stranger to controversy, concluded as he read the life that England's "clerical enemies . . . hated him because he was so big. . . . Here was a man of extraordinary ability," O'Connell went on, thinking perhaps about himself as much as the historical character, "a noble soul of endless devotion and zeal, and all his life he was harassed and impeded right and left, not by Turks, infidels and Jews, but by priests and unfortunately even Bishops." The spectacle was a sad one, and although he praised

1

Guilday's study, O'Connell mused aloud whether such historical work had any lasting value. "But now, dear Doctor," he wrote the author, "I often ask myself how much permanent good comes out of digging up the bones of dead Bishops, spending years in musty archives to find in the end such sordid quarrels, such mean animosities, such contemptible intrigues. . . . Is all this edifying to the public? I wonder."[2]

What, indeed, is the good of digging up the bones of dead bishops? Why should anyone undertake either to write or to read the biography of a bishop such as Cardinal O'Connell almost fifty years after his death? What can an account of his life possibly have to say to the contemporary world? For one thing, history is a very different enterprise today from what it was in Peter Guilday's time. Historians are now inclined to look at the past from the bottom up rather than from the top down. Leaders and elite groups may still have their roles to play, but of greater interest are the lives of average men and women. In such circumstances, would not a wide-ranging social history of religion be more appropriate? Has historical fashion not made obsolete the study of one white male, a man whose own beliefs would have argued that because of his office he was fundamentally different from other people?

In the same way, how can a study that hopes to shed light on a large, modern urban area be focused so precisely on one man from one religious tradition? Even if the reader indulges an author's specialty, has the age of denominational narrowness not, thankfully, passed? Must not any work in American religious history be more broadly based? In Peter Guilday's generation the only people who would read a work of Catholic history (aside from a handful of scholars) were other Catholics. Each denomination had its own history, guarded by its own historians and unlikely to interest outsiders. Today, historians must look to a wider audience by describing the impact of religious belief and practice on American life as a whole, especially American public life.

Though on the face of things it appears to be hopelessly narrow and old-fashioned, the story of the life of one Catholic bishop can indeed contribute to an understanding of broader themes. The biographical form remains useful because it must necessarily address the tension between the one and the many. The biography's subject may be a single individual, but that person inevitably influences and is influenced by the other actors on the historical stage. A complex relationship binds the leader and the led, and the dynamics of that relationship are rooted in the public culture—the ideology and symbolism—of leadership, whether in the religious or secular sphere. What was it that made certain leaders influential in their own times and on their own terms? What was it in the conditions and expectations of their people that produced the leaders and symbols of particular periods? Properly conducted, a biography can begin to answer these questions too.

If they are to do so, however, modern historians must study the lives of bishops as they really were. Like Cromwell, we have come to expect that both painters and biographers will present their subjects "warts and all," although earlier chroniclers of American Catholic bishops left this admonition largely unheeded. Their work too often veered into the realm of hagiography—the lives of the saints—glossing over a great deal and fundamentally altering the nature of the actual lived experience. In those accounts everyone was good and getting better; everyone was holy and getting holier. All problems were overcome by an unfailing combination of vision, determination, ability, and divine guidance. Progress was steady, never in doubt, and the Great Man was the guarantor of success.

Along the way, insufficient attention was paid to many important subjects. The bishop's private life and interior spirituality were left unexamined. Either that private character was a clear, polished mirror of his outward rectitude, or it failed to measure up to his public persona and therefore deserved to be disregarded. There was a persistent fear that scandal might be given to the laity, who were assumed to be naive and immature in such matters, needing in effect to be protected from their history. Absent too was any consideration of the day-to-day management of the complex organizations that American churches had become in the modern era. The man of God was expected to be adept at manipulating the things of this world, but he was not to be seen actually doing it. A Victorian sense of propriety enveloped the whole historical effort, and anything negative was carefully excised for fear of not being, in O'Connell's own phrase, "edifying to the public."

As O'Connell's story amply demonstrates, history, like life itself, is not so simple. A realistic approach to a bishop's life must look at trouble as well as triumph, at limitation as well as expansion, and failure as well as success. It cannot avert its glance from subjects that show human frailty if it hopes to be taken seriously when it describes others that reveal human nobility and achievement. It must account for moral failure as well as probity. It must consider disagreement and dissension, even among the "faithful" who still accepted the bishop as their leader while at the same time pressing for goals that were different from his or even at odds with them. The picture cannot be sketched in black and white only—there is plenty of gray, and many other colors besides, and the biographer, like the painter, must use them all. Little advantage is gained by merely replacing all the white with black, yielding to the easy temptation to knock down previously exalted figures simply because they offer such tempting targets. Reputations and pious myths may not always survive scrutiny, of course, as Lord Acton, the great nineteenth century Catholic pessimist, predicted. "What archives reveal," said Acton, "is the wickedness of men. . . . The one constant result is to show that people are worse than their reputation."[3] Still, if it is to represent the past accurately, episcopal biography must be balanced and fair, but it must also be complete and unsentimental.

Who was William Henry O'Connell and why is he a candidate for this kind of study? On the grounds of sheer longevity alone he is noteworthy, for he lived through most of the events that have shaped modern American life. He was born on the eve of the Civil War and died near the close of World War II. He lived through the Great Depression, America's emergence as an international power, and the arrival of automobiles, electricity, and routine travel through the air. He was a big man in an age of big men, an era that is just now passing beyond the reach of living memory. Recovering his story with all its drama and richness therefore has an innate appeal.

For the church in which he found his vocation, his years were marked by changes that upset centuries of stability. In 1870, when O'Connell was a boy of ten, the pope had his temporal kingdom in central Italy forcibly taken away from him. Concurrently, he achieved spiritual supremacy by being proclaimed infallible in matters of faith, a direct channel to the Holy Trinity. During the remainder of O'Connell's life, the papacy, which only a few decades before had seemed on the brink of extinction, expanded its control over Catholicism worldwide, seeking in every country the aid of churchmen willing to be the agents of its expanding influence. William O'Connell was such a man for the Catholic church in America, but not everyone welcomed the standard of Roman loyalty as readily as he. He faced lasting opposition from churchmen who were not afraid to resort to the quarrels, animosities, and intrigues he had complained of in Bishop England's case, and for O'Connell's part he enthusiastically responded in kind. Still, in large measure it was O'Connell who set the terms of debate: American Catholics either had to accept his position wholeheartedly or challenge it cautiously. The influence of that division endures to this day.

The place of Catholics in Boston society was also changing dramatically. Catholics had come to Massachusetts in the previous century as a despised and suspect immigrant minority, but by O'Connell's adult years they were the majority. In politics they swept all opponents before them, seizing control of the commonwealth's major cities and its state government as well. In the world of affairs they were also making their mark, rising increasingly to influential professional positions. Boston had become the foremost Catholic city in the nation, and the cardinal himself coined the epigram that summarized the change: "the Puritan has passed," he said, "the Catholic remains." As the head of this rising political, social, and religious force, O'Connell emerged as a public figure, an authority recognized by the people at large, not just the members of his own flock. His influence was not narrowly denominational but broadly moral. He helped define standards for the community as a whole, upholding traditional values against the onslaughts of the modern world, defending stable truths in a time of relativity and change.

In the process he helped determine both the content and the style of early twentieth-century American Catholicism. O'Connell's church was, as the ancient formulary had it, both militant and triumphant. It turned a combative face toward the secular world and prepared for battle against what O'Connell's newspaper would identify shortly after his death as "all of the polite lusts which our society condones—but which God's law has never ceased to forbid." Metaphors of warfare and strife came naturally to O'Connell and the Catholics of his generation. He took for granted the notion that the church would be more or less constantly at odds with the modern world, and he prayed for strength in the battle. What is more, he believed that steadfastness would guarantee victory, that militance would bring triumph. "We shall compel peace terms" from the world, he wrote confidently in 1917.[4] Victory was neither swift nor total, and indeed barely twenty years after O'Connell's death the Catholic church would remake itself in a very different image—this one more at ease with the modern world—at the Second Vatican Council. If the church today seems far from the one he knew, he was nonetheless instrumental in creating that unified and simple world we have now lost.

O'Connell not only accepted an expanded definition of his role in church and society, he embraced it. He lived in an intentionally grand and relentlessly public manner. He was "the ideal of what a prince of the Church should be," as the Boston writer Henry Morton Robinson said of the thinly disguised O'Connell character in his novel, *The Cardinal*. In the age of emerging mass journalism, O'Connell was consistently "good ink," and he learned early how to use the press to construct and reinforce his image as a central player in the public drama. His style is outmoded and faintly offensive today: even immensely powerful personages are not supposed to be quite so full of themselves as he often appeared. To a community eager for self-assertion after years of persecution (both real and perceived), however, such a style was welcome. The most domineering of a generation of American Catholic bishops who sought this wider impact, O'Connell never shied away from visibility. Like the president, the governor, or the mayor, what he had to say on any subject was news simply because he said it.[5]

In this way O'Connell was able to cross the barrier between actual leadership and symbolic leadership. He was stern and imposing, carrying himself rigidly erect, never really loved or even lovable in a way that some other churchmen were. Despite this apparent aloofness, two generations and more of Boston's Catholics accepted him as the one who embodied their church. They found that they could live vicariously through him, sharing in the reflected glory when his counsel was sought by kings and presidents, by leaders in society, business, and the arts. Full social acceptance still lay in the future for most Catholics, but they had come far enough to covet it secretly, and O'Connell's successes were theirs as much as his. They themselves might never be on familiar terms with popes and princes, with financiers and opera singers; they might never acquire summer homes at the shore among the Yankee elite. O'Connell did all these things and more, making him both agent and avatar of their own future success.

Unfortunately for the clarity of this public projection, O'Connell was also troubled throughout his life by a darker personal side hidden from his people. Like many who had risen to high places from unpromising beginnings, he came tacitly to believe that the rules of behavior he unhesitatingly enjoined on the community did not apply to himself, simply by virtue of who and what he was. Morality was for others. With a startling ease he was able to exempt himself and those around him from ordinary accountability. His management of archdiocesan finances, for example, was capable and shrewd, and the Boston church generally prospered under his stewardship. At the same time he was too willing to confound his official position with his personal benefit, diverting money to his own use and to advancing the fortunes of his family.

More seriously, he tolerated and condoned for many years two members of his inner circle who, though ordained and active priests, were simultaneously and secretly married: one of them, his own nephew, was also actively embezzling money from the church. O'Connell's ecclesiastical enemies pounced on the scandal, feeding a steady flow of information and gossip to Rome in an effort to have him removed from office, "kicked upstairs" to an important-sounding but powerless position. Through a combination of luck and skillful maneuvering, he managed to survive the crisis, and he never faced the embarrassment of public exposure. Still, his moral obtuseness was well enough known by churchmen both above and below him that he became a hated outsider in the very institution he had sought to dominate. He retained the appearance of moral leadership but not its substance.

Throughout his long life, O'Connell was a hard man to ignore. Whether one ultimately approved or disapproved of his program, whether one knew of the private scandal or not, he was always there, difficult to get around. From historians, too, he has demanded consideration, if only because he was so successful at fixing his self-image in the opinions of others. The present study seeks to understand this admittedly difficult man and his meaning for his church and his times. It seeks to discover whether he was what we think he was, whether our image of him is myth or reality—or, more precisely, how much is myth and how much reality. New sources from many archives, no longer the "musty" repositories to which the cardinal referred, are used here for the first time. Finally, a biography of him is appropriate because, in so many places, O'Connell's life is simply a very good story, a critical ingredient for any worthwhile history. O'Connell can occasionally charm, just as he can more often anger, exasperate, and baffle, but he seldom disappoints. He may be appealing or unappealing to modern eyes, according to one's taste, but he is never dull.

1

THE PATH TO POWER:
O'CONNELL'S EARLY LIFE AND CAREER, 1859–1901

O<small>N</small> D<small>ECEMBER</small> 8, 1859, Catholics celebrated the feast of the Immaculate Conception. This holy day, officially proclaimed by Pope Pius IX just five years before, was part of a new, worldwide wave of religious devotion to Mary, the mother of Jesus. By defining as dogma that the Virgin herself, like her son, had been conceived without original sin, the pope was rebuking those within the church who relied too much on the rationalism of the Enlightenment in questions of belief, reasserting instead the centrality of the miraculous and supernatural. At the same time, he was flexing his own ecclesiastical muscles, establishing a new article of faith in part simply to prove that he could do it.[1] This addition to the church calendar was thus freighted with larger meaning, even if few ordinary Catholic laypeople fully appreciated it.

The burgeoning industrial city of Lowell, Massachusetts, was a great distance, both geographically and otherwise, from the theological and political world of Pius IX. If Rome was a city that styled itself "eternal," Lowell was by any measure a very new place, scarcely thirty years old. Still, it was already at the center of the American industrial revolution, attracting large numbers of weaving mills and an ever increasing population of immigrants, especially from Ireland and French Canada, to work in them. For one immigrant family, the feast of the Immaculate Conception in 1859 was important not for the religious occasion, but because it saw the birth of a baby. A boy, the new arrival was the youngest of eleven children born to a couple that had come to America only a few years before. In keeping with the practice of the time, the infant was taken immediately by his godparents (in this case, an aunt and an older brother) to the local parish church, Saint Peter's, where he was baptized only a few hours after birth by the pastor, Father Peter Crudden. The names conferred in baptism were William Henry; the family name, O'Connell.[2]

The route to Lowell for the O'Connell family had been a long one. This particular branch of the large clan came from County Cavan in north-central Ireland, in the parish of Lurgan near a town called Virginia. More heavily Protestant than most Irish towns, Virginia had been a center of the linen industry, and it stood on the high road that led from the hinterland into Dublin. The new baby's father, John O'Connell, had been born in Lurgan in 1809, and in January 1838 he had married a twenty-year-old named Bridget Farrelly from a nearby village. Over the next decade, six children (all of whom, like their later siblings, were lucky enough to live to adulthood) were born of the union with clockwork regularity: Julia in November 1838; John in June 1841; Bridget in February 1843; Luke in January 1845; Mary in February 1847; and Matthew in January 1849. The family was engaged in farming and, despite later claims of extensive landholdings, there is only spotty and circumstantial evidence to suggest that they were perhaps slightly better off than most of their countrymen.[3]

The Ireland of the 1840s was teetering on the brink of disaster, and Cavan was among the hardest hit of the nation's thirty-two counties. Commercial agriculture (grain production, mostly) coexisted uneasily with subsistence agriculture (largely in the form of raising potatoes), and the resulting strain on both the supply of land and the demand for labor left the county's economy in a precarious position. The once extensive linen industry was long since in decline, and when the repeated failure of the potato crop in the middle of the decade caused prices to collapse, large portions of the population plunged into destitution. Some vigilantism and rural violence occurred in Cavan and elsewhere, but, as one historian has noted, "by mid-1847 the peasants were too famished and demoralized to riot." Getting out seemed the only solution. By the early 1850s, Cavan had the highest emigration rate of all the counties in the province of Ulster, tenth highest for the country as a whole. Between then and the end of the century it was to lose more than 40 percent of its people to foreign shores.[4]

The O'Connells were a part of that great exodus. Sometime in 1850 the family left its home and boarded an emigrant ship which landed them, after the usually rigorous Atlantic crossing, in

Montreal. That they emigrated as a group, while not uncommon for the period, may indicate that they had more resources than some: they could sell off their property and travel all together, rather than crossing the ocean one by one, as poorer migrant families were forced to do. The choice of Montreal as a destination, however, dispels the notion of entirely comfortable circumstances: the fare to Canada was cheaper than that to the United States, and passengers who chose a northern destination still had a genuine need to economize. Crossing the border, the O'Connells settled first in Malone, New York, a small town roughly halfway between Ogdensburg and Plattsburgh, and another child, Simon, was born there in April 1851. John O'Connell found work as a laborer, but the family's stay in those remote and snowy reaches was brief. Bridget Farrelly had a sister living in Lowell, so the family relocated there by the time the next child, Sarah, arrived in May 1853. This proved the end of their travels, and it was there that the family was completed: Richard, born September 1855; Edward, born September 1857; and William Henry, born December 1859.[5]

Lowell at mid-century was full of great opportunity and great exploitation. In the rapidly expanding world of textile manufacturing, fortunes were being made, fortunes that were not shared with the immigrant workers, both male and female, on whose labor they depended. Still, many of the Irish found stability and happiness there. By 1855 the city had approximately 15,000 Irish immigrants and their children—almost half the total population—clustered in enclaves scattered on both sides of the Merrimack River, which provided the mills with power. Their family life was cohesive, offering many advantages in the struggle to accommodate to new surroundings. Children married late, seldom wed anyone who was not also Irish, and maintained extended family networks, often by living on the same streets as their parents and other relations.[6]

The O'Connells conformed to this pattern and achieved a measure of upward social and economic mobility. They settled in Saint Peter's parish on Gorham Street, a long road leading south out of town, and both the father and his older sons went to work. John O'Connell found employment in one or another of the city's fifty-two mills until his death in September 1865, when his youngest child was only five years old. The future churchman's brothers, however, worked at better trades. Luke took up blacksmithing, Matthew became a mason, and Simon a plasterer. Two of the younger boys learned skilled work, Richard as a tinsmith and Edward as a coppersmith. The family was also able to accumulate enough capital to buy its own houses and eventually owned four of them, renting out flats for additional income. John O'Connell, Jr., the oldest boy, had a varied career. After working in the bleachery of a mill as a teenager, he enlisted in the navy in 1862 as a "coal heaver," serving on several vessels and rising to the rank of fireman, first class, before his discharge at the conclusion of the Civil War. He was subsequently a member of the Lowell police department. For young William, with his brothers providing a measure of financial security, the future held more extended schooling than gainful employment. He attended the public schools of Lowell and then, perhaps after a brief period of work in the mills himself, he enrolled in the city's high school, from which he was graduated in 1876.[7]

At some point in his early years, the boy began to discern a religious vocation. Individual motivation in such matters is always hard to reconstruct, and there can be no telling when or how the idea of becoming a priest first occurred to him. The O'Connells were as observant as most Irish-American families in the practice of their religion, the result of a "devotional revolution" that had swept their homeland. The clergy enjoyed high prestige among recent immigrants, adding appeal to a clerical career. Not surprisingly, William and his brothers had served as altar boys. Historical work has identified the broad characteristics of the young men entering the priesthood in this period, and young Will was representative of the aggregate picture. Like him, priests came increasingly from the second generation and were drawn from families that were achieving some success. Like him, their fathers were mostly unskilled, but their brothers were moving up the economic ladder and resisting pressures to slip back down. The influence of his mother may have been decisive for O'Connell, as it had been for others, and he later recalled feeling "a gentle attraction, which seemed like nothing else but a mother's love," an attraction he subsequently concluded was "a call which could come from God alone."[8]

He was still young when he responded to this call, though not unusually so for an era in which young men typically enrolled as teenagers in a "minor" seminary to conclude their secondary education before pursuing theological studies and ordination in a "major" seminary. Since the Boston archdiocese, of which Lowell was part, did not yet have a seminary of its own, however, he had to look elsewhere for this training, and he decided, perhaps on the urging of a priest-alumnus, to enroll in Saint Charles's College in Maryland. He traveled south in September 1876 at the age of sixteen, surely his first extended time away from home, to begin his clerical studies.

Saint Charles's was conducted by priests of the Society of Saint Sulpice, originally a French group that took as its special mission the training of candidates for the priesthood. Their curriculum was a traditional one, combining studies in Latin, Greek, English, and French with such other general and useful subjects as mathematics, bookkeeping, geography, and history. Church history and Christian doctrine also received due attention. Tuition was $180 per year, and the college's firm rules requiring payment in advance would seem to indicate that the O'Connell family had a sufficient level of disposable income by this time to spend on the education of its youngest member. William O'Connell entered that fall with sixty-seven other boys from all around the country, of whom about half were eventually ordained to the priesthood. There was one other lad from Lowell who enrolled with him and six more from elsewhere in Massachusetts, but the remainder of his classmates came from as far south as Florida and as far west as Wisconsin.[9]

William O'Connell's stay at Saint Charles's was to be a truncated one of only about two years. He was never happy in Maryland. Discipline at the school was strict, certainly more so than any he had previously known, and he afterward remembered thinking that "our teachers were expecting rather too much in too short a while." More than likely he suffered from simple homesickness and a kind of culture shock at plunging into a French-dominated clerical world after the close family circle of home. He also seems to have been unpopular with his fellow students. He was stiff and awkward, and one of his teachers later recalled that, although the young O'Connell "gave no especial trouble," he was frequently the butt of jokes. Part of a group sarcastically dubbed "the Sewing Circle" by their classmates, he was upset by apparently constant jibes. On one occasion, an anonymous satirical poem about the Sewing Circle was posted on a bulletin board, and the boy from Lowell was angry when none of the school's professors took the matter as seriously as he did, refusing to track down and punish the perpetrators as he demanded. An official biographer later reported that a death in the family forced O'Connell's withdrawal, and he himself would maintain that his own health gave out; this assertion may have been true, his condition (whatever it was) aggravated by his dislike of the place and a longing for home. Whatever the reason, he failed to return to Maryland after the fall term in 1878, remaining instead in the more comfortable surroundings of Lowell.[10] His first encounter with priestly life was thus an unhappy one, but it nonetheless had enduring effects. Among other things, it left him with a life-long animus against the Sulpicians, a grudge he nursed for many years and acted on after he became archbishop of Boston.

* * *

Giving up neither his plans for education nor his desire to become a priest, O'Connell enrolled in March 1879 in Boston College. Located in the heart of the city's bustling South End district, a neighborhood that seemed always just on the verge of becoming fashionable but that never quite made it, the college had opened in 1863 as a day school for the area's Catholic boys. Combining the elements of a secondary school and a college, "B.C." was smaller than Saint Charles's, and for O'Connell the students and the surroundings were reassuringly familiar. The first baccalaureate degrees had been awarded just two years before, when there were only thirty-six students in the college division. The school's Jesuit faculty was drawn from the religious order with the longest tradition of Catholic higher education in America, and their curriculum followed the classical *ratio studiorum* that had been developed and perfected by their confreres in Europe.[11] O'Connell's attendance required of him a long train ride (about an hour each way) back and forth from Lowell every day, but this was a price he gladly paid.

If pursued from start to finish, the full track of courses at Boston College lasted seven years, beginning with "rudiments," followed by three years of grammar, and then a year each for poetry, rhetoric, and philosophy. Because of the secondary schooling already behind him, O'Connell entered the poetry class, roughly equivalent to the sophomore year of college. Together with twenty-two other students, he studied Latin (especially Cicero, Livy, and Horace), Greek (the *Iliad*, Demosthenes, and Sophocles), and English (with an emphasis on "Compositions, especially Poetical"). Mathematics (geometry and trigonometry) and French rounded out his schedule. If there had been any doubt of the wisdom of his transferring from Saint Charles's, it was dispelled by the end of the academic year, when prizes were distributed. The new student received a "premium," the second-rank award, for his overall performance, and he was "honorably mentioned" in both French and math. "I found the atmosphere of the College most genial," he remembered long afterwards, discovering that his daily journey to school "gave me a combination of study, open-air exercise, and home care which . . . was precisely the combination desired."[12]

In the next two years he maintained his good academic record while participating in extracurricular activities. In the rhetoric or junior year, the outline of courses was much the same, with increased emphasis on Latin and Greek translations, and the addition of calculus. He received an honorable mention for his general record and also served as treasurer of the student Sodality of the Immaculate Conception, a devotional club. As a senior, he really began to shine. This was the time which the curriculum devoted to philosophy and the sciences. The study of "mental philosophy" embraced logic, ethics, and metaphysics, while "natural philosophy" encompassed chemistry, physics, and mechanics. He took one of two medals for his general performance and one of three medals in each of physics and chemistry. He rose to first assistant prefect of the sodality and was corresponding secretary of the senior debating society. At graduation ceremonies in June 1881, he presented one of the six traditional student orations, with "Philosophy and Literature" as his assigned topic. His work completed, he was awarded his degree along with fourteen other scholars. In later years he always spoke fondly of his days at alma mater, and he was remembered in one account "as the best-dressed man and the owner of the most luxuriant crop of side whiskers on the campus."[13]

Graduation from college brought him back to his desire to pursue seminary studies, and after application to the appropriate diocesan authorities O'Connell was accepted as a student in Rome. The Catholic church in America was at that time superintended by the Vatican department known as the Sacred Congregation de Propaganda Fide ("for the spreading of the faith"), the church's missionary agency; all of the United States was still considered mission territory. American seminarians who studied in Rome attended classes at the Propaganda's university in the Eternal City, and they lived at what was known as the American College, a house on Rome's Via dell'Umiltà ("Humility Street") only a few blocks from the Pantheon. No formal courses were given there, but it nevertheless became the central point of reference for those Americans who had come to prepare for the priesthood close to the heart of the reinvigorated papacy. The American College had been organized in the middle of the 1850s with the support of Pius IX as a means of promoting the development of an American clergy that would look instinctively to Rome as the center of church life; its official opening had taken place, prophetically enough, on William O'Connell's own birthday, December 8, 1859. When O'Connell arrived in October 1881, after a journey that had taken him through Ireland, England, and France, he found a young New Yorker, Father Louis Hostlot, as rector of the college and an entering class of twelve seminarians.[14]

Rome was an interesting place to be in the early 1880s. Only a decade before, Italian nationalist troops had stormed the city, bringing to an end the reign of the pope-kings and relegating the successor of Saint Peter to the self-imposed status of "prisoner of the Vatican." In response, the papacy struck back, asserting its primacy in matters religious, the one sphere left to it now that temporal power had been taken away. Under Pius IX (1846–1878) a church council formally declared the pope to be infallible in matters of faith and morals, a doctrine many American bishops had their doubts about, and under Leo XIII (1878–1903) the papacy laid the intellectual foundations of orthodoxy by reasserting the authority of Saint Thomas Aquinas in philosophy and theology. For seminarians in particular, literally undergoing their seminal experiences in such an atmosphere, the direct, personal impact of these events was decisive. Above all, it left most of them with an abiding sense of what was called *Romanità*— "Roman–ness"—an intuitive belief that only from the pope and his expanding administrative apparatus could the definitive expression of Catholicism proceed. A few Roman alumni would adopt broader views once they returned home, but the majority tended to a more conservative, centralized outlook. "The Roman mind is the Church's mind and the mind of Christ," William O'Connell wrote later, having himself fully absorbed this attitude. "The Roman mind is neither Italian, nor French, nor German, nor American. It is catholic. In its best phases it truly represents the world. . . . That, undoubtedly, is the unique gift of Christ to the See of Peter."[15]

Quite apart from intellectual stimulation and a broadened cultural outlook, study in Rome also brought with it certain practical advantages. On their return to America, priests who had been trained at the church's emotional center became a sort of de facto elite. Their time in Rome brought them to the attention of the papal bureaucracy, making contacts and alliances for them with the men who, both at that time and later, would be in a position to influence and make appointments. As his career went on, O'Connell benefited from his associations with two of his Roman professors: Francesco Satolli, later apostolic delegate to the United States, and Antonio Agliardi, a member of the Propaganda Fide at the time of choosing a new archbishop of Boston.[16] That the young man from Lowell had access, however limited by his student status, to such men certainly seemed to bode well for his future prospects.

Student life at the American College followed an established routine. The new seminarians arrived in the middle of October, participated in a week's spiritual retreat, and began their classwork early in November. Each student occupied a small, simply furnished cell, and he was expected always to wear a straight black cassock. Only this garment's red buttons and sash and its blue piping, together with the stiff white of the clerical collar, identified his nationality. Rising each day was at 5:30 in the morning, followed by private prayer and mass at 6:30, breakfast, and then a walk to the Propaganda college for the start of lectures at 8 o'clock. All instruction was in Latin. After midday dinner and siesta, the late afternoon and evening were taken up with classes or private studies, organized recreation, and religious observances, before retirement at 10:00 P.M. Coursework concluded in the spring, and the graduates would generally be ordained in June before returning home. Underclassmen spent the summer months at the college's villa outside the city at Grottaferrata, acquired in 1882, O'Connell's first summer there.[17] Continuing students seldom returned home for summer vacation, so William O'Connell remained in Italy for three full years, avidly drinking in Roman culture and experiencing none of the homesickness that had troubled him in Maryland.

Very few records of the American College survive for O'Connell's time there, and thus it is not possible to describe or assess his particular experiences within the general pattern. He always spoke glowingly of his seminary days, however, and he quickly became a thoroughgoing *Romano*. He added fluent Italian to his language skills and indulged an interest in music that had begun with childhood piano lessons. He sang in the choir, sometimes played the organ for house ceremonies, and began to compose little religious tunes, a practice he continued in later life. He even claimed to have done some painting, but this was probably never serious, and it did not continue as he grew older.[18]

Having successfully completed his studies, he approached his priestly ordination, which took place on June 8, 1884, in the great Basilica of Saint John Lateran. As was the case with his classmates, none of his family was present either for this solemn ceremony or for his first celebration of the mass a few days later. He remained in Italy through the summer and into the fall, temporarily serving a parish in a fishing village south of Rome and then staying at the college villa. He enrolled in classes again in the fall, perhaps with the intention of pursuing the graduate doctor of divinity degree.[19] At the end of that term, however, he left Rome and returned to America, prepared to take up his first assignment.

* * *

On arrival home, the twenty-five-year-old priest presented himself to Archbishop John J. Williams, the leader of Boston's Catholics for nearly two decades. From the crowded heart of the city, Williams's diocese stretched out like a great half-moon: north to the New Hampshire border, south to Plymouth, and west to the edge of Worcester County. Its 300,000 people were predominantly Irish, but by the 1880s there were also significant numbers of French, Italians, Germans, East Europeans, and others. There were parishes in cramped urban districts where recently arrived immigrants huddled together, and there were parishes in pleasant country towns, most of them still dominated by Yankee Protestants. A new priest could expect an assignment to any of these places. Father O'Connell met with the archbishop in December 1884, and just before Christmas Williams placed him as an assistant in Saint Joseph's parish, Medford.[20]

A seventeenth-century settlement located less than ten miles from Boston, Medford was still a quiet rural village when O'Connell arrived. It claimed only 7,500 residents, though it was just about to undergo a burst of growth. Its large estates were being divided up for the construction of new homes, the ready access to Boston making it an ideal "streetcar suburb." A Catholic parish, Immaculate Conception, had been established on the town's border with Malden as early as 1854, and the separate parish of Saint Joseph had been founded just a year before O'Connell's assignment there. Its pastor, Father Richard Donnelly, was an older man who welcomed the help a young curate could give. The parish was not a large one, and the archbishop had assigned O'Connell there deliberately, so he could accustom himself to parish life and learn from the experience of the older priest. Part of the learning process was for him to take on more than his share of the day-to-day work. O'Connell performed virtually all the baptisms during his two years there and most of the marriages as well. He helped prepare a confirmation class of almost ninety students when Williams came to administer the sacrament in October 1885.[21] O'Connell's time in Medford was brief, but it did successfully introduce him to the regular routine in the life of a priest.

Donnelly died early in the fall of 1886, and he was replaced by a priest from Saint Joseph's parish in Boston's crowded West End. That promotion created a vacancy in the city, and William O'Connell was transferred to fill it in November of that year. This urban Saint Joseph's parish was presided over by the Reverend William Byrne, vicar general of the archdiocese and a man with whom Father O'Connell would find himself in competition for advancement twenty years later. The parish lay in the heart of one of the city's most complex and diverse neighborhoods, a marked contrast to the sleepy little world of Medford.

The West End, extending along the curve of the Charles River from downtown, had a population of a little less than 30,000 people, almost half of whom were members of the parish. The area consisted largely of tenements, originally occupied by Yankee "native immigrants" from outlying farms, but these had quickly been displaced by foreign newcomers. It boasted plenty of theaters and saloons but precious little industry. Politically, it was Ward Eight, home of one of the most efficient of the city's rising Irish Democratic machines, presided over by Martin Lomasney, a man whose skills had earned him the title of "the Mahatma." Ethnically, the West End was a

hodgepodge: the largest single group of inhabitants was Irish, but
there were also pockets of Yankees and Italians, as well as the greatest concentrations of blacks and Jews in the city. Its birthrate was
high, second only to that of the teeming North End. It was hardly a
fashionable address, but neither was it a slum. Crime was a declining
problem, and job prospects were reasonably good: roughly half of the
adult males found work in the professional, clerical, or skilled jobs
that were at the top of the employment scale. Almost two-thirds of
the West End's families lived in houses that had yards of some kind,
and nearly 90 percent of them had indoor plumbing and sanitary
facilities.[22] A number of prestigious institutions made their homes
there, including several hospitals and charitable agencies, as well as
the Suffolk County jail.

The people who worshipped at Saint Joseph's were not excep-
tionally well off, but they were far from the bottom of the pile. A reasonably accurate sense of their standing can be reconstructed
because, unlike most parishes in the archdiocese, the priests assigned
there at this time habitually recorded the birthplaces and the occupations of the people who came to them to be married. The majority
of these had been born abroad and, given their ages, had probably
come to America as children. Skilled and semiskilled trades were
extremely common among them. The single most frequent occupation given for the men was the relatively lowly laborer (13 percent),
but there were more respectable and lucrative jobs as well, including
clerks (11 percent), waiters (4 percent), plumbers (3 percent), car-
penters and bookkeepers (2 percent each). For women a similar pattern held. Their single most common occupation was listed as
domestic (26 percent). While an equal number were described either
as being simply at home or having no occupation, others displayed a
wide range of skills. More than 12 percent were involved in one
aspect or another of dressmaking, and 6 percent were either clerks or
saleswomen. A few unusual occupations appeared for both sexes,
including a detective, a bookbinder, two artists, and a "japanner."[23]
The people of Saint Joseph's were thus not the poorest of the poor,
such as might be found in the parishes of the North and South Ends.
These were people who were already on their way up.

O'Connell found life here more active and demanding than in
his previous assignment. He was the junior man of four curates in
addition to Father Byrne, an unusually large parish staff, and the

range of activities was wider than he had previously known. Besides the regular round of masses, confessions, baptisms, and weddings, he participated soon after his arrival in a major fund-raising effort to construct a parish school. He also encountered a host of programs for lay people, including a literary society, a "total abstinence" temperance league, and an annual parish mission. The number of bars and taverns in the West End prompted fears about prostitution and other crime associated with saloons and, although Saint Joseph's parish was not as rife with these activities as were others, there was still some cause for concern. Accordingly, Byrne and his staff led efforts to get at least the Catholic bar owners to close their establishments on Christmas day, a campaign that was not uniformly successful. Young Father O'Connell threw himself into this crusade avidly, attending temperance missions and minstrel shows and preaching on the subject in Saint Joseph's and at other parishes, including his native Saint Peter's, Lowell.[24]

One of O'Connell's particular duties was the superintendence of the Sunday school. He presided over the annual awards ceremonies, prepared the classes for confirmation, and participated in the regular outings (sleigh rides or picnics, depending on the season) that were provided for the teachers. He likewise took an active part in the devotional life of the parish during what was the heyday of new Catholic religious practices worldwide. The Forty Hours devotion, a form of eucharistic adoration that moved from church to church on a fixed schedule, came to Saint Joseph's each year, usually in March. Activities in honor of the Sacred Heart, one of the nineteenth century's most popular devotions which emphasized the suffering love of Jesus, also found expression in the West End. The parish boasted a League of the Sacred Heart, the Advanced Ladies of the Sacred Heart, and even a Mandolin Club of the Young Ladies of the Sacred Heart. Priests from various religious orders also visited the parish to conduct missions, periods of especially intense preaching designed to encourage a return to the sacraments on the part of those who had temporarily "fallen away." The resident priests encouraged these programs, and at least one of them at Saint Joseph's was phenomenally successful: during a mission in 1887, about 3,000 women and 2,000 men received communion, a response which a local newspaper said "reflects great credit on the zealous pastor and his assistants."[25]

These special events supplemented the normal work of the priest, which consisted mainly of saying mass every day and presiding at the administration of the sacraments. As he had in Medford, William O'Connell did more than his share of this work. The pastor, Father Byrne, was not a factor here at all. His position as vicar general and close adviser to Archbishop Williams removed him from much of the mundane parish routine: during O'Connell's years at Saint Joseph's from 1886 to 1895, Byrne officiated at only two baptisms and only a single marriage. These duties were performed instead by the younger clerics, and not always in equal proportions. The junior man in the rectory seems to have been kept busiest with baptisms, perhaps as a way of breaking him in. In O'Connell's first two years at Saint Joseph's he performed more baptisms than any other priest, close to one-third the whole number, with the remaining two-thirds divided among the other three curates. He was the most active baptizer again in 1890 and ranked second in four other years of his tenure. Only after he achieved some seniority in the middle 1890s did he yield these duties to others: in 1895, for example, he performed only forty-six of the almost three hundred baptisms in the parish. In marriages, too, O'Connell did his part, though here the pattern was reversed: he performed relatively fewer marriages during his early years, and only after he achieved some seniority (and presumably came to be better known by the young couples being married) did his rate of presiding at weddings increase. He officiated at only 21 percent of the marriages during his first full year (1887) at the parish, but by 1892 he was in charge of about 41 percent of them, the remainder spread out unequally among his four colleagues. The demands of clerical life were constant and unpredictable, frequently requiring response to calls from parishioners at all hours of the day and night, but O'Connell seemed to flourish. "Much of it," he said, referring to his work, "very much of it, was trying and even repulsive to mere human sensibilities, but the 'God bless you, Father,' of the homeless and the friendless lightened our hearts and brightened our way."[26]

As time went on Father O'Connell came to be known beyond the borders of the parish, and he assumed the wider role in Catholic Boston for which his Roman training prepared him. In particular, he acquired a reputation as an orator. Later recordings indicate a full baritone voice, and he spoke in the formal, rolling style of public address that was common in the days before electronic amplification. By the early 1890s he was in wide demand as a speaker. His previous association with the Jesuits at Boston College brought an invitation to preach "the panegyric of Saint Ignatius Loyola" at the celebration of the feast of that order's founder at Immaculate Conception church (the college's chapel) in August 1891. O'Connell was also chosen to preach during the celebration at Saint Joseph's of the 400th anniversary of the landing of Columbus in October 1892. The local Irish newspaper, the *Pilot*, identified him the next year as one "who is fast coming to the front as a preacher and orator" after he had presented the toast to "Civil and Religious Liberty" at the annual dinner of Boston's Charitable Irish Society.[27]

Like all good speakers he got several uses out of the same talk, lecturing on "The Poetry of Ireland" before three different audiences in Boston and Lowell. He preached at the dedication of churches and orphanages. He spoke to a range of groups, even providing "a delightful intellectual entertainment . . . in the form of a 'smoke talk'" for the Catholic Club at Harvard College, describing "Clerical Student Life in Rome." This performance was a hit, his remarks containing "so much beauty of expression, such fine descriptive passages, so much humor and feeling" that the club elected him an honorary member.[28] Among his colleagues in the clergy—there were about 400 priests in the Boston archdiocese at this time—William O'Connell was becoming identified as a rising star, one to whom advancement, most likely in the form of early promotion to the pastorate of a church of his own, was sure to come.

* * *

Promotion came in 1895, after nine years in the West End, but it came in an unexpected form. It led him back to the city that had captured his heart, Rome, and to his old haunts, the American College. The college had frequently been controversial throughout its forty-year history, but the decade after O'Connell's departure from it as a student had been especially stormy. Factionalism within the American hierarchy, turning as much on matters of personality as on questions of policy, had always clouded the place. The turmoil surrounding the office of rector, who was always the most visible and influential American at the papal court, had only increased with the arrival in 1885 of Denis J. O'Connell, a brilliant and ambitious priest from Richmond. A slim, handsome man, this O'Connell (no relation to the Lowell O'Connells) was an alumnus of the college who had caught the eye of Baltimore's Cardinal James Gibbons, the de facto primate of the American church, and who excelled at the art of church politics. During his rectorship the college managed to achieve financial stability, and it successfully fought off an attempt by the Italian government to confiscate its property.

Denis O'Connell had larger goals in view, however, goals that were fired by a thoroughgoing faith in the American spirit and a belief that the rising fortunes of American Catholicism offered a model to be emulated by the church universal. Highlighting differences of opinion among the bishops of the United States dividing those who envisaged a distinctly American church from those who, like the so-called ultramontane party in France, sought closer allegiance with Rome, Denis O'Connell sided with the "Americanists," using his position as rector to become the chief lobbyist at the Vatican for that group. These Americanists enjoyed high favor, especially during the early years of the papacy of Leo XIII, but by the middle 1890s the tide had begun to turn against them. A number of issues arose that led Roman officials to question whether church affairs in the United States ought to be entrusted to a faction that seemed to put such faith in a particular national expression of Catholicism, with insufficient reliance on central authority. The 1893 establishment of a permanent apostolic delegation in Washington (a liaison to the American church which did not achieve formal diplomatic standing until 1984) only underlined these concerns. Increasingly, Denis O'Connell emerged as a partisan for that one side—the losing side—in these disputes, and his position as rector thus became problematic. His enemies gathered their forces, and in June 1895 he was compelled to resign.[29]

The resignation necessitated the appointment of a successor, and on October 2 of that year the archbishops of Baltimore, Boston, New York, and Philadelphia, who together constituted the college's board of trustees, gathered in Baltimore for that purpose. With the recent history of the partisanship of Denis O'Connell as background, the four prelates began a spirited discussion of potential candidates. As the leader of the conservatives among the American bishops, New York's Archbishop Michael Corrigan proposed the name of Augustine Schulte, a Philadelphia priest who had served as interim rector of the college in the 1880s, a nomination that was seconded by Patrick J. Ryan, the archbishop of Philadelphia. Gibbons (a liberal sympathizer) objected to Schulte, however, expressing concern over the "national question." Schulte was of German extraction, and Gibbons and his Americanist allies feared that his promotion would exacerbate German-Irish antagonism within the American church, a longstanding and multifaceted dispute. Three other candidates for rector were also discussed: Thomas Kennedy, also from Philadelphia; Nathaniel Mooney, a curate at Chicago's Holy Name Cathedral; and William H. O'Connell of Boston.[30]

How and why O'Connell's name had come into consideration is curious and surprising. The official Boston archdiocesan historians maintained that it was Gibbons who had suggested him, though this seems virtually impossible since the Baltimore prelate had had no occasion to know the young Bostonian. More than likely he had been suggested by Archbishop Williams, who had perhaps taken notice of him in the parish of his aide and confidant, William Byrne. There were also rumors at the time, openly discussed in later years, that the ambitious O'Connell himself, suspecting that the nomination might be a disputed one, had taken a quick train to Baltimore to lobby on his own behalf with Gibbons and the others.[31] Regardless of the circumstances that led to his consideration, O'Connell eventually did make the list, called a "*terna*," of names submitted to the Propaganda Fide for approval and final selection. Arranged in order of preference the three were Kennedy, Mooney, and O'Connell; the controversial Schulte was excluded.

The Roman congregation acted relatively quickly on the matter, but not before the American ultramontanes weighed in with additional opinions. Corrigan was upset with the outcome of the selection process, and he asserted angrily that his Americanist opponents, including Gibbons, Denis O'Connell, and Archbishop John Ireland of Saint Paul, Minnesota, were engaged in a conspiracy to promote their cause. "It *looks* like another intrigue," he wrote, "starting from the Clique in Rome, and fostered at St. Paul and Baltimore." He warned that Father Kennedy was a man of too much good humor to maintain the requisite discipline at the American College. Brooklyn's Bishop Charles McDonnell also wrote to Rome, supporting Corrigan's views and arguing that the new rector should "not be a partisan or agent of one party." Francesco Satolli,

O'Connell's former professor and now apostolic delegate to the United States, submitted no formal recommendation, though he praised Kennedy's virtues and said that he did not know the other two well enough to speak about them one way or another. Thus, there was no shortage of opinion when the eleven cardinals of the Propaganda Fide met on November 18, 1895, and selected William O'Connell as the college's new rector. The surprise choice was ratified by the pope three days later and then communicated to the Americans. O'Connell himself was informed in early December, and he began immediately to make plans to depart for Rome and his new assignment.[32]

O'Connell, who had placed last on the list of the American archbishops, had vaulted over his two rivals. His selection seemed a plausible compromise, perhaps the result of Rome's desire to steer a middle way between the contending factions in the American church. If neither side could have its own man—Schulte for the conservatives, Kennedy for the liberals—a seemingly less controversial selection had merit. Corrigan had expressed a slight preference for O'Connell as just such a compromise, but more telling was the association with Archbishop Williams. A man of solid orthodoxy who maintained close personal relations with both sides, the Boston prelate was a scrupulous neutral in American hierarchical disputes. Rome may well have imagined that the best way through the turmoil was to place the rectorship in nonpartisan hands by promoting the candidate most closely connected with such a figure.[33] O'Connell's steadily advancing tilt in the conservative, ultramontane direction after his appointment would demonstrate the futility of trying to predict the outcome of disputes in the shifting sands of nineteenth-century church politics.

Thus, on the eve of his thirty-sixth birthday, William Henry O'Connell took the first giant step of his career. If the promotion did not come so completely out of the blue as he later protested—"I awoke one fine morning to find myself . . . Rector of my Alma Mater," he wrote, a little too innocently—it was nonetheless a noticeably rapid promotion.[34] He had been ordained barely more than a decade and had had no experience in the formation of priests, other than his own training. Though he had achieved something of a local reputation, there had been little to predict this sudden jump into an international position. Now he held one of the highest offices his church had to offer short of a bishop's miter. What is more, this appointment seemed a sign of advancements yet to come, positioning him as the principal American in clerical Rome. Here he would receive a first-hand education in the workings and ways of the Vatican organization, meeting the key shapers of policy, both current and future. Here he would see virtually every American bishop or priest passing through the Eternal City. He would necessarily have correspondence with members of the hierarchy at home as he supervised their seminarians. As rector he would arrange papal audiences for visitors, both clerical and lay, Catholic and non-Catholic, from the United States, giving him access to prominent people of all sorts. Even the manner of his selection foreshadowed his future promotions, achieving disputed positions even when his chances seemed thin. Assertions of diffidence notwithstanding, he cherished his new position and the opportunities it offered. While we cannot know what ambitions he may have harbored beforehand, his appointment to the rectorship of the American College gave him grounds to believe that this would not be his last promotion.

O'Connell left Boston by steamer shortly after New Year's Day and by the middle of February 1896 he was safely installed on the Via dell'Umiltà. He found life there substantially unchanged from his own days as a student. Great emphasis was still placed on discipline and obedience, virtues that were considered at least as important as formal learning in preparation for a priestly career. "The life of a Roman student is not an easy one," an alumnus of this era reminisced later, "but the life, too, of a zealous, earnest priest, whether in city or country, is essentially laborious and attended with hardship and self-sacrifice." The schedule of studies and devotions remained much as O'Connell remembered it. Daily mass was of course obligatory, though in keeping with the custom of the time that frowned on frequent communion, students took the sacrament less regularly. Student recreation was confined largely to daily walks through the streets of Rome, where the robed seminarians sometimes had to endure the jeers of the Italian nationalist citizenry. O'Connell supervised all these activities of the student body, which numbered about seventy on his arrival, and his first impressions were favorable. "I find the spirit of the house excellent, and so I begin my new life with fair hopes and courage," he wrote Cardinal Gibbons shortly after his arrival, explaining later to Archbishop Corrigan that, "as I am with my students at all their exercises, I am able more and more to see for myself what matters need more personal correction and supervision."[35]

From the outset the new rector from Boston was careful to draw a distinction between his own activities and those of his more political predecessor. Aware that the other O'Connell had spent as much time looking after the interests of his allies in the hierarchy as he had in attending specifically to college business, the Bostonian shunned the role of factional agent. He assured Corrigan that the college would be a truly national one, not favoring one group of American bishops over another. He recalled later that "I took the firm stand, and kept it, that my work was in the College, in the management and administration of the institution. . . . There, said I to myself, is where my work begins and ends." He may not have known how near the end was for the faction for which Denis O'Connell had spoken—papal condemnation of Americanism was only three years away—but he was shrewd enough to know that by aligning too closely with one party he risked making at least as many enemies as friends. He was careful to pacify both the liberal Gibbons and the conservative Corrigan on this score, telling the cardinal explicitly "we are entirely non partizan [sic]—interested only in the proper training of the young men committed to our charge, and glad and willing to be of service to any and all the bishops of America." This policy was widely recognized and generally greeted with relief by those at home. "You were sent to Rome to run the American College, and nothing else," Rochester's crusty and blunt Bishop Bernard McQuaid told him, "and by so doing you have won the approval of all, from the Holy Father down."[36] Nonpartisanship quickly brought its rewards: in the middle of O'Connell's second year as rector he was raised to the rank of monsignor.

Because the college was a residential facility rather than an academic one, the duties of the rector were more nearly those of a house manager or dean of students than those of a university president. A good deal of O'Connell's time was therefore spent in looking after the financial affairs of the institution and in watching the accounts of the students. Most of the college's assets were deposited with the Drexel bank of Philadelphia, with additional resources also held in Rome and Paris. Checks were drawn from these periodically to meet normal expenses for food and clothing for the students, maintaining and repairing the college and its out-of-town villa, and such varied necessities as books for the library, medicines, and postage. The rector kept a particularly watchful eye on student finances, tightening restrictions on the practice of permitting seminarians to borrow money from the college for passage home. Since each student's bishop had eventually to repay the funds thus borrowed, O'Connell required every applicant for such a loan to have specific permission in hand before the money was advanced. He managed all these affairs effectively during his years as rector, and the school's endowment grew along with the number of burses, or scholarships, that were available. The financial aspects of the job pleased him. The work was "very absorbing," he wrote, "but exceedingly interesting."[37]

The most serious financial transaction of his rectorship was the purchase of a new villa as the summer quarters for the students. Like most other institutions in Rome, the American College shut down almost completely in the hot weather, as its inhabitants sought relief in the cooler hills outside the city. The American residence had used several different summer homes over the years, most recently the one at Grottaferrata to which O'Connell himself had repaired as a student. Now, as rector, he found this place inadequate. The grounds were much too small, and a neighboring field had been appropriated by the Italian government, "who impose such conditions upon its use and restrict in such a manner the time allowed that it has ultimately become practically unavailable." Accordingly, O'Connell purchased an estate of the Orsini family, an old Roman noble clan now down on its luck, near the town of Castel Gandolfo, the traditional summer retreat for the pope himself. After some negotiation in 1899 O'Connell acquired the place, consisting of a large house and a few out-buildings, for a little over $22,000, a price that was considered a steal. He was pleased with the acquisition of this "respectable, healthy and sufficiently roomy Villa," which stood "in the midst of a splendid park fully 7 acres in extent, with room for base ball, tennis, etc."[38]

O'Connell's duties at the college left him with enough free time to begin making the rounds of Roman social life, and he liked what he saw. Perhaps more than anything else, this opportunity to know and to be known in return by important people from all walks of life marked the turning point in the young priest's career. Far behind him he put the immigrant tenements of Lowell, the unsophisticated rustics of Medford, the crowds and noise of the West End. In their place he substituted the apparently limitless possibilities of the cosmopolitan scene. Despite his later, too-loud protests that his life in Rome was that of a lonely hermit, he missed few chances to take advantage of the contacts he now made. He put in regular appearances in "Black Society," the aristocratic circle that still huddled around the pope and shunned the secular court of the House of Savoy. Another young American O'Connell encountered in these circles spoke for both of them when he remembered years later the thrill of those times. "Making a new acquaintance always seemed . . . to be fraught with the savour of adventure," the Indianapolis-born Francis MacNutt recalled of the Rome of the 1890s. "Who knew or could foresee what interest was to be created in one's life or what relationship was going to develop?"[39]

O'Connell took this message to heart, forming friendships and beneficial alliances that would last a lifetime. Foremost among these was his association with Monsignor Raphael Merry del Val, the shrewd and worldly son of a Spanish diplomat and a English gentlewoman. At the time he and O'Connell met in the late 1890s, Merry was one of the private secretaries to Leo XIII, but he was destined for higher things. After a brief stint as papal legate to Canada, he became secretary for the conclave in 1903 that chose Leo's successor, Pius X. He then served the new pope as secretary of state, right-hand man, and ecclesiastical enforcer. Merry was a regular visitor at the American College during O'Connell's rectorship, and he became a great favorite of the students on account of his fluent English and his better than average abilities as a tennis player. In later years he would become O'Connell's closest—perhaps his only—friend among his fellow cardinals, and the two men always did what they could to promote one another's interests.[40]

O'Connell's contacts with ecclesiastics like Merry del Val foreshadowed not only his future friends but also his future enemies. Despite the fond hopes that he maintain his neutrality, O'Connell fell increasingly into line with the more conservative, ultramontane, Roman forces within the church, both in Europe and in America. This course was easier to follow after the papal rebuke of the liberal Americanist forces in 1899, and O'Connell was smart enough to see where the path to the future lay. He came to favor and adopt the outlook of Archbishop Corrigan, later praising the New Yorker as "Roman to the core." Contact with "the great universal atmosphere

of Rome" aligned the young Bostonian with the forces of papal tri-
umphalism and set him in opposition to those churchmen in
America he would accuse of lacking the "innate Roman and
Catholic sense." From this time onward, "Roman" and "Catholic"
became synonyms for William O'Connell. Thus, if conservative
churchmen had found a rising star in the young rector, the liberals in
the American church had found a formidable new opponent. What
is more, these potential enemies came to fear what they perceived as
O'Connell's overactive ambition. The story that he had actively
campaigned for his job fueled these fears, and his considerable *amour
propre* led one American observer at the Vatican to dub him
"Monsignor Pomposity."[41] The contentious episcopal generation of
Gibbons, Corrigan, and John Ireland may have been drawing to a
close; the rise of O'Connell and of an opposition to him indicated
that the disputes dividing the older men would endure.

Just as important for O'Connell's expanding horizons as the
church contacts he made during his rectorship were the friendships
he formed among the sizable circle of Americans he found living in
Rome. Expatriates were flocking to the Eternal City at the turn of
the century, seeking an older, more advanced and noble culture they
thought unavailable at home. "The spirit of the place," Henry James
said as enthusiastically as he ever said anything, was "the master-
conductor of a great harmonious band. . . . No one, really, could be a
bore about Rome. . . . People might elsewhere be stupid, might elsewhere be vulgar or cross or ugly," but the "harmonizing charm" of
Rome smothered every offense.[42]

William O'Connell was no more immune to that charm than
the rest of the varied cast of American characters he encountered:
political figures like Bourke Cockran and former vice president Levi
Morton; the diplomat Bellamy Storer and his politically active wife,
Maria Longworth; writers like Marion Crawford and Hall Caine; the
architect Samuel Abbott; the sculptor William Story; and men of
affairs like Francis MacNutt and Benjamin Franklin Keith, a
vaudeville theater magnate. More than a few Bostonians were sprin-
kled through these ranks, including the widow of Senator Charles
Sumner and a physician from the West End named William A.
Dunn, who had followed the former curate from Saint Joseph's to
Rome and who had connections among the Italian nobility.
Monsignor O'Connell stood near the center of this American colony

since all visitors from the United States seemed to want papal audiences, the arrangements for which he skillfully handled. Thus O'Connell regularly enjoyed the pleasure of the visitors' company, and the relationships proved mutually beneficial. Keith underwrote the cost of some artistic improvements at the college, for example, and for his part O'Connell secured papal honors for MacNutt. Doctor Dunn proved to be a particular friend, though his personal life—he was a homosexual—would later threaten to damage O'Connell when the churchman's career was at its most precarious. For the present, however, no such threats were foreseeable, and the two men took a hiking trip together around Lake Como in the summer of 1900.[43]

O'Connell came home for vacation only once while he was rector, visiting his family in the summer of 1898. The separation did not mean that he had forgotten them, however, and indeed he took a keen interest in their affairs. His unmarried, oldest sister, Julia, had assumed the position of head of the clan following the death of their mother in August 1893, and he corresponded with her regularly on the full range of family business. He offered unsolicited advice on the rearing of his growing number of nieces and nephews. The O'Connells owned four houses in Lowell by this time, and the rector was always anxious to know if these were rented and if family finances were secure.[44]

He seems to have sent home most of his annual salary of $1,000 to help the family, and he saw his own advancement as contributing to that of his siblings. He badgered members of the hierarchy for mass intentions—contributions for masses and prayers on behalf of the dead—as a means of supplementing his income. In explaining a testy exchange with one of his brothers just before his departure for Rome, he outlined the motives for this concern over money. "I know I was fussy and cranky," he wrote, "but it was only because I wanted you all to be respectable and respected. I am sure you see it all clearer now when I am no longer with you to scold and worry."[45] Not unlike many second-generation immigrants, O'Connell was "making it," moving into a life in which he was "respectable and respected." He found he liked the experience, particularly after he had tasted the high life of Rome. His family too had to achieve the same respect and respectability if his own status was to be secure. He was prepared to do whatever he could to aid their achievement.

Both within the circle of his family and outside it, William O'Connell had come a long way in his first forty years. From humble and generally undistinguished circumstances as the youngest son of an immigrant couple, he had pursued an education and embarked on a career which he believed offered him rewards both in this world and the next. He had risen early above his peers and by the time the new century opened was in a position to distinguish himself even further. He had shown a number of talents and had acquired an unusually wide variety of experiences and allies. Awakened to a growing ambition, he apparently awaited only the opportunity to apply himself to greater tasks. As he approached his fifth year as rector of the American College, that opportunity unexpectedly presented itself.

2

DRY RUN:
O'CONNELL AS BISHOP OF PORTLAND, 1901–1906

ON SUNDAY, AUGUST 5, 1900, James Augustine Healy, the second bishop of Portland, Maine, died at the age of seventy. One of the most remarkable men ever to serve the Catholic church in America, Healy had been the son of a white Irish immigrant to Georgia and a black former slave. Because Georgia law classified him and his ten equally remarkable siblings as slaves, the young Healy had been sent north to be educated, first at Quaker schools in New Jersey and then at the College of the Holy Cross in Worcester, Massachusetts, where he was a member of the first graduating class in 1849. Ordination followed seminary studies abroad, and then came a career as a priest in Boston during the turbulent years surrounding the Civil War. He had gone to Maine in 1875 to lead what was then the northernmost and the easternmost Catholic diocese in the United States.[1]

Catholicism had come early to Maine with the French explorers of the seventeenth century, but the growth of the church there had been slow. At Healy's death there were only fifty-seven settled parishes scattered over 33,000 square miles of shoreline, potato farms, and dense forests. These churches, together with thirty-one mission chapels, were served by just over one hundred priests. About three hundred nuns staffed hospitals, schools, and orphanages, serving a Catholic population of about 97,000 in a state of almost 700,000.[2]

The Catholics of Maine, a small minority surrounded by an overwhelmingly Protestant population, were themselves hardly unified. However much the frequently hostile and suspicious Yankees viewed it as monolithic, the Catholic community was cracked by ethnic and linguistic fissures. English-speaking Irish struggled with French-speaking Canadians for supremacy within individual parishes and in the diocese as a whole, each side convinced that the other represented a threat to the preservation of authentic Catholic culture. Bishop Healy, generally siding with the Irish though he was fluent in the French language and sympathetic to Canadian interests, had attempted to pacify these tensions, but he was not always successful. Like other ethnic groups elsewhere who protested the domination of the hierarchy by Irish Americans, the French of Maine pressed for a greater say in diocesan affairs.[3]

In the midst of these rivalries, the search began for a successor to Healy, whom the apostolic delegate remembered as "so good, holy [and] zealous a Bishop." Contemporary canon law permitted a greater degree of local participation in the selection process than would later be the case, with both the diocesan clergy and neighboring bishops canvased for their nominations. The appropriate archbishop—in this case John Williams of Boston—appointed an interim administrator for the diocese, choosing Father Michael O'Brien, the longtime pastor of Saint Mary's parish, Bangor. Williams also convened the Portland diocesan consultors (a six-member council comprised of the senior pastors in Maine) and the seven other bishops of New England. Each group was charged with preparing a ranked list or *terna* of three candidates thought appropriate for appointment as the new leader of the diocese. The implicit assumption was that Rome would choose one of the names on these lists, though technically it was not bound to do so.[4]

The diocesan consultors met first, shortly after Healy's funeral on August 9, 1900. They chose, in order of preference, Fathers Thomas H. Wallace, pastor of Saint Patrick's parish, Lewiston; Michael F. Walsh, pastor of Immaculate Conception, Calais; and Edward F. Hurley, pastor of Saint Dominic's, the oldest parish in Portland itself. The New England bishops, meeting in Boston a week later, chose the same three priests but ranked them in a different order: they placed Walsh first, followed by Hurley and then Wallace.[5]

The nominees were noteworthy in light of Maine's contentious ethnic situation. All three men were Irish, and only Hurley was originally from Maine. Wallace was an older man who spoke no French, drawbacks sufficiently serious to account for the bishops' dropping him from first place on the consultors' list to third place on their own. Walsh had had extensive contact with the French in his far northern parish on the Canadian border, but Hurley was better known because his parish was in the center of Maine's largest city.

This last factor brought an endorsement of Hurley by Archbishop Sebastiano Martinelli, the apostolic delegate to the United States, whose opinion was also sought.[6] These names had no sooner been submitted to the Propaganda Fide in Rome than the principal French pastors of the diocese began a campaign to throw out both lists and to have one of their own appointed bishop instead. Their agitation clouded an otherwise routine procedure, and it opened the way for the selection of a completely unlikely candidate.

The opening shot was fired in early October when eighteen French priests wrote to Rome. They argued (not entirely correctly) that Canadians were the largest proportion of Catholics in Maine and that preservation of the French tongue was critical for them and for the church. "It is a constant," they told Propaganda, "that once the French-Canadians forget the language of their fathers, they lose their faith." They decried a consistent lack of sympathy between Irish priests and French parishioners, and they even invoked Bishop Healy from beyond the grave, alleging that he had said his successor should be French. Father Wallace (who, unknown to them, had withdrawn his name from consideration) was specifically denounced as unsympathetic, and subsequent letters similarly attacked both Hurley and Walsh.[7]

The weakness of their strategy was that the French pastors had no obvious candidate of their own on whom they could agree. Some leaned toward Father Narcisse Charland of Saint Francis de Sales's, Waterville, while others supported Father F. X. Trudel of Saint Joseph's, Oldtown, but neither man was very impressive. Trudel wanted the job and even tried clumsily to bribe the apostolic dele-gate with a conveniently timed charitable contribution, an insignifi-cant sum that was immediately returned to him and that ended whatever chance he may have had. As time went on, the French priests began to despair of controlling the appointment, and they feared that failure would leave them with an openly hostile bishop. Accordingly, they rallied behind the diocesan administrator, Michael O'Brien, an Irishman to be sure, but fluent in French and apparently willing to listen to them. O'Brien's advanced age perhaps allowed them to hope for a brief, caretaker reign, after which they could renew their demand for a Francophile. His "transcendent talents and his orthodoxy" were praised as qualifications.[8] By the beginning of 1901 a full-fledged effort was underway to deny the bishop's miter to any of those on the lists and to give it instead to the aging administrator.

At this point, the pastors overplayed their hand by enlisting several French-Canadian businessmen in their cause. Nothing was more likely to raise eyebrows in Rome than the meddling of the laity in a matter, like the selection of a bishop, that was thought not to concern them. In early February 1901 a number of leading French laymen addressed a letter to Propaganda describing their many trials in "this heretical and infidel country." Though they did not endorse O'Brien by name, they did support the position already set forth by their pastors in commending "his virtue, his wisdom, his perfect knowledge of the two languages, French and English, and enjoying a considerable prestige among the population, Catholic as well as Protestant." The precise contents of this letter remained unknown in the diocese, but the fact that private citizens were campaigning for O'Brien was something of an open secret. If nothing else, the unusually long delay in designating Healy's successor aroused suspicion. Years later, in his autobiography, William O'Connell felt constrained to mention the entire affair, absolving the clergy (incorrectly, as he probably knew) and placing the blame squarely on "the political and professional leaders, stimulated, no doubt, by some of their leading politicians in Canada."[9]

So much agitation convinced Propaganda that the Portland case warranted special attention. The sharpness of the ethnic conflict over the local candidates called for caution and perhaps for a compromise that would choose sides with none of the contending factions. As the months ticked steadily away, the idea of selecting an outsider, unencumbered by factional connections, grew more appealing. Given "the divisions that . . . have arisen," Providence's Bishop Matthew Harkins (an Irishman) wrote, "it seems to me that a choice of a clergyman from without the diocese would be preferable to any thus far suggested." Bishop John Michaud (a Frenchman) of Burlington agreed, suggesting a priest from Vermont or Monsignor Thomas Conaty, head of the Catholic University of America in Washington. Similar compromise suggestions came in from other neutral observers.[10]

Propaganda Fide did not formally consider the Portland appointment until April 22, 1901, fully nine months after Healy's death. Only the surprising result of that meeting is known with certainty: that Monsignor William Henry O'Connell, rector of the American College, would be the next leader of Maine's Catholics. Presumably, all the contending parties were disappointed that their candidate had not been chosen, but relieved that at least their opponents' choice had not been ratified either. As a compromise, O'Connell had merit. He spoke French fluently, though he had no other special qualifications for the task of pacifying the ethnic dissension. If he was largely unknown in Maine, he was certainly well-known in Rome, the result of his workmanlike management of the college and his equally deliberate cultivation of those in authority. He had been on the spot at the Vatican as the matter was being debated, and he could therefore promote or reinforce the idea that he, a loyal clergyman from a diocese not very far from Portland, was the perfect choice. He had not hesitated to put himself forward for the rectorship six years before, and there is little reason to doubt his readiness to do the same for this larger prize. It is a reasonable speculation that he had renewed his ties to his old professor, Francesco Satolli, by now a cardinal and a member of the Propaganda congregation, and that Satolli had either put his name forward or had supported it once presented. In any event, the appointment did not simply happen "one fine day," as O'Connell later remembered.[11] He was consecrated a bishop in the Lateran Basilica on May 19, with Cardinal Satolli officiating, assisted by Archbishops Edmund Stoner, a leader of the English Catholic colony in Rome, and (perhaps inevitably) Raphael Merry del Val. The new bishop remained briefly at the Vatican and then set sail for America, arriving in Boston on July 2.

* * *

Promotion to the rank of bishop was unquestionably an honor for O'Connell, but his assignment to this rather insignificant see was not universally acclaimed among his friends. "We think our congratulations should be more than shared with your new diocese," wrote an American lady who had known him in the Eternal City, "for if I remember Portland rightly it is a very bleak and cold place with an equally cold and placid population and I fear that you will notice this all the more after your long sojourn in Rome." Even those who looked on O'Connell with more jaundiced eyes had their doubts. Ella B. Edes, a Bostonian convert to Catholicism who now enjoyed dabbling on the fringes of Vatican politics, took a more cynical view.

She, who had previously dubbed O'Connell "Monsignor Pomposity," derisively accused him of hurrying through his episcopal consecration, "afraid that the Powers that Be might change their minds and not permit the mitre to rest on his head, after all." O'Connell himself had no such reservations, however, interpreting his new dignity as both "a reward and an encouragement for my services" and giving him "the very greatest satisfaction."[12]

More important, O'Connell viewed his appointment as an opportunity to establish in the American church a "tighter and stronger link of union and attachment to the Holy See." He was by now a confirmed member of the Roman, ultramontane camp among American churchmen, and he made no effort to disguise that loyalty as soon as he arrived home. On July 3, 1901, he said mass in his old parish of Saint Joseph's, Boston, took the train to Portland that afternoon, and was installed as bishop in the Cathedral of the Immaculate Conception on the next day, the great national festival. "As I am American in patriotism," he declared in taking possession of the diocese, "so am I, and shall ever be, Roman in faith and love of the Church." Rome was a "second fatherland" to him, he said, adding that "we turn Romeward as naturally . . . as the needle seeks the North." He proclaimed that his one goal would be "by word and example to strengthen the bond of love and faith between our diocese and the primate of the world."[13] O'Connell set forth no grand ecclesiastical master plan for his diocese. Still, he knew that his time in Maine would give him important practical experience at being a bishop. He had never been the pastor of his own parish, but now he was responsible for nearly sixty of them. If he was ever to progress beyond "cold and placid" Portland, he would have to demonstrate his ability at managing diocesan affairs.

Accordingly, he spent his first six months getting to know his large territory, a course that seemed to border on hyperactivity. In the summer he administered confirmation in Augusta and Biddeford and dedicated new churches in Portland and Lisbon Falls. In September he participated in an interreligious memorial service for the assassinated President McKinley and delivered a five-minute oration. In October he was received at the state capitol by the governor. Later that month he presided over a commemoration of Pope Leo XIII's golden jubilee as a priest, an occasion when, a local newspaper observed warily, "for the first time in the history of Catholicity in

Portland a Roman Catholic bishop headed a procession through the public streets." He spoke to the Portland Knights of Columbus, organized a Catholic club for the city's young men, and even traveled home to Massachusetts on occasion. He was still a young man, only forty-two years old. He cut a substantial, striking figure, and he was determined to be vigorous and visible in his leadership of the diocese. He moved throughout Maine, aided by free passes provided by railroad executives. "I travelled from village to village," he recalled thirty years later in a romantic mood, "sleeping wherever the night found me, and gathering along the whole wearisome route the inspiration which all the scenes breathed forth into my very soul."[14]

If he had a larger goal in view, it was to create a new image of who and what the Catholic bishop of Portland was. His was to be a public office, conducted in a public manner, a program whose underlying purpose was as much social as it was religious. Conscious of the gulf that had long existed between the Catholic minority and the Yankee Protestant majority, he was resolved, he later said, "to work to the best of my ability to lead our good people forward in the estimation of the people who are often prone to misunderstand us." To achieve that end he determined to take "whatever opportunity comes naturally in my way to mingle among the professional and influential men here," a task at which he had already demonstrated his considerable ability in Rome.[15]

This reliance on high visibility was widely noted by the Maine press, which took to regular reporting of his activities. "He is a very manly sort of a man and is rapidly winning friends," the *Bangor Commercial* said less than two months after he assumed office. "His personal popularity here promises to overflow all church barriers and take in all his fellow citizens." Significantly, the paper also remarked that reporters liked him, "and they believe in him." Another journal approved of the "grand and inspiring spectacles" that characterized his every move, while yet another congratulated him on his first anniversary in Portland for having "won the respect and esteem of the community."[16]

O'Connell's sense of public display was carefully cultivated, with a view toward enhancing the self-esteem of Maine's Catholics. His emergence as a public figure could serve as both a source of pride for his people and a spur to their own assertiveness. Still, such a plan was not without its underside. Accustomed to the simpler lives of their earlier bishops, O'Connell's flock were at least surprised that their new leader was covered so regularly in the newspapers, often socializing with non-Catholics. Many Catholics were put off by O'Connell's grand, often pompous style, complete with a personal retinue that included a valet, a housekeeper, a driver, and even an Italian singing-master for his cathedral choir.[17] The mixed reaction to this odd combination of autocratic and democratic impulses would continue throughout O'Connell's career. His people might accept and even welcome his symbolic significance for their own advancement, but they would always feel a certain distance between him and themselves.

Nevertheless, as the newspapers noted, O'Connell made a distinct impression on Maine's non-Catholics. If the "placid" Yankees expected little from this son of immigrants from Lowell, they were pleasantly surprised by the polished cosmopolitan who had emerged from Rome and who was now making his mark in Portland society. He was befriended by William L. Putnam, a federal judge from an old Protestant family, and through his patronage O'Connell joined the exclusive Cumberland Club. The new bishop also took up the fashionable game of golf, integrating the previously all-Protestant links on Little Diamond Island in Casco Bay, where he pursued what he called "that most excellent game." When Theodore Roosevelt visited Portland in August 1902, the president stood in his carriage as it passed O'Connell's reviewing stand, "bowing gracefully to the bishop who," a reporter observed, "politely acknowledged the courtesy." Later that evening the two met privately at the home of Maine's foremost citizen, the now retired lion of Congress, Speaker Thomas Brackett Reed. O'Connell believed that "a bishop must take his rightful place [in] the life of his community for the good of all and for the honor of his position."[18] In the near past, Catholics in Maine had been the object of hostile political rhetoric; now the president of the United States bowed gracefully to their bishop in public and conversed with him in private.

Although his was not a particularly tolerant era, O'Connell even took some minor steps toward religious rapprochement. He entertained the theological doubts of an Episcopal clergyman with the unlikely name of Saint Ethelbert Yates, who was considering conversion to Catholicism, and he helped find places in convent schools for the daughters of prominent Protestants. He cordially received a suggestion from Robert Codman, the Episcopal bishop of Maine, that he establish a new parish in the town of Camden, though he refrained from arguing when Codman took High Anglican umbrage at his remark that "there is no Catholic church in Camden." (An Episcopalian in the high church tradition, Codman maintained that his denomination was a legitimate branch of the Catholic church—a view Roman Catholics rejected—and that the Episcopal parish in Camden was thus "a catholic church.") O'Connell corresponded with other well-to-do Protestants who asked him to establish parishes near their summer residences for the convenience of their servants, most of whom were Irish. Though he was not always able to satisfy such requests, he took them seriously, suggesting to one pastor whose domain had many servants "that you keep all these well-disposed persons [i.e., the Yankees] as friends." Careful cultivation of religious and social leaders paid off. "The bishop is personally a great and successful worker," said one newspaper, while another concluded that "it is not too much to say that he made friends as rapidly as he met people."[19]

O'Connell's public style was inseparable from the substance of his episcopate. Indeed, he could concentrate on his visible role because, as he himself observed on several occasions, the management of diocesan affairs was not an overly demanding task. He described for a fellow bishop "the numberless difficulties with which my path is strewn," but later, recalling his Portland days, he judged the rectorship of the American College to have been "far more difficult." The diocese offered him "little really to do," he said, "scarcely enough to keep a strong energetic man busy." He even claimed to have found time for the intensive study of languages, "as the work of the Diocese was never excessively absorbing." These were remarkable admissions for a man who always characterized his work with images of adversity overcome and who had chosen as the motto on his episcopal coat of arms the phrase *"Vigor in Arduis"* (Strength in Difficulties).[20] He was capable of managing whatever real trials did come his way, but he was also keen enough to turn them to advantage in building his own public image and reputation.

* * *

His tasks as bishop may not have been "excessively absorbing," but they were multifaceted, and O'Connell threw himself into the job. He constructed an intensely personal management system, with all matters referred ultimately to him. His only close associate was Father Charles Collins, a curate at the cathedral, whose role as chancellor and secretary to Bishop Healy was continued in the new regime. Collins served as a general adviser to the new bishop, but it was O'Connell who supervised almost every aspect of church administration. All outgoing letters from the chancery office were signed by him, a procedure that was more than simply *pro forma*. Concern with even the smallest details of life among the parishes, clergy, religious, and laity gave reality to O'Connell's view of himself as an active presence, constantly at work.

Perhaps because he knew—and, equally important, knew that others knew—that his appointment as bishop had been unexpected, he was swift to pacify the important pastors in the diocese, particularly those whose names, unlike his own, had appeared on the *ternae*. He immediately sought the friendship of Michael O'Brien, the former administrator, now returned to his parish in Bangor. He made a special point of telling O'Brien (who nonetheless reacted testily when the new bishop failed to use his newly acquired title of "Monsignor") that his "first visit of courtesy . . . outside of Portland, should be to you." In November 1901 O'Connell designated Father Edward Hurley, who had placed second on the bishops' list of candidates, as vicar general of the diocese, a largely honorific position. As time went on O'Connell also deferred to Father Thomas Wallace of Lewiston, who had ranked as the first choice of the Maine clergy. Wallace was assigned curates of his own choosing, and O'Connell sought the benefit of his counsel in financial matters, praising "the perfect accord that has always existed between the Bishop and yourself." At a meeting of all the bishops of New England in 1903, O'Connell raised the question of singling out priests who gave "evidence of qualities which would indicate fitness for the episcopal office and dignity," and then promptly put forward the names of Hurley and Michael Walsh, whose name had also been under consideration.[21] Conscious that he was an outsider, O'Connell wisely moved to defuse any potential resistance to his authority, either from his former rivals or from those who might rally around them.

Though he deliberately mollified these Irish priests, he gave curiously little thought to pacifying the French clergy and laity whose intervention in the selection process had opened the way for his appointment. Once in office O'Connell did little to show himself particularly solicitous of French-Canadian interests. He insisted that French nuns learn to speak English, a policy sure to antagonize those who saw their cultural survival, their "*survivance*," tied intimately to the endurance of their mother tongue. Symbolically but pointedly the new bishop always referred to Saint André's parish in the French stronghold of Biddeford as "Saint Andrew's," and the parishioners interpreted this, said their historian, as "another attempt by the Irish hierarchy to Americanize them." The French accepted these slights for as long as O'Connell remained in Portland, but the tension built steadily and finally exploded early in the tenure of his successor, as French-speaking Catholics sought unsuccessfully to strip a host of legal powers from the bishop.[22]

As the overseer of diocesan affairs, O'Connell was above all concerned to see that local parishes were run peacefully and smoothly. For Catholics, the parish was the enduring point of contact and participation in their religion. O'Connell's concern for the operation of parishes was multilayered, and it began with solicitude for the soundness of their finances. Because state law made him alone the legal corporation that was the church, the owner of all property and at least theoretically responsible for all indebtedness, he was particularly concerned that parishes live within their means. He personally had to approve loans in any amount for the construction and maintenance of parish property, and he demanded regular financial statements in return. A priest who failed to follow these procedures could expect a swift and pointed dressing down. When Father Adolphe Lacroix of Notre Dame de Lourdes's parish, Skowhegan, negotiated an unauthorized loan in late July 1901, only weeks after O'Connell's arrival, the bishop granted him retroactive permission "*this once*" but reminded him that "the Bishop of the Diocese is the responsible party, and he is bound in conscience to acquaint himself with the facts in detail. When that is done you will need have no fear," O'Connell continued. "Your promptness in seconding the plans of your Bishop will be the best guaranty of your future success."[23]

"Acquaintance with the facts" was crucial. O'Connell's administration rested on his mastery of the flow of information about his diocese. He enforced the previously ignored requirement that each parish submit an annual report. What is more, he carefully scrutinized those reports, and he did not hesitate to ask for more details when he found them lacking. Not even the remotest place escaped examination. The pastor of the small church in Saint David, a tiny village on the Canadian border at the far northern tip of the state, was told that his report was not only "very late in arriving," but also "very meagre in facts." What was the amount of the parish's debt, O'Connell wanted to know, and why had the prescribed collections for charities, seminarians, and other causes not been taken? What was the weekly attendance at mass, and how many children were enrolled in catechism classes? When the priest failed to respond after a month—thinking perhaps that his distance from Portland (more than 250 miles) insulated him from his bishop's anger—he received a second letter demanding a correct and full report in two weeks. Nothing, neither the amount of insurance on church property nor the arrangements for parish fairs, escaped O'Connell's attention.[24]

His concern for the supervision of parish life extended beyond financial affairs. The pastor of a new parish in Rumford Falls, a town in the Rangeley Lakes region near the New Hampshire border, was asked about the best site for a new church building. The priest proposed one location, but O'Connell, who was probably briefed on the details of local geography by Father Collins, suggested a different one because it was situated on a larger and busier street and had room for an expanded school as well. He distrusted pastors who sought to introduce new devotions on their own—"Do not institute any pious practice . . . without my permission," he told one; "you must await official authorization"—and he tried to promote the use of Gregorian chant in even the smallest villages. He occupied himself with the redecoration of his own church, the Cathedral of the Immaculate Conception in Portland, asking repeatedly for sketches of the artwork, suggesting color schemes, and insisting on precision in the painting of the angels that were to surround the windows.[25]

This attention to minutiae may seem, from an historical distance, petty and interfering, and to some extent it was. Many other American bishops managed their dioceses successfully without this manic eye for detail. For O'Connell, however, it was entirely natural, part of the functions of an active, involved prelate in superintending his charge. "The Bishop of the Church stands like a sentinel," he wrote in a pastoral letter to the diocese on Ash Wednesday 1904, drawing an oddly martial analogy. "His see is a watch tower whence he scans his own peaceful camp, ever alert against aught that could work disorder in the ranks."[26] Guarding against spiritual disorder was, of course, essential, but mundane administrative disorder had to be checked as well. To that end O'Connell took seriously his intention to be the "sentinel" watching all facets of church life.

Care for both the spiritual and the practical well-being of parishes found special expression in his supervision of parochial schools. American bishops, assembled at the Third Plenary Council of Baltimore in 1884, had demanded that there be a desk in a Catholic school for every Catholic child, but this call had gone largely unheeded in many dioceses, including Portland. In 1901, when O'Connell arrived, only twenty-one of his fifty-seven parishes had schools, and the situation was not significantly different (three more parishes; two more schools) when he left in 1906. Still, he expressed vocal support for parochial schools and took some limited action, without embarking on a massive building campaign. He reluctantly continued a policy established by Bishop Healy, selectively enforcing the Baltimore council's sanctions of excluding from the sacraments those parents who refused to send their children to parochial schools where available. Father Stephen Ferrier, pastor of churches in Lewiston and Auburn, was permitted to deny absolution in the confessional to such parents because, the priest claimed, the policy had a "salutary effect." O'Connell sent a circular letter to all pastors at the beginning of the school year in 1905, making some specific suggestions on their administration. Among these was care in the choice of textbooks; he reserved to himself the right to approve all texts, though he seems never to have exercised that right. He also urged greater attention to reading and to "strictness in promoting children from one grade to a higher one."[27]

Even so, he rarely interfered in the administration of the schools themselves, expecting the individual pastors to negotiate with the communities of religious sisters who staffed them. Nor did he generally attempt to influence or control the curriculum. The Portland diocese had no central administrative department for its schools until long after his departure. Still, he could become actively involved when school matters touched on larger issues. Two of these were the teaching of Latin and the enforcement of Pope Pius X's policy of "reforming" church music by restoring the primacy of Gregorian chant. Pius had issued his decrees in November 1903, and by the following February, O'Connell was seconding the pope's call to revitalize "the language of the Church, which to our great regret is becoming less and less familiar to the faithful." Accordingly, every child was to be taught to say the Our Father and Hail Mary in Latin, as well as to sing the *Te Deum, Tantum Ergo*, and other hymns, a task, the bishop rightly recognized, that "will no doubt mean patience and perseverance on the part of those in charge." Little evidence remains as to how successful this program was, though O'Connell himself liked to believe it so. Years later he recalled being told by an improbable group of children he had found praying in Latin that "we like it better." With an eye toward Rome as usual, he wasted no time in telling the apostolic delegate how hard he was working "in the Diocese of Portland in conformity with the wishes of the Holy Father."[28]

Few issues in the management of local church affairs were more critical than the establishment of new parishes as the Catholic population grew and shifted. O'Connell proceeded in this area very cautiously. His tenure in Portland was too short for any significant trends to emerge, but he was certainly in no rush to create parishes, preferring instead to add mission stations (which were served from established churches) to the parishes he already had. The number of churches with a resident priest grew only from fifty-seven to sixty between 1901 and 1906; the number of mission chapels they served increased during the same period from thirty-one to forty-four.[29] Such a policy put a greater strain on the clergy, who had to serve more communities without the rewards, financial and otherwise, that the regular parish structure offered. O'Connell was fearful of overextending his resources, however, and he thus preferred a slower approach to growth.

No case demonstrates this caution better than that of the town of Lubec, which was located at the northern end of the coastline, opposite Campobello Island. Lubec was a small town, but it had a significant Catholic population and a Sacred Heart chapel, which was served by priests from Machias, almost twenty-five miles to the south. Led by their most prominent layman, Thomas E. Vose, the local Catholics began pressing O'Connell for designation as a separate parish late in 1901. The bishop's first concern was financial. "We shall have to see by the amount you can raise that a clergyman can be supported," O'Connell told them. "While I am happy to organize distinct parishes, I must in duty see to it that such parishes will be self-supporting." Vose repeatedly assured him on this score, even going so far as to send two separate lists of names of parishioners and the amount each had pledged to contribute annually. O'Connell continued to hesitate, however, now claiming that he did not have enough priests to spare one for Lubec, though he did scold the pastor of Machias for paying insufficient attention to his remote station. The negotiations continued for several years, but it was not until 1914, well into the tenure of O'Connell's successor, that Lubec's Catholics got a parish of their own.[30] O'Connell's public image as a man of bold action sometimes masked a more hesitant reality.

Though Vose and his friends did not get what they wanted from O'Connell, the bishop was at least willing to hear their case. For most American Catholics at the turn of the century a bishop was a remote figure, someone to be approached with reverence and awe if at all. O'Connell's imposing personal style reinforced this sense of distance. Nevertheless, he occasionally associated with the laity, if only because they constituted useful allies in his occasional struggles with priests who, though technically subordinate to him, were accustomed to doing as they pleased in their own localities. In considering the ambitious plans of Father John M. Harrington, pastor of Saint Mary's, Orono, for a handsome new stone church, he demanded proof of broadly based lay support. "I have reason to think," he told Harrington, "that the sentiment which you believe to be almost universal in your parish in favor of this plan is not so." Later he scolded the priest for "violent conduct in Church towards the people," after receiving several reports of public denunciations of parishioners. Another priest was similarly warned, and two laymen from his parish were secretly assigned to monitor his sermons and to send O'Connell a signed, witnessed account of any abuse from the pulpit.[31] O'Connell was at least as infected as any prelate of his age with a spirit of clericalism. Still, he knew that the laity had their uses and, since all financial support came ultimately from them, their needs had to be addressed.

Complicating every facet of diocesan life was the ethnic character of Catholicism in Maine. Other groups—including several tribes of Catholic Indians, converted centuries before and concentrated in the northern towns of Eastport, Oldtown, and Calais—played their parts, but it was the enduring cultural and linguistic tension between French and Irish Catholics that demanded regular attention.[32] If the diocese's French pastors had complained to Rome about Irish domination of the hierarchy, so too had Irish parishioners frequently chafed under unsympathetic French pastors. One such parish was Saint Francis de Sales's, Waterville, long a predominantly French territory but with a growing Irish contingent. Fearful of upsetting established patterns of local church life, O'Connell reluctantly entertained pleas from the Irish for separation, and he asked the French pastor, Father Narcisse Charland, for his opinion. Initially in favor of partition, Charland quickly changed his mind. He was dissatisfied with the proposed boundary line between the two churches, and he fretted over the loss of revenue that would result from the split. He objected to the means the Irish were using to raise money for their new parish, including fairs and bazaars at which there was dancing. "I have always been against such amusements at anything Catholic," he explained, pointing out that his French parishioners were scandalized by them and that local Protestant ministers were also clucking their tongues.

The priest went too far, however, when he denounced the separation from his pulpit. However unwillingly O'Connell had become involved with this dispute, the question now was one of his own authority. Since "the matter of increasing accomodation [sic] for the faithful of Waterville is a matter which pertains to me alone," he snapped, the priest's public comment was an act of "serious insubordination." Accordingly, Charland was ordered "in your sermon next Sunday, . . . using the greatest caution and prudence, to unsay what you said to the people about the matter and to send me a faithful copy of your discourse."[33] The rancor of this dispute, which persisted long after O'Connell had left Maine, reinforced his hesitancy in parochial affairs, further limiting whatever inclination he may have had to create new parishes. Though in later years he would pride himself in these as in other matters for his boldness, he was from the beginning of his episcopal career extremely cautious.

* * *

O'Connell's sharpness with Father Charland was by no means unusual when he was dealing with a prickly subordinate, but at the same time it was not entirely characteristic of his supervision of his priests. As bishop he was responsible for the eighty-six diocesan priests he had inherited on his accession, as well as sixteen clerics associated with religious orders who also performed parish and other duties. During his tenure the ranks of the clergy grew modestly, increasing to ninety-nine diocesans and twenty-two order men. In overseeing their activities O'Connell demonstrated the same absorption in detail he exhibited in his administration of parishes. He personally approved routine requests for vacations, provided that another priest could cover the vacationer's responsibilities, and he enforced attendance at an annual spiritual retreat. He made sure that all priests paid uniform fees for canonical dispensation petitions from their parishes, and he even directed one pastor to give a series of sermons on church law when the large number of mixed marriages with Protestants in his parish seemed to evince a lack of "true Catholic spirit."[34] Priests who crossed their bishop in particular cases could expect a severe verbal reprimand, but these situations were never so strained that O'Connell actually had to remove or demote one of his men. His relations with the clergy remained correct, if cool.

A recurring problem was the shortage of priests in Maine. As early as March 1902 O'Connell wrote the superior of a seminary in Montreal, where several Portland students were enrolled. He asked that their training be accelerated by placing them immediately in "the class in which the ceremonies of the Mass are taught," hoping to make them serviceable for routine parish work as quickly as possible. Shortly afterward he wrote the bishop of Springfield, Massachusetts, asking if he could borrow some priests, "even if the men were not strong and would be benefited by a vacation at the sea shore." Eager to add to the number of his priests, he was likewise careful to hold on to those he already had, denying one permission to become a navy chaplain and demanding the return of another who had been working for several years in West Virginia. Despite these concerns, however, O'Connell did not take simply any clergyman who applied, and indeed he seems routinely to have turned down requests by priests for adoption into the diocese when the initiative came from them rather than himself.[35]

O'Connell also had to supervise the diocese's communities of women religious. Distributed among ten different orders, most of the sisters, who outnumbered Maine's priests by three to one, staffed schools in the French-speaking centers. The largest single group was the Sisters of Mercy, a "diocesan" community, meaning that its work was organizationally limited to the Portland see and that it depended on the bishop for its support more closely than other sisterhoods. These nuns were concentrated in the city of Portland itself, running several parish schools with a combined enrollment of 1,200 pupils. They also managed a small orphanage and foundling home in the city.[36]

Despite this limited geographical range of their work, the nuns were given the same close scrutiny O'Connell gave his parishes and his priests. Between August and October 1902 he ordered a series of weekly "instructions" for them at the Mercy convent in Portland. He himself gave the first lecture, on humility, with later topics assigned to various priests: work, prayer, obedience, self-sacrifice, community life, and devotion to the eucharist. He also enforced the regulations, common at the time, of rigid and harsh separation from the world. In approving the rule of the Sisters of Mercy in 1901 he noted that, while these constitutions permitted a sister to remain overnight in the home of a sick or dying relative, "this exception will never be made, unless the presence of a Sister be a legal necessity."[37]

Above all, he expected the sisters' institutions to meet the rigorous standards of sound finances and regular reporting demanded of priests and parishes. When reports were tardy or incomplete he was quick to go after them. In early March 1903, for example, he scolded the superior of the Healy Asylum (an orphanage for boys) and her counterpart at the Hospital of Our Lady of Lourdes (an orphanage for girls), both in Lewiston, for laxity. "I am surprised that you do not seem to know that this is one of your duties as directress of that Institution," he told the latter summarily, "and a very important duty too. I want this complete and itemized statement immediately, and I do not wish to be compelled to make this demand another time."[38] Both these institutions were staffed by the Sisters of Charity known as "Grey Nuns," a "pontifical" religious community who had a motherhouse in Quebec and owed their primary allegiance to their own superiors rather than to the local bishop. O'Connell's ultimate sanctions against such sisters were therefore limited: technically he could not, as he could with the diocesan Sisters of Mercy, simply remove or transfer them. He could and did, however, demand the right to be informed about their work, thereby attempting to influence their operations in a way that was beyond the specific powers given him by the canon law. Still, armed with a strong sense of his rights and duties as a bishop—and also perhaps with contemporary assumptions about the practical capabilities and incapabilities of women—he attempted to exert control over all Catholic institutions within his jurisdictional reach.

His chief worry for these institutions was, as always, for their finances. Despite later claims to financial wizardry, O'Connell possessed no particular economic talent, relying instead on the commonsense frugality he had learned as a boy. Fiscal management in the Portland diocese was a reasonably straightforward proposition: the assets other than real property were kept readily on hand in a few local banks, with liabilities distributed among an equally small number of accounts, including the cathedral, the chancery office, diocesan cemeteries, and a number of trust funds established for charitable purposes. O'Connell mastered this simple system by seeking to avoid debts at all costs and to reduce them as quickly as possible whenever they occurred. To this end, several pastors received letters in March 1903, informing them that their accounts showed too much red ink, and one of them was told bluntly: "I wish the next Report to show a reduction of this indebtedness."[39] Here as elsewhere, he relied on his access to information about money to expose potential problems early enough to correct them.

If these simple financial standards were applied to parishes and institutions, priests and nuns, they were likewise applied to his own household and office, at least outwardly. At times they approached the fanatical. As the winter of 1903 set in, he had Father Collins write to the treasurer of Saint Mary's College in the town of Van Buren, inquiring whether he had any spare potatoes that could be given to the bishop's household. (When told that the college had had some earlier in the season but had already given them away, Collins promised to write sooner next year.) The diocesan chancellor likewise dickered with butchers over the price of meat and complained when lobster hit the "prohibitive price of 18 cts. per lb." Though O'Connell insisted that "there is nothing I dislike more than a long and varied dinner," preferring only "a small lunch sufficient for the needs of the body," he nonetheless maintained both a physique and a lifestyle he thought appropriate for a bishop—a tendency that would become exaggerated as time went on.[40]

More significant financial matters got greater attention, and in particular O'Connell was eager to bolster the special collections taken in parishes on behalf of common causes. Most of these supported particular projects, including charitable agencies and the expenses of educating seminarians, or contributed to the cathe-draticum, a tax on parishes to meet the bishop's own expenses. If a parish's receipts were adjudged to be inadequate, the pastor could expect from O'Connell a letter urging higher returns, as often as not with a quota to be met. How the priest got the money, whether through especially fervid promotion of the cause from the pulpit or by making up the difference from regular Sunday collections, was up to him.[41]

The diocesan collection in which O'Connell was most inter-ested was the annual one for support of the papacy, the so-called Peter's Pence. As he explained to one pastor whose total seemed low, the returns of this collection were a direct reflection of "devotion to the Holy See." Because he was "Rome's man," appointed to Portland specifically because of his Vatican connections, O'Connell avidly sought to bolster the Peter's Pence in his diocese, thereby making both it and himself look good. That he was presumably interested in advancement beyond Portland only served to redouble his efforts. His success at this was less than spectacular. The collection taken in the summer of 1901, just at the time of his appointment and installa-tion, amounted to slightly more than $2,500, and it grew to $3,100 in 1902. That increase could not be sustained, however, and in 1903 the total slipped back to $2,800, though O'Connell apparently sup-plemented the amount from other sources and sent an even $3,000 to Rome.[42] These variations should not be vested with more impor-tance than they deserve: Portland was a small, not particularly wealthy diocese, and its people, though like most American Catholics loyal to the Holy See, could afford only so much for far-flung and poorly understood causes. Still, if O'Connell had hoped to make his mark by establishing a strong record of financial support for Rome, he was disappointed for as long as he stayed in Maine.

* * *

On the surface, the Portland diocese during O'Connell's tenure was healthy and well-managed. An activist, if sometimes stern and demanding, bishop managed the temporal affairs of the church, allowing it to fulfill its religious mission. Beneath the surface, how-ever, there was another story. Throughout his time in Portland, while

O'Connell was enforcing rigorous administrative standards on his subordinates, he himself showed a too-easy willingness to bend the rules. He failed to distinguish between his personal and corporate status, assigning to his own use funds that were not his. Civil law vested control of all church property in him as a "corporation sole," but it expected nonetheless that his official and private capacities would be kept distinct. Despite that, O'Connell's accounting was often irregular, and he consistently treated diocesan money as his own. Like many who achieve positions of authority, he came to believe that the ordinary standards of behavior simply did not apply to him.

The evidence for these irregularities comes from an audit of diocesan accounts conducted by his successor in Maine, Bishop Louis Sebastian Walsh. A native of Salem, Massachusetts, Walsh was a year older than O'Connell and had graduated from Holy Cross College before taking his seminary training under the Sulpicians in Montreal and Paris. Following ordination in 1882, he studied further in Rome before returning to America, where he eventually joined the faculty of Archbishop Williams's seminary, Saint John's, in Brighton. Besides teaching history and canon law, Walsh also served as treasurer of the institution before Williams made him supervisor of the fledgling archdiocesan school system in 1897. This post he held until his appointment to the Portland bishopric after O'Connell's departure in 1906. Walsh's varied administrative experience made him fastidious in accounting for diocesan funds, a trait he found lacking in his predecessor.

Walsh's first scrutiny of Portland's books on his arrival in September 1906 revealed what he cautiously called "some original methods of keeping accounts," and the more he looked the more disturbed he became.[43] Not only were many significant transactions omitted, but some account books were missing altogether. Inquiring of Father Collins, the chancellor, Walsh discovered that some of the Portland records had actually been taken to Boston by O'Connell. Worse, the new bishop said, many of "the books presented to me were made up on and off at various times, and in a large measure during the last few months" of O'Connell's tenure. No accurate day book or cash book remained. Though Walsh allowed for the possibility of imprecision in record-keeping, he believed that O'Connell's actions were the result of something other than inattention to detail.

His conclusions were startling. Adding up all the ready assets of the diocese in various accounts he found a total of almost $21,000. A computation of the liabilities and obligations yielded a figure of just over $46,000, resulting in a deficit of more than $25,000. The trouble did not stop there. The assets of two trust funds were not shown on their books, but had instead been transferred to an account in O'Connell's own name as early as December 1901—"and the check itself is on file," Walsh noted. Other deposits listed among diocesan assets had been made "the day before or [the] very day" of Walsh's arrival as bishop, "and as I found out later many were made from the 'personal account' of my predecessor." O'Connell had even carried off to Boston with him the 1906 cathedraticum offering of almost $5,000, even though, since he was no longer bishop of Portland, he had no right to it. What emerged before Walsh's eyes was a systematic pattern of misconduct.

How should we judge Walsh's extended financial analysis, which, for all its controlled language, reads like an indictment? Personal animus cannot be entirely discounted. Both men had strong personalities, and to this stylistic clash was added a political dimension. Walsh was aligned with the liberal, Americanist wing of the hierarchy that was wary of O'Connell, and he was therefore presumably inclined to put the worst possible interpretation on any given set of facts. The most conclusive evidence for the validity of Walsh's charges, however, was to come from O'Connell himself. After satisfying himself that the deficit was suspicious, Walsh wrote to O'Connell, now archbishop of Boston, in June 1910, presenting him with "a summary and detailed account of liabilities and cash assets" of the Portland diocese. The result was a tacit but swift admission of guilt. With a perfunctory letter, O'Connell enclosed a check for "$25,576.09, the balance deficit in full." The "affair was closed," and with a dramatic flourish Walsh wrote "Amen" at the end of his audit and signed his name to it.[44]

In retrospect, O'Connell's financial irregularities cast an unfortunate pall over his tenure as bishop of Portland—unfortunate because he was not without accomplishments in Maine. He kept the church's centrifugal ethnic forces generally in check, and by enforcing frugality on those under him he prevented the accumulation of debt beyond the ability of the state's Catholics to repay. The diocese may have experienced no inspiring growth under his leadership, but it nonetheless expanded modestly. More important, O'Connell experimented successfully with a new role for himself as bishop, the role of a visible public figure whose influence extended beyond the Catholic community alone. He became, as one newspaper noted (not entirely in sympathetic terms), "an aggressive prelate. . . . In every possible way the claims of the church [were] brought to the attention of the people."[45] Before his tenure, Catholic prelates in Maine and around the country had been inward-looking, concerned with their own people; from this time onward, a wider role was possible and more appealing.

O'Connell stood on the edge of a sharp generational shift in the American Catholic church, as an older leadership group, which had come to maturity in the era of the Civil War, was passing. Fully one-third of all the bishops in the United States would die in the first decade of the twentieth century, including the leaders of the major Catholic centers: Boston, New York, Chicago, Cincinnati, and Saint Louis. Of the nine bishops in New England other than O'Connell, all but two would die in that decade. In their places, a new generation would arise, and William O'Connell assumed the most prominent place in it. His tenure in Portland, brief though it was, gave him the opportunity to experiment with the new episcopal style, to work out in practice what would become the standard by which to judge the church's leaders.

At the same time, O'Connell's years in Maine also had a darker aspect, one most clearly defined by his misappropriation of diocesan funds. Just as his detailed oversight of church affairs was a portent of his future, so was the willingness—to modern eyes, it looks like nothing so much as avarice—to take for his personal use money that properly belonged to the institution he headed. He formed the habit of failing to distinguish between himself as an individual and his role as trustee for the larger, ongoing organization that existed apart from him. The underside of his clear and aggressive public persona was a readiness to act like a law unto himself, a divided sense that the rules he vigorously enforced on others did not apply to him simply because of who he was. He had a larger mission in mind; he was in control, and he could therefore do whatever he wanted.

O'Connell served as bishop of Portland from July 1901 until his installation as coadjutor archbishop of Boston in April 1906. In fact, the time he actually spent in Maine was much shorter than that: for six weeks in the winter of 1903 he vacationed in Florida, and he spent the six months between November 1904 and May 1905 in Rome. In September of the latter year he was appointed a special papal emissary to Japan, and he left the diocese that month, never to return to it as bishop.[46] Even apart from these extended travels, he was during his tenure increasingly preoccupied with the advancement of his own career, particularly in an effort to be designated as the future archbishop of Boston. It is to that advancement we must now turn.

3

AMBITION:
THE CAMPAIGN FOR BOSTON, 1904-1907

NO VERY SOPHISTICATED SENSE of church politics was needed as one century gave way to another to know that a new archbishop of Boston would soon be appointed. John J. Williams, who had held the office since the spring of 1866, bore his age well. He had a spare, wiry frame, was abstemious and regular in his habits, and had maintained an active liturgical and sacramental schedule. Though slowed somewhat by deteriorating eyesight, he submitted to cataract surgery in 1905 and recovered with remarkable ease, with eyeglasses as the only lasting effect. Still, it was clear that he could not live forever and that he would need a successor.[1]

Nor would the transition from Williams to whoever came after him be of merely parochial significance, for this change in the church would coincide with equally important shifts in the political and social life of Boston. John F. Fitzgerald, one of the prototypical Irish ward heelers, would be elected mayor in 1905, defeating the rapidly collapsing remnants of the city's Yankee Republican elite. The first Irish Catholic governor of Massachusetts was less than a decade away. "People here are really in a transition state," one observer reported, and the influence of the church was destined to grow steadily more powerful as Catholics approached an absolute majority of the population. Like the O'Connell family itself, Boston's Catholics were becoming "respectable and respected." They were establishing themselves, accumulating some property, and their children were acquiring higher education and the sense that the world was not a uniformly hostile and uncertain place. A new archbishop would speak to and for this emerging generation of Catholics who were moving from the margins of society to its center. If church activity had understandably slowed somewhat under the

58

aging Williams, one local layman told the Vatican overdramatically, a new archbishop "will take the Catholic body out of the slough of despond in which it has so long lain."[2]

For the American Catholic church as a whole, this would likewise be a critical period. Not only would there be a new generation of leaders, but they would face the challenge of defining their place in the church worldwide. Catholicism had made impressive gains in the United States, but the future held a number of uncertainties. Pope Leo XIII had condemned what he called "Americanism" in 1899, rejecting the notion that the church in the United States ought to develop its own style. Adherence to central, Roman standards in all things was now to be strictly enforced. After Leo's death in 1903, his successor, Pius X, began to move against what he saw as the even more serious threat of modernism, the notion that the church had to adapt itself to changing times and the "higher criticism" of biblical and other traditional sources of authority. Though the precise extent of modernist belief remains uncertain, independent intellectual inquiry became theologically suspect, and ultramontane orthodoxy was the order of the day.[3] As one of the first appointments in a major Catholic center to follow in the wake of these developments, the new archbishop of Boston would be seen—and he would be intended—as a bellwether for the future.

* * *

From the beginning of public and private speculation on Williams's successor, the vigorous bishop of Portland was recognized as a leading candidate. He had been in Maine only a year when a newspaper there described him as "ready to occupy any field likely to be opened to him." Boston papers too considered his promotion a likelihood. "Unless things have changed very much in Rome since the elevation of Pius X," one of them quoted an unnamed priest in 1903, "Bishop O'Connell will be the next archbishop of Boston." The rumor spread early that he would be named as Williams's coadjutor, a title that bore with it the right of automatic succession on the older prelate's death. Other names were also mentioned, but O'Connell was thought to have the inside track because of his personal and ideological ties to the Vatican. No other New Englander was as well known there as he, and his appointment would mark "a new epoch," another newspaper said, "a strong Roman epoch."[4]

O'Connell's Roman associations helped promote his candidacy for Boston, but they also ensured that he would face opposition. Identified as he was with the American ultramontane faction, he was a lightning rod for the hostility of those leery of too exclusive a reliance on the Roman tradition. Liberal churchmen in America, led by Archbishop John Ireland, had elaborated the vision of a Catholicism more in accord with the self-confidence and democratic idealism of the United States. They clung to the Americanist positions that the pope had condemned, embracing the separation of church and state, for example, as good for both. They hoped to forestall the forging of tighter links to Rome, which, they feared, only emphasized the "foreign" character of their faith. That this faction had been chastened by Leo's denunciation of this view as heretical did not mean that they had given up hope for a continuing influence, particularly by securing the appointment of like-minded bishops. If, therefore, O'Connell could be expected to press for designation as Boston's next archbishop in order to forge (as he had said of Portland) a "tighter and stronger link . . . to the Holy See," other Catholic leaders in America could be expected to oppose him in the hope of heading off that very result. Indeed, Ireland and Cardinal Gibbons seem to have kept a wary eye on O'Connell from an early date.[5]

For his part, Bishop O'Connell did little either to encourage or discourage speculation about his future. He never commented publicly on any rumors, and his private responses to anyone who broached the subject of his advancement were appropriately circumspect. Still, he did what he could to present himself, his abilities, and his Roman loyalties in the best possible light. Through the apostolic delegation in Washington, O'Connell sent the Vatican a steady stream of news about his activities as bishop, connecting them whenever possible to issues in which he knew Rome was interested. He made much of his efforts on behalf of Italian immigrants, for example, even though their presence in Maine was negligible. When Leo XIII died in the summer of 1903, O'Connell presided at an impressive memorial in the Cathedral of the Immaculate Conception, attended by the governor and the mayor, an event that was, he proudly maintained, "surpassing in its character even the memorial service here on the occasion of the death of President McKinley."[6] O'Connell's program of aggressive visibility was perfectly suited to keep both his diocese and himself in the public eye, fueling the assumptions that he would be moved to a higher place.

Behind the scenes, too, he worked to maintain his curial contacts. Though he did not visit Rome until the time of his regularly scheduled *ad limina* report (a formal account of diocesan activity required of bishops every five years) at the end of 1904, he was never shy about keeping in touch with his Vatican associates. He was overjoyed when a puzzled Cardinal Merry del Val, now the papal secretary of state, wrote him, asking for an explanation of an American organization with the curious name of Elks. O'Connell responded with a painstakingly helpful letter, denouncing the "excessive conviviality" of the lodge, making it "a sort of recruiting agency of secret societies [like the Masons] already condemned by the Church." More to the point, he signaled his readiness to undertake other tasks, thanking Merry profusely "for the privilege offered me of being even in the smallest way of any service to Your Eminence." O'Connell traveled to Washington twice in 1903 to meet with the apostolic delegate, and when his old mentor Cardinal Satolli visited the United States the next year, O'Connell quickly invited him to Portland. This was seen as a significant visit, particularly since the powerful Roman had called on no other bishops in New England, not even the venerable Williams. From far-off Saint Paul, Archbishop Ireland saw in these arrangements a "fatal mistake."[7]

O'Connell also relied on an American layman by the name of Francis Augustus MacNutt to be an agent promoting his cause at the Vatican. A friend of O'Connell's since his college rector days, MacNutt was a flamboyant character with large mustaches who would probably have been more at home in an earlier century. A native of Indiana, he had enrolled as a young man in an Italian seminary, where he had been a classmate of Merry del Val and others who were now assuming important church positions. He left the seminary well before ordination, married, and pursued a successful business career, finally settling in Rome. There he presided over a salon society that included traveling Americans, random European aristocrats, and prominent churchmen. By the turn of the century, MacNutt was holding weekly card parties on Friday afternoons, to which he regularly invited a number of cardinals for talk of church affairs. He described these occasions, giving detailed accounts of who had said what to whom, in long letters to O'Connell.[8]

MacNutt sent O'Connell blunt assessments of his supporters and detractors, charting the ups and downs of his prospects. "You may certainly count on me," MacNutt wrote, "to leave nothing undone to further your interests, and I sincerely hope you may be transferred to Boston in which wider field you could find fuller play for your energies." Of their chances for success, he said simply: "I think we can do it." In return, O'Connell did what he could to repay MacNutt's favors, writing to several officials in an effort to secure various papal honors for "Franz," whom he described as "*the American Catholic in the Eternal City . . . persona gratissima to the Holy Father.*"[9]

If the bishop of Portland had one eye focused on Rome, he kept another on Boston. He made the short trip to Massachusetts frequently, often to assist Archbishop Williams: for two weeks in June 1903, he administered confirmation at nine suburban churches. He read the metropolitan newspapers regularly, and he spoke to a number of lay groups, giving the Lowell Knights of Columbus permission to hang his portrait in their "parlor," hoping that "it will keep me in the memory of my old friends." He attended priestly functions at Saint John's Seminary in Brighton, telling the rector: "I am much interested in the Seminary"—a phrase that would later take on an ominous tone. At the same time, he was careful not to overstep the bounds that prevented one bishop from interfering in the diocese of another. When the rising politician John Fitzgerald sought an endorsement for his newspaper, the *Republic*, the Portland bishop demurred. "It would be discourteous if I were to write a letter commending its merits," O'Connell told Fitzgerald at the beginning of their sometimes friendly, sometimes stormy relationship, "before any action had been taken on the part of the Bishop of your own Diocese [i.e., Williams]."[10] Without seeming pushy or meddlesome, O'Connell continued to be a public figure of at least secondary importance in Boston.

His first real chance for advancement came in the spring of 1903, shortly before the death of Leo XIII, and the opportunity was as unexpected as it was unlikely. The archbishop of Manila in the Philippines had died, and Rome was about the business of finding a successor. Since the islands had been seized from Spain in the "splendid little war" of 1898, an American seemed a sensible choice for the job. After a bishop from California turned down the appointment for reasons of health, the Vatican offered the position to William O'Connell. He had little to recommend him by way of particular knowledge of Southeast Asia, but he was an American and, in Rome's view, reliable. As he recalled afterward, the decision was entirely in his own hands, "an invitation which I was at liberty to accept or reject, without offense or prejudice." He gave the matter serious thought, even traveling to Washington to discuss it with the apostolic delegate and with officials of the American state department. Though the offer was a flattering one, he turned it down. If accepting Manila were "a duty," he wrote later, he would have been willing to go, but "if they left me entirely and absolutely free in the matter, for very strong reasons, which to me and other wiser heads seemed exceedingly valid, I would remain in Portland. . . . I have never had cause since to doubt the reason which prompted me to make my decision."[11]

"The reason which prompted" him was two-sided, as he explained in his letter of refusal. First, he argued, since the Spanish-American War had been unpopular in certain quarters in the United States, the appointment of any American was problematic, inevitably raising the touchy political question of imperialism. This scruple bothered O'Connell more than it did those in Rome: when he refused the job, it was given instead to a priest from Saint Louis. More boldly, O'Connell rejected Manila because of the impending appointment of a coadjutor for Boston, a post for which he thought himself better suited. He knew the diocese and its people, he told the Vatican, and he alone could give it the Roman discipline he said it needed. He even reported that Archbishop Williams had privately expressed a preference for him as a successor, an assertion that was almost certainly false. O'Connell's frankness in alluding to the possibility of his promotion to Boston was striking. In fact, Francis MacNutt, perhaps one of the "wiser heads" he had consulted, thought it a tactical blunder. Although widely expected, no formal request for a coadjutor had yet been made by Williams, and O'Connell thus appeared overeager in talking about it so openly. The slip was potentially serious, but MacNutt conferred with his ecclesiastical grapevine and happily reported, "I have not at all discovered that this has been taken amiss."[12] By giving up the opportunity to be an archbishop on the other side of the world, O'Connell hoped to have another chance closer to home.

* * *

He did not have long to wait. Archbishop Williams had been considering the step as early as the preceding Christmas, and in September 1903 he made a formal request to Propaganda Fide for a coadjutor. He had been a priest since 1845, Williams pointed out, and a bishop since 1866; he was now supervising a diocese of more than 700,000 Catholics, 560 priests, and 1,500 religious women. He had an auxiliary bishop, John Brady, but he too was old and in failing health. "It requires a younger and more vigorous hand," Williams concluded, "to attend properly to the affairs of the diocese." Rome found these reasons persuasive and granted permission to proceed with the preparation of the *ternae*.[13] The high-level maneuvering began almost immediately.

Williams was characteristically discreet about his own preferences, but in subtle ways he made it clear that he favored Bishop Matthew Harkins of Providence. A native of Massachusetts, Harkins had, like Williams, studied at the seminary of Saint Sulpice in Paris, and he had served in several parishes in Boston, Arlington, and Salem before his appointment to the Providence bishopric in 1887. There he had presided over a modest and peaceful expansion of diocesan services in the face of an increasingly diverse ethnic population. He regularly traveled the short distance between Providence and Boston to advise and assist the archbishop. Williams signified to the apostolic delegate that this was his man and, equally important, as Harkins confided to his diary, he "seemed desirous not to have a certain prelate"—undoubtedly O'Connell. At Williams's urging, Harkins spoke to several other New England bishops, apparently to convey the archbishop's sentiments.[14]

For all his desire to have a successor appointed, Williams was curiously slow in setting the procedure in motion, waiting several months before convening the necessary meetings of the senior Boston pastors and of the New England bishops. The gathering of the clergy on April 4, 1904, was a calm, businesslike affair. The twenty priests eligible to participate voted, in order of preference, for Harkins, Auxiliary Bishop Brady, and O'Connell's former pastor, Monsignor William Byrne, still in charge of Saint Joseph's parish in Boston's

West End. The meeting of the bishops three days later was more strained, since both of the leading contenders were present. Harkins absented himself from the room for fifteen minutes while his own name was discussed. O'Connell, who had been designated to keep the minutes, remained coolly aloof throughout, refusing to participate in what he took to be an active conspiracy against him. With his name apparently not even mentioned as a candidate—he could not nominate himself, and no one else seemed willing to do so—he reported that "for good and legitimate reasons [he] took no action in the election." When the voting was completed, the bishops agreed with the priests on their choice for first place ("*dignissimus*"—most worthy): Matthew Harkins. The other two names proposed by the clergy were set aside, however, and replaced with Monsignor William McQuaid, pastor of Saint James's parish in downtown Boston, and Father Richard Neagle, pastor of Immaculate Conception, Malden, who had served for ten years as Williams's chancellor. These names were submitted to the apostolic delegate, who forwarded them to Rome.[15]

O'Connell was furious over his exclusion. Abandoning the icy silence he had adopted during the meeting, he sent Rome a damning assessment of the competition. Harkins he described as chronically sick, possessed of a "most ordinary" education (including, pointedly, no fluency in Italian), and incapable of managing the affairs even of the Providence diocese, "the smallest in America." Brady was "practically useless," O'Connell sneered, and Byrne was at the center of a plot by the Boston pastors to ensure a weak, pliable successor to Williams so they could have their own way in diocesan affairs.[16]

Posing as the innocent victim of Americanist intrigue, O'Connell also sought to invest the selection process with a larger, ideological significance. He offered to meet the apostolic delegate in New York to expand on this notion—a proposal the shrewd prelate prudently rejected—but O'Connell found others who would listen. Those preparing the lists of candidates had "one frank and avowed motive," he told Merry del Val: "to keep off the *terna* at all costs any name which stood for Rome, for Roman views and for Roman sympathies." Taking the high ground himself, he maintained that "my only thought is to save, in this awful hour of peril, the honor of [the] Church. . . . Boston is at this moment," he concluded ominously, "in the balance between Rome and her enemies."[17]

O'Connell had few supporters among the Boston priests, but a handful, most of them younger alumni of the American College, sounded similar themes in backing their former rector. Father Patrick Supple, a *Romano* now at Saint Peter's, Cambridge, complained that the electors had "purposely set aside the man who of all others . . . is best fitted to advance the interests of Catholicity in New England." A "strong anti-Roman bias" was on the loose among the bishops, he asserted; "is it to men of such character that Rome intends to leave the choice of the future Archbishop of Boston?" Father John Cummins of Sacred Heart parish, Roslindale, concurred. Loyally maintaining that the "Roman influence" was "the best bulwark of society," Cummins noted sadly that "the name of him who is preeminently the best exponent of the Holy See in these parts was invidiously omitted." If the Vatican were wise, it would reject the recommended names and appoint O'Connell instead. "No better opportunity has ever been open to Rome to eradicate a disease [i.e., Americanism] foreshadowed by the lamented Leo XIII," Supple concluded.[18]

O'Connell's friends made both a positive case for him and a negative one against Bishop Harkins and even Archbishop Williams himself. In particular, they raised the question of the appropriate public image for the next archbishop, an area in which the man from Portland had already distinguished himself. Though Boston now had a majority Catholic population, one layman observed in a not-so-veiled slam at Williams, "the voice of the Church is never heard except in trumpeting some trivial parochial exhibition or whining over an injustice which the inefficiency of the great body at large and the supineness of its leader has permitted to exist." The writer perhaps had in mind the construction only two years before of a branch of the Boston Elevated Railway directly in front of the Cathedral of the Holy Cross: the superstructure blocked the view of the church's rose window, and the rumble of trains along the track drowned out whatever ceremony was taking place inside. Catholics had to stand up to such indignities, the writer argued. Williams's leadership had grown "sluggish, inert, inactive and without fruit," but now Catholics were ready for the more assertive leadership that only William O'Connell could provide. "A man of large parts ought to be appointed," one priest maintained, while another said that Boston Catholicism needed an archbishop who was "*big* enough, and *great* enough, and *grand* enough to grace and represent this great Metropolitan see."[19]

O'Connell was particularly well suited to this task, a non-Catholic newspaperman told the apostolic delegate, because he knew how to work through the medium of mass journalism to touch a wider audience. The daily press, said Matthew Hale of the *Boston Globe*, was "open to anyone who can, to use a phrase of the newspaper world, 'talk . . . news.' Even in his diocese of Portland Dr. [*sic*] O'Connell has used this opportunity . . . to good effect." Predicting (not inaccurately, as it turned out) that O'Connell as archbishop would rival Harvard's president Charles W. Eliot as an influential public figure, Hale asserted that O'Connell's "commanding presence [was] no small attraction among a people who like dignity and manliness."[20]

Despite this support for O'Connell, Harkins remained the more likely choice. Not only was he the senior bishop in New England after Williams and the unanimous choice of those qualified to express a formal opinion, but he also enjoyed a wide national reputation. In keeping with traditional practice, the Vatican had solicited the opinion of the eleven other archbishops in the United States, and every one of them (excepting only the archbishop of Santa Fe, who said he was too far away to have an opinion) endorsed Harkins. The leading figures of the liberal wing of the hierarchy, including Cardinal Gibbons, John Ireland, John Keane of Dubuque, and Patrick Riordan of San Francisco, joined this chorus enthusiastically. Williams at last told Rome formally that Harkins was "my choice." Father Supple's carping that Harkins was infected with "the Americanist spirit" and an affinity for "what is known as Higher Criticism" (the code phrase for modernism) notwithstanding, the bishop of Providence seemed a better bet for promotion to Boston than his brother of Portland.[21]

Such broad support for his competition was problem enough for O'Connell, but he soon faced a challenge that threatened to render him unacceptable to the public at large. During the same spring months of 1904 that he hoped would bring his advancement to Boston, he had to defend himself against charges that he had been disloyal, and perhaps even treasonous, during the Spanish-American War six years before. The story had surfaced first in February, when the *New York World* carried a report that O'Connell, while rector of the American College, had given Merry del Val a thousand lire to outfit a Spanish battleship. Asked by a Portland newspaper for comment, O'Connell called the story "rascally and cowardly," and he promised to "prosecute to the full extent of the law if I can find him the originator or the propagator of this vile lie." With the struggle for the Boston coadjutorship intensifying, O'Connell knew he had to meet the rumor with a vigorous retaliation. At his prompting, several political figures from Maine and Massachusetts (led by Boston's respectable mayor Patrick Collins) sent Rome an endorsement of O'Connell's "sound, patriotic . . . sentiments" and denouncing "the story, evidently designed to injure his prestige. . . . The falsity of this calumny is evident," these leading citizens concluded, "and we deplore its mischievous invention and intent."[22]

The charge of disloyalty, especially a disloyalty carried out in so bold and personal a way, was almost certainly the deliberate slander O'Connell thought it. He had indeed been close to the Spaniard Merry del Val at the time of the war, but the attachment was hardly strong enough to lead him into treason. American Catholics generally had seized on the brief conflict enthusiastically as a way of countering persistent nativist claims that they made unreliable citizens. Even when their country did battle with an overwhelmingly Catholic nation, they had argued, their duties as Americans took precedence. Some churchmen, including O'Connell's predecessor in Portland, James A. Healy, had expressed private reservations about the war, and O'Connell himself had predicted sadly to his sister in 1898 that fighting would have "a bad effect upon the business of the country, and of course as usual the poor will suffer." For his part, Merry del Val had appreciated the delicacy of his American friend's position, telling him at the outbreak of the war: "it is all so unholy, so unnecessary, so terrible."[23] O'Connell undoubtedly had a clear conscience on the subject, but more to the point in 1904 he feared the effect even a falsehood could have on his chances to succeed Archbishop Williams.

O'Connell's desire to find and expose the source of the story was no idle threat, and he was quickly satisfied that he had done so. On the very day that he denounced the unnamed rumor-monger to the press, he wrote a long letter to Denis O'Connell, his predecessor at the American College and by now rector of the Catholic University in Washington. There followed several exchanges in which the New England O'Connell pressed his southern colleague for what he knew of the matter. Denis was at first evasive, and he then took simply to ignoring William's letters. The silence from Washington convinced the Portland bishop that his colleague had at least actively spread the story, if he had not actually been its origin. "It is simply a lie," William O'Connell said sharply to his supposed accuser. "I say—a lie—advisedly, because I know that it was a false-hood invented to deceive others and to calumniate me." These sus-picions were well-placed: though not as influential as he had once been, Denis was still a leader among the episcopal liberals who backed Harkins for the Boston position. What is more, the effort to embarrass William O'Connell publicly gave substance to his private belief that he was the object of an Americanist conspiracy. The two O'Connells had never been particularly close before this episode; after it, their relations became decidedly frosty.[24]

O'Connell was able to defuse the charges of disloyalty, but the affair had an impact nevertheless. Coupled with the efforts to get Rome to reject the official *ternae*, the uproar made the Vatican think twice before designating a coadjutor for Boston. As with O'Connell's appointment to Portland only a few years before, the apparently straightforward process became clouded by controversy. Propaganda Fide did not meet until August 22, 1904, when it voted to postpone a selection indefinitely, a decision that was itself long delayed in reaching Archbishop Williams, who did not receive word of it until shortly before Christmas.[25] For the present, no appointment would be made.

O'Connell soon got the chance to press his case personally, for on November 19, 1904 (before Propaganda's decision to delay was known in America), he sailed from Boston to make the regularly scheduled *ad limina* report on the affairs of his diocese to Pius X. Planned long before, the visit was routine enough, but its timing seemed particularly auspicious for O'Connell. He remained in Rome until the end of the following May, an unusually long stay for such an occasion, during which time he met with the pope at least twice and made the rounds of his other allies at the Vatican. His tarrying at the center of power naturally sparked rumors at home, including a far-fetched one that he would be appointed apostolic delegate to Cuba and that Harkins would receive the Boston coadjutorship. Nothing came of these reports, but O'Connell still made progress toward his true goal. Francis MacNutt recalled later that it was during this sojourn in Rome that "his nomination became as certain as anything could be in a world of uncertainties."[26]

On his return to America, O'Connell briefly went back to his duties in Portland before receiving a surprising temporary assignment, one that seemed at first to diminish his prospects for promotion to Boston, though it eventually enhanced them. On September 1, 1905, the Vatican announced that he would be sent on a special diplomatic mission to Japan, recently triumphant in its war with Russia. O'Connell afterwards described this commission as coming "like a bolt from the blue" and, if he had received hints of it while in Rome the previous spring, it was no less genuine a surprise to most observers.[27] By the middle of the month he left Portland for San Francisco, sailing from there on Columbus Day and arriving in Tokyo on October 29.

The mission to Japan was long on ceremony and short on substance. Carrying a letter of greeting from the pope to the mikado, O'Connell acknowledged that "the mission was an entirely friendly one, with no other purpose" than the show of goodwill. Though the rise of nationalism during the war had increased Japanese hostility toward all things foreign, O'Connell was received respectfully, especially when he expressed the pope's thanks for the mild treatment of Catholics in Manchuria during the fighting. This was an era of relative religious toleration in Japan, a policy perhaps made easier because the number of Catholics there had effectively leveled off at a scant 10,000.[28] O'Connell met with the emperor in the middle of November 1905, attended lunches and dinners with the diplomatic corps and with prominent Japanese, and delivered speeches to the Imperial Education Society and to the students of Tokyo University. Besides the capital, he also visited the Catholic centers of Kobe and Nagasaki, setting sail again in early December, bound for home by way of China, Singapore, India, and through the Suez Canal to Rome.

The diplomatic results of the mission were slim: the Vatican and Japan would not establish formal relations until 1942, although the opening of Sophia University in Tokyo in 1913 by the Jesuits may have been loosely connected with the visit. On the whole, the trip probably did O'Connell more good than vice versa. He got to observe the church in Japan at first hand, though he found it entirely too French. The cathedral in Tokyo was unfortunately known as *l'église française*, he noted, and the diplomatic alliance between Paris and Saint Petersburg had exacerbated antagonism toward Catholic missionaries, most of whom were French. In broader, cultural terms, he brought home with him a reinforced Western sense of the potential threat of "the East," a caricature made that much stronger because he now fancied himself something of an expert on the subject. His final assessment, written almost ten years afterwards, concluded expansively: "I am thankful for the great privilege I have had in being able to see the East as few are able to see it. . . . But never again! Never. Let me live where there is a Sunday, a church bell, and the necessaries of life—but never again in this awful gloom of paganism . . . where human life seems next to hopeless."[29] The young man from Lowell, as experienced as he had become in the ways of the world, remained to the end a believer in the superiority of Western civilization.

* * *

O'Connell's homeward journey landed him in Rome at the beginning of 1906. By then the movement to appoint a coadjutor for Boston was again gathering steam, and his arrival was, therefore, particularly timely and hardly accidental. Much had happened since Propaganda Fide's postponement more than a year before. Williams had written to the Vatican twice, asking for an end to the delay. "The 'Boston affair' is still unsettled," Fall River's Bishop William Stang (a staunch liberal ally) wrote a colleague, expressing the fear that no news was most likely bad news. "Things are growing desperate."[30] These entreaties, together with Williams's steadily advancing age (he was now eighty-three), led Propaganda to consider the matter again, after eighteen months of inaction, on January 22, 1906.

O'Connell had conveniently arrived in Rome just ten days before, devoting himself to an intensive lobbying effort. He went immediately to see Cardinal Merry del Val, who was reported to be "overjoyed to see him," and he presented Pius X with a full report on the Japanese mission. Meeting again on several occasions with the secretary of state, O'Connell also waited on a number of other cardinals, one of whom "spoke very plainly of [the] need of recompense" for O'Connell's services.

January 22, a Monday, was "a day of subdued excitement." O'Connell kept demurely to his hotel room, but his traveling companion, Father Charles Collins, stood like a spy at the foot of the

Spanish Steps, watching the Propaganda's office, which was located nearby. Cardinal Girolamo Gotti, the head or "prefect" of the congregation, was sick, and that threatened to postpone the deliberations yet again. At midmorning, however, Collins was cheered to see the carriages of several cardinals pulling in and out and to watch the shades of the upstairs meeting room go up. Not hearing word of a decision by noontime, however, his spirits fell again. He feared that no action would be taken and, together with Father Patrick Supple, a fellow traveler and O'Connell's principal backer among the Boston clergy, he "began to wonder how long we would have to remain in Rome," presumably for more lobbying, before a decision would be made.[31]

That evening brought happier news. Summoned to O'Connell's room, the party found an Italian monsignor, one of Merry del Val's secretaries, who (paraphrasing the usual announcement of papal elections), intoned, "*Habemus Pontificem*"—"We have a bishop." Explaining the deliberations, he reported that one cardinal had proposed adding O'Connell's name to the official *ternae* and that two others had seconded this nomination, which then received the unanimous endorsement of the entire group. Though Pius X would not confirm the choice until a week and a half later, the appointment was nevertheless official. "We fell on each other's necks," Collins said, "and there was hilarity." The goal had at last been achieved: William O'Connell would be coadjutor archbishop of Boston with right of succession. "It was clearly God's Will," O'Connell wrote in his memoirs.[32]

Those who had opposed his selection thought they discerned something other than the hand of the Almighty at work. Once the decision became known in America on January 26, expressions of shock were commonplace. Archbishop Williams was publicly restrained as usual, saying he would accept anyone the pope sent him. Privately he told Bishop Stang that he was "disappointed and depressed," and he remarked sadly to Harkins, the runner-up: "I did not think that Rome would treat me thus." From Baltimore, Cardinal Gibbons was equally discreet, though he could not keep from expressing surprise at the speed of O'Connell's advancement. "I little thought," he wrote in a carefully worded congratulatory message, "when I recommended you as Rector of the American College that your rise would be so rapid."[33]

Other churchmen were not so docile. Stang was beside himself with rage, calling the selection of O'Connell "an affliction" and "a shock from which the present generation will scarcely recover." His friend Archbishop Riordan of San Francisco concurred, bluntly describing the choice as "the most disastrous thing that has happened to religion in a century." The manner of the appointment was as objectionable as its outcome, and supporters of Harkins began immediately to plan a formal protest. "He who was 'dignissimus' in the conscientious opinion of Bishops and priests is pushed aside," Stang fumed. "Things have come to such a state that American bishops are treated like a lot of unreliable schoolboys." Springfield's Bishop Thomas Beavan likewise objected to the behind-the-scenes maneuvering, saying "all are astonished . . . but attribute it to the influence of [Merry] Del Val." Encouraged by John Ireland, the godfather of all liberal causes among the hierarchy, Stang drafted a letter of protest to Pius X, a letter signed by all the bishops of New England except Williams, Manchester's John Delaney (O'Connell's one friend among his colleagues), and of course the new coadjutor himself. Even so, it was too late: the "memorial" was received but not answered, and Williams's acceptance of the decision put an end to any effort to block it. Pius was reported to be "in sympathy" with Williams over the rejection of his choice, but the matter ended there. "So we must be satisfied with the 'sympathy' of the Pope," Harkins told Ireland bitterly.[34]

O'Connell knew the extent and the virulence of the reaction to him. He was more convinced than ever that there was a conspiracy against him by those who sought to limit Rome's influence in America, and each new objection by Harkins, Stang, and their allies only proved it. Rather than linger in Rome as he had after his appointment to Portland, he wasted no time in 1906, hurrying home to claim his prize. He had a farewell audience with Pius X on February 6, and on March 12 (delayed several days by rough seas) he landed in Boston. He made a brief trip to Portland to arrange affairs there—and perhaps to concoct the unusual bookkeeping practices Louis Walsh later found—and then he returned to Boston. On April 3, five hundred priests gathered in the Cathedral of the Holy Cross for the ceremony of installation.

O'Connell's address to the priests of Boston that day was startling in its frankness. He and his audience both knew that his promotion had been irregular; many of his listeners had been overtly opposed to it. Alluding to the "long delay which the weightiness of the question demanded," O'Connell rested his case on the principles of authority and allegiance to Rome with which he thought no Catholic—and certainly no priest—could argue. "Ecclesiastical power and authority are derived," he lectured, "not from the votes of the clergy or from the suffrages of Bishops, but solely from the Apostolic See." If his selection was a surprise, it was nevertheless made "with the perfect observance of every detail of law." Regardless of how anyone in America might feel about it, "Rome has made her irrevocable decision." More to the point, the approval of the papacy implied an even higher sanction. "I believe as strongly as I believe that there is a God," O'Connell said, "that that God has placed me where I am."[35]

Lapsing into the military metaphor he so often used to characterize the church, he spoke next of obligation. Every priest was akin to the church's "humblest soldier"; bishops were the "greatest generals"; and the laity were "that vast militia" who needed to be "regulated and protected." The call of duty to all ranks was now clearly sounded: "upon the day when we enlisted we gave our solemn vow to God to respect these relations." Thus, regardless of their private opinions, the whole army that had "enlisted" at baptism or ordination was bound to unite and obey their orders. Accordingly, O'Connell asked for acceptance, demanding "the right respected by all honest men[:] to be judged only by my own acts." The plea was coupled with a warning: "He who from this day breaks the sacredness of order and harmony in this Diocese will have small claim to the respect of any of us who rule it and labor in it." Perhaps unconsciously slighting Williams, who sat close by, he averred that "the past is dead[,] the future is at the door." Finally, he exhorted all to "turn now to Him who has already given the order to march," and concluded: *Procedamus in pace*"—let us go forth in peace.

Having signified that he was firmly in place, O'Connell settled into his new duties as coadjutor. After a round of civic and religious receptions, he moved into a spacious townhouse across the street from the cathedral and began performing liturgical functions. He administered confirmation in several parishes, especially those in outlying towns whose distance from Boston made travel by Williams burdensome. He dedicated new church buildings, partici-

pated in priestly ordinations, and presided at school commencement exercises, including those of his alma mater, Boston College.
He took no real role in the administrative affairs of the archdiocese,
but for the seventeen months until Williams's death, he fulfilled the
role of a coadjutor, assisting his archbishop in whatever ways were
required.[36]

* * *

In following to its conclusion the story of O'Connell's pursuit
of power, the historian must inquire into its larger significance. Is
there more to it than merely the prurient appeal of an involved tale
of intrigue and maneuver, of power and conspiracy? Is it just an
ironic account, given particular piquancy because it unfolds in a religious context, where base motives are not supposed to govern
behavior? Does it tell us anything about its times and its characters?
Is it, in short, anything more than just an ecclesiastical soap opera?

The story of O'Connell's ambition does indeed highlight
important aspects of American Catholicism at the opening of the
twentieth century. To begin with, his triumph was the first conspicuous and successful display of personal ambition by an American
prelate. He had mastered the intricacies of church politics in a way
no American before him ever had. His long years in Rome had
taught him the rules of the game. He accepted those rules on their
own terms, and he played the game to win. The constant contacts
with Vatican officials, the readiness to be seen as obedient to Rome's
slightest wish, the use of MacNutt as an agent and promoter at court,
the marshaling of support for his own cause, and the denigration of
his enemies—all displayed his willingness to use methods whose
principal justification was that they were likely to succeed. The
church in Europe had known such shrewd, worldly, and even cynical
men for centuries. O'Connell was the first, and assuredly not the last,
such figure in America. His careerism was thus a sign—an ironic one,
to be sure—of the maturity of the American church as it entered its
second century. American Catholicism had formerly been an uncertain missionary outpost of dubious durability; now it was an established and powerful institution whose rewards, both internal and
external, were worth contending and scheming for.

The struggle had implications, too, for the whole church of
Boston, both then and in the future. That O'Connell had received

not a single vote on the official lists from either the local pastors or the New England bishops marked him permanently as an outsider. That he was able to secure his position only by playing his Roman trump cards reinforced that perception. He would enter his tenure as archbishop only by further antagonizing those already inclined to view him with suspicion. What should have been an occasion of rejoicing within the church—the coming of a new leader—was turned instead into a polite but sharp confrontation. He would never escape the reality that he had been imposed on a local church that did not want him. For the remainder of his life, O'Connell might be respected, obeyed, and even feared. The circumstances of his appointment guaranteed that, unlike his predecessor, he would never be loved.

More broadly, O'Connell's rise to power shows just how substantial the divisions within the American Catholic leadership were. Though competing personalities exacerbated this "war of the prelates," something more important was at stake. The issues that divided American bishops from one another were sharp, undisguised, and enduring. The conflict was grounded in differing conceptions of what the church in America could be and what kind of model, if any, it provided for Catholicism worldwide. One group, the Americanists, saw no necessary antagonism between the church and democracy, and they welcomed the development of a distinctive American flavor to the church. What is more, they thought the experience of pluralism could be replicated in other nations to good effect, and that the church would only flourish as it abandoned its European traditions of privilege and closed-mindedness. The loss of temporal power by the papacy was liberating, they thought, and the severed connection between church and state only freed the church to carry out its true mission. Rome's Catholicism, defined so often by its hostility to the modern world, was not the only, objective standard. National expressions of religion, in tune with the particular genius of particular peoples, were signs of health, not of sickness. The pope remained the spiritual leader of the church universal, but collegiality among the bishops in each country determined how that international unity would be expressed in local terms.[37]

The opposing group (called "ultramontanes," because they followed the lead of earlier continental churchmen who looked for leadership "beyond the mountains" in Rome), found such views dangerous, and probably heretical. There neither was nor should be such a thing as "American Catholicism," they maintained. The church was one and indivisible, literally catholic, the same everywhere. It was perfectly defined by its infallible leader, the pope, and the administrative apparatus that depended on him. The "jurisdictional power of the Roman pontiff" was "immediate" everywhere in the world, the First Vatican Council (1869–1870) had proclaimed, and the responsibility of Catholics, "both singly and collectively," was "to submit to this power by the duty of hierarchical subordination and true obedience." What is more, this centralized authority had to extend to all things, even into the secular world. Catholicism in America might have flourished under the separation of church and state, but that was a fluke and no model to be emulated. How much better off the American church would be, Pope Leo XIII had written in 1895, "if, in addition to liberty, she enjoyed the favor of the laws and the patronage of the public authority."[38]

In this context, the appointment of a coadjutor archbishop of Boston was, for supporters of O'Connell and Harkins alike, a struggle for supremacy. It was the latest battle in a very long war. When O'Connell told Merry del Val in 1904 that Boston was hanging "in the balance between Rome and her enemies," he meant it, investing his own advancement with an international and even theological meaning. When he accused his opponents of excluding his name because it "stood for Rome," he was declaring his loyalty to one side, the side of triumphant papalism. When he compared the church to an army in which those on top gave orders and those below obeyed them, he deliberately identified with a familiar conception of how religion operated. His was a victory for the ultramontanes of America, whose earlier leader had been New York's Archbishop Michael Corrigan. With his death in 1902 this conservative faction had been left without a champion.[39] By placing himself in that tradition William O'Connell was preparing to assume its leadership and to carry out in the new century the program it had outlined. This monolithic approach would later seem inevitable, the only option for American Catholicism, and that inevitability is itself a testament to O'Connell's success. Before his appointment, another option had seemed possible. For a generation and more after it, there would be little choice: American Catholics would come to glory in being at least as Catholic as the pope.

The successful outcome of O'Connell's ambition was thus the decisive nail in the Americanist coffin. It was part of a larger Roman program, advancing swiftly during the pontificate of Pius X. A new sense of discipline in the church was on the rise everywhere. O'Connell's final accession to the position of archbishop in August 1907 would coincide, almost to the week, with the papal denunciation of modernism in the encyclical *Pascendi dominici gregis*, a document that ushered in an unrelenting, ironclad orthodoxy. The appointment of William O'Connell as archbishop of Boston was the American expression of that worldwide phenomenon.

4

VIGOR IN ARDUIS:
THE MAKING OF A NEW EPISCOPAL STYLE,
1907–1915

WILLIAM O'CONNELL FINALLY REALIZED his ambition on August 30, 1907, the day John J. Williams died. The eighty-five-year-old archbishop had taken his usual vacation that summer with Rochester's Bishop Bernard McQuaid in upstate New York, but on his return home he had been immediately confined to bed. He suffered from "no particular disease," the diocesan historians wrote later, but simply from "the gradual and painless decline [of] extreme old age." After ten days of confinement he died quietly on a Friday evening, and O'Connell automatically became archbishop of Boston.[1]

In pronouncing over his predecessor a eulogy that occasionally damned by faint praise, O'Connell noted Williams's spiritual sincerity, but he also drew implicit comparisons between the deceased and himself. Williams was, O'Connell said, too often "credulous" in his dealings with others, and he exhibited "the sensitiveness of a woman," even in circumstances that demanded sterner stuff. The dead prelate's "reticence" and "modesty almost amounting to shyness" were not traits his successor would imitate. Rather, O'Connell promised to embrace his new responsibilities and to "struggle . . . through storm and tempest" in the years ahead. By thus invoking the metaphors of struggle, storm, and trial, O'Connell signaled that his motto, "Vigor in Arduis," would be the hallmark for his tenure in Boston as it had been in Portland. "No one knew better than I the tremendous weight of the burden," he recalled a quarter-century later, adding disingenuously, "but I had come to my post not by any wish of my own, but by the command of him who represents Christ on earth. . . . So I faced the future with the fullest and most absolute confidence in God and the determination to do . . . well."[2] Whatever the future held, O'Connell would rely on his characteristic self-confidence to see him through.

O'Connell's reign as archbishop would extend over the better part of the next four decades. It was not the uniformly turbulent and burdensome struggle he foresaw at his accession, but it was nevertheless filled with its share of both triumphs and defeats. Like any long regime, his was marked by periods of activity and inactivity, times of intense labor balanced by times of more predictable momentum. The years between 1907 and 1915 were the most significant, however, because they set the patterns that would characterize the remainder. It was during this period that he established himself, despite the opposition to his appointment, as a man firmly in charge. It was then that he achieved his most enduring successes, elaborating a personal style of leadership that was different from that of earlier bishops. Wider accomplishments would elude him, and personal scandal would later block his achievement of other goals. Still, in his first years in office he managed to change the nature of expectations for Catholic bishops in America, thrusting on them the role of public figures they have generally sought to play since.

* * *

Anyone who had followed O'Connell's career in Portland was not surprised to see him adopt the same highly visible approach to his duties in Boston. His schedule was a demanding one, and if, as time went on, he mitigated this pace with long vacations he was nonetheless a man who seemed constantly on the go. From the time of Williams's funeral in September 1907 until the end of the year, he seemed to be everywhere. He spoke at the opening of classes at Boston College and consecrated a new bishop of Fall River to replace the recently deceased William Stang, his erstwhile opponent. He laid cornerstones for new churches in Roxbury, Cambridge, Lowell, and Brookline. He visited the Catholic students' club at Harvard University, administered confirmation at the House of the Angel Guardian, an orphanage in Boston, and ordained eighteen new priests at Saint John's Seminary. His first months culminated in January 1908 with a grand public spectacle in Holy Cross cathedral as he received the pallium, a small yokelike liturgical garment that was the symbol of his office as archbishop, from the hands of

Cardinal Gibbons. "There is a general expectation," the *Pilot* commented on all this busyness, "that the Catholic life of Boston will make vigorous strides under the active sympathy and guidance of Archbishop O'Connell."[3]

In the hectic years that followed, he maintained his pace and expanded his scope. The leaders of national organizations chose Boston for their meetings, in part to bask in the reflected glory of this rising star of the hierarchy. Accordingly, he welcomed gatherings of the American Federation of Catholic Societies (August 1908), the National Catholic Young Men's Union (September 1909), and the Catholic Church Extension Society (October 1913). He put in regular appearances before the local branches of the Knights of Columbus, the Ancient Order of Hibernians, the League of Catholic Women, and the Holy Name Society. Appropriate fanfare accompanied celebrations both official and personal: the centennial of the diocese in October 1908, a canonical synod in February 1909, the twenty-fifth anniversary of his ordination the following June, and his fiftieth birthday that December.

In contrast to Williams, who had seldom ventured onto the public stage, O'Connell appeared at numerous civic functions. He was an attraction on the banquet circuit, taking dinner with President William Howard Taft (September 1909), lunch with Massachusetts Governor Curtis Guild (January 1908), and even attending the dinner meetings of Boston's jocular and sarcastic Clover Club (September 1915). He met with such nonreligious organizations as the American Guild of Organists (March 1910), the Associated Charities of Boston (November 1910), and the American Cancer Society (January 1915). He prayed over the opening of the new term of the Suffolk County Superior Court in January 1910 and at John Fitzgerald's inauguration for a second term as mayor of Boston the following month. He helped dedicate the new Customs House (January 1915) and a memorial for former mayor Patrick Collins (November 1908), and he visited battleships docked at the Charlestown Navy Yard. He was prominently seen with a host of dignitaries visiting Boston, including the British ambassador, Lord Bryce, in February 1908, the Italian tenor Enrico Caruso that spring, and John Redmond, the Irish parliamentary leader, in the fall.[4] In short order, O'Connell had become a celebrity, recognized not only by his own flock but by every inhabitant.

The newspapers cheerfully reported his comings and goings, and they also covered his every public utterance. When he issued a pastoral letter (the local analog of a papal encyclical, a practice previously unknown in Boston), echoing Pius X's condemnation of modernism, the full text was published in the secular as well as the religious press. The papers kept a keen eye out for his appearance in unlikely places, including a tour of the "motor boat show" in the winter of 1908. (This may have been a shopping trip, for shortly afterward a published report indicated that he had given a boat to his old friend, Cardinal Merry del Val, as a present.) A dog fancier who kept a succession of large black poodles, each of them named "Moro" (Italian for "the Moor"), O'Connell also visited the annual dog show. He took in other sporting events as well, including football and baseball games between the Jesuit rivals Boston College and Holy Cross. He appeared in the society pages when he presided at weddings, most notably that of Joseph P. Kennedy and Rose Fitzgerald, the mayor's daughter, in his private chapel in October 1914. His achievement of celebrity status was rapid and complete. "The high degree of dignity you have given by your presence . . . to every public act since your installation," one observer told O'Connell, all "superbly reported in [the] secular press, must have raised many stages . . . Catholic prestige in the Archdiocese."[5] As the journalist who wrote the Vatican during the coadjutor struggle had predicted, O'Connell knew how to make news and he was relentlessly good ink.

O'Connell's success at securing favorable press coverage was not entirely accidental. His advent to power coincided with the expansion of mass journalism at the beginning of the twentieth century, when newspapers fought each other for circulation. Competition among the papers in Boston was intense, and several of them were actively seeking to expand their audience among the city's Irish, Catholic, and Democratic readers. The *Post*, long the favorite in those circles, made it a policy to run stories about O'Connell on the front page, while the tabloids, the *American* and the *Record*, seized on him as a figure who always attracted attention. Even the Republican *Herald* and the Brahmin *Transcript* recognized the benefit of regular features about the archbishop. Thus, the relationship between O'Connell and the press was mutually beneficial: they helped him publicize his activities and personality; he helped them sell newspapers and advertisements. At the same time he did not leave his treatment in the public prints wholly to chance. He used the archdiocesan attorney, Henry V. Cunningham, to plant or suppress stories as necessary, while a reporter for the *Globe* named Frank Flynn served as his "quasi-official" conduit to the remainder of the journalistic brotherhood. As time went on, the *Globe* assigned other senior staff members to be the contacts with O'Connell's office.[6] The new archbishop had quickly become a public figure and, like all such figures, he was eager to stay in the public eye and, insofar as possible, to control what was said about him.

Concern for the dissemination of what he called "authoritative" news even led O'Connell into the newspaper business himself. Local Catholics had been reading one weekly newspaper, the *Pilot*, for almost eighty years. Founded in 1829 by Boston's second bishop, Benedict Fenwick, the paper had had an on-again, off-again relationship with the diocese, but for most of its history it was independent, both financially and editorially. In its heyday it attracted a substantial national circulation, especially among recent immigrants, and it was known informally as "the Irishman's Bible."[7] By the turn of the century, however, it had fallen on hard times. Many Boston Catholics were switching to the *Republic*, a livelier paper edited by John Fitzgerald, and nationally the *Pilot* faced tough competition from official diocesan newspapers, sponsored and underwritten by their bishops.

O'Connell realized that a newspaper owned and operated by the archdiocese would be the best way to bring his efforts to the attention of the public. "The immense progress from day to day should be made known as a stimulating influence for good," he wrote some time later, "and this could best be done by a diocesan organ of news and proper publicity." To accomplish this purpose, in early 1908 he hired James T. Murphy, an experienced securities dealer and former reporter, to investigate the *Pilot*'s financial condition and to buy up the available stock. This was done by that autumn, and on September 14 O'Connell announced that the journal would henceforth be the official diocesan newspaper, the reading of which was enjoined on priests and people alike. The editorship was given to a bright young priest, David J. Toomey, a decision the archbishop would later have cause to regret. In order to maximize its distribution, O'Connell consulted with a canon lawyer at Boston College about the permissibility of selling the paper in church vestibules.

When this Jesuit expressed reservations about overt commercial activity in churches, the archbishop sought a second opinion from a New York Redemptorist, who more readily approved the idea, which was immediately put into effect.[8]

In every respect, the acquisition of the *Pilot* was a great success. O'Connell's hope that the head of every Catholic household become a subscriber was probably not realized, but circulation did increase markedly and with that came greater advertising revenues. By the end of 1909 the paper was turning a healthy profit. Any pastor whose parishioners seemed reluctant to subscribe could expect a letter inquiring into the reasons for this apparent laxity and encouraging greater zeal in promoting subscriptions. Not everyone was convinced, however, and one pastor bluntly described the new version of the paper as "fearfully dull. . . . People unfortunately do not like it. This is our great difficulty." To meet this challenge, a Catholic Literature Campaign was organized to expand readership, with a recently ordained priest named Francis J. Spellman as its director. O'Connell hoped that the *Pilot* would become "a powerful influence for the spreading among the people of sane Christian principles and popular Christian instruction."[9] Just as important, it became the official outlet by which he extended his own campaign of visibility. So minutely did the paper report his every move, providing always "proper" publicity, that he could count on extensive newspaper coverage, even in those rare weeks when his activities went unreported in the secular press.

This sustained public presence was the centerpiece of O'Connell's style as archbishop, and it was a new role for Boston's preeminent Catholic. Gone was Williams's "modesty almost amounting to shyness." In its place was an imposing, unapologetic, forceful figure who was at ease in the spotlight. Here was a real leader, described in glowing terms by one newspaper as "a big man— big in every sense of the word. He is tall, thick framed, presenting the appearance of a very solid wall of flesh. Without the slightest suggestion of stiffness he is nevertheless straight, and one always gets the impression that he is standing squarely upon his feet and is drawn up to his full height."[10] In an age in which size equaled substance and "a solid wall of flesh" was presumed to be healthy rather than unhealthy, O'Connell (who in fact was only about five feet, eight inches tall but weighed over 250 pounds) was compared favorably with William McKinley and the redoubtable Thomas Brackett Reed. Like an ecclesiastical Theodore Roosevelt, he was vigorous and outgoing, one who always had to be taken into consideration.

Even his leisure time attracted attention. A reporter followed him on one of his frequent late afternoon walks along Commonwealth Avenue in the Back Bay, the main promenade of respectable Boston, and came away describing him as "one of the most enthusiastic pedestrians in Boston. . . . Attired in silk hat, overcoat and frock coat of clerical black broadcloth and carrying an ebony cane, the only thing about [his] appearance to suggest his high ecclesiastical office is the little triangle of crimson silk just below his collar. . . . He believes in devoted and consistent walking, as good for the brain and good for the body, and the results show that, in his case, the theory is sound."[11] Surely this was a public man in a way no Catholic bishop before him had ever been: a simple walk was an event worthy of newspaper coverage. The other regular strollers along the mall included A. Lawrence Lowell, the president of Harvard, and his cousin William A. Lawrence, the Episcopal bishop of Massachusetts. Now, the leader of Boston's Catholics moved in that world, too, both literally and figuratively.

As a result, there developed an aura around O'Connell's personality, a perception that he was different from ordinary people and had to be treated as such. When a local Catholic association wanted to invite both him and Governor Guild to a reception in May 1908, O'Connell was unwilling to share the limelight. "I think one or the other of us, the Governor or myself, is sufficient for the occasion," he told the event's organizer. "You must choose between the Governor and me."[12] The priest in question made the obvious choice, and not for the last time did the leader of Boston's Catholics trump the leader of the entire commonwealth. That such a "him-or-me" choice could be so readily posed and just as readily made demonstrated how far O'Connell had succeeded in asserting his enhanced stature.

Other things were due him because of his position. In the interest of maintaining him in suitably fine surroundings, a group of priests gathered as early as October 1907 to raise a subscription for a new residence for him in the fashionable Back Bay. The rectory at the cathedral was small and located in Boston's South End, a neighborhood that had never quite become the desirable district its nineteenth-century promoters had hoped for. "There is unanimous and hearty feeling," Father John O'Brien of Cambridge told him, "that 'the Archbishop ought to have his own home,' and one outside his office and one that must be entirely satisfactory to himself." O'Brien took the lead in negotiating with a real estate agent, arranging for the mortgage, and hiring an architect to make appropriate renovations. Later, a $50,000 addition doubled the size of this house, located on the banks of the Charles River at the corner of Granby Street and Bay State Road, providing a combined residence and chancery office.[13] Nor would this be the last time O'Connell would relocate to a fancier neighborhood. When the Back Bay lost some of its luster, he moved to spacious Fisher Hill in suburban Brookline in 1916 and ten years later to a Renaissance *palazzo* in Brighton which he built for himself. Archbishop Williams had been content with a room at the cathedral rectory; Archbishop O'Connell required lodgings that were, in Father O'Brien's deft euphemism, "entirely satisfactory to himself."

A grander episcopal style was evident in other ways. He moved in settings that had once been reserved for the Yankee elite, including the summer colony on Boston's tony North Shore. An estate at Bay View, Gloucester, a former residence of the flamboyant Civil War General Ben Butler, was purchased for $20,000 in 1908 as a summer home and grandly rechristened "Villa Santa Croce." A group of well-to-do laymen presented O'Connell with an $8,000 Pierce Arrow, "tastefully finished in dark blue with nickel trimmings." A proposal was even made to abandon the Cathedral of the Holy Cross, barely thirty-five years old, and to build a more visible cathedral on "a proposed island in the Charles River Basin." Though Mayor Fitzgerald was a keen backer of this plan, O'Connell rejected it as too costly.[14]

The new archbishop's persona also embraced activities not previously expected from a Catholic prelate. His interest in golf he brought with him from Maine, and he joined clubs in Watertown and Allston before being voted, over a waiting list of more than three hundred, a member of "The Country Club" in Brookline. "It really is a bully game," the newspapers quoted him as saying—he even talked like Theodore Roosevelt—though there is no evidence that he ever actually ventured onto the links to swing a club. "I hope to play it every day, if I can only find the time." Transported from Maine, too, was his participation in gentlemen's clubs, of which Boston had more than its share. The Winter's Night, Wednesday Evening, Thursday Evening, and Puddingstone clubs—Yankee Protestant bastions all—elected him to membership, and he took his turn at entertaining his fellow members. (Lacking fixed clubhouses, the clubs dined at members' homes.) More often, however, he declined their invitations, and the conclusion that these groups sought him more than he sought them seems warranted. His emerging place in Boston society was so secure that he was even credited with spiritual influence over its most powerful figure. His friendship with Isabella Stewart Gardner, the great "Mrs. Jack" (who patronized artists and served as the city's arbiter of taste), fed rumors that she either would or already secretly had become a Catholic, stories on which neither of them commented and which were in the end untrue.[15]

Travel at home and abroad continued to exercise a fascination for him, and it too became a feature of the new role of the archbishop of Boston. Between his accession in 1907 and the outbreak of the First World War, O'Connell went to Europe seven times, an average of once a year. These were not pleasure cruises—with the exception of a May-through-September vacation in 1911 that included a leisurely trip down the Rhine, with a pause to take the cure at Carlsbad—but rather they combined relaxation with official business in Rome. Still, O'Connell's photograph was often enough in the newspapers, getting on or off some ship, to earn him the nickname "Gangplank Bill," a sobriquet of which he himself never took any notice but which greatly distressed the members of his family.[16] He traveled to Washington every spring for meetings of the board of trustees of the Catholic University of America, of which he was an ex officio member. Other trips included a visit to a eucharistic congress in Montreal in 1910, a vacation (his second that year) in Atlantic City in 1911, journeys to New York City, and summer months spent at the villa in Gloucester.

O'Connell's high visibility and personal projection, as gratifying as they may have been to his own ego, served a larger purpose. Like other figures of his era—most notably Theodore Roosevelt on the national stage; John Fitzgerald and James Michael Curley on the local scene—he understood the symbolic role leaders could play. He sensed intuitively an emotional need among Boston's emergent Catholics for an assertive kind of hero-leader, and by dramatizing his office and his activities, he provided them with just such a figure.

When he dined with presidents and governors, when he received dignitaries from around the world, or when he appeared as a sought-after guest among the local elite, he was transformed into what one social scientist has called a "vehicle for identification" among the people he represented. The boy from Lowell had come a long way, but his successes were not merely personal ones. Catholics in the kitchens and parlors of South Boston and Roxbury—or even of the more middle-class suburbs—might never experience those same thrills personally, but they had come far enough both to desire them and to dare to hope for fulfillment of that desire. When Archbishop O'Connell achieved these little triumphs, therefore, his people did so vicariously as well. As his correspondent had predicted, he "raised the prestige" of Catholics by his own behavior. A contemporary journalist agreed, observing that O'Connell taught his own people to realize "their full duty to themselves"—a code phrase for self-esteem—while teaching the community at large "a fair attitude toward the Church," the respect and deference their numbers now demanded. This gave the prelate "impact."[17]

O'Connell's own significance was thus magnified, achieving a larger meaning, well beyond mere social climbing. Armed with a well-grounded understanding that his was an age of social and cultural transition in Massachusetts, O'Connell was determined to speed that process. In earlier times the leader of Boston's Catholics might have been justified, or at least forgiven, for being quiet and largely invisible, keeping to himself and his own flock. Now the era of the Catholic Uncle Tom was over. "The child of the immigrant is called to fill the place" of leadership in society, he proclaimed, and that responsibility demanded no timidity, no retiring modesty. The transition was still very much underway, not nearly so complete as he made it seem, and marked by steps backward as well as forward. Still, the direction of the change was clear. "They wrote the history of the last century," he told his people, without having to explain who "they" were; "we must make the history of the coming one."[18]

* * *

If O'Connell's policy was designed to influence local affairs, it was no less deliberately intended to enhance his impact within the church. His long years of involvement in ecclesiastical politics, honed sharp in his struggle for the coadjutorship, now paid off. He was prepared to exert the influence one would expect from the leader of the third largest diocese in Catholic America. His Vatican connections in the reign of Pius X and Merry del Val seemed to guarantee that he would play the roles of kingmaker and power broker for the American church. He exerted his influence in other dioceses both close at hand and far removed.

In April 1908, for example, he took the unusual step of traveling to Vermont in order to preside personally over the selection of candidates for the vacant bishopric of Burlington. The following month he began a correspondence with a priest from Cleveland on the subject of a new bishop there. The midwesterner described conditions in that frequently troubled diocese and sought the Bostonian's intervention. "It is pretty hard for your friend here to do anything directly," O'Connell's secretary wrote back, "but he does see a few things that may be done. The thing is to work cautiously, prudently, and surely." He was being too modest, for in March 1909 O'Connell's former vice rector at the American College was named bishop of Cleveland. Closer to home, he was similarly interested in the succession in the diocese of Hartford. "Give us at Hartford a man like yourself," a Connecticut priest wrote him, as if the choice were up to O'Connell rather than the pope. "Give us such a man, Your Grace, and we will bless you."[19] O'Connell was always on the lookout for "a few things that may be done" in promoting the careers of churchmen who shared his outlook.

Among his fellow bishops O'Connell sought a position of prominence. Until Cardinal Gibbons's death in 1921 he deferred to the great Baltimore prelate, but he could still strike out on his own. He joined Gibbons in endorsing the Catholic Church Extension Society, a Chicago group that promoted domestic missions, but he discouraged an annual collection to support it. "My own opinion is that we already have too many national collections," he said. When presented with the text of a prayer for peace, drafted in 1918 by the National Catholic War Council (NCWC), he submitted a new prayer of his own, explaining that "it was easier for me to write the substitute than to say what I did not like in the original."[20] The differences in wording were less important than O'Connell's desire to stake out a position that was distinct from that of his brother bishops.

This emerging role earned mixed reviews from other members of the hierarchy, depending on their predispositions toward

O'Connell. In 1919, for example, Patrick Hayes, the newly appointed archbishop of New York, promised to defer to the Boston archbishop as senior in tenure. "Catholic New York will gladly follow or lead, as duty demands," Hayes said. "I as archbishop will seek and welcome . . . the counsel, the wisdom, and the experience of my more venerable brethren." Not everyone was so deferential. Saint Paul's aging John Ireland, who had not changed his mind about O'Connell, worried that the younger man's forceful personality had a smothering effect. In advising Gibbons on appointments to the various departments of the NCWC, Ireland urged him, "Do not be too favorable to your colleagues" in the East. "I mean especially 'Boston,'" Ireland continued; "where he dominates cooperation will be lacking." Other bishops viewed O'Connell with an even more jaundiced eye. Providence's Matthew Harkins, the loser in the struggle over the Boston succession, wrote sarcastically to a colleague in 1910, "It is not every one who is such a wonderful man as the Archbp. of Boston, at the early age of 51."[21]

Looking abroad, O'Connell had similar ambitions for influence in the international church. As always, he focused his attention on Rome and in particular on Pope Pius X and Cardinal Merry del Val. He still lost few opportunities to demonstrate his adherence to their program of conservative orthodoxy. The two had decided that modernism was the "synthesis of all heresies" and needed to be suppressed. Pius condemned it in an encyclical at the beginning of September 1907, and before the end of November O'Connell published an "echo of the Holy Father's voice." Admitting that modernism had "few if any open advocates in America," let alone in Boston, O'Connell nonetheless counseled vigilance. He was the first bishop in the United States to issue a statement endorsing the pope's view—he took the occasion to scold some of his enemies for their refusal to do likewise—and this precedence was not lost on Rome.[22]

O'Connell found other ways to let his Roman backers know that he was still their man. As in Portland, he appointed a commission to promote the Gregorian chant favored by the pope. He publicly took the Vatican's side in a dispute between Pius and former president Roosevelt, who was refused a papal audience in the spring of 1910 because of his contacts with Italian Protestants. He sent frequent reports of his activities, sometimes including newspaper clippings, to those he was eager to impress. "You have every reason to rejoice and thank God for the great success attending your work in Boston," Merry wrote him on receiving one such package in 1911. "Let me congratulate you most warmly and assure you that the Holy Father rejoices with you and affectionately blesses your work, which he is following with the deepest sympathy and interest." The significance of such formal sentiments should not be exaggerated: most likely, neither the pope nor his prime minister were hanging on every dispatch from Boston. Still, they were gratified that O'Connell was justifying their confidence in him. "There is no danger of my forgetting you," Merry told him, adding encouragingly: "how often we speak of you."[23]

O'Connell could be subtle in his courting, but he could also be direct and even a little pushy. In 1910, during a "dreadful agitation in Spain" (protracted anticlerical demonstrations that resulted in a break of diplomatic relations between Madrid and the Vatican), O'Connell unabashedly pleaded for a supporting role. "I felt as if it was cowardly and mean of me to be resting here in comparative peace," he told Merry expansively, "and not take the next boat for Rome, so that I might at least say to His Holiness and yourself, 'Here I am, give me something to do to prove that some of us at least are faithful.' . . . Dear friend, can I be of any service?, or is there anything I can do?, or have I anything that I can offer?, or is there any way in which I can alleviate your burdens? If so, do me the honor and let me know." The secretary of state had no assignment for his American friend but told him that "it is a great consolation to me that you are there and to know that we can reckon on you. When occasion arises I shall not hesitate to appeal for your help."[24]

As time went on, the close private connection between Boston and Rome was noticed in public. Amid almost constant rumors, beginning immediately after his accession as archbishop, that O'Connell would be created a cardinal, the newspapers were ready to report the slightest evidence of papal favor: a gold watch Christmas present, an audience for O'Connell despite a papal illness, a jeweled pectoral cross presented personally by the pontiff.[25] O'Connell was firmly in possession of his office, but the years of striving to acquire it had left him with the habits of ambition. One cannot "campaign" to be made a cardinal, since the honor comes entirely at the pope's discretion. Still, in hindsight O'Connell's pleading "give me something to do" sounds like a request for another promotion. Like a perennial candidate, he instinctively sought higher positions.

O'Connell's usefulness extended beyond ringing letters of support. In particular, now that he had moved to a larger and wealthier diocese, he used the power of the purse to further his cause. By the early twentieth century most European churchmen had come to look on all Americans as rich by definition, and O'Connell did little to discourage that perception. He made a point of contributing to charities in which he knew Pius and Merry del Val were personally interested. In 1909 he collected $5,000 from the parishes of the archdiocese for the relief of sufferers from an Italian earthquake. He gave a substantial sum later that year to the Pontifical Biblical Commission, which Pius had reinvigorated as a counter to modernist "higher criticism." He endorsed the idea of a "school of sacred music" in Rome, but before contributing to it he wanted to know whether the project really had the pope's backing. "I am anxious to do what is right in the right way," he told the cardinal secretary of state, "especially in all those matters in which our venerable Holy Father is interested." Similarly, he contributed frequently to an orphanage in the Trastevere district of Rome that Merry del Val had founded. These contributions were all duly noted. "I should never dream of appealing to your generosity, tho' I know that I can reckon on it," the infinitely shrewd Merry wrote in thanks. "I think Boston never forgets the Holy Father."[26] Officials of the curia were accustomed to fawning words from underlings in the provinces. A regular flow of cash was a better measure of loyalty, and in that O'Connell did not disappoint.

More important than these informal gifts in establishing O'Connell's reputation was his regular contribution to Peter's Pence. Taken every February, this collection had been instituted in the 1860s, and by the turn of the century American dioceses were giving roughly $80,000 annually to the Vatican. Even under Archbishop Williams, Boston had done its part, contributing respectable and growing amounts. In 1908, O'Connell's first year as archbishop, he made a special effort to insure that the amount raised would be noticeably higher than usual. He knew the value of a good first impression. "I dare to hope confidently," he wrote all his pastors, "that the collection for the Pope this year will double the ordinary Peter's Pence of the diocese." In some parishes, he noted sharply, the donation "has been in the past practically insignificant." He even urged that, "as a personal manifestation of their own devotion to the Holy Father," priests take up the collection themselves, a practice that had been generally forbidden because it smacked of intimidation.[27]

The special effort paid off handsomely. Returns from the parishes showed a solid increase, and when the figure approached $40,000 O'Connell added funds from other accounts to boost the total over that appealingly round number. This initial burst of monetary enthusiasm could not be sustained over succeeding years, but the results still hovered annually around $20,000. The significance of this accomplishment O'Connell stated proudly. "While the amount of Peter's Pence in former years was usually about $10,000," he said, understating Williams's true record slightly, "it is now quite assured that it will never fall below twice that amount." Equating dollars with devotion, he told Merry del Val bluntly: "our good Catholics are faithful and loyal, and the cheque for $20,000 proves it."[28]

* * *

These proofs of loyalty made it likely that O'Connell would receive the further honor of the red cardinal's hat. Since the 1870s America had always had one cardinal, first John McCloskey of New York and then James Gibbons of Baltimore. By 1910 the number of Catholics in the United States and the extent of their financial support for the Vatican seemed to demand that other Americans be added to that number. With his every trip to Europe speculation grew that O'Connell would be the favored one. As he set sail in May 1911 a local newspaper wrote: "It has been intimated in Catholic church circles that should the Pope honor America with another Cardinal his choice would be Archbishop O'Connell." Their meeting was thus "being watched for with much interest in Boston."[29] No announcement followed that particular encounter, but neither O'Connell nor Boston's newspaper readers had long to wait.

Appropriately enough, it was Merry del Val who broke the news to his American friend. In mid-October 1911 he wrote to O'Connell, telling him of the "very great token of esteem and affection, with which the Holy Father wishes to honour you, and to recognize your services to the Church. Nobody," he added significantly, "will know how to appreciate this great dignity better than yourself."[30] The public announcement came on October 28: O'Connell would be named a cardinal, together with two other Americans—New York's Archbishop John Farley and Archbishop Diomede Falconio, the apostolic delegate to the United States, who was a naturalized citizen.

The news caused a sensation in Boston. Never was the vicarious identification between O'Connell and his flock stronger. "I congratulate Your Grace and congratulate myself as one of your children," wrote Emma Forbes Cary, a convert to Catholicism who was the founder and grande dame of the Radcliffe Catholic Club. James M. Prendergast, a Brookline businessman and sometime financial adviser to O'Connell, sent a telegram directly to Pius X, thanking him for "the great honor you confer on Boston." Elsewhere, the honor was received with similar acclaim. A Chicago priest told the new cardinal that he had happened to be with President Taft when the announcement came over the wire, and he quoted Taft as saying that "it would be a great pleasure to me if the news is true." The feeling of honor persisted. A decade later a Boston nun was still, like Miss Cary, "congratulating herself" because of her leader's high position. "For the first time in my life I have the honor to address a *Cardinal*," this sister enthused while writing about a routine financial matter.[31]

In some church circles, however, O'Connell's further advancement was not greeted with the same joy. The liberal faction understood immediately that it had lost yet another battle and that O'Connell's elevation only ratified their continuing decline. Cardinal Gibbons was reported to have wept when he learned that O'Connell would join him in the most exclusive club in the world. More than one churchman wrote to John Ireland, expressing dismay that the archbishop of Saint Paul had been passed over for the honor he had coveted for twenty years. "The ways of Providence are surely not to be fathomed," Portland's Louis Walsh told Ireland sorrowfully, while Matthew Harkins reported that he was sending congratulatory notes to Farley and Falconio but could not bring himself to send one to O'Connell. For their part, O'Connell's friends also understood the ideological significance of his selection. Francis MacNutt, with whom O'Connell had had little contact since securing the Boston appointment, crowed that the pope's choice would "sound the final requiem over the noisy hopes and struggles of an element—a faction—in our church, at whose definite interment all wise Catholics assist with feelings of heartfelt relief."[32]

O'Connell himself was outwardly demure about the distinction and claimed to have disbelieved the first reports of it. While he was not shy about his accomplishments, he asserted with deliberate modesty that they were "the merest matters of daily duty, certainly meriting no special reward." He also remembered the experience of "worthier prelates than I" (perhaps an ironic barb aimed at Ireland) who had been "genuinely injured by this sort of dangerous publicity, which finally ended in smoke." No such fate befell him, and he issued a public statement sharing the honor with his diocese. It was "through your faith," he told his people, "your unflinching loyalty to Holy Church, your undying attachment to the See of Peter, your splendid generosity, even to sacrifice," that the distinction had come to him. Now, all of Catholic Boston would get its reward through him. "Even in the smallest hamlet of the farthest East today Boston is known as never before, honored as never before."[33] Like the other great cities of the world, Boston now had a cardinal.

O'Connell set sail for Rome on November 11 and arrived two weeks later. Though they are telescoped today, the events of a consistory creating new cardinals then stretched over several days, beginning with a private ceremony in Saint Peter's Basilica. Pius X placed the red hat on the cardinal-designate's head and reportedly told him, "O'Connell, my trust in you is unlimited." He also took possession of the Roman "titular" church to which he was now entitled—in this case the ancient basilica of San Clemente in the heart of the city—and he attended receptions with the diplomatic corps.[34] Most of his entourage returned home shortly afterwards, but O'Connell himself remained behind, spending Christmas at the American College and finally sailing from Naples in mid-January 1912.

Back home, the ceremonies were followed with keen interest, crowning O'Connell's transformation into a public figure. "The papers have spoken of little else than the great events in Rome since the day of your departure," wrote his nephew and secretary, Father James P. E. O'Connell. "No doubt was left as to whom the great[est] importance was attached among the three Cardinals from America, and for that matter, among any of the newly created Cardinals. . . . Everything you do or say is heralded in the papers as if you were right here." Boston was also making ambitious plans for the triumphant return of its local hero. A welcoming committee of distinguished citizens was formed, and there were plans for a parade and a round of congratulatory receptions and dinners. A collection of nearly $25,000 was taken up in the parishes, and several prominent laymen (joined by a number of Protestant gentlemen) raised a considerable sum to underwrite archaeological excavations at San Clemente. "Your Eminence," James O'Connell told him, delighting in his uncle's new title, "will have every reason to be proud of Boston, clerical and lay, Catholic and non-Catholic." His homecoming would "outdo in beauty and dignity anything Boston has known." Eyeing competitors for publicity and influence, the young priest added cheerily: "We are beating New York to a *frazzle*." O'Connell's new rank had other privileges. While nieces and nephews had been permitted as children to call him "Uncle Will," now when they came to be considered adults (generally at their confirmation) they had to abandon this familiar form and refer to him as "Uncle Cardinal."[35]

When O'Connell docked on January 31, 1912, Boston's enthusiasm was unbounded. Not even a blinding snowstorm could dampen the high spirits or cancel the parade. For Catholics, O'Connell's elevation was a mark of ultimate distinction, a talisman to be grasped as a sign of their coming of age. Emerging from a century of struggle in not always congenial surroundings, they now had a leader who ranked as a prince of the universal church. What better way to show the Yankees that the once-despised immigrants had achieved respectability? There were only fifty cardinals in the entire world; less than half of them were non-Italians. One of their own was now admitted to that select number, and Catholic Bostonians felt justifiably proud. Non-Catholics, too, could share in the reflected glory, for O'Connell's distinction elevated Boston to a place they thought it deserved. With him, the consistory had elevated to the cardinalate the archbishops of New York, Paris, London, and Vienna.[36] That Boston should be ranked with such cities seemed only fitting to those who, like Oliver Wendell Holmes, thought they lived at the "hub of the universe."

The celebrations continued for a month. A mass of thanksgiving in the cathedral on February first was followed by a banquet for priests on the fifth, a banquet for the laity (led by Mayor Fitzgerald and the new Massachusetts Governor Eugene Noble Foss) on the seventh, a reception for Catholic women on the seventeenth, and a welcome home parade in Lowell on the twenty-fifth. Some discouraging words were occasionally heard: a Protestant church group objected to including the Ninth Massachusetts Regiment, the Civil War "Irish Brigade," in one ceremony on the grounds that its participation compromised the separation of church and state. New rules of etiquette also had to be learned, rules with which not everyone was happy. Governor Foss testily refused to attend a Saint Patrick's Day dinner that year in a dispute over protocol. O'Connell, now considered royalty because of his status as a "prince of the church," was ranked second in seating and speaking behind the evening's special guest, President William Howard Taft, leaving the governor an unacceptable third. The crusty *Boston Evening Transcript* justified Foss's boycott as motivated by "a desire to see that the Commonwealth received its just honors," but the public at large sympathized with O'Connell, whose newness in his rank made him still their favorite.[37]

The general adulation also fell short of convincing his once and future enemies. One wag commemorated the lavish display at the various receptions with a Kipling parody called "The Charge of the Gold Brigade." The Boston priests who had not wanted this man as their archbishop quickly grew weary of the cult of personality. Several close associates of Archbishop Williams grumbled on the sidelines, while Father Hugh Roe O'Donnell, pastor of Saint Anthony's, Allston, channeled his hostility into creativity. O'Donnell privately circulated a satirical poem entitled "How History Is Made, 1912," which spoofed the unremitting newspaper coverage:

> The journals produced illustrations
> Of red hats and garments galore;
> And this most democratic of nations
> Saw princes, in print, by the score.
>
> The supplement sheets issued photos
> Of churches and palace hotels,
> With His Eminence riding in autos,
> The prince of American swells. . . .

> We are told in a way that convinces,
> How blue blood now flows in his veins;
> How, ranking with royalty's princes,
> This prince over governors reigns. . . .
>
> In fine, it is hardly surprising
> That people exclaim—quite aghast—
> "For lime light and big advertising,
> Old Barnum is nailed to the mast!"[38]

The carping of clerical naysayers notwithstanding, O'Connell's transformation into a first-class public celebrity was now virtually complete. His early years as archbishop were full of pageantry and practically unbroken success. In a remarkably short time, he had succeeded in staging a series of public dramas in which he was the central character. In the new, publicity-minded century, he was setting a new standard of behavior for himself and for other bishops. The "lime light and big advertising" were both the medium and the message. Boston's Catholics were beginning to accustom themselves to the notion that they could influence and control larger events, and the emergence of their leader as one who could instantly command the attention of the entire city and state reconfirmed this self-assertion. When O'Connell returned from Rome with his red hat, Archbishop Williams had been dead for barely four years, but already his era seemed longer ago than that. O'Connell had lodged permanently in the mental world of the average citizen, Catholic and non-Catholic alike.

* * *

But what of the private man behind the public figure? Where was the core of personality that he brought home with him after all the public appearances were over? Penetrating to the private man is difficult with O'Connell. He seemed always to be playing his predetermined public role, never distinguishing clearly between the celebrity he had become and his individual character. Theologically, he would even have denied that he had a personal nature different from what the world saw or in any way significant. For Catholics of his generation, priesthood and episcopacy were both seen as essentially objective in character. Ordination was akin to the action of a seal making an impression in soft wax; what mattered was the seal, not the wax. Public role and private nature were one and the same. "There is no such thing as the personality of a Bishop," he would say in 1930. "We do not follow any priest or Bishop or anybody else merely for his personal qualities. We follow because that is the law of Christ. The Church is founded that way."[39]

What is more, O'Connell's inner self remains elusive because he exercised such rigorous control over it. A lifelong concern for "authoritative" news and "proper publicity"—phrases he had used in acquiring the *Pilot*—meant that he was eager always to control both the text and the context of what was said about him. In later life, for example, he would refuse permission to a local reporter who wanted to publish in book form a biography previously serialized in the newspapers, not because it contained anything negative but simply because he himself had not been the origin of it. From an early date, he was the sole creator of his own outward personality, and he believed implicitly in the aptness of his creation. He was self-made, and if it was necessary to change his inner nature or even his own life history to support his larger public role, then so be it.[40]

Nowhere is O'Connell's self-creation more evident than in the collection of letters that was published in 1915.[41] Intended to be the first of a multivolume series that never in fact appeared, the book contained letters, addressed principally to members of his family, covering the first forty years of his life. All great men were expected to publish their letters, especially from their younger days, so that interested readers could see how they had become great. Brahmin Bostonians (from the Adams family on down) had engaged in the practice for years and, in conformity with his belief that Catholics were now supplanting those people as the leaders of society, O'Connell followed suit. These apparently very personal items from his youth, from the time before the bright light of publicity had shone on him—items that therefore seemed more reliable than any self-conscious autobiography—would, he hoped, provide the personal underpinning to his public persona.

Unfortunately for this hope, O'Connell's *Letters* were not genuine. They bore dates between 1876 and 1900, but they had in fact all been composed by him between 1911 and 1915, in some cases upwards of thirty years after the events they purportedly described. The surviving manuscripts of the published versions (together with manuscripts describing his years in Portland and the trip to Japan, for a proposed second volume which was never issued) are on uniform sheets of paper and written in the hand of the mature O'Connell. Letters that appeared in print with such salutations as "Dear W.," ostensibly edited to protect the privacy of the addressee, contain the same cryptic greeting in the original, indicating that no such person ever existed. Many of the manuscripts contain O'Connell's marginal notes to himself, including suggestions for precise dates to be assigned them later. They are full of overly meaningful asides and an unusual number of prescient statements about people and events.[42] Not really forgeries in the usual sense, the letters are rather a form of early autobiography in epistle form. They were O'Connell's attempt to correct a deficiency—the absence of any authentic early letters— supplying something he did not have but which, now that he was a great man, he needed.

He was thus inventing, or rather reinventing, his own life so that it would be serviceable for the present. Accustomed as he was to favorable treatment by contemporary journalists, he sought by this deliberate remaking of his own past both to confirm his image in his own time and to pass it undiluted to posterity. Like others whose influence depends on the public perception of them, he succumbed to the temptation to look on history as "past public relations." Accordingly, he felt both the right and the responsibility to create a personality that would be, as he himself would phrase it, "edifying to the public." Edification was more important than accuracy.

In the last analysis, this passion to control all aspects of his public persona was the key to understanding his private psychology. His outward image was a deliberate creation because it was useful for his broader religious and cultural purposes. As a result, he developed an oddly detached way of looking at himself, confirming his belief that he was unlike other people solely on account of who and what he was. The view, brought with him from Maine, that he was a law unto himself only became clearer in Boston: he had gone from being a big fish in a little pond to being a big fish in a big pond.

He came to rely on the force of his own personality, and he believed in that forcefulness wholeheartedly. He was always supremely self-confident, never unsure. Doubts about himself and his actions, second thoughts of any kind, seemed never to occur to him. Despite the efforts of his enemies to "minimize and even defeat my efforts," he told Merry del Val proudly, he remained undaunted: "I simply smiled and went ahead—and now they are busy saving their own skins."[43] If the consternation in the ranks of his detractors was not really so complete as that, it mattered little. If his blustering self-assurance masked a deeper insecurity, he could nonetheless over-power it in his conscious mind. The public and the private man merged together, and when the latter had to be rearranged to fit the purposes of the former, he accomplished the task without hesitation.

No aspect of O'Connell's life must be treated with greater care than this delicate matter of self-image, if only because he seems on the face of things to be such a disagreeable man. To observers several generations removed from him, his stern nature seems merely arro-gant and, perhaps, offensive. A public man who is always, as the newspaper had said of him, "standing squarely upon his feet" and "drawn up to his full height" seems more imperious than appealing today. We have come to expect more humility and even self-depreca-tion from those in high positions. These later styles must not, how-ever, be projected back into a different era. Nor should they be allowed simply to dismiss O'Connell, who used his very self-posses-sion as part of the larger public effort on which he was embarked. "I have lived to see my entire program carried out with . . . complete success," he wrote in his memoirs.[44] His success was neither so abso-lute nor so readily achieved as that, but he was nevertheless able to command broad and sustained public attention, altering for years to come the world in which both he and his church lived. Later American Catholic bishops might not exhibit the same need to create and recreate themselves, but they still followed O'Connell's path by attempting to be public men, recognized and influential on a broad scale.

5

"THE MAXIMUM OF EFFICIENCY":
ADMINISTRATIVE MYTH AND REALITY, 1907-1920

Newspaper readers who got used to seeing their cardinal archbishop covered almost as regularly as other local personalities saw only half the story. The public aspects of O'Connell's position were always balanced by more mundane responsibilities. This was still a period of institutional expansion for Catholicism in America, and churches were coming in many respects to resemble the corporations of the contemporary secular world. By 1907 the archdiocese of Boston was a big operation. Covering some twenty-five hundred square miles, it had almost two hundred parish churches, with nearly six hundred priests and almost sixteen hundred religious sisters. Fifty thousand students attended church-related schools from the elementary to the university level, and the diocese's hospitals and charitable agencies handled 70,000 cases each year.[1] Like the head of a business with an extensive network of branch offices, Boston's archbishop oversaw the varied affairs of this conglomerate—not the spiritual affairs only, but also the practical details of personnel, finance, and real estate. Concern for the things of the next world demanded that he be adept at the things of this one.

O'Connell immersed himself in his managerial duties, aided by a small group of assistants, carefully chosen for their loyalty. Like many a new boss, he began by clearing out the remnants of the old regime. First to go was Archbishop Williams's chancellor, Father Thomas MacCormack, who was made pastor of a parish in suburban Norwood. Replacing him as principal administrative officer of the diocese was Father Michael Splaine, an alumnus of the American College during O'Connell's rectorship. Next, Father John Mullen, the somewhat curmudgeonly rector of the Holy Cross cathedral, was dispatched to the even more remote town of Hudson. Mullen, an ally

of those who had opposed O'Connell's appointment, was passion-
ately hostile toward the new archbishop, and his motives were partly
personal: a teetotaler, Mullen was horrified when O'Connell
demanded wine with meals at the cathedral rectory. Solidifying his
hold on things, O'Connell took the unusual step of designating
himself as rector of the cathedral, thereby assuming personal control
over the finances of that prosperous parish. Most important of all in
the rearranged scheme of things, O'Connell created a new position
of secretary to the archbishop and gave it to his own nephew, Father
James P. E. O'Connell, only twenty-three years old.[2] As secretary,
and later as Splaine's successor as chancellor, he became his uncle's
alter ego, the key man in the early years of the O'Connell era.

With this team in place, the archbishop announced the new,
rigorous procedures that would characterize his administration.
Williams had been informal about such things, but O'Connell
arranged to "receive" only on Monday and Wednesday mornings. He
discouraged pastors from seeking audiences "in all matters which do
not absolutely necessitate a personal interview." All business had to
be conducted by mail, never by telephone. Even decisions reached in
personal interviews were not considered official until confirmed by
an exchange of correspondence. Matters of finance were watched
closely. Special collections in the parishes were not to be taken without O'Connell's specific permission, and "permission to collect will
be rarely, if ever, granted." All church property was to be insured at
80 percent of market value, and this insurance was to be bought
through a firm the chancery would select. A diocesan synod (a
canonical gathering of priests that took the form of a legislative
debate but in fact served simply for the promulgation of centrally
prepared rules) was held in 1909, confirming these and other
policies. Pastors had to seek explicit approval for any expenditure
over $100, for instance, and parish account books were to be brought
to the chancery office every year for inspection.[3]

As in Maine, O'Connell sought to control his diocese by mas-
tering the flow of information about it. His system was designed to
allow him, he said later, "to take complete cognizance" of church
affairs. He and his immediate subordinates stood at the center of this
communications system. Mail was delivered to his office twice a day,
and it was handled with impressive speed: a two-day wait for a reply
was unusual. Pastors and the directors of diocesan agencies were

required to address all letters to him personally, though the replies they received were more remote. The chancellor or secretary would sign the response, which nevertheless ran in O'Connell's name: the formulaic "His Grace, the Archbishop [and, after 1911, "His Eminence, the Cardinal"] directs me to say" became the ritual opening of all communications from his office. Extensive chancery office files accumulated, and these "paper brains" were at once the symbol and the substance of O'Connell's administrative style. They were useful but not universally popular. "You sent me a special delivery letter [on] the 13th and wanted to know about the letter you sent the 5th," sighed one pastor, scolded for not answering promptly. "I receive a great many letters from your office but just can't remember what the letter of the 5th was."[4]

O'Connell's management system was efficient enough, but it was not really as forward-looking as it appeared. The early twentieth century was an era of business consolidation in America, with complex bureaucratic organizations evolving to replace the small, highly personalized companies of the previous century. Middle-level managers, whose power was increasingly structural rather than individual, were taking over responsibilities formerly discharged by the owner and his immediate circle. The archdiocese of Boston developed no such structures until much later, and under O'Connell it was too small and much too personalized to keep pace with the changes elsewhere. The Boston church still resembled the industrial concerns of the nineteenth century—John D. Rockefeller's Standard Oil, perhaps, where everything turned on the genius of the founder—more than its own contemporaries in the new century — Henry Ford's motor company, for example, with its multiple layers of managers. Church administration in America had always been a cautious affair, and despite the busy activity on the surface during the O'Connell years, in Boston it remained so.[5]

Still, hard work at the job of being archbishop became as much a part of O'Connell's image as his roles of public figure and Catholic exemplar. The "*arduis*" that demanded his "*vigor*" was temporal and worldly as well as theological and spiritual. He liked to quote Pope Leo XIII as having told him on his appointment to Portland that a bishop could not afford to be a "mere mystic," but had to be a "man of action." From the beginning of his tenure in Boston, O'Connell used frenetic activity to portray himself as just such a man. He was, the *Boston Herald* reported in 1912, "far busier than even the Catholics of his own archdiocese dream." The chancery office on Granby Street was a bustling place where "the steady clickety-clack of typewriters, the clack of adding machines and the rustle of paper" indicated that "a really appalling amount of business is handled expeditiously." O'Connell was personally in command: after brief conferences with him, his aides returned to their desks "with enough work on hand to keep busy throughout the day," the *Herald* went on. There were brief respites for "frugal" meals of "plain, substantial food," but for the rest of the day "everything is business-like."[6] No empty celebrity, O'Connell appeared before the public as an efficient manager with a sure touch, a suitable character for an age in which many of the public's heroes were "go-getters."

This image of O'Connell as a reformer bent on rearranging the practical affairs of the archdiocese and putting them on a sound basis was one to which he himself returned repeatedly. The longest and most detailed chapter in his 1934 autobiography was devoted to the "Reorganization of the Archdiocese," detailing point by point the administrative actions of his first fifteen years in office. Above all, he wanted to be remembered as the leader who saved the church from the lackadaisical ways of its simpler past. The "laissez-faire attitude on the part of those who were entrusted with the administration of the Archdiocese" before his arrival, he said, had left "an almost incredible state of disorganization." Taking a not-so-veiled swipe at Archbishop Williams, O'Connell accused him of allowing the church "to drift as it would," bumbling along "in a haphazard way without any sort of supervision or inspection."[7] What the archdiocese needed in 1907 was what it got: a vigorous leader who would bring order out of this chaos. O'Connell presented himself as the man of the hour.

This self-image as the very kind of manager-shepherd the Boston church needed was taken up by other observers, both then and later. Near the end of O'Connell's life, a journalist compared him favorably to a sledgehammer whose task had been to "smash down precedent and diocesan custom, and [then] rebuild." The official historians O'Connell commissioned in the 1930s struck the same note, crediting him with providing "the maximum of unity and efficiency" and "introducing up-to-date businesslike methods, such as the administration of a great diocese required." Even subsequent writers who disapproved of O'Connell accepted the notion that he had readily accomplished an administrative revolution. One historian found him "authoritarian" and "medieval," but no less "superb and visionary" in his "swift and total centralization of the diocese."[8] Not even a negative assessment of what he had done to and for the archdiocese could dislodge the conviction that he had, in fact, done it.

The picture of the hardheaded bishop equally at home in the sanctuary and the boardroom was a good one, offering O'Connell and his flock yet another point of pride—but was it true? Was the Boston church an administrative shambles on O'Connell's arrival, and did he restructure it in measurable ways? What was the financial condition of archdiocesan institutions, and how did they respond to O'Connell's leadership? Notwithstanding the apparent clarity of the managerial image, how successful was O'Connell in this aspect of his work? Beyond that, what did the image itself say about him and his people?

* * *

Other than his acquisition of the *Pilot*, O'Connell's clearest administrative victory came in restructuring the diocesan seminary after a brief but bloody battle. Given his experience at the American College, he considered himself something of an expert on the training of seminarians. This background, coupled with a dislike of the increasingly beleaguered Sulpician priests that stemmed from his own student days, made a new order for Boston's clerical education a high priority.

Saint John's Seminary in the city's Brighton district had been opened by Archbishop Williams in the fall of 1884 and placed under the direction of the same Sulpicians who had been responsible for his own education in Montreal and Paris. From its founding until Williams's death, it had trained almost six hundred candidates for ordination, and on O'Connell's accession it had eighty-six students, a good-sized institution for its day. From the very beginning, O'Connell expressed an interest in the school and its affairs. He asked immediately for a complete accounting of its programs, and he appointed a separate Board of Examiners of the Clergy, composed of diocesan priests, to test the candidates prior to ordination, a task formerly carried out by the faculty. He dropped in on classes unannounced and introduced changes he thought more "Roman" in character, including a directive that philosophy and theology courses be conducted exclusively in Latin. Very early on, he admitted later, he formed a resolve to "place the Seminary under the care and instruction of my own priests."[9]

O'Connell's plan had some ecclesiastical underpinning, but it was also a matter of culture. The Sulpicians were largely French in origin, and for O'Connell that was a disadvantage. The rector of Saint John's, himself an Irishman, concluded simply: "He dislikes the French. He connects in some way the 'Gallican' or 'national' spirit [that is, an insufficient reliance on Rome] with Sulpician training." O'Connell wanted a stricter, more orthodox formation for his priests since "Rome has the world-outlook." The archbishop told another priest waspishly that the Sulpicians were "filled with spiritual pride" and thought themselves "the only ones who know how to run seminaries, and the fact is that they know nothing about it." Personal factors, too, played a part. He gave in to a long-nursed grudge against the group who had been in charge of his own first, unsuccessful attempt at the priesthood at Saint Charles's College in Maryland. Sometimes, he lapsed into simple name-calling: "their system [is] a combination of Jansenism, Gallicanism, and Frenchism." Long afterward, O'Connell was still denouncing Sulpician institutions as "foreign" places "where American students never seemed at home."[10]

After three years, O'Connell moved against the seminary. The occasion was a visit to Boston in late September 1910 by Father Henri P. Garriguet, the Paris-based superior general of the Society of Saint Sulpice. Garriguet was touring several seminaries in America, and he called on the archbishop on September 29, together with Father François-Xavier Herzog (another officer of the society), and Father Francis Havey, the rector of Saint John's. Garriguet had a ten-minute private meeting with the archbishop, after which the others were called in, joined by Fathers Splaine and James O'Connell. The archbishop declared that Williams's contract with the Sulpicians, which gave them control of the seminary "in perpetuity," was "obsolete." Garriguet and the others acquiesced. O'Connell next asserted that he was necessarily "the first or chief authority in matters concerning the Seminary," and the Sulpician superior concurred, saying his men were "but the helpers of the bishops, and would never hold a seminary against [a bishop's] wishes." In particular, they agreed that if O'Connell decided that, "for the good of the Diocese . . . , the Sulpician Fathers [should] depart from the Seminary, they will do so, the Archbishop giving them two years' notice and, if necessary, three years's [sic] notice to leave." The parting was amicable enough under the tense circumstances, but Havey concluded sadly that "the Seminary was lost to us." Herzog saw a more devious plan at work, believing that O'Connell was trying to force them out in a way that made it look like their own idea.[11]

Having won agreement in principle, O'Connell saw no need to wait, and the three-year transition was summarily shortened to less than a month. At the end of October, he wrote Garriguet, saying that "to delay this any longer would only complicate the situation and enlarge the difficulty." At the same time, he secretly assigned Father John B. Peterson, a seminary alumnus now teaching there, to prepare a restructured curriculum using an entirely new faculty of local priests. Peterson worked on this project throughout the fall, and by Christmas he was instructed to notify each of the new teachers in confidence, deliberately creating the false impression that a few reassignments would be made, rather than a wholesale changeover. The public announcement of the Sulpicians' departure and Peterson's appointment as rector, made on May 18, 1911, was circumspect, even including references to "the excellent work of the Sulpician Fathers during the past twenty years." Still, insiders knew at the time, as others came to learn, that O'Connell had won the power struggle.[12] In a final retaliation against the Sulpicians in 1928, he ordered the bodies in their graveyard on the seminary grounds disinterred and shipped back to their Maryland headquarters.

Elsewhere, the "swift and total centralization" attributed to O'Connell was less impressive, even among the social service agencies that were, he claimed, in the most serious trouble. "Many of our own charitable Institutions are in a deplorable financial condition," he said at the end of 1907, "staggering under enormous debts." The last fifty years had brought an impressive growth in the number of orphanages, hospitals, and other facilities operating under church auspices. Most focused on a particular locality, independent of central diocesan authority, and they were staffed by orders of sisters, brothers, or priests. Some had developed out of a fear that if there were no Catholic services available, public or Protestant agencies (usually thought of as amounting to the same thing) would fill the void and "steal" Catholics from their faith.[13] All charged modest but easily waived fees for their services, and they relied on small endowments and private donations to stay afloat. Few turned a substantial profit—that was not their purpose—but all the evidence indicates that, O'Connell's warnings of disaster notwithstanding, most were financially sound.

The annual diocesan charities collection, taken on the first Sunday in October, was divided among these agencies to help them meet expenses. In the Williams era, this collection always ran well ahead of Peter's Pence, indicating a strong popular sense that charity began at home. After the turn of the century, it grew steadily, yielding about $10,000 in 1900 and as much as $18,000 three years later. Correctly surmising that parishioners would be more generous if they could see the results of their giving, Williams permitted the money taken in some parishes to go for the support of specific institutions near them. Thus, for example, the proceeds from Holy Trinity parish, Boston, were given to the Saint Francis Home, a nursing home affiliated with that German church, and the returns from several North Shore parishes were applied to the City Orphan Asylum in Salem. O'Connell ended this localist practice, requiring that all funds be sent first to his office for subsequent redistribution.[14]

In only one institution was there the kind of financial trouble O'Connell attributed to all of them. This was the Working Boys Home in Newton, an industrial training school. It had been opened in the 1880s, the dream "of a rather easy-going impractical curate," O'Connell said, and it was managed by "a Board of Directors which did everything in the world but direct." Never particularly well-off, the home was land-poor, occupying a beautiful parcel of suburban real estate but saddled with a $75,000 mortgage and revenues that barely met expenses. O'Connell's first impulse was to stop throwing good money after bad and simply allow the place to close. "The Institution was blighted from the beginning," he told the superintendent, Father James J. Redican. "You are in the breach[;] I expect you to stand manfully by." Thinking better of this, however, he decided in February 1909 to pay off the existing mortgage and issue a new one from the archdiocesan corporation. He also supported a fund-raising bazaar which realized an almost incredible $86,000. There was still about $12,000 of indebtedness, but this was to be met as time went on. "I am sure that everyone will be relieved to learn that this institution is finally on a solid financial basis," O'Connell said.[15] In its difficulties, the Working Boys Home was the exception among charitable agencies, though he later described it as the rule.

Comparable facilities were stable and well-managed, and the archdiocese had several of them. Saint Vincent's Orphan Asylum, a home for girls originally situated in Boston's South End but soon relocated to Cambridge, dated from 1832; the House of the Angel Guardian, a residence for boys, had begun in 1851; the Home for Destitute Catholic Children, housing both girls and boys, had been in existence since 1864. All were governed by independent boards of trustees, and all were running distinctly in the black on O'Connell's arrival. Saint Vincent's ended each year with substantial bank balances and, while expenses sometimes slightly exceeded revenues, contributions and individual bequests were more than enough to make up the difference. The Home for Destitute Catholic Children, a pleasant facility despite its austere name, was equally sound. Revenues consistently outran expenses, and an impressive investment portfolio cushioned any small shocks along the way. The value of the home's property and investments had grown to a quarter of a million dollars by 1910, and it had no outstanding mortgages or other debts.[16]

The House of the Angel Guardian came closer to the break-even point, and in 1907 it borrowed $1,500 (against receipts of more than $47,000) to overcome a temporary cash-flow problem. O'Connell seized on this as evidence of mismanagement. "There was neither head nor tail to the financial report," he charged later. Accordingly, he attempted to reorganize the house, which was legally owned by the French-Canadian Brothers of Charity who staffed it. They resisted this effort to put the orphanage more directly under his control, hiring a prominent Catholic attorney to defend their interests. A judge concluded that the archbishop's authority was severely limited and that the brothers had "the unqualified right to determine the way this Institution shall be conducted." Annoyed by this opposition, O'Connell curtly pointed out that canon law required the general oversight of the archbishop and that the judge's reference to the brothers' "unqualified right" was therefore an overstatement. He may have won this technical point, but it had no effect, and O'Connell's practical recourse was limited. He struck back by blocking a fund-raiser for the house at Easter 1909. In 1914 he tried to assert his authority again, demanding reincorporation this time because of what he took to be a legal loophole. The house's charter, dating from the 1850s, had limited the value of its holdings to $50,000, a figure it now exceeded. Hence, O'Connell argued, it needed restructuring, and he again demanded that he be installed as president of the corporation. The brothers were a few steps ahead of him, however, and their superior coolly refused "to enter into any negotiations," informing him of a bill "we had passed through the Legislature" three years before which raised the monetary limit.[17] The autocratic, monolithic regime attributed to the cardinal was very different from the world of give-and-take in which O'Connell and this brother superior really lived.

Hospitals, too, came under O'Connell's scrutiny, and here again the financial picture was far from dismal. The fastest growing was Saint Elizabeth's, founded in the 1870s as a hospital for women but by the turn of the century expanded into a general facility. In the 1890s it was paying its bills and simultaneously reducing a substantial mortgage. By 1904 it was reporting a cash balance in excess of $50,000 and property holdings (some of which it rented out to supplement its income) valued at more than $100,000. A rising demand for services exposed the need for larger quarters than were available on its crowded South End site, and with O'Connell's approval the hospital purchased a spacious estate in Brighton. It mounted a successful fund-raising campaign in 1914 under the cardinal's general patronage, realizing more than $250,000.[18] O'Connell deserved some credit for this happy outcome, but the hospital had a sound enough basis that it required from him no rescuing from mismanagement and calamity.

Saint Mary's Infant Asylum, an orphanage in Dorchester, was not quite as well fixed, though it was still secure. A small operating deficit of $1,600 in 1911, however, sent O'Connell into a rage, directed against Saint Mary's lay board of trustees. While the Daughters of Charity who staffed the asylum were doing their part, he said, "the men seem to lag in the performance of their duty. It appears to me incredible that . . . men of such experience as those

who form the committee in charge cannot raise a goodly sum
of money each year." He designated Father Peter Ronan, pastor of
the nearby Saint Peter's parish, to keep an eye on things and in
particular to block any expensive plans for growth. "I have found,"
he told Ronan, "when heavy debts are incurred in this manner by
institutions, I have to stand back of the bills in the end." No such
obligations were incurred, and the institution rushed headlong into
solvency when it expanded its maternity section into an affiliated
entity, Saint Margaret's Hospital. The new facility's construction was
made possible by substantial donations from Father Ronan and his
brother Michael, who was pastor of Saint Peter's parish, Lowell, and
it produced impressive revenues that outstripped expenses and grew
as steadily as the Catholic birthrate.[19]

The hospital that concerned O'Connell most was the Carney
in South Boston. Opened in 1863 and endowed by Andrew Carney,
Boston's first Catholic philanthropist, it served a predominantly
immigrant population, many of whom could not afford to pay for its
services. When O'Connell questioned its stability at the end of 1908,
the sister superior responded sharply that any suggestion of trouble
"is not only unfounded, but is also gratuitously unkind." Every possible economy had been made, even though about 40 percent of its
patients were charity cases. Money was raised through private donations, three-quarters of which came from non-Catholics, and steady
payments were being made on a $60,000 mortgage, a loan to which
"Your Grace's predecessor and my predecessor gave consent."
O'Connell accepted this explanation but was not happy with it, and
he grumbled in return: "I wish you to keep in mind that debts are
debts, and that they must be paid." As usual, his first principle of
management was "pay-as-you-go": no institution was allowed to keep
outstanding notes as soon as money became available to liquidate
them. The pastor of a struggling parish was pleased to report one year
that he had accumulated a $3,000 cushion. Instead of the congratu-
lations he probably expected, he received an order to pay off all of a
$2,600 mortgage.[20]

O'Connell's shortness with the managers of the Carney highlighted the one issue that was more important to him than money:
authority. What really preoccupied him was not the prospect of
bankruptcy, but rather the question of who was in charge. He possessed what the official historians of the archdiocese (hardly neutral

observers) would call a "deep and very Catholic sense of the Church's peculiar constitution." It was a view which held that all power was concentrated at the top and only sparingly parceled out to those below. Every institution in the diocese needed what he himself described as the "authoritative supervision" that he alone could give.[21] The idea that subordinates could get along without him was unacceptable, a view they did not always share.

As he had done with the House of the Angel Guardian, therefore, he attempted to reorganize both the Carney Hospital and Saint John's Hospital in Lowell, another facility owned and operated by the Daughters of Charity. He pressed his case with all the forcefulness of his personality, but he met his match in the nuns who ran the two hospitals. "The administration of our houses is under the jurisdiction of our Superior General, as declared by the Sovereign Pontiff again and again," Sister Gonzaga of the Carney told him, adding shrewdly: "Hence we could not, without infringing on his [that is, the pope's] authority elect Your Grace President of our corporation." Sister Raphael of Saint John's told him the same thing in almost precisely the same words, a coincidence that suggests collusion on the part of the nuns as to strategy.[22] By wrapping themselves in the Roman flag that had always been his own, the sisters successfully resisted O'Connell's administrative advances, and he dropped his plans to restructure the hospitals.

The view from the top may have been that everyone had to be obedient to the archbishop. Those below took a different view of the church, and if they had the nerve to stand up to O'Connell's admittedly intimidating presence, they could derail his efforts at consolidation. "I do not think," an officer of the Daughters of Charity told one of O'Connell's aides, "the diocese has any more right to ask the Carney for an account of the $25.00 it receives for board and treatment of any patient . . . than it has to ask the Jesuits for an account of the hundred dollars they receive for the tuition of a boy at their college."[23]

The religious who pointed to the independence of the Jesuits and "their college" might not have spoken so quickly had the struggle already taking shape over that institution been known. Boston College had prospered in the years since O'Connell's graduation, and it commanded fierce loyalty, even from those "streetcar alumni" who had never attended the place but hoped that their sons might. The school enjoyed O'Connell's patronage and was proud to welcome him to the campus several times each year. He was a generous supporter of its projects, giving money to endow scholarships, to support athletic programs, to open an evening division, and to help erect new buildings.[24] Still, O'Connell's interest in his alma mater was not without its disadvantages, as the college's president, Father Thomas I. Gasson, S.J., was to learn.

Serious conflict between O'Connell and Gasson was probably inevitable: they were too much alike for theirs to be a uniformly calm association. Though small in stature, Gasson, an English convert to Catholicism, was quick-witted, strong willed, and ambitious for the success of the college whose presidency he assumed in January 1907.[25] He envisioned a grander school than was possible on its original inner-city site, and thus he purchased the spacious farm of that redoubtable Yankee, Amos A. Lawrence, in Chestnut Hill, a rural district on the boundary line between Boston and suburban Newton. The college would relocate there and become, in Gasson's dream, an educational institution far beyond a simple day school for city boys; instead it would become, almost overnight, a great university. He commissioned Charles Donagh Maginnis, Boston's leading Catholic architect, to draw up plans for a vast complex of collegiate Gothic buildings.

In the face of Gasson's unbridled enthusiasm O'Connell felt constrained to apply the brakes. The Catholics of Boston had always supported the college, he pointed out in June 1910, but it was important that Gasson not move too quickly. "The rushing up of enormous buildings at a tremendous outlay is a most serious blunder," O'Connell told the president, "one that will cripple the best efforts of the College for a long time. . . . For the present the obvious duty of myself and yourself is to go cautiously." Fear of red ink was, as usual, the motive for this caution, but the matter of authority also entered the picture. "All such large projects as that before Boston College have their difficulties to face," he wrote Gasson in a long, frank letter, "and the only way to overcome them is by complete and sincere submission to the direction of Holy Mother Church, even in the smallest details. The lack of this submission breeds only disunion and trouble." Taking for granted that the church's direction came exclusively from his own mouth, O'Connell concluded with a direct warning to the mercurial Jesuit: "Naturally I look to you as the responsible head of Boston College to direct all those under your immediate charge to observe scrupulously the Diocesan regulations and to show the whole Diocese that your work is not as if of some private corporation. . . . Every single evidence of a lack of unity and harmony is a block in the way of the progress of Boston College."[26]

Gasson's apparent tractability in slowing down his plans led the archbishop to press his case further. The college was legally owned by the Jesuits, and a charter from the state vested in them all responsibility for its management. Now, however, as he had done with independent Catholic hospitals and orphanages, O'Connell sought direct control over Boston College. The university Gasson wanted to build, complete with a law school, a medical school, and other graduate departments, was a fundamentally different institution from the old college, O'Connell reasoned, one that required "authoritative supervision." Accordingly, he said, a new legal structure was needed, one in which "the Archbishop consulting with Rome should be the head and director," with the Jesuits stripped of legal authority. He claimed that both Gasson and the superiors of the Jesuit order had already agreed to such an arrangement orally, and he demanded that it now be put in writing.[27]

At this point, Gasson began stalling, a tactic that eventually allowed him, like the Daughters of Charity, to outmaneuver his allegedly irresistible archbishop. Gasson waited five months before responding to O'Connell's request for written submission and then answered only by saying that the problem was being studied. Finally, shortly before Christmas 1910, he gave a formal reply that was cunningly crafted. He acknowledged that "the opening of courses, which belong strictly to the sphere of a University" was a matter that required consultation with the archbishop. He referred to a document from the Vatican curia which seemed to demand such consultation and said that the college would of course abide by it. "As we hold this view," Gasson added, coming quickly to the punch line, "and no one will ever dream of any other position, may we be excused from signing a formal document, as such a procedure would imply the possibility of a contrary position." O'Connell let the matter rest there, either unwilling or unable to grapple further with a man who, like the sisters, knew the usefulness of an appeal to Roman authority. O'Connell continued to watch the college warily and periodically lectured Gasson and later presidents on their "duties toward the Holy See and towards the Archbishop."[28] He could not, however, accomplish the substantive changes he desired in the face of resistance from those who were supposedly submissive to his every wish.

* * *

This kind of widespread resistance to O'Connell's authority continued throughout his tenure. The Catholic church in that era (and in other eras, too, for that matter) was often viewed as monolithic, an institution in which unquestioning compliance with the commands of those on top was the only option for those below. "In her," Boston's diocesan historians instructed their readers, "authority proceeds from above downward—and not in the contrary direction, as in democratic civil states."[29] To be sure, the church was no democracy, but neither was it an absolute monarchy in which an all-powerful king (in this case, the archbishop) had merely to give the word and all his subjects would fall submissively into line. Rather, American Catholicism in the age of O'Connell was feudal in character. There were many different sources of power, both central and local, and the relationships among them were complex and unpredictable. There were interlocking obligations, extending both up the chain of command and back down it. Subordinates did not forfeit their freedom of action simply by virtue of being subordinate.

The bishop certainly possessed real authority because of his position. He was, after all, specifically consecrated to his office and was thought to share fully and directly in the priesthood of Christ. Clergymen participated in that divine priesthood only by extension, and of course other religious and the laity shared in it not at all.[30] On paper at least, such an understanding allowed for the kind of precision that made O'Connell's frequent military metaphors seem appropriate: he gave the orders and everyone else simply obeyed. In practice, however, the system was more flexible. Though hierarchical in nature, the church was an unalterably local institution. Catholics identified, not with the diocese as a whole, but with their own parish. The representative of the church they recognized most clearly and followed most willingly was a person they saw every day or every week: the pastor; the mother superior of the local convent, hospital, or orphanage; the sisters or brothers in charge of their school. That identification by ordinary Catholics with local figures—the lesser feudal lords, in effect—invested them with an authority their overlord, the bishop, could neither ignore nor exterminate. The bishop remained their superior, and they remained his loyal "subjects"—the language of kingly rule came readily—but each had to find a way of living with the other. There was room in the system for resistance, negotiation, and accommodation.

The victories of Father Gasson and the Daughters of Charity who held off O'Connell's attempts at centralization were not won merely through fine points of law or clever maneuvering. They were part of a larger pattern, one in which O'Connell's own diocesan priests, those most directly subject to his will, played their part as well. No case illustrates this better than that of John O'Brien, the remarkable pastor of Sacred Heart parish in East Cambridge. An Irish immigrant to western Massachusetts, O'Brien had become a priest of the Boston diocese and served what had been the original Catholic church in Cambridge from 1873 until his death in 1917. An unabashed supporter of the public school system, he had served a term on the city's school committee. He constructed an impressive complex of parish buildings, located directly across the Charles River from downtown Boston, and he organized activities ranging from a debating society to a bowling league for his parishioners. Most important of all, he edited and published a weekly magazine called the *Sacred Heart Review*. Begun in 1888 as a kind of glorified parish bulletin, the *Review* had grown into a popular journal with an impressive national circulation. It attracted well-known writers and a wide readership with its lively combination of political commentary, devotional literature, household hints, and advice on proper social behavior for the emerging Catholic middle class. O'Brien was a prototype of the baron-pastor of his age. He could be charming and urbane, but he also had a temper, and he was a suitable adversary for O'Connell.[31]

The two had begun their association on friendly terms, when O'Brien took the lead in raising the subscription for the archbishop's new residence. He had even offered to resign as a member of the diocesan consultors so that O'Connell could appoint a replacement of his own choosing, an offer the new archbishop had declined. More significantly, in an era when the size of a parish was directly related to both the prestige and the financial security of its pastor, O'Brien had offered Sacred Heart for division into several new parishes. "Dividing ours first may remove objections" elsewhere, he told

O'Connell in 1907, explaining that "a small or a large parish can have little interest for a man in his seventieth year."[32] Though O'Brien later retracted this proposal to carve up his domain, he went along with its division and achieved an uneasy truce with the archbishop. Still, when O'Connell indicated a desire to move against the *Sacred Heart Review*, the apple of the pastor's eye, he touched a nerve that drove the Cambridge priest into protracted warfare.

When the *Pilot* first passed into archdiocesan hands, O'Brien thought it inevitable that the *Review* would follow suit. "It seems incongruous now to see one of your priests publishing a rival paper," he told O'Connell. As time went on, however, he resisted the idea of shutting down his own presses. He flatly refused to give the archbishop any reports of the *Review*'s financial condition, and he accused O'Connell of looking for any possible excuse to put it out of business. He would suspend publication, he said, only if he could state publicly that the *Review* was being suppressed at the explicit wish of the archbishop. O'Connell tried both carrots and sticks to suspend the *Review* or merge it with the *Pilot*. He lectured O'Brien on priestly obedience, but he also arranged with Rome for the aging pastor to be raised to the rank of monsignor, an honor the Vatican granted but found puzzling. O'Connell continued to watch the *Review*, scolding O'Brien if he found objectionable material in it, but the magazine survived until 1918, a year after O'Brien's death. A bishop who was an absolute monarch would have simply suspended the *Sacred Heart Review*, no questions asked or reasons given, but that was impossible for Boston's cardinal. O'Connell won this struggle with his uppity feudatory only by outliving him, and he was reduced to petty acts of revenge: the cardinal drove home from O'Brien's funeral in the monsignor's shiny new limousine, simply appropriating it as his own. Even at that he was the ultimate loser, forced to return the car when one of O'Brien's heirs threatened a lawsuit.[33]

At issue here were competing views on the nature and structure of the church. Was the church centralized and orderly, or was it diversified and occasionally chaotic? For much of the previous century, the local and decentralized view had been predominant. Archbishop Williams approached his duties as a kind of first among equals, one who presided over a fragmented kingdom in which individuals and institutions operated on their own initiative under his general oversight. He found nothing objectionable in diversity, and that outlook endured. O'Connell, by contrast, adhered to a model he thought more "Roman" and therefore more correct. He sought to check and control the centrifugal forces of diocesan life and to replace them with a centralized system that depended entirely on himself.

Trying was not succeeding, however, and for every centralizing triumph there was countervailing failure. For every Father Garriguet who resigned himself to O'Connell's will, there was a Father Gasson, a Father O'Brien, or a Sister Gonzaga who resisted success-fully. For every *Pilot* that became a direct instrument of diocesan policy, there was a *Sacred Heart Review* that retained both its Catholic loyalty and its independence. For every Working Boys Home that needed O'Connell's help in averting financial disaster, there was a Home for Destitute Catholic Children or a Carney Hospital that needed none. For every institution "floundering about in a very precarious moral and financial condition," there were many more that continued a long tradition of service in the work they had chosen to do.[34] The archdiocese was neither so badly off before O'Connell nor so completely changed by him. He did not save Catholic Boston from financial ruin and organizational chaos, because it did not need saving.

Perhaps typically for O'Connell, however, appearance was almost as important as reality. He promoted the notion that he was the managerial genius on the episcopal throne because that image was a useful one. To those within the diocese who had opposed him in the past and continued to do so, the picture of the omnicompetent administrator was a demonstration that he had been right and they wrong from the beginning. They may not have wanted him as arch-bishop, but now, that image seemed to suggest, because he was the one who had "so well systematized" the church, even they would have to admit that he had been the best choice all along. He might never be honored as Williams had been, but he would have to be respected because he was rescuing the Boston church from the "slough of despond" into which his predecessor had let it slip. His self-projection as the man who had imposed "the maximum of unity and efficiency" was designed to legitimate him despite the clouded circumstances under which he had secured his office.

More broadly, his people also responded to the pose of the effi-cient man of affairs. As Boston's Catholics increasingly left behind them their isolated physical and mental worlds and emerged into respectability, they needed something more than a "simple pietist" for a leader. They were advancing steadily in politics and society, assuming more substantial positions in the professions: law, business, insurance, real estate, and the civil service. In so doing, they were acquiring the practical, worldly abilities that had been unnecessary for their immigrant parents and grandparents. They were "making it," and they found the new outlook that went along with that experience inevitable and even enjoyable. What is more, if they possessed those new skills and attitudes, it was somehow necessary that their leader possess them, too; and precisely because he was their leader, he had to possess them—or at least seem to possess them—to an extraordinary, almost perfect degree.

Both O'Connell and his people, therefore, latched onto the myth of his singular administrative ability because each liked what it said about them. The image reassured the cardinal that he truly merited his position after all, even though most other churchmen had thought otherwise. It reassured his flock that they were indeed achieving the dream of advancement that America had promised them and their families. For O'Connell the picture was altogether too useful in underlining the symbolism of his leadership, and so, just as he had invented a boyhood that never existed, so he invented an ecclesiastical career different from his real one. The picture of an efficient, docile church, obedient to his every command, was more an expression of O'Connell's hopes than a description of his true experience. Unfortunately, that image was far from harmless, for it necessarily slighted the contributions of many others—priests, sisters, brothers, the laity—who were just as responsible as he for the church's works of devotion, education, and charity. He could exalt his own contribution only by minimizing theirs. In the end, Catholic Boston was more than merely an extension of the personality of its leader.

6

RENDERING TO CAESAR:
O'CONNELL AND THE POLITICIANS

ON THE MORNING OF WEDNESDAY, October 28, 1908, 3,000 people crowded into the Cathedral of the Holy Cross to begin five days of ceremonies marking the centennial of the Boston diocese. The governor of Massachusetts and the mayor of Boston, both non-Catholic descendants of old Yankee stock, occupied the front pew, while Archbishop Diomede Falconio, the apostolic delegate of Pope Pius X to the American church, celebrated the mass. Women in black gowns and lace mantillas joined men in cutaway coats for the long service that began at midmorning. Two hundred policemen held back the throngs outside, and the elevated trains that usually rumbled along the tracks in front of the imposing stone cathedral were diverted to other routes. As William Henry O'Connell rose to deliver a sermon entitled "In the Beginning," Boston was witnessing the most impressive public display of Catholicism in its history.

Anniversaries usually call forth speeches that reflect on the past, and O'Connell's hour-long address was no exception. He reviewed the saga of the Catholic church in New England in the one hundred years since Pius VII had appointed the first bishop in Boston. The completeness with which the land of the Pilgrims had become home to Catholic immigrants and their offspring intrigued the archbishop. Despite recurrent friction between the two groups, a shift of historic proportions had been accomplished. O'Connell summarized the change with an epigram: "The Puritan has passed; the Catholic remains."[1]

Nowhere was the transition from Puritan to Catholic more apparent than in the political life of Massachusetts. At all levels Catholics, and especially Irish Catholics, were dominating the electoral process. Though neither of the major civic officials present as

121

O'Connell spoke that morning was a Catholic, they were increasingly the exception to the rule. The change was gradual and by no means complete, but the trend was both unmistakable and irreversible. Hugh O'Brien, born in Ireland, had been elected Boston's first Catholic mayor in 1884, and he was followed a decade later by his countryman, Patrick Collins. In the next generation, Irish, Catholic, and Democratic machines rose to power in wards and cities from one end of the commonwealth to the other.[2]

On the state level too the changeover proceeded. David Ignatius Walsh became the first Catholic governor in 1914, and he would go on to serve for nearly thirty years in the United States Senate, occupying the seats once filled by the Brahmins George Frisbie Hoar and Henry Cabot Lodge. Before the century was half over, Walsh would be succeeded as governor by his fellow Catholics James M. Curley, Charles F. Hurley, Maurice J. Tobin, and Paul A. Dever. Other offices had a similar Irish Catholic succession. The post of state treasurer, for example, was held between 1931 and 1952 by four different men, each of them named Hurley. They were followed by an upstart named Kennedy, who profited by sharing a name, though not any kinship, with the state's most powerful political clan. The legislative chambers, which had rung with Know-Nothing denunciations of popery in the 1850s, were passing into the hands of Catholic majorities. Even the prayers over the deliberations of government took on a Romish flavor: in the decade after O'Connell's death, both branches of the legislature would appoint Catholic priests as their chaplains. More than ever, politics in Massachusetts was a matter of ethnicity and religion, as the passing Puritan yielded to the rising and remaining Catholic.[3]

Catholic political success demanded the evolution of a new relationship between the leaders of the church and the wielders of power. The worst of the nativist fears that Catholics were un-American by definition were finally being laid to rest (though some of them proved remarkably resilient), but the positive contributions of Catholics to public life had yet to be defined. How should Catholic officeholders respond both publicly and privately to their religious leaders? How much influence should churchmen like O'Connell exert in matters of public policy, and when should they exert it? What were the proper spheres for religion and politics, and when did one impinge on the other? If, as the archbishop observed,

Catholics were now filling the place vacated by the earlier elite, did they assume certain responsibilities along with the benefits of power?

Over the course of his thirty-seven-year tenure, O'Connell necessarily addressed these questions—sometimes forcefully, sometimes in a halting and uncertain manner. He was navigating in largely uncharted waters, with few precedents from Boston's earlier bishops on which to rely, and his political activity thus had an occasionally experimental quality. His predecessors had often been in a purely defensive position, marshaling what little political authority they commanded to hold off hostile advances. O'Connell lived in times that were less stark and foreboding, with many new opportunities, as a journalist would say, "to teach the community at large a fair attitude."[4] O'Connell took advantage of those opportunities and emerged as a powerful political figure in his own right, a position he was able to pass on to his successors.

* * *

The early twentieth century is viewed today as something of a heroic age in Massachusetts politics, a time when figures of mythic proportions occupied center stage. Best known of these is James Michael Curley, a perennial candidate who served as congressman, mayor, and governor during a career that spanned fifty years. Later immortalized in Edwin O'Connor's novel, *The Last Hurrah*, Curley was an urban folk-hero, a man who could do no wrong in his constituents' eyes despite the faint odor of corruption that lingered about him. John F. Fitzgerald, whose sweet-voiced oratory earned him the nickname "Honey Fitz," was mayor, a congressman, and a member of the patronage-rich port authority: his grandson and namesake rose even higher. From a West End powerbase called the Hendricks Club (named inexplicably for Grover Cleveland's obscure vice president), the great "Mahatma" Martin Lomasney was a force to be reckoned with: seldom holding elective office himself, Lomasney was perhaps the most powerful—and assuredly the most feared—man in Boston politics. Operating from less cosmopolitan Worcester County, David I. Walsh achieved enduring success. These figures often vied with one another for control of the state's Democratic party, but together they dominated Massachusetts politics in the age of the bosses.[5]

Despite the emerging hegemony of these men, who regularly drove their Republican and reform-minded opponents before them, Massachusetts politics remained a fragmented and faction-ridden affair. Each leader had his own safe district in which he was supreme, but outside it he was nothing. The Bay State lacked an equivalent of New York's all-powerful Tammany Hall, and no single boss could consolidate or hold power for very long. "All politics is local," an alumnus of this system is supposed to have observed: allies and supporters became enemies if one ventured too far into their territory. What is more, competition among ethnic groups only enhanced the fragmentation. French-Canadian and Italian distrust of the Irish, for example—feelings the Irish usually reciprocated—often drove those groups into the welcoming arms of the Republican party. Thus, in Worcester at the turn of the century, even though nearly 70 percent of the city's population was foreign-born, city hall remained in Republican hands.[6]

William O'Connell was a worthy ecclesiastical match for this potent cast of political characters. The priestly supporter who had described him to the Vatican as "big enough, and great enough, and grand enough" for the job of archbishop had accurately gauged O'Connell's suitability for the political hardball of his diocese. The cardinal's success at constructing a vigorous public persona enhanced his stature even further: he would learn to use his political power sparingly, choosing his battles with care, but he used that power to good effect. He acted independently, distancing himself from those politicians who were most like him. In that way he established his own authority, apart from those who constituted his closest rivals for influence within the Catholic community.

On the surface O'Connell's relationship with the rising Irish politicians looks like simple overcorrection, a bending over backwards to prove that he was different from them. Given the coolness with which archbishop and layman often viewed each other, not even the most suspicious nativist could maintain that a monolithic popish conspiracy was afoot. Curley and O'Connell, for example, seemed constantly at odds. The grand old man of Boston politics always assumed that the cardinal was in league with his enemies, whoever they happened to be at any given moment. He blamed O'Connell's interference for several electoral defeats, as well as for President Franklin Roosevelt's refusal to appoint him ambassador to

Italy in 1933. "There were times when the Cardinal abused the privileges of high office," Curley wrote years later, adding the understatement: "I must admit that he never became one of my ardent supporters."[7]

With his usual astuteness Curley had characterized the relationship precisely. Nor was he alone in realizing that the mutual suspicion between O'Connell and himself could be exploited. During one of Curley's many mayoral reelection campaigns, his opponents took advantage of the widely acknowledged hostility between the cardinal and the politician, who was a faithful communicant with a son in the priesthood. "VOTERS OF BOSTON!" the anti-Curley *Post* cried above its masthead on the morning of election day 1937—it happened to be the feast of All Souls, and many Catholics picked up the paper as they emerged from mass on their way to vote. "Cardinal O'Connell, in speaking to the Catholic Alumni Association, said, 'The walls are raised against honest men in civic life.' You can break down those walls by voting for an honest, clean, competent young man, MAURICE J. TOBIN, today. He will redeem the city." Only the most careful reader of the *Post*'s punctuation noticed that the out-of-context quotation from the cardinal ended at the word "*life*," thus stopping significantly short of endorsing the handsome but inexperienced Tobin. Still, the damage was done. Curley and his lieutenants spent the day frantically calling O'Connell's office, demanding a correction, but the cardinal (who was perhaps not as upset as he might have been with the misattribution) made no reply, and Curley went down to blazing defeat.[8]

O'Connell knew that Curley was slippery, and he was constantly on guard against the maneuvers of "the purple shamrock," who often tried to create the impression that he enjoyed the cardinal's support. On one such occasion, O'Connell lashed back in a long handwritten letter. "You might very naturally like me to do something which would from *your* point of view . . . seem not only possible but even urgent," O'Connell told Curley. That was "an unfair constraint to which (quite independent of personal likes or desires) I will be *bound* to return a refusal." Like other political leaders, O'Connell had prerogatives and even "turf" that Curley had to respect, regardless of the bond of religion. "I should do precisely the same thing to a Protestant official. Our religion has nothing whatever to do with it," O'Connell concluded, adding somewhat cryptically: "I am always praying for your success—I mean of course true success." The O'Connell character in *The Last Hurrah* cried out in exasperation at the "schemer in City Hall who would stop at nothing, absolutely *nothing*, to bend and twist the Church to his own purposes." No less than this fictional cardinal, the real one might complain that "this man cheapened us forever."[9]

O'Connell's associations with the other Catholic politicians of his day were carried on within the same carefully defined limits. Martin Lomasney was by all accounts a "practical Catholic," pious in his private observance and the benefactor of church-related charities, but he did not hesitate to cross his archbishop on political matters. When he and O'Connell disagreed over an issue before the state's constitutional convention in 1917, for example, Lomasney said bluntly: "Tell his Eminence to mind his own business." John Fitzgerald fared little better. During his scandal-ridden terms as mayor just after O'Connell's arrival in Boston, the churchman seemed to align himself with the Yankee reformers—Curley called them "Goo-Goos," a derisive abbreviation for their Good Government Association—who opposed the Irish upstart. Relations between the two men grew more cordial during Honey Fitz's long period of political decline, however, and the politician even credited O'Connell with providing decisive advice on the religious education of his growing brood of children.[10]

O'Connell's only personal friend among the politicians was David I. Walsh, and even at that the discussion of political questions was always off-limits. Walsh was less flamboyant than his Boston counterparts, and these stylistic differences made him more appealing to the cardinal. A bachelor who lived at home with his three unmarried schoolteacher sisters, Walsh was a little too saturnine and diffident for the career he had chosen: so sparing was he with patronage in his central Massachusetts home base that even his supporters dubbed him David "Ignore-Us" Walsh. O'Connell became a kind of spiritual adviser, writing the politician personal letters and receiving him at home, especially during Lent.

Despite their friendship, O'Connell and Walsh were eager to avoid the appearance that they were somehow in cahoots or that one was merely a mouthpiece for the other. Soon after Walsh began his first gubernatorial term, O'Connell wrote him a long letter setting forth the terms of their public relationship. "You know very well that personally I shall never attempt to inject any views of my own," the cardinal said. "I never have done so, and I never will do so. I believe, in fact I know, that I am as conscientious as anyone can possibly be." As time went on, O'Connell would make his political opinions known, but he held to his resolve to leave Walsh out of the matter. He never tried to exploit the relationship or to manipulate the governor into an unthinking parroting of some kind of church "party line." For his part, Walsh often took positions that were at variance with those of O'Connell. He supported adoption of the initiative and referendum in Massachusetts, for example, a practice the cardinal thought too unpredictable for orderly government.[11]

Still, something more than mere appearance was at stake as O'Connell defined himself in relation to the Catholic politicians of his day. With all of them he needed to make clear that he had a sphere of influence just as they did. His might not be defined in terms of a specific ward, but his authority within it had to be respected nonetheless. He was one of them, another powerbroker in a fractious political world, and he was prepared to play according to the generally accepted rules. In effect, his church was the ward of which he was boss. "I'm not exactly sure, by the way, that His Eminence would appreciate his inclusion in a group of politicians," the fictional Curley said of the fictional O'Connell in *The Last Hurrah*, "but I'm inclined to believe he qualifies." An angry woman with the otherwise orthodox name of Mary O'Hara agreed with this analysis, telling the cardinal at one point: "All the folks around call you Big Bill the politician. You're the Curley of the church"—an equation that surely stung.[12] Thus, when O'Connell criticized or even opposed "one of his own," he was moving to ensure his own freedom of action and to preserve the public influence he had worked so hard to achieve.

He faced no such problems with non-Catholic, generally Republican politicians, whose natural constituency did not impinge on his. He could be closer to them than to those who were members of his own flock. He was especially friendly with Curtis Guild, a Yankee mugwump who served as governor from 1906 to 1909, and with his wife Charlotte, who eventually converted to Catholicism under the cardinal's instruction. The only man ever to address his letters to O'Connell "My dear William," Guild saw in their friendship across religious barriers "the opening of a door that will I hope give a truer meaning to the fraternity of American citizenship." In the same way, O'Connell stood by another Yankee governor, Alvan T. Fuller, even when he approved the execution of the radicals Sacco and Vanzetti. O'Connell's association with such men of substance came to seem natural, even on the national level: he remained on familiar terms with William Howard Taft, visiting the president's summer home in Beverly, Massachusetts, and corresponding with him long after he had left the White House.[13]

One possible inference from the pattern of O'Connell's choice of political friends is that he was simply more partial to Republicans than to Democrats. Such a view has some merit. He never spoke openly in favor of the GOP (as his longtime ecclesiastical rival, John Ireland, had done), but it was widely rumored that he regularly voted the Republican ticket. "That you have not the people's interest at heart is well known," an angry anonymous parishioner wrote him just before the election of 1928. "It is even said you are a Republican," she added, perhaps calling him the worst name she could think of.[14] The cardinal's conservative social outlook probably did indicate that he was at heart more of a Herbert Hoover Republican than a New Deal Democrat, but he was not a simple partisan.

O'Connell's dealings with the political leaders of his day reveal an effort to draw the lines of influence with care and subtlety. He was closer to non-Catholic politicians and to the "safer" Catholic politicos (like Walsh and the out-of-office Fitzgerald) because he could do so without seeming to overstep proper boundaries. The virulent nativism of the nineteenth century was alive enough in memory so that alarms over Catholic subversion, organized and directed by the hierarchy, could not be simply ignored. Indeed, during the 1920s a revived Ku Klux Klan made some headway, especially in rural Massachusetts, by raising those old fears. The often irrational response to Alfred E. Smith's candidacy for president showed that Catholics still had to be sensitive to the charge that they made unreliable citizens, and O'Connell therefore had to maintain a distance from Catholic politicians that would demonstrate the falsity of the charge. At the same time, since he was inevitably a competitor with those men for influence, he had to be careful to protect his own position and to respect theirs. Contact with Yankee politicians presented no such risks, and O'Connell could thus be freer with them. If anything, his friendship with men of such obvious probity only helped underline Catholic patriotism.

O'Connell's view of the role Catholics were rightly coming to play in public affairs, however—"We must make the history of the coming [century]," he had asserted without apology—demanded an active political role on many occasions. Because they were supplanting the Puritans who "passed" into oblivion, Catholics had both the right and the responsibility to influence public policy and to push it in deliberately chosen directions. "The march toward our duty here," O'Connell said in his centennial sermon, "not merely to ourselves, but to our surroundings, must proceed. God wills it." Just as the Protestant establishment had once shaped public life in conformity with its moral and religious outlook, so now Catholics would do the same. As the emerging force in Massachusetts politics, Catholicism assumed both the benefits of ascendancy ("duty to ourselves," in O'Connell's phrase) and its obligations ("duty to our surroundings"). If politicans like Curley and Fitzgerald said to their people, in effect, "Now it's our turn," O'Connell added the cautionary, "Now it's our responsibility."[15]

* * *

The view that Catholics had a duty to their surroundings led O'Connell into several substantial political battles during his career, but he took to heart the message of Ecclesiastes that there was a time for speaking and a time for keeping silent. When he wanted to, he could influence the course of public events. He was known in the slang of the state legislature simply as "Number One," a title that correctly measured his authority there. He relied on carefully placed observers to keep an eye on pending legislation for him, looking out for church interests.[16] Still, he was smart enough to know that there were simply certain disputes in which the wiser course was inaction.

Most notable of these was the culmination of the long struggle over women's suffrage. Many Catholic priests and politicians had long opposed extension of the franchise to women. Voting was beyond the proper female sphere, they thought, and the alliance of the suffragists with the rising birth control movement, as well as with the remnants of political nativism, gave suffrage a suspicious cast. By the time of the First World War, however, Catholic opinion was beginning to shift. A few American bishops came out in support, and Catholic trade union leaders took up the cause as a means for improving wages and working conditions. In Massachusetts, Governor Walsh became the most ardent Catholic supporter of women's suffrage. He lobbied hard on behalf of an amendment to the state constitution, and in 1916 he campaigned for reelection on that platform. Both he and the amendment were defeated, but the loss only confirmed him in his support. Running for the United States Senate two years later against a hardened antisuffragist, he swept to victory, adding another first (that of the state's first Catholic senator) to his list of accomplishments.[17]

Cardinal O'Connell was known to oppose women's suffrage, but he did little about it. The *Pilot* voiced some doubts, but otherwise the cardinal kept his own counsel. He declined to speak out himself, and he forbade the state's largest antisuffrage association from speaking to parish women's clubs on the question. Like most Catholic prelates, once the Nineteenth Amendment was ratified he urged all Catholic women to vote, recognizing the power that came with numbers. A similar conspicuous silence prevailed in O'Connell's reaction to the strike by Boston's police force in the fall of 1919, an event that catapulted the state's taciturn governor, Calvin Coolidge, into the White House.[18] Perhaps because he knew in both instances that any public position would win him as many enemies as friends, O'Connell wisely kept quiet.

When the church had an identifiable interest in an issue, however, he did not hesitate. This happened first in 1917, during debate over the sectarian or "anti-aid" amendment. A convention was called that year to consider a major revision of the Massachusetts Constitution of 1780. Adoption of the initiative and referendum and a two-year (rather than one-year) term for the governor were the principal concerns of the body, but the question of state aid to private educational and charitable institutions was also hotly contested. Massachusetts had a long tradition of granting such aid: Harvard had received appropriations from the state treasury well into the nineteenth century, and the original constitution had endorsed the use of town tax money for the support of "public, Protestant ministers of the Gospel." Now, however, the convention debated an amendment that blocked aid to schools "wherein any denominational doctrine is inculcated" or to any social welfare agency "which is not publicly owned and under the exclusive control . . . of public officers."[19]

Approved by the convention, the measure was submitted to the voters in November 1917.

The amendment touched a raw nerve. The *Pilot* had been monitoring debate on the proposal and referred to its backers simply as "the bigots," who were always identified as anti-Catholic ministers or members of sinister nativist organizations like the Guardians of Liberty. State support for private institutions was a long-established practice, the diocesan newspaper argued, one that no one had questioned until it became likely that Catholic agencies would receive some share of the money.[20]

Unfortunately for the clarity of this "us-them" characterization, some of the measure's leading sponsors were themselves Catholics, including Martin Lomasney and the young John W. McCormack, then a rising politician from South Boston and later Speaker of the U.S. House of Representatives. They acknowledged the tradition of assistance to Protestant agencies; fairness seemed to demand sharing that aid with Catholics. Age and prestige meant that Protestant institutions would continue to get a larger share of the pie, however, even if some small amounts were available to Catholics. Cutting off aid for everyone, Lomasney and McCormack reasoned, was at least a way of reducing a perpetual Catholic disadvantage. A wide majority of the convention, including all but nine of the ninety-four Catholic delegates, agreed and voted for the measure.

Cardinal O'Connell took another view. He had been hesitant to seek state support in the past—he had directed the head of the Catholic Charitable Bureau to kill a bill in the legislature in 1908 that would have given $10,000 to the Carney Hospital—but he now saw the issue as one of blatant anti-Catholic discrimination. The *Pilot* undertook a vigorous editorial effort aimed at defeating the amendment at the polls. Echoing the ethnic hostility that had served Irish politicians like Curley and Fitzgerald so well, the paper denounced the amendment's Yankee supporters, including "Mr. A. Lawrence Lowell, President of that well-known real estate and educational incubus [in] Cambridge."[21] O'Connell could not indulge in such open Harvard-baiting himself, but an unsigned editorial gave him just enough cover.

A week before election day, the cardinal entered the dispute publicly. Speaking to a layman's group on October 28, he denounced the measure as "a gratuitous insult" to Catholics. Church schools and hospitals saved millions of dollars for the state, which would have to expand its own services without them, he maintained, and it was pure bias that pushed for a change in the long-standing policy. Now, when "at last our voice, too, might at least begin to be audible," O'Connell said, mixing his metaphors slightly, "even before we have a chance to speak, the door is slammed violently in our faces." The diocesan newspaper made the same argument right up until election day, but the cardinal's public enunciation of the "distinctively Catholic side" of the question had no effect. Voters approved the anti-aid amendment overwhelmingly, forcing the *Pilot* to notice Catholic support for the measure at last. It shook its editorial head over "a lot of dead wood calling itself Catholic, but really mere time servers, servile politicians and cheap toadies."[22]

O'Connell's definition of the church's interest in political questions extended well beyond money. Larger moral and family issues were more important to him. Seven years after the anti-aid fight, he became even more active in an electoral battle over child labor. After several laws on the subject had been invalidated by the courts, an amendment to the federal Constitution was introduced and submitted to the states. The question was on the Massachusetts ballot in 1924 as an advisory referendum, seeking citizen opinion on ratification. Supporters presumed ready approval, since the amendment embodied regulations that had been in effect in the Bay State for some time. Nationwide, Catholic opinion on the matter was divided, although it generally leaned more in favor of restricting child labor than against. The *Catholic Charities Review* and other national periodicals (with the notable exception of the Jesuit weekly, *America*) supported the amendment. The National Council of Catholic Women expressed its support. Monsignor John A. Ryan, a faculty member at the Catholic University and director of the social action department of the National Catholic Welfare Conference (NCWC), was an active campaigner on its behalf.[23]

Several members of the hierarchy opposed the measure, however, including Baltimore's Archbishop Michael J. Curley and Boston's Cardinal O'Connell. Some local Catholic politicians shared this opposition. Lomasney advanced the libertarian argument that any government strong enough to restrict child labor was strong enough to impose compulsory military training and a draft, and he denounced all three ideas. Curley and Walsh, candidates for governor and senator respectively that year, initially supported the amendment, but when the cardinal's opposition became known both changed their minds. Walsh lapsed into an embarrassed silence, but Curley, never one to let principles stand in the way of expansive oratory, immediately took to the stump to denounce the amendment as so much "bolshevism." The abrupt switch did neither man any good, and both were defeated.[24]

For once, O'Connell and Lomasney agreed on something. "Beneath this measure, couched as it is in apparently innocuous language," the cardinal told an opposition group with the unlikely name of Citizens Committee to Protect Our Homes and Children, "lurks a grave menace to family life, parental control and the sovereignty of the individual States." Combining conservative social views with traditional notions of the proper limitations on the jurisdiction of the federal government, O'Connell saw the question as an invasion of the family circle. "For parental control," he argued, the amendment would "substitute the will of Congress and the dicta of a centralized bureaucracy more in keeping with communism than the base-rock principles of American government."[25]

Because he thought the church the unique protector of the family, O'Connell launched an active campaign against the child labor proposal, organizing archdiocesan priests and parishes to get out the anti-amendment vote. By circular letter to his pastors, he ordered that all sermons delivered on Sunday, October 5, just a month before election day, be devoted to presenting "the dangers hidden in the proposed Child Labor Amendment." Priests were also expected to remind their parishioners of the "necessity of registering . . . and of voting on election day to protect the interests of their children." Two women from each parish, selected by the pastor, were invited to a meeting at the Notre Dame Academy in Boston for instruction in how to spread the message and organize their neighbors. The *Pilot* editorialized on the subject every week, and denunciations from the pulpit continued until the Sunday before the vote. The amendment "takes away from parents the right to regulate the labor of their children," proclaimed the pastor of All Saints' parish, Roxbury. "It gives Congress that right. It is Socialistic as it puts the State above the Parents. . . . Therefore, my good men and women, vote no, put an X in the no column of the Referendum. It is your solemn duty to do so."[26]

O'Connell was also working behind the scenes to neutralize Catholic support for child labor restriction. He was particularly angry at Monsignor Ryan and other prominent Catholics who endorsed the amendment. O'Connell and Ryan had always viewed each other warily: the professor from Catholic University held what O'Connell considered strange social opinions, and he also came with suspect church credentials, since he was a protégé of Archbishop Ireland. Now the cardinal complained to Archbishop Curley (technically Ryan's superior) and to Albany's Bishop Edmund Gibbons, who was head of the legislative department of the NCWC. Ryan and his "agents" were "sending out propaganda in favor of that nefarious and bolshevik amendment," O'Connell told Gibbons, and in so doing they were exceeding their authority. "How anyone who knows Catholic principles and practice can have any part of this infamous proceeding is a mystery," he went on. "Give some clear talk to this coterie, and tie their hands before they get a rapping that they will regret." Gibbons intervened and, in the closing weeks of the campaign, Ryan and his allies toned down their support rather than risk further antagonizing the Boston cardinal. Even so, O'Connell could not resist the temptation to continue harassing Ryan on the subject: a week after the election, the *Pilot* wondered "just how and why . . . a certain professor in our Catholic University" could have supported "a movement widely regarded as radical and socialistic."[27]

The church's opposition was not the only factor in the voters' minds as they went to the polls on November 2, but it combined with others to send the amendment down to overwhelming defeat. Statewide the vote was 241,000 in favor to 697,000 opposed, a margin approaching three to one. In the predominantly Catholic urban centers, the vote was even more lopsided: just over three to one in Fall River and almost four to one in the city of Boston itself. Other powerful interests, including the National Association of Manufacturers and the Associated Industries of Massachusetts, both of which had put large sums into anti-amendment advertising, helped affect the outcome, but the *Pilot* nonetheless trumpeted that "the greatest credit for the defeat of the ratification . . . must be accorded to His Eminence the Cardinal." What is more, the national impact was substantial. Since everyone had expected easy approval, the defeat in Massachusetts served to kill off the movement against child labor nationwide.[28]

Though it looks harsh and reactionary to modern eyes, O'Connell based his opposition to the child labor amendment on a defense of the family and its autonomy. That concern led him to political action again, late in his career, over the question of birth control. Like many states, Massachusetts still enforced nineteenth-century laws severely restricting the dissemination of birth control information. As some jurisdictions began to modify their laws, a similar movement got under way in Massachusetts, and the issue quickly became politicized. Several attempts to change the statutes through legislation failed, and the proponents of liberalized birth control laws resorted in 1941 and 1942 to a ballot initiative.

Though he was approaching the end of his long life and was increasingly feeble, O'Connell needed little prompting to marshal his forces to block any change in the law, which coincided with the traditional Catholic outlook on birth control. A first effort was carried out behind the scenes, and his chief aide in this work was Frederick W. Mansfield. The son of Irish immigrants from County Mayo with a Yankee-sounding name (a circumstance that helped him in some circles and hurt him in others), Mansfield had been active in the conservative wing of the Democratic party since the turn of the century. He had run unsuccessfully for governor in 1910 and served as mayor of Boston from 1933 to 1937. Long a favorite whipping boy of Curley, Mansfield (like David Walsh) was the cardinal's kind of respectable Irish politician, and the two had been close for years. After becoming the official archdiocesan attorney in 1939, Mansfield was the logical choice as O'Connell's political spear-carrier.

When the advocates of birth control reform introduced their measure in the state House of Representatives in April 1941, Mansfield swung into action. He testified against it at a committee hearing and helped block it from reaching the house floor. When the backers changed tactics to the initiative procedure, Mansfield raised objections before the state's ballot law commission and in court. Heavily annotating his argument with constitutional citations, Mansfield argued that the proposal related to "religion, religious practices, or religious institutions," and that it therefore could not be resolved by direct appeal to the voters. "The proponents did not rest their arguments upon . . . reasons of health," he said, but rather stressed "the religious aspects of the matter." At the same time, the ban on "artificial and external" methods of birth control was a genuine and important religious matter for Catholics: "it is a law of their Church; it is a natural law and a moral law; and it is a law of God."[29] Since the constitution expressly barred religious questions from the referendum ballot, Mansfield maintained, the proposal was out of order.

The state supreme court rejected these arguments, finding that the measure pertained more to the state's regulatory authority than to religious questions, and thus the way was cleared for its appearance on the ballot in November 1942. Echoing Mansfield's themes, O'Connell began a low-key but effective campaign to hold off any change in the law. The cardinal himself never issued a personal denunciation, but the *Pilot* editorialized on the subject weekly from the middle of the summer until election day, denouncing birth control as "this unholy, unpatriotic, loathsome thing." Apologizing to its readers for even having to talk about the subject openly, especially in front of children, O'Connell's newspaper encouraged voters to oppose "a practice which God Almighty has forbidden."[30]

Priests were enlisted as they had been in 1924, encouraging voter registration (especially by women) and explaining the procedures by which Catholic servicemen could obtain absentee ballots. The pastor of Saint Charles Borromeo parish in Waltham distributed anti-birth control literature at his church after mass, and he urged his parishioners to "make a house to house canvas in your neighborhood and leave the folders." His colleague at Saint Thomas Aquinas, Jamaica Plain, summarized the church's opposition succinctly the Sunday before election day when he announced from his pulpit: "Birth Control is against God's Law! Every registered voter of this parish should go to the polls Tuesday and vote *NO* on Question number one."[31] These efforts proved effective, and the birth control referendum was defeated statewide by about 200,000 votes. As with the child labor proposal, the heavily Catholic cities led the way: the margin of defeat in Fall River was more than two to one, and in Cardinal O'Connell's native Lowell it was more than three to one.

* * *

The cardinal had amply demonstrated his political muscle, but why did he speak out on some issues and not on others? The reasons were not primarily tactical, not based solely on decisions about whether he could win. Rather, they were grounded in an enduring ambiguity toward politics as such. Since neither he nor his predecessors had ever had such power at their disposal before, he had to learn as he went along how to exercise it. At the same time, a recurring sense that he had to remain somehow untainted by politics complicated his response to public questions. A mixed attitude toward political life affected his decisions on when and how to use his influence.

Whenever O'Connell used the word "politics," he meant explicit partisanship in favor of a particular candidate or party. Involvement in that kind of politics was unacceptable for the church and its leaders. "I want to say," he told an audience of seminarians shortly after the defeat of Al Smith in 1928, "that I have never contributed a cent in my whole life to any campaign or individual who was running for office or to any party." Some years later he took to task churchmen who became involved in "purely political affairs [and] passing political phases of civil life." It was dangerous, he thought, to trust "too much in the sinuous arts of politicians."[32] Negative connotations were everywhere. Politics was of only "passing" interest, and politicians were necessarily "sinuous" and "artful." Suspicion of "purely" political matters, therefore, was always necessary.

It was for these reasons that O'Connell criticized priests like the NCWC's Monsignor Ryan who seemed too ready to get involved with specific issues or candidates. Even more distressing was the case of the famous radio preacher, Father Charles Coughlin of Royal Oak, Michigan. A genuine celebrity because of his immensely popular Sunday afternoon broadcasts from the Shrine of the Little Flower, Coughlin took to discussions of economic and social issues. An early and open supporter of Franklin Roosevelt, he turned bitterly against the New Deal, eventually mounting a rival candidate for the White House in 1936 under the banner of his own newly christened National Union for Social Justice. Increasingly frenzied and anti-Semitic, Coughlin nevertheless enjoyed a huge following among Catholics and non-Catholics alike, including many in O'Connell's own backyard: Jim Curley had dubbed Boston the "most Coughlinite city in America," and the label seemed to stick. When Coughlin visited the city in the summer of 1935, politicians tripped over one another to be seen with him.[33]

O'Connell strongly disapproved of both the medium and his message. Addressing a group of Catholic dentists in April 1932, the prelate issued the first of several denunciations of the charismatic priest. "Almost hysterical addresses by ecclesiastics" had no place in political discourse, O'Connell said. Casting a figurative but direct glance in the direction of Michigan, he observed without ever mentioning Coughlin by name that "if a priest talks about things purely religious, established Catholic truths and teachings, we do not mind. . . . If the speaker begins to talk nonsense, or indulges in mere emotionalism or sensationalism he is stopped, and that is the end of his talks." That Coughlin was "only" a priest and not a bishop may have added to O'Connell's sense that he was overstepping his authority, and in any event silencing Coughlin was not quite so easy: the radio priest remained on the air for several more years. At the same time, O'Connell's rebuke brought forth floods of angry letters from Coughlin's supporters, but the cardinal neither responded nor let them dissuade him from further denunciations, once in 1933 and again in 1934. O'Connell was on slightly thin ice, since he was competing for influence with Coughlin among some of his own flock. Nevertheless, his belief that "the Catholic Church does not take sides with the rich or the poor, the Republican or Democrat," led him to reject any partisan mixture of religion and politics.[34]

When political issues became moral issues, however, O'Connell thought he had both the right and the duty to take direct political stands. The church's proper teaching function, together with its responsibility to act as the guardian of the family and indeed of all public morality, demanded action. "There can be no true morality," he declared, "unless it is founded on religious principle," and the church had to make both clear.[35] Thus, O'Connell's political activism was justified not only when church interests were directly at stake but also when public issues were moral issues. In 1917, he thought, the existence of Catholic schools, the right of parents to send their children to them, and the question of equal treatment for all denominations seemed at issue. In 1924 and 1942, the very structure of the family and the enforcement of moral standards—"God's law," in fact—were in jeopardy. In those cases, defense of the church's moral role justified political action.

A more dramatic, if less consequential, example of the transformation of politics into morality came in 1935 over the issue of a state-supported lottery. Curley, serving his only term as governor, had proposed a lottery as a relatively painless way of raising revenue in a depression-ravaged economy. When his bill was introduced, it sped through the legislature, destined for easy passage despite the opposition of some newspapers and several Protestant church groups. Just before the final vote, however, the cardinal joined the opposition. Asserting that several unnamed persons had solicited his opinion, he declared flatly: "I am opposed to a state lottery. . . . You can use polite phrases for it if you like, but it is out-and-out gambling." More to the point, however, were the cardinal's reasons. "This is not merely a political question," he said. "It is a very serious moral problem," since lotteries were "a tremendous source of corruption and demoralization." These same considerations had led him at the time of the First World War to oppose legislation permitting the playing of baseball and golf on Sunday.[36] Now he took a similar stand in the face of legalized gambling.

The effect of this statement by "Number One" was swift and devastating. He had spoken to the press on a Monday morning, and by Tuesday afternoon the lottery bill had crashed to defeat by a margin of 187 to 40 in the House of Representatives. One embarrassed legislator after another took the floor "in what was not a debate," one newspaper said, "but a retraction of views." Representative Martin Hays of Brighton led the stampede: originally one of the measure's backers, he was smart enough to know the battle was lost once Cardinal O'Connell—his own constituent!—had spoken. "I am not so vain that I will presume to place my opinion over both press and clergy," Hays gulped, a scruple that had not troubled him so long as the only "clergy" involved had been Protestants.[37]

For O'Connell, the church's role as the only reliable defender of public morals was clear. Sounding themes about the organic nature of society that had been part of Catholic thought for some time, he guarded jealously the boundaries around governmental activity. He shared with many of his contemporaries, regardless of political affiliation, the ideal of strictly limited government: there were certain things that the state simply could not and should not do. He expressed this philosophy repeatedly over the years, never more fully than in a speech to the National Catholic Educational Association at Saint Louis in 1919 entitled "The Reasonable Limits of State

Activity." The greatest threat to modern society, he said, was the way in which all governments were taking on new responsibilities, edging out the individual and the family. "Our democratic institutions are endangered by the present tendency of the State to increase its power and to absorb the individual in its paternalistic legislation," he argued, trends that "exalt unduly the State" and "degrade the citizen." These were the same trends that had led to "Caesarism" and "despotism" in other countries. The "real menace" of the modern era was "governmental absolutism," leading the average American "to expect from the State omniscience and omnipotence—both attributes of God alone."[38] With totalitarian regimes on the rise elsewhere in the world, O'Connell feared something similar for America.

Earlier that same year, he had voiced similar opinions in a letter to a midwestern congressman. The lawmaker had introduced a bill to create a federal education department, and he sent a copy to the cardinal for comment. The *Pilot* would soon get into the habit of condemning such proposals whenever they appeared (fearing that restriction or even abolition of the parochial school system would be the inevitable result), and O'Connell anticipated that opposition. The bill proved that the United States was "well along the road to the centralization of legislation concerning every phase of human life," he told the surprised congressman, and it heralded the advent of "an autocracy far more iron than any ever devised by the rulers of Germany. What we eat, what we drink, where and how we shall do both; . . . how we shall think, and whether we shall think or not, or whether we shall even be allowed to think;—all these seem to be well advanced in becoming entirely controlled by a centralized bureaucracy." If that was to happen in America, he wondered, why had the nation even bothered to fight the great war just concluded? No, the best government was the least government.[39]

The cardinal's reference to regulation of "what we drink" was particularly timely, since his letter was written less than two weeks after the Eighteenth Amendment had ushered in the era of prohibition. O'Connell had said nothing during the debate on this divisive political and moral question, though the general Catholic position was widely known. Legally enforced prohibition was the solution to the "liquor problem" espoused by many Protestant denominations, but the Catholic church had usually preferred the idea of voluntary abstinence from drink—"taking the pledge." Many, including Archbishop Williams, had supported this view, and hundreds of Father Mathew Total Abstinence societies dotted the Catholic land-scape, inspired by a traveling Irish priest who fought a disease to which many thought Irish Americans particularly susceptible.

O'Connell avoided public comment on prohibition until the beginning of 1926, by which time the movement for repeal was already gathering steam. Pressed by reporters for his opinion, he finally issued a statement enunciating what he modestly identified as "the true Catholic standpoint." He repeated the preference for absti-nence and denounced compulsory prohibition as contrary to Scripture and tradition. He was concerned about a supposed "con-spiracy on prohibition," dominated by Protestants, and he feared that wooing Catholics away from their church was the real motiva-tion behind it. His remarks were picked up by the wire services and reprinted around the country, calling forth a flood of mail both favor-able and unfavorable. "The liquor interests are using you for a pawn," one anonymous writer told him, though another praised him for speaking against "the all too easy seeming remedy of legislation for social ills." When prohibition was repealed in 1933, O'Connell felt vindicated, expressing satisfaction that it had been "wiped from the constitution. It never had a place there."[40]

The image of an overblown government managed by a faceless bureaucracy and controlled ultimately by crafty politicians preoc-cupied O'Connell whenever he thought about politics. Bureaucracy characterized absolute states, and he associated it with socialism and "bolshevism." In such systems, individual liberty was inevitably eroded, and the loss of religious liberty was never far behind. Thus, for O'Connell anything that promoted "Caesarism" or "govern-mental absolutism" had moral and religious as well as political implications. Entering the public lists to prevent such dire con-sequences was accordingly justified and correct.

O'Connell's political opinions and involvements were thus a complicated mixture of theory and practice, of action and inaction. Because he had made himself such a potent and visible public figure, he acquired a power that earlier bishops had not enjoyed, the power to influence the world of public affairs, often by a simple word or gesture. At the same time, a lingering distaste for the vagaries of practical politics made him somewhat unpredictable, choosing to fight on some issues and not on others. He could keep silent on momentous questions, like women's suffrage; he could speak out after long restraint, as in the case of prohibition; he could boldly enter the political debate and organize his forces in order to win, as with child labor and birth control. When he chose this last option, he was usually powerful enough to see his position prevail, and he accustomed political leaders to deferring to him and respecting his power. His successors as archbishop later in the century, including Cardinal Richard Cushing (who seemed to many at least as natural a politician as a churchman), inherited that power and exercised it gleefully.[41]

O'Connell's sure guide was a belief in the role of his church as the protector of morality, a morality he was never unsure of or reluctant to express. His Catholic who "remained" now enjoyed both the advantages and the responsibilities of power, and as the preeminent local Catholic leader, he expected to guide the application and the enjoyment of power. In the generation that came after him, Catholics would exercise their influence more forcefully, directly, and unapologetically. They would even see "one of their own" elected to the highest office the political world of the United States had to offer. That was a world O'Connell may have glimpsed on the horizon, though it was a world in which, for all his assertiveness and authority, he never fully lived.

7

"THE NEWER CATHOLIC RACES":
THE VARIETIES OF ETHNIC CATHOLICISM

In the winter of 1921, Father Michael Scanlan spent some time on the docks of South Boston. Scanlan, whose own parents had come from Ireland barely fifty years before, wanted to see for himself the "Catholic immigrants arriving at the port" and to assess "the religious welfare of same." In just two days he met about three thousand passengers from many different lands: they were Italians, Poles, Lithuanians, Portuguese, French, Germans, and even Syrians and Lebanese. He saw all the noise and confusion that went with mass migration. He saw too the sharpers and scoundrels who took advantage of the naive with no one to greet them. Even more alarming, he saw Protestant ministers passing among the newcomers, conveying the message—often subtly, often in so many words—that to be true Americans, they had to relinquish the faith of their fathers and join the Protestant mainstream of the United States. Scanlan, who was director of Boston's Catholic Charitable Bureau, quickly concluded that the need of the hour was for "one responsible agency under Catholic auspices with workers representing the dominant elements among the immigrants."[1]

Scanlan submitted a plan for such an agency to Cardinal O'Connell, and within weeks an immigrant welfare department had taken shape in his bureau. Mary A. Cotter, a "trained worker of large experience in organizing charitable and social agencies," was hired to oversee the effort. She was joined by a corps of assistants, most of them women, each one fluent in a different language. The demand for their services was great: in 1921 alone, Scanlan estimated, more than 56,000 immigrants, the majority of them Catholics, arrived in Boston. Cooperating with federal authorities, the Catholic workers offered a variety of help: "they assist in the details of travel, give correct information, extend courtesies that lessen the difficulties, protect from serious dangers, . . . and when necessary accompany young women or children to their destination or to a place of safety." Many were coming to America to marry and thereby become citizens, and Scanlan's agents pointed the way to the appropriate parishes, smoothing out canonical technicalities that were barely understood. The cardinal appointed an advisory board made up of priests representing all the nationalities of the immigrants, a committee, the *Pilot* said, "of which every Catholic may feel proud." Reserving the greatest share of the credit to O'Connell himself, the paper proclaimed the work "a tribute to the zeal and vision that have made Boston one of the nation's strongholds of the Faith."[2]

Since the middle of the nineteenth century immigration and ethnicity had never been very far beneath the surface of life in Boston. Containing perhaps the most homogeneous population of all the original thirteen colonies, Massachusetts quickly found itself crowded with newcomers from very different backgrounds. The accommodation of new and old peoples was seldom smooth, and the resulting tension seared itself into the thinking and behavior of both groups for generations. What is more, the ethnic fault lines, dividing "us" from "them," generally coincided with religious differences. The "native" population—which was of course no more native than the new arrivals, merely the product of a more remote migration—had been overwhelmingly Protestant; indeed, it was both aggressively Protestant and aggressively anti-Catholic. Now they found themselves surrounded by Catholics. No wonder they resorted to the terrifying images of natural disaster, speaking of immigrant "floods" and "tidal waves" to describe the change.[3]

At first, the most significant immigration to Boston had come from famine-devastated Ireland, and thus, for most of its first century, Boston Catholicism had meant Irish Catholicism. New parishes and institutions came into existence to serve overwhelmingly Irish populations. Every bishop from the 1840s onward was of Irish stock, and the clergy and religious who assisted them had similar backgrounds. In this way Boston was different from many other emerging centers of American Catholicism because it lacked broad ethnic diversity. In New York and Chicago, for example, other groups (particularly Germans) were represented in greater numbers, and friction inside the Catholic community was more painfully apparent. In Boston, though tensions with non-Catholics persisted, the absence of significant rivals to Irish hegemony within the church muted ethnic hostility: non-Irish groups could be, and were, happily accommodated without seriously fragmenting local Catholicism. So completely did the Irish dominate the church that for all practical purposes they almost ceased to be recognizable as a distinct group within it. In the Boston archdiocese, those who were not expressly something else were Irish.[4]

By the turn of the century, the character of Catholic Boston was changing. The Irish were increasingly identified as the "old immigrants," and their successors on the ships of passage came from a wider variety of places. Southern and eastern Europe began to hemorrhage, and the diversity of the Catholic people broadened. These newcomers presented no serious challenge to the Irish hierarchy, but they nonetheless placed new demands on the church and its leaders. Archbishop Williams responded to the challenge admirably, almost doubling the number of parishes for non-Irish groups, even in the last years of his life: the archdiocese had just seventeen ethnic or "national" parishes in 1900; at the old archbishop's death seven years later, it counted thirty-two. The percentage of churches devoted to particular groups continued to grow until 1925, when they constituted nearly one-quarter of all archdiocesan parishes. (See Figure 1.) O'Connell thus ascended the episcopal throne at a time of social change, a change his official historians would later refer to with gentle condescension as "the coming of the newer Catholic races."[5]

O'Connell was not a bad choice to lead the Boston church during this shift toward greater ethnic variety. He had carefully cultivated a sense of internationalism, and he deliberately projected a cosmopolitan image. Ever eager to demonstrate to Boston's Yankee Protestant elite that Catholicism could be respectable, he made much of his own broad experiences. He had, after all, literally traveled around the world during the mission to Japan in 1905 and 1906. He had lived abroad for extended periods (though, as a matter of fact, so had all of his predecessors as bishop). He was fluent in two foreign languages, French and Italian, and he could get by in several others.

His view of the church also gave him a particular perspective on the ethnic differences among his people. Other denominations might be rooted in singular national or cultural circumstances, he

Figure 1

Ethnic Parishes in Boston Archdiocese, 1900–1940
(Source: *Official Catholic Directory*)

	1900	1907	1910	1915	1920	1925	1930	1935	1940
French	9	10	12	14	21	21	22	23	23
German	1	1	1	1	1	1	1	1	1
Italian	2	5	7	8	10	13	13	14	14
Lebanese/Syrian	1	2	3	3	3	4	4	4	4
Lithuanian	1	4	5	7	5	6	6	6	6
Polish	1	5	8	11	12	13	13	14	14
Portuguese	2	3	5	5	5	5	5	5	5
Total Ethnic	17	30	41	49	57	63	64	67	67
Total Parishes	150	194	225	243	256	272	288	305	323
% Ethnic	11.3	15.4	18.2	20.1	22.2	23.1	22.2	21.9	20.7

would tell a crowd gathered for the dedication of a French-language church in Waltham in 1929. "The great Catholic Church," however, "was not meant for one nation, but for all nations; it was not meant for one race, but for all races." Because the church was international in scope, he believed, literally catholic, it subsumed a variety of peoples without being fragmented by them. If all Catholics, regardless of ethnic background, dutifully accepted the direction of their properly appointed leaders (men like himself), O'Connell thought, harmony would be preserved and progress assured. "Difficulty seems to arise with every new incoming group of strangers to this country," he wrote the apostolic delegate philosophically in 1928, "and until they settle down to the only possible solution, moral unity, it is almost futile to attempt to remedy the situation." Still, by exercising "eternal patience," he sought to address the challenges that ethnic diversity presented him.[6]

Each ethnic group had its own history and internal dynamics, but O'Connell was right in saying that they shared a common experience. The issues that stirred the waters of Catholic ethnicity in Boston could be seen across the particular lines of national division so apparent to the people themselves. As different as Poles were from Portuguese, Lebanese from Lithuanians, Boston's Catholic ethnics experienced many similar problems in accommodating themselves to their changed circumstances. Cardinal O'Connell had to respond to these demands, and if he was not always so completely in command of the situation as he had suggested to the delegate, he was still guided by a few consistent principles. He tried to balance the survival of Old World ties with acculturation to America, and he sought above all to maintain the immigrants' loyalty to Catholicism as the solution to all their other problems. Religion and ethnicity both offered his people a form of self-identification. For O'Connell, the religious identity was always paramount.

* * *

Pastoral concern for the newcomers began with life in their particular parish, the primary institutional reference point for all Catholics. Contemporary theology defined a parish in territorial terms. Parishes were little fiefdoms; they were geographical units, based loosely on population, which encompassed a specified area and required the participation of all Catholics who lived there. Solidarity regardless of ethnic background was the ideal, a principle enunciated early by John Carroll of Baltimore, the first bishop in America. Writing to the tiny Boston church in 1790, Carroll had expressed the hope that, "since it has pleased divine providence to unite all parts of the United States under one Episcopacy, all would lay aside national distinctions and attachments, and strive to form not Irish, or English or French Congregations and Churches, but Catholic-American Congregations and Churches."[7] With time, the patterns of Catholic settlement challenged this standard, however, as non-English-speaking immigrants understandably clung to their "national distinctions and attachments."

Ethnic change only complicated the matter. The neighborhood was essential for maintaining group cohesiveness, but what happened as people moved around? What were large numbers of Italian families to do, for instance, on moving into a previously all Irish district, with the territory of its English-speaking parishes already fixed? The mass and the sacraments were all conducted in Latin, a language uniformly foreign to all Catholics, but immigrants who understood little English had other needs. They wanted, for instance, to hear sermons in their mother tongue. Even more important in an era when the sacrament of penance was central to Catholic spirituality, they wanted to make their confessions in their own language to priests who could understand and respond. Priests sought to provide these services, fearful that a language barrier might keep immigrants and their children away from church, resulting in dangerous "leakage" to other denominations. Accordingly, American bishops took advantage of a canonical loophole that permitted formation of parishes along linguistic lines rather than strictly according to geography. The Vatican sanctioned this approach first in 1897 and granted full approval in the revised canon law code of 1918.[8] Ethnic parishes were formed in every major American city, thereby superimposing a second, language-based system of parishes on the existing grid of territorial parishes. Catholics whose first language was not English were free to attend a church of their own nationality regardless of where they lived.

Viewed from the archbishop's office, each ethnic group was perceived as a separate "colony," a linguistic outpost that was the exception rather than the rule. For the people in each colony, however, the closely knit structures of family and neighborhood, together with their shared language and customs, filled an important need during the time of adjustment to new circumstances. The ethnic group provided a ready-made sense of belonging, a "psychological halfway house" between two cultures. Ethnic identity, neighborhood, and parish all merged together, providing a safe haven of traditional values, a place where people who were otherwise on the fringes of society could have their chance at being in the center.[9] Establishing churches of their own was particularly important to every immigrant group.

Like his predecessor, Cardinal O'Connell was prepared to satisfy this demand. The crucial question for him was whether the group demanding a parish had reached the critical mass needed to build a church and pay the salary of a pastor. In 1917, for example, he assigned a local Irish priest to investigate the growing number of Poles in the South and West Ends of Boston. When the priest determined that "there are sufficient Polish people to form a substantial parish," O'Connell approved a new church, Our Lady of Ostrobrama. Similarly, when the Lebanese of Brockton, claiming six hundred people, worried about delays in opening their church, O'Connell's secretary explained the procedure. The "preliminaries" of determining parish viability "do not indicate any diffidence in the matter but are for the purpose of securing a test of good will and proof that a Priest can be supported." They had to wait a few years before O'Connell was entirely satisfied on this score, but the Lebanese did get a parish of their own (with the unlikely name of Saint Theresa's) in 1931. The Italians of Everett achieved their goal more quickly. They were concentrated in one corner of that relatively compact city, and thus barely six months passed between the time the issue was raised and the establishment of "a Church of their own where they can attend Mass and understand just what is going on."[10]

Though he was generally accommodating, O'Connell's familiar fear of debt removed all reluctance to say no if he had to when an ethnic group petitioned for a parish. Since each pastor had to rely wholly on the financial resources of his own people, the practical questions were often the most important ones. O'Connell was particularly cautious in dealing with requests from the Merrimack Valley cities of Lawrence and Lowell, where the differing ethnic populations were more evenly balanced than in Boston. Attracted by a heavy concentration of manufacturing jobs, new arrivals came in such numbers that Lawrence was known popularly as "Immigrant City." Still, the pace of parish formation there was slow. The city's Portuguese attended the mission chapel of an established parish, but the cardinal decided against granting it independent status. "I fail to see how they shall be able to support a Priest," a Portuguese cleric from neighboring Lowell reported to him in 1915, "when the revenues of the Church have not been sufficient even to pay the full amount of the annual interest on the mortgage." A Portuguese-speaking priest was assigned to Lawrence, but O'Connell warned that "in nowise was he to understand that he was a Pastor or in charge of any Parish."[11]

A nearby German congregation met a similar lack of success. Their chapel of the Assumption of the Blessed Virgin was attached to Saint Mary's, the original Catholic church in Lawrence, which was superintended by Father James T. O'Reilly, the longtime parochial baron of the entire region. By 1917 the Germans were complaining that "the more our church is Prospering the more Fr. O'Reilly is asking for more money." The people asserted that "we can amply support our own Priest," but O'Reilly took a different view, saying that the need for a separate parish had already passed. Germans were "scattered all over the city," he told O'Connell, "they speak English, intermarry with the Irish, and attend the other parish churches." Those who went to Assumption were simply lazy English-speakers who "find it a five minutes shorter walk than that to their own church."[12] The cardinal was swayed by this argument—he was also perhaps politically wary of establishing a new German-language parish only three months after American entry into World War I—and Assumption never achieved its desired independence.

Complicating the decision to form new ethnic parishes was the problem of the boundary lines between different groups and their parishes, together with all the possibilities for conflict that the setting of limits entailed. O'Connell's office regularly received complaints from pastors that other parishes were siphoning off their people. An Italian priest in Lawrence confessed to performing six Lithuanian baptisms in 1915, for example, and he was directed to return the offerings he had received for them to the local Lithuanian pastor. Similar charges were lodged against a Polish pastor in Cambridge for overstepping his bounds with regard to Lithuanians, a people ethnically and linguistically quite distinct from his own but often confused in popular thinking and in the minds of Irish hierarchs. This priest stoutly denied the accusation, lodging a countercharge that the local Lithuanian pastor was stealing Poles, but he hit on the reality of shifting demographics: "the polish [sic] people in our parishes frequently change boarding places," he explained, "and this is only occasion for misunderstandings." Changes of residence were always unpredictable, and they could have a disastrous effect on parochial life. Saint Joseph's, Salem, for example, ceased to be a French-speaking parish following the great fire in that city in 1914. The pastor was eventually ordered even to stop trying to recover those who had moved to other parishes and to accept a diminished status.[13]

If anything, the problems of parish boundaries were even worse when disputes arose within a single ethnic group, as the Lithuanians of Boston and Cambridge demonstrated. Saint Peter's, South Boston, had been opened in 1895 to serve all Lithuanians in the metropolitan area. By 1910, however, their numbers were sufficiently large to justify the opening of a second parish, Immaculate Conception, in East Cambridge, just across the Charles River from downtown. The two pastors fell into almost immediate competition for communicants, each one jealously guarding the people he considered "his." They besieged O'Connell with complaints about one another, and the cardinal sought to pacify them by setting the river as the dividing line: any Lithuanian living north of the Charles was declared a member of Immaculate Conception; anyone south of it was part of Saint Peter's. This neat solution came to grief over the growing Lithuanian community of Boston's Allston neighborhood, located south of the river (and thus belonging to South Boston) but handier by means of bridges and trolleys to the Cambridge church. Tiring of the constant bickering and reluctant to create yet a third parish, O'Connell threw up his hands in exasperation. "His Eminence leaves the Lithuanian Catholic people . . . free to attend, for their spiritual needs, any Lithuanian church they may choose," his secretary wrote.[14] O'Connell's "eternal patience" gave out rather quickly in this instance, and the "moral unity" he hoped for was noticeably absent.

More often, ethnic tension crossed national lines and manifested itself in hostility between groups that chance had thrown together. International affairs sometimes intruded as well. When the pastor of Saint Jean Baptiste, Lowell, published an overtly anti-German piece in the summer of 1915, he received a warning not to allow the battles of the European war to affect him. Since the papacy remained officially neutral and nonintervention was still American policy, O'Connell told this French priest "to be careful that nothing which appears in your Parish Bulletin hereafter may be in violation of our neutral attitude or offensive to Catholics of any nationality." American Catholic opinion on the war was sharply divided along ethnic lines, each group naturally siding with its country of origin, a circumstance that caused some consternation to President Woodrow Wilson. Any bishop, such as O'Connell, who had a broad national mix in his diocese had to be doubly sure that Old World antagonisms remained "over there" until American participation in the war permitted a flowering of rally-round-the-flag patriotism.[15]

The most typical expression of interethnic hostility came in the form of tension between the "newer Catholic races" and the dominant Irish. A parishioner of Saint Adalbert's, a Polish parish in Hyde Park, complained to the cardinal that the pastor "keeps an American organist in our Church," only one of many signs that "the Irish . . . are being catered to." The writer's easy equation of "American" and "Irish" showed how readily the area's oldest Catholic immigrants were accepted by their latter-day successors as the standard against which everyone else was measured. This particular musician was especially offensive: "She does'nt [sic] like Polish people and she makes fun of them," the parishioner reported. "When an old person comes to the church and kneels down on both knees or bows to the Blessed Sacrament, she said, 'Look at the Polish mull' [i.e., mule] in front of the children."[16]

The Irish, too, found grounds for complaint. A city official in Cambridge charged the French pastor of Notre Dame de Pitié church in that city with endorsing "a mostly Protestant ticket as against a ticket composed entirely of Catholics" because the latter was exclusively Irish. Adding pointedly that "every Baptist pulpit in Cambridge did the same," the Irish candidate (reelected despite the priest's alleged antagonism) concluded, "We English speaking people feel that Father Pirennes has gone too far." Tensions of this kind frequently degenerated into simple name-calling, a measure of the strength of ethnic consciousness throughout Catholic Boston. A Lithuanian pastor, quarreling with a curate of the same nationality,

The O'Connell Family, ca. 1866. Front row (left to right): Richard, William, Edward; middle row: Matthew, Julia, Bridget (Mrs. John Sr.), John Jr., Bridget; back row: Luke, Mary, Simon, Sarah. Photo courtesy of Michael T. K. Sullivan

O'Connell (front row, center) as Rector of the American College, Rome.
Photo: Archives, Archdiocese of Boston

Boston traveling party for O'Connell's elevation to the cardinalate, Rome, December 1911.
Standing next to O'Connell (holding hat) is Monsignor Michael Splaine; standing at the rear (in front of pillar) is Dr. William A. Dunn.
Photo courtesy of Michael T. K. Sullivan

Two Irish Catholic politicians, 1931: Mayor James M. Curley (left) and Senator David I. Walsh (right).
Photo courtesy of Archives of the College of the Holy Cross

The nephew:
Monsignor James P. E. O'Connell (above)
and Mister James P. Roe (right).
Photo: Vatican Archives

The Antagonists: Father John T. Mullen (left) and Bishop Louis S. Walsh (right).
Mullen photo courtesy of Rev. William Wolkovich; Walsh photo courtesy of Diocese of Portland

O'Connell (far left) congratulating graduates, Boston College commencement, June 1925.
Photo: Burns Library, Boston College

O'Connell addressing Daughters of Charity, Holy Cross Cathedral, October 1932.
Photo: Archives, Archdiocese of Boston

could think of nothing worse to call his troublesome young associate than the epithet "Irish priest!" that he blurted out during a heated confrontation.[17]

The dominance of the Irish, however, also yielded examples of interethnic cooperation. Many pastors genuinely tried to be helpful, recognizing that everyone would be better off if distinct national parishes could be formed. The Irishman in charge of Saint Mary's, Waltham, for example, described for the cardinal his well-intentioned but risible efforts to assist the growing number of Italians in that city. He had provided several special services, including "four festivals a year," for his non-English-speaking parishioners. "I have even tried preaching in Italian," this priest reported, "but I fear it was a sorry effort, and productive only of derision." Thinking at first that an Italian-speaking curate would solve his problems, he quickly concluded instead that a separate Italian church was a more satisfactory solution. O'Connell agreed, establishing a national parish, Sacred Heart, within the month.[18]

Irish laypeople also joined in efforts to help recently arrived ethnic groups. The fledgling League of Catholic Women, a predominantly Irish organization formed under O'Connell's active patronage for educational and devotional purposes, made a commitment to work in Boston's increasingly Italian North End. Barely a year after its first meeting, the league hired a full-time social worker, fluent in Italian, who formed a nursery school, a mother's sewing club, a folk dancing group, and various classes for adults. The league's motives may not have been wholly unalloyed: only a generation or two removed from the immigrant experience themselves, the women were perhaps motivated by some of the same *noblesse oblige* that had led an earlier generation of Yankee reformers to seek to "improve" the Irish. Interethnic tensions were not easily erased, and enough sources of irritation remained: Irish control of local labor unions, for instance, was an enduring problem for other ethnics.[19] Like their leader, however, Boston's Catholics addressed the specific demands of ethnic groups with their own assessment of self-interest and common interest.

* * *

The formation of national parishes was as much the beginning of O'Connell's practical problems as the end of them. Churches serving ethnic groups often took a very different approach to religion from the one he was used to. Like many other bishops, he looked suspiciously on the special devotional practices and styles of particular groups. A contemporary Italian priest in New York spoke for many Catholic ethnics when he recalled that, as a general rule, the Irish clergy had always been "against" singular ethnic devotions, saying that "they thought we were Africans, that there was something weird" about them. O'Connell was always on watch against any irregularities and swift to stop them when they came to his attention. A French parish in Lowell, for example, was denied permission to use a six-piece string orchestra, playing the music of Gounod, during its twenty-fifth anniversary celebration; the unadorned music of mass and benediction was all that O'Connell, ever the champion of Gregorian chant as advocated by Pius X, would permit. Other unfamiliar practices were also vigorously suppressed, including the scheduling of weddings and funerals on Sunday mornings and one Lithuanian priest's highly unorthodox practice of "demanding money for confessions at Easter time."[20]

O'Connell worried especially about the Italians in his flock, people whose "theology of the streets" placed greater emphasis on open-air festivals than on the decorous, regular mass attendance that characterized Irish-American Catholicism. One Italian priest, assigned by the cardinal to investigate these practices in the North End, identified the problem. "To the Sacraments they do not care to go," he said of the people in Saint Leonard's parish, "but feasts and processions yes." The priest was fearful that these devotions were "too" Italian and insufficiently American, and he worried that they brought "disgrace and irreverence to religion." Tighter control was needed. "If the procession is made with proper reverence, in a religious manner, it dus [sic] some good," he wrote, "and bring[s] many to Church."[21] O'Connell allowed the festivals to continue, though he never graced them with his own presence, the ultimate sign of official favor in his church.

The proliferation of national parishes also raised the question of what to do with organizations of lay people which, although made up largely of Catholics, were not specifically operated under church auspices. Who would determine the policies and activities of these groups? Would the laity be left free from any kind of authoritative, clerical supervision? The idea of such latitude was not one the cardinal was even willing to entertain. He was, after all, the same man who had assumed office with the expressed goal of "subjecting . . . all [church-related entities] to proper control and supervision," and he was not about to give in on this point with any group that could be remotely regarded as part of his diocese. Thus, he viewed with a wary eye the plan to form a group called the "Saint Joseph's Lithuanian Roman Catholic Association of Labor." Particularly troubling was the clause in its charter that supported strikes "brought about for very important reasons, and which were prepared in a careful and proper manner."[22]

Several Portuguese societies presented similar difficulties, especially after a change of government in that Iberian nation brought to power a party that churchmen considered anticlerical. The pastor of Our Lady of Good Voyage, Gloucester, explained the problem in 1915. A local fraternal organization wanted to carry the Portuguese flag into church during a special mass, though they were quick with assurances "that in using it they don't mean any adherence to the infidel regime of the new portuguese [sic] government but simply because they have no other flag to represent their . . . nationality." Such assurances were unconvincing, and O'Connell's secretary told the pastor sharply that "you know perfectly well" that national flags were forbidden in church. The dilemma turned squarely on the thorny question of the identity of ethnic Catholics: were they ethnics, or were they Catholics? To O'Connell they were always Catholics first, part of a church that was "neither Italian, nor French, nor German, nor American."[23] It was as though Catholicism itself were an ethnic group, one that always took precedence over the "lesser" identity of nationality. Accordingly, O'Connell sought to apply the church's rules and outlook, even when there may have been mixed feelings on the part of the people themselves.

Ethnic clergy were of more immediate concern to O'Connell than the laity. National parishes needed priests to staff them, and the cardinal faced a continual shortage of ethnic clerical manpower. The demands this shortage imposed on individual priests were considerable and tiring. In 1908 Father Anthony Jusaitas of Saint Francis, the Lithuanian parish in Lawrence, was also pressed into service saying mass twice a month for a congregation in nearby Haverhill, and he was even dispatched to far-off Brockton to hear Christmas confessions. Such multiple arrangements could last for a long time simply because there was so little infusion of new personnel. O'Connell spoke hopefully of "the desirability of having Lithuanian young men trained in our own Seminary," but his wish for them and for other ethnic seminarians remained largely unfulfilled. As late as 1919 he was still "waiting to hear . . . of a good Lithuanian Priest who would be willing to come to Boston," but he had to continue to make do with those he already had. Strangely enough, it never occurred to him to take Irish priests or seminarians and give them the training in foreign languages necessary for service to immigrant communities, a failure that serves as evidence of just how immutable the cardinal thought ethnic barriers to be.[24]

Shortages of ethnic priests meant that O'Connell tolerated men he would otherwise have transferred elsewhere simply because he had no other choice. Ethnic priests were more likely to be scolded than their English-speaking counterparts, but they got consistently more lenient treatment, even when their performance did not measure up to the perceived standard. One Portuguese priest in Cambridge had "a record of constantly incurring debts that he cannot meet," the cardinal's nephew-chancellor told him, but the two men in the chancery recognized (as, indeed, the troublesome cleric may have) that there was little they could do. "It might be well," the chancellor concluded, "that he be taken to task for these failures to the extent of threatening to send him back to the Azores." The threat would remain a hollow one, however, until "a suitable Portuguese priest could be found to take his place." Another Portuguese of somewhat dubious skills, on assuming parochial duties in Gloucester, was assigned a countryman as a kind of watchdog "to assist him in every way possible, to guide him in his work and, more pragmatically, teach him how the parish accounts are kept."[25] Throughout O'Connell's tenure ethnic clergy found a "seller's market," and the cardinal was often frustrated in his attempts to enforce discipline, because his options were so limited. He could not summarily get rid of trouble-makers, because he seldom had anyone to take their places.

The shortage of personnel might have tempted O'Connell to accept virtually any foreign-language priest who came along, but he tried to resist this temptation. Extending well back into the nineteenth century, America had served as a magnet for European clergymen no less than for other immigrants, and control of these wandering, sometimes irresponsible, priests had been a problem for many bishops. Thousands of Irish clerics had come to the United States in just this way and, in the twentieth century, those of the newer immigrant groups continued the pattern. Conditions in the New World compared favorably to those in the Old, and the benefits of finding a position in a parish in America seemed obvious. One Portuguese priest told O'Connell that a suspect compatriot was looking for a local assignment "because . . . the American Dollars dazzle him." For his part, the cardinal was on guard against the abuses of opportunism. One visiting Italian priest was given permission to remain in the archdiocese only as long as he was visiting his sick brother, while another was reminded that his "stay in this diocese will depend entirely upon his conduct and his work."[26] In managing his ethnic parishes, O'Connell was torn between his need to meet the demands of foreign-speaking Catholics and his need to exercise control over his priests. Despite the usual stern talk about authority, service usually won out over control.

The problem was compounded further because, quite often, newer ethnic priests manifested poor administrative skills in overseeing the affairs of the parishes entrusted to them. Many seemed oblivious to the procedures O'Connell had so painstakingly established, and they persisted in irregular habits even after repeated correction. A Lebanese priest in Lawrence was "not much of a success." Saddled with debt and incapable of meeting his people's demand for a school, he was in over his head. "He seems to mean well enough," a neighboring Irish priest reported, "but is incapable of getting results." A Portuguese priest in Cambridge neglected for a period of two years to file records of the marriages he performed with city officials as the law required, apparently because he simply forgot. In September 1923 an Italian pastor in Boston's South End attempted to patch over what O'Connell took to be poor preparation of the confirmation class by sending the cardinal a sizable check. In a highly uncharacteristic move O'Connell returned the money and had his secretary explain that "he would be much more pleased if he could see more evidence that the children attending the Church of Our Lady of Pompeii were being properly trained in Christian Doctrine." The priest's subsequent request for a meeting with the cardinal brought years of administrative exasperation to the surface. "Let him speak to Secretary," O'Connell wrote angrily across the bottom of the letter of request. "Always late and whining."[27]

Poor managerial ability was clearest in matters of parish finance. Monsignor James O'Connell, his uncle's chief aide in financial and other practical matters, mused to the archdiocesan attorney on "the subject of how these foreign priests can contract bills away beyond their financial resources." Creditors regularly wrote the chancery demanding payment on overdue accounts from national parishes, a necessity that was rarer in the case of territorial parishes. A French pastor in East Boston had a $150 bill for candles that remained outstanding for three years, while another left a bill twice that size for lumber unpaid for eighteen months.[28] More often than O'Connell would have liked, even greater sums were at issue, and huge parish debts threatened complete collapse.

In such cases, O'Connell relied on neighboring Irish pastors to investigate in the hope of straightening out the tangled affairs. The task was never easy. Father Joseph McGlinchey, who presided for decades over the Irish preserve of Saint Mary's, Lynn, was sent in 1932 to investigate the troubles of Holy Trinity, an Italian parish in Lawrence. On examining the books, McGlinchey readily found indebtedness of almost $320,000, together with another $48,000 that, although disputed, was probably also a part of the parish deficit. Worse, the pastor of Holy Trinity had been keeping three different sets of account books, no one of which had much relationship to any other. The problem was solved only by the removal of the offending priest (a process that itself took almost three years) and by pooling the resources of several nearby churches to wipe out the red ink.[29] The Irish priests sent to check up on their confreres were generally sympathetic, but the results of their work did little to mitigate the chancery's suspicion of "these foreign priests" in managing the things of this world.

* * *

Factionalism among parishioners, frequently centering on the clergy, was equally troublesome. Boston's ethnic Catholics were not always as deferential as their more acculturated Irish counterparts, and many came from places in Europe with stronger anticlerical traditions than Ireland. Parishes often divided into one group that supported the pastor and another that opposed him. Virtually every ethnic group experienced such turmoil in the O'Connell years. Typically, one faction would write to the cardinal, presenting a predictable catalog of accusations against their priest: inattention to parochial duties; charges of immorality with the rectory housekeeper or other women; drunkenness; too great a concern for raising money. These letters would be answered by parishioners who denied the charges of impropriety and impugned the motives of the accusers. The more lurid charges were usually found to be groundless, but not before O'Connell had had to investigate each situation thoroughly. Lawrence's plenipotentiary, Father James O'Reilly, was dispatched to one such troublespot (this one Lithuanian) with instructions to "investigate, tactfully and in a friendly spirit, the cause of the trouble that [the pastor] seems to be constantly having. . . . If you could . . . impress upon him in a kindly manner the importance, and even the necessity, of so dealing with the parishioners so as to avoid having these complaints coming to His Eminence, it might be productive of good results."[30]

Internal parish divisions sprang from several sources. The first of these was the replication in America of Old World struggles. Social distinctions, such as those dividing northern and southern Italians, proved remarkably resilient. "They are the snares of Italy everywhere they go," one southern priest said to O'Connell, describing the "malignity and worse" of a northern confrere. Old political differences also interfered with the maintenance of harmony. One Lebanese pastor found himself shunned and opposed by his people because, "before coming here, [he] was a sort of go-between between the Turkish government and the people in Beyrouth [sic]." This seemed to O'Connell's Irish observer to be "the cause of the lack of confidence on the part of his people."[31]

Closely related to this persistence of foreign divisions were rivalries between extended ethnic families. One priest, seeking to capitalize on dissatisfaction with a particular pastor, "incited his few relatives . . . to unjust actions and remarks" in the hope of securing the parish for himself. This brought a retort from a parishioner who claimed to speak "for his family and relatives, who number fifty (50) persons." Even though they had settled in a new land, these extended families still carried with them the mental baggage of their former homes. With one foot in each world, they were to some degree marginalized in both: no longer pure expressions of their old national identity, not yet fully adapted to their new one.[32]

A third cause of division among Boston's ethnics was more serious: the intrusion of radical secular politics into religious affairs.

The early decades of the twentieth century were troubled times in the European homelands of many recent immigrants, and there was widespread fear of correspondingly undesirable effects in America. Eastern Europeans were presumed to be particularly problematic, especially after the Bolshevik revolution in Russia in 1917 led many American Catholics to view that part of the world warily. A faction filing complaints against the Polish pastor of Saint Adalbert's, Hyde Park, for example, was "a group of Bolsheviki who want to control the little funds which the Parish has," according to an O'Connell informant in 1923. Lithuanians, too, were plagued by such problems. "The principal cause of the constant troubles in every, almost without exception, Lithuanian parish in America," one pastor opined, was the work of "unbelievers and socialistic papers."[33] O'Connell himself needed little encouragement to find bolshevism at the root of whatever was wrong with modern life, from child labor laws to prohibition, and in the decade after his death American Catholics would become the quintessential anti-Communist crusaders. That preeminence had its origins in the fear that radicalism found too congenial a home in ethnic communities that were traditionally Catholic.

It was not so much the fear of radicalism abroad that troubled the leadership of Catholic Boston as the domestic version. Such concerns usually centered on labor turmoil, especially in the Merrimack Valley. O'Connell's own hometown of Lowell was generally calm, but neighboring Lawrence was a livelier place. General strikes by textile workers in 1912—the famous "Bread and Roses" strike, named for the workers' joint demand for higher wages and an improved quality of life—and again in 1919 were protracted and bitter, in both cases requiring the mustering of the National Guard. The strikers included a high percentage of Catholic ethnics, especially Italians and Poles, and the church tried to preserve the peace without alienating its own people, a particularly keen dilemma for O'Connell himself. Placing a high value on discipline and order, he was nonetheless close enough to his own roots among the workers that he could not simply dismiss their demands. As the strife persisted, however, he gave in to his worst fears, particularly when he thought Catholic laborers were going over to secularized radicalism. "Lawrence is a city of constant strikes and great disorders," he told the apostolic delegate in 1920. Most of the strikers had originally been Catholics, but now "many of them are socialists and members of I.W.W." For that reason, the parishes in that area were among "the most difficult . . . in this part of the country."[34]

Concern that the strikes would get out of control—a fear embodied by hostility toward the anarchist Industrial Workers of the World—came to dominate the church's response to unrest. During the 1912 strike, several Lawrence pastors said special masses for the soldiers called out to keep the peace, but they offered no such services (beyond those normally available in their churches) for the strikers. In one sermon the indomitable Father O'Reilly "explained the Catholic doctrine on the question of the strike. He said that while all the clergy were in sympathy with the strikers as regards the question of wages, yet there could be no compromise when it was a question of anarchy or violation of the law." Many workers had reason to doubt O'Reilly's sincerity, claiming that he was more sympathetic to the mill owners than to them. During the 1919 troubles, a group of strikers wrote to O'Connell, complaining about the priest's "bitter invective, villification [sic] and vituperation" and asserting that "he persists upon every occasion in repeating charges which he cannot prove, and in villifying [sic] those who do not agree with him." Accordingly, the people decided to look elsewhere for support: "we must repudiate utterly his moral and spiritual leadership."[35]

That kind of talk was bound to be worrisome to O'Connell, and he launched his own investigation in the hope of salvaging the church's position. He chose Father Patrick Waters of Saint John's Seminary to go to Lawrence, study the situation, and make a full report. Waters was quick to recognize both the structural causes underlying the strike and the dangers presented by the presumed susceptibility of recently arrived immigrants to radical blandishments. He found that the majority of the strikers were in 1919, as they had been seven years before, Italians; English-speaking mill workers, most of whom were also Catholics, generally remained on the job. Many of the protesters were "illiterate and of an excitable character, easily swayed by their leaders," Waters reported. Too few of them had or even wanted to become citizens, and the "leaders among the Italians are bad men, . . . anti-clericals of the worst type." Public sympathy, which had been substantial in 1912, had largely evaporated by 1919. There was widespread opinion that the "trouble is created not for the benefit of the workers but for the advancement of radical principles" set forth by "irresponsible I.W.W. Bolsheviki parasites"—a wonderfully compact characterization that managed to lump together all the recognizable villains. Unfortunately, Waters concluded, there was little chance to pacify the situation, since "the great majority of those out on strike do not come within Church influence at all." Though he was personally "sorry that a better case can not be made out for the workers," Waters concluded that time alone would solve the problem, time in which the workers could be brought to "understand American institutions and ideals."[36]

The collapse of the 1919 strike and a return to general prosperity in the 1920s removed the immediate source of tension, but Waters was probably correct in saying that church influence among the strikers was negligible. O'Connell himself carefully refrained from speaking out on the turmoil, waiting two full years before issuing, in November 1921, a pastoral letter entitled "Religious Ideals in Industrial Relations." Attempting to satisfy both labor and management, the cardinal spoke generally of the need for workers and businessmen alike to behave responsibly. Urging both employers and employees "to avoid extremists and disturbers," O'Connell tried to chart a middle course: "to-day, [the church] condemns the cruel arrogance of wealth and power; to-morrow, with voice no less authoritative, she condemns mob law and mob violence."[37] The strikes had only served to underline O'Connell's enduring concern that Catholic ethnics had too great a capacity to absorb pernicious political dogmas. His worries were probably exaggerated: ethnic radicalism achieved less enduring success in the Boston area than elsewhere in the country. For Cardinal O'Connell, however, it remained a constant concern in overseeing the non-English-speaking portion of his flock.

Still, the struggle for influence between the church and radical political ideologies continued, and the real battleground remained the Italian populace. The protracted case of Nicola Sacco and Bartolomeo Vanzetti kept the tensions alive, leaving almost no one neutral. Convicted in 1921 for the robbery and murder of a payroll clerk, the two Italian immigrants came to symbolize many things to many people. To their supporters, they were innocent victims of an anti-immigrant, antiworker frameup, and their persecution was a case of "justice crucified." To others, they were precisely the kind of recent immigrants O'Connell feared: both had rejected their Catholic faith in favor of socialist politics. As their legal appeals dragged on in the courts through the 1920s and the day of their execution neared, they became a *cause célèbre* in Boston and around the country.[38]

Though the case was unfolding in his own backyard, Cardinal O'Connell tried to keep his distance from it for as long as he could. The *Pilot* was noticeably silent amid the national and international press coverage. Privately, the cardinal and his staff were watching the situation closely. Proceeding cautiously, O'Connell sought advice from his old friend Father Michael Scanlan, who had become an all-purpose adviser on ethnic questions because of his role in promoting the diocesan charitable bureau's immigrant department. Scanlan looked into the case but found it a mine field which the leadership of Catholic Boston would do well to avoid. "A great many members of the Radical Labor Element have been speaking for the past few months in behalf of these two men now convicted," Scanlan reported, and the problems of making common cause with such people were obvious. Any plea on behalf of Sacco and Vanzetti, whether for a new trial or for commutation of their sentence, he concluded, "was not a situation we could very well take any particular interest in."[39] This cautious recommendation confirmed O'Connell's own reluctance, and official silence remained the cardinal's policy.

With their last appeals exhausted, "the good shoemaker and the poor fish peddler" moved steadily closer to execution in the summer of 1927. Responding to public pressure, the governor of Massachusetts, Alvan T. Fuller, appointed a special commission, headed by Harvard's president, A. Lawrence Lowell, to review the trial and its verdict, a move that won public support from the Episcopal bishop of Massachusetts (he was also President Lowell's cousin), William A. Lawrence. Despite his acquaintance with all three—governor, academic, and bishop—O'Connell continued to keep his own counsel. Other Catholic leaders, including New York's Archbishop Patrick Hayes, were pressured for public statements on the case, but they refrained for fear of publicly embarrassing the

Boston prelate. Luigia Vanzetti and Rosina Sacco, the sister and wife respectively of the condemned men, called on the cardinal at his summer home in Marblehead with a plea for clemency, but they were greeted only with "tea and sympathy." They came away with little more than O'Connell's otherworldly hope that "God's clemency and mercy [will] reach both these men."[40]

O'Connell's public silence on the question has made him seem somewhat heartless in the matter, but he did make an effort behind the scenes to prevent the administration of the death sentence. His attempt came in response to prompting from Rome. The Vatican had been no more willing than he to state an opinion on the case, but as the final hours counted down the semiofficial newspaper, *L'Osservatore Romano*, began to run stories and editorials on the condemned men, emphasizing their Italian nationality. Not even their explicit rejection of the consolations of religion kept the paper from pleading for pardon for the two men. Against this background came a more direct, though private, action. On August 10, 1927, only two weeks before the scheduled execution, an official of the apostolic delegation in Washington telegrammed a direct request from the papal secretary of state, Cardinal Pietro Gasparri, for "charitable intercession in favor of Sacco Vanzetti." Though O'Connell replied that he had "already done so and will continue as long as there is hope," this official request was the spark that led him to act for the first time.[41]

His intervention came in the form of a personal letter to Governor Fuller. O'Connell had long been friendly with Fuller, whose wife was a Catholic, and the two had corresponded before on public and private affairs. Now the cardinal presumed on that friendship, explaining that, while he sympathized with the governor's "trying position," he himself had been "implored by people whose request I cannot ignore" to intervene. Accordingly, he asked Fuller "to do whatever is possible in this matter and I offer you my application for clemency, trusting that it may be favorably received."[42] The governor's response to O'Connell does not survive, and his decision in the celebrated case was unchanged: Sacco and Vanzetti went to their deaths in the electric chair at the state prison in Charlestown on August 23, leaving their ultimate fate to historians to argue over. Cardinal O'Connell had stepped carefully—perhaps too carefully— around their case, a sign of how seriously he took the problem of

Catholic ethnics and radical politics and of how cautiously he moved in those tricky, often shifting, currents.

* * *

O'Connell's political fears had a parallel religious concern: that ethnic Catholics were too readily converted to Protestantism. The efforts of non-Catholic churches to win over recent immigrants, efforts identified by the code word "proselytism," were watched closely by Catholic authorities. This was the concern that had led Father Scanlan to the docks in the first place, and there seemed good reason to fear. An Episcopalian chapel for Italians, complete with a high-church sanctuary lamp, had opened in the North End in 1914, and several Methodist missionaries were active in the city. Even the Unitarians were having a crack at converting ethnic Catholics, an attempt that brought a scornful howl from the *Pilot*. "Is it possible to imagine a Unitarian Italian?" the newspaper wondered. "It is another of those vain things which Unitarianism is always imagining. . . . The Italian can be nothing else but a Catholic." Placing Catholic children who had become wards of the state in Protestant foster homes was a longstanding concern, one that became more intense as the number of non-Irish children increased. Social workers who "carry on a religious propaganda among the immigrants under the guise of Social Service work" troubled O'Connell, and many Catholic agencies provided comparable services in hopes of counter-acting this influence. Any attempt to win over immigrants was misdirected and nefarious, since the objects of the proselytizers' desires were, in the *Pilot*'s view, "people who by every tie of tradition belong to the Church."[43]

Protestant inroads among those who "belonged" to the Catholic church were cause for alarm for O'Connell, underlining the fear of leakage that had led to the formation of national parishes. "The Anti Catholic propaganda amongst the Portuguese people is unfortunately very intense," a priest serving that group reported in 1929. The problem was particularly troubling in the coastal towns south of Boston, where the fishing industry had attracted large numbers of immigrants from Portugal, the Azores, and Madeira. "In Plymouth," this priest said, "the matter seems to be more serious, because there is no Portuguese Catholic church there and there are two Protestant Sects working amongst the

Portuguese people." Another Portuguese priest assured O'Connell that he was doing everything possible to combat Protestant missionary efforts, vowing that "this detestable tare will not germinate in this field," while a French pastor investigated people from his parish suspected of attending a local rally led by the flamboyant evangelist Billy Sunday. Among Poles and Lithuanians, fear of Protestants was matched by concern over the so-called Independent Catholic churches, which rejected the authority of Rome and of the American hierarchy. In some clerical minds all the possible opponents of Catholicism blurred together. An excited Lithuanian pastor in Cambridge told the cardinal that socialists among his people had affiliated with a local Baptist congregation and then plotted "to have a [sic] Independence priest and Church." Assuring his boss that he himself was doing all he could, this priest modestly reported to O'Connell that "with my sacrifice I drawed the Catholics away from the wrong road."[44]

Adding emotional fervor to the fight against any Protestant attempt to "steal" Catholics was the patronizing attitude that so often seemed to go with it. O'Connell and his church flatly rejected the assumption, whether implicit or expressed, that Catholic ethnics needed to be uplifted and civilized. The *Pilot* decried "holier-than-thou proselytisers" who pitied the immigrant "because he never had the chance to see the light. . . . The immigrants as a rule do not feel the need of such pity." Catholics from rich Old World traditions had as much, if not more, culture to be proud of as their supposed American betters, the paper argued, commenting bluntly that "we cannot be blamed for resenting the slur that Catholics are unregenerate pagans." Adopting a sarcastic tone O'Connell himself could not so readily use in public, his official newspaper even drew a barbed comparison with "our boasted Pilgrim Fathers," who were after all immigrants too. "Perhaps the native Indians considered them undesirable citizens," the editorial writer mused. "Perhaps they debated how they might Americanize them."[45]

Even more pointedly, the *Pilot* observed that large numbers of American Protestants had no faith and that "the American religion is indifferentism." Protestants seeking to convert "immigrants who should be Catholics" would be better advised to look to their own affairs. "Why all this talk about the religious needs of the immigrant?" the paper wanted to know. "Is he as unchurched as the

American Protestant?" The zeal of those seeking conversions was hypocritical when directed at "people who, even though they do not speak English, are more moral than the average American." The newspaper's sentiments were those of its owner and publisher, who occasionally launched himself a well-aimed shaft at his Protestant antagonists. Observing in his autobiography that New Englanders had often associated worldly success with godliness, O'Connell observed drily that, as Catholic immigrants advanced themselves to "places of power, civilly and commercially, all this must have been considered by some Puritans as a mistake on the part of Jehovah."[46] In O'Connell's mind, immigrants had little to apologize for and no reason to abandon their long-established religious culture.

O'Connell's sympathy for Protestant efforts to convert traditionally Catholic groups was not measurably affected when the tables were turned and Catholics tried to convert those who had traditionally been Protestants. In particular, archdiocesan efforts aimed at blacks remained small in scope and achieved only limited results. The black population of the Boston area was never very large during O'Connell's tenure, and the Catholic percentage of that population was smaller still. The cardinal himself estimated in 1927 that Boston had just over eighteen thousand black people and that only about one thousand of them were Catholics. The number was not insignificant and, for another ethnic group, it might well have been enough to warrant establishing a separate parish: a thousand Poles or Portuguese could probably have successfully demanded a church of their own. Blacks were not a "national" group as O'Connell was used to thinking of them, however—they did not, for example, speak a foreign language—and the idea of establishing a distinct black parish seems never to have occurred to him.[47]

In limited ways, however, O'Connell did support special efforts for black Catholics, centering on the convent of the Blessed Sacrament Sisters in the South End. This religious community had been founded by Katherine Drexel, a white Philadelphia heiress and convert to Catholicism, specifically to work in what were known then as the Negro and Indian missions. The group had come to Boston in 1914 with O'Connell's enthusiastic support. He met with Drexel personally and wrote her with repeated encouragement. He underwrote the South End convent's expenses from central archdiocesan funds, a step that was both generous and necessary: in 1919, for example, the sisters reported expenses of almost $2,400, matched by receipts and contributions of only $56.66. O'Connell did not appoint a priest to work specifically with the sisters, who had reported that, while they were generally successful in their contacts with black women, they needed a priest to make similar progress with men.[48] Still, he endorsed the convent's limited programs and continued to pay its bills for several years, an act of beneficence he granted to virtually no other local institution.

The Blessed Sacrament convent gave O'Connell the chance to do a little proselytizing of his own. The majority of the city's black Catholics were Cape Verdeans, one of the sisters explained to him, most of whom had been baptized as children but had since fallen away. Many had intermarried with American blacks, who tended to be Protestants, and the rate of leakage was therefore thought to be quite high. An Episcopalian clergyman, associated with that denomination's Cowley Fathers, was active in the area, for example, and he had "perverted" two or three hundred "careless or indifferent Catholics who do not attend church at all."[49]

The cardinal was therefore eager that the convent be visible in the black community. He sanctioned a set of lectures and devotions, "provided these plans are carried out in such a way that the Catholic Church gets credit for them." Similarly, he gave his approval for the sisters to conduct public benediction of the Blessed Sacrament every Sunday evening and for their intention to ask every person attending to bring along at least one non-Catholic friend. "Our hopes," Mother Katherine Drexel explained, "are that it be the means of converting many if the sermons were given by one thoroughly in sympathy with the people and knowing their needs."[50] All these efforts were no more broadly successful than Protestant attempts to convert Catholic ethnics, but they had some result. Boston's black Catholics remained a cohesive, if small, group, and they briefly had a parish of their own, which opened in 1946 and closed in 1966.

* * *

No reliable figures are available to judge how real was the danger of leakage among ethnic Catholics, but the vast majority of immigrants did indeed "keep the faith." Few converted either to a Protestant church or to the religion of radical secular politics because, for most of them, ethnicity, religion, and their native language were all parts of the same larger whole. Language and culture were inseparable, and the church, which could help them preserve both, for the most part held their loyalty. The *Pilot* recognized the desirability of immigrants' learning to speak English, but it rejected the notion that "ignorance of the English language is a crime." It was "the height of insolence," the paper argued, for Protestant "Americanizers" to demand that ethnics "put aside their old racial customs" or to think that "one is saved by the very fact that he is an American, English-speaking Protestant, and . . . damned because he worships God in a foreign tongue."[51]

O'Connell's parishes found several means to preserve ethnic language and customs. All attempts to emphasize English at the expense of the native tongue were resisted, even when shifting urban populations meant that the people in the pews were becoming more varied. The cardinal warned a French pastor in Lowell against "attempting to destroy the French spirit" of his people by preaching in English, and an Eastern rite parish for Lebanese in Brockton was forbidden to conduct its rituals in Latin (rather than the Syriac used in the Maronite liturgy) in order "to attract the American element." The cardinal's pastoral letters and other announcements were translated into the appropriate languages, and the hymns he composed, which were sung widely in English-speaking churches, were made available for use by other language groups.[52]

Most often, ethnic parishes sought to preserve their language and cultural traditions in their parochial schools. Non-Irish ethnic groups built parish schools at a higher rate than their Irish neighbors—more than 70 percent of the Polish and Lithuanian parishes had schools—and this support required special sacrifices. One pastor in Lowell hired teachers to provide language instruction in his Sunday school, while another ran a summer program to improve the fluency of young people in his parish. The willingness of Catholic ethnics to bear the expense of schools was viewed admiringly, even by the Protestant social workers O'Connell eyed so suspiciously: the sociological pioneer, Robert Woods, in his studies of Boston's urban neighborhoods, found it "inspiring . . . that a great body of relatively poor people support an expensive institution" like a school. The cardinal could take comfort in the conclusion that schools evinced "a greater degree of spiritual vitality than is likely to be found in Protestantism today."[53]

O'Connell's concern to maintain the linguistic character of his national parishes had practical as well as philosophical roots. Because ethnic churches were superimposed on the map of territorial parishes, there was a constant danger that the national parishes would siphon off English-speaking parishioners who really belonged elsewhere if the language barrier were lowered. The pastor of a territorial parish faced serious financial trouble if his people performed their religious duties somewhere else on a regular basis. Thus, an Italian pastor in Revere was scolded for preaching in English, and another Italian in Cambridge was cross-examined when he asked permission to publish a booklet on the church's patron saint. O'Connell wanted to know "why the pamphlet is written in English in view of the fact that you are supposed to be in charge of an Italian-speaking congregation."[54] The cardinal tried to accommodate the ethnic members of his flock, but in the feudal kingdom that was his diocese he could not risk antagonizing English-speaking pastors by granting too much leeway to those who spoke other languages.

The priest who wanted to publish in English explained his motives by pointing to the dilemma he and all his ethnic colleagues faced. Their parishes had been established to serve populations that did not speak English, but the balance shifted as one generation succeeded another. The immigrants themselves continued to be most comfortable in their original tongue, but their children and grandchildren found their parents' speech increasingly foreign. Virtually every ethnic pastor faced this generational problem in trying to address both the older and younger members of his community. The priest in charge of Boston's Holy Trinity, the city's only German church, put the matter succinctly. "The only persons in the parish who can be properly reached by the German language are the old people," he wrote in 1919, and they were "becoming fewer every year." The younger parishioners were "American citizens and all their business, social, domestic and civic affairs are carried on in English, as is proper for Americans." In this case, the problem was compounded, since, during the recently concluded World War, the teaching of German had understandably fallen off because it was viewed as unpatriotic. To continue to adhere to the requirement for preaching and instruction exclusively in German would mean increasing irrelevance and the loss of younger parishioners. O'Connell recognized the problem, and Holy Trinity became bilingual.[55]

A layman of Sacred Heart parish in the Italian North End made the same observation. "Altho' we are Italians we are living in the good old U.S.A.," he told the cardinal, "and we want to bring up our children in the American ways and ideas." This required priests who could communicate with young people in, as the writer would have it, "Inglish." Likewise, a Portuguese priest from Lowell observed that, in his parish, even "real portuguese [sic] children" were more at home in English.[56] In none of these cases could O'Connell solve the problem save by allowing the parishes to operate in both languages, a testament to the fluidity of life in America's ethnic enclaves. People who were identified, by themselves and others, as being one thing—Germans, Italians, Poles, Portuguese—were in the process of becoming something else—acculturated Americans of differing, but increasingly distant, origins. The phenomenon predated O'Connell's tenure in Boston, and it endures to the present day. The cardinal had to remain flexible, attempting different solutions and bending the general rules which he could still state forcefully as if they admitted of no exception.

* * *

The tenacity of ethnic identity among Boston's Catholics was powerful. At its best, ethnicity provided a means for transition to new circumstances; at its worst, it reinforced an "us-them" way of looking at the world that was not always healthy. Patterns of ethnic thinking and behaving would never simply go away, however, and everyone who lived within the confines of the archdiocese had to come to terms with diversity.

For William O'Connell, himself a first-generation American, the problems of immigrant Catholics and their offspring were played out in this larger context. Unlike many of his fellow bishops—including his contemporary, Cardinal George Mundelein of Chicago, and even his erstwhile opponent, John Ireland of Saint Paul—he was not an unremitting Americanizer, as that term is normally understood.[57] O'Connell was tolerant of national divisions and the survival of ethnic traditions, while at the same time trying to push his people toward acceptance of a new order of things in the United States. His responses to ethnicity were fundamentally reactive, and they were sometimes subtle: if a priest or layperson wrote him in a foreign language, even one in which he was perfectly at home, his reply would invariably be in English. The point was deftly made: older cultural habits were acceptable and perhaps even necessary, but the way of the future lay in setting some of those traditions aside.

As with so many other aspects of his administration of church affairs, O'Connell spoke the language of centralized control while simultaneously permitting the continuance of local autonomy. "In every single case of what appeared exaggerated nationalism," he wrote proudly in his memoirs, he had managed to check the splintering of his people.[58] In reality, the dynamics of ethnic life in Catholic Boston were more complex than that. The cardinal opened new national parishes as circumstances seemed to demand, but virtually all the "newer Catholic races" remained turbulent for greater or lesser periods of time. No matter how much he wanted to, he could not prevent such turmoil, and he was forced to react to it: he had to put out the fires he could not keep from erupting in the first place. He applied the same theoretical standards for managing national parishes that he set for territorial parishes, but his discipline often broke down in the face of an enduring shortage of ethnic clerical manpower. He was attentive to the danger of leakage, whether to Protestantism or secularism. He was generally sympathetic to the preservation of native languages and cultures, so long as all Catholics submitted to constituted church authority with docility and "moral unity."

The ethnic Catholics themselves experienced varying degrees of difficulty at adjusting to life in the New World, a problem the Irish had, by and large, addressed in the previous century. The powerful pull of the "American Way of Life," particularly as one generation succeeded another, meant that old and new loyalties existed in constant tension with one another. These larger forces were beyond the control of any single individual, even the cardinal archbishop himself. He responded to events as best he could, sometimes gruffly, sometimes sympathetically. Still, the identity of his people could not be changed overnight.

8

SCANDAL AND SURVIVAL:
THE CRISIS OF O'CONNELL'S CAREER, 1915–1925

As HE NEARED THE END of his first decade as archbishop, William O'Connell was a familiar figure in church and society. His success at constructing a vigorous public image as leader of the local Catholic world was striking. Notwithstanding occasional political uncertainties and administrative limitations, the notion of who O'Connell was and what he had accomplished was fixed in the popular mind. Mayor Fitzgerald had said it best: "His many-sided accomplishments and magnetic charm, as well as his lofty character, have made him a wide circle of admirers both inside and outside the church."[1]

Fitzgerald was right, but only up to a point. O'Connell's circle of admirers, especially within the church, was not nearly so wide as the mayor thought. The wounds opened by the troubled manner of O'Connell's appointment to Boston continued to fester long afterward, and they never really healed. Despite his call that the Boston clergy close ranks and accept him as the choice of both pope and God, passionate divisions remained. The archbishop had few real friends among his priests, and the opposition—hatred is not too strong a word—he evoked from other churchmen took on an enduring life of its own. His enemies scrutinized his every move, looking for opportunities to strike back, to take revenge for their loss in the struggle for control of the local church. In the years surrounding 1920, they got their chance.

The average lay man and woman remained piously unaware of trouble, but animosity was strong among O'Connell's own subjects. A number of local priests, particularly those older men who remembered Archbishop Williams fondly, coalesced into a faction dedicated to resisting O'Connell's efforts to become the alpha and the omega of Catholic life. They choked on each new piece of self-promotion and self-congratulation that issued from O'Connell's office. Prominent among them were two of Williams's former chancellors: Father Michael Doody, now pastor of Saint Mary of the Annunciation parish, Cambridge, and Father Thomas MacCormack, pastor successively of three large churches in Boston and its near suburbs. Father Hugh O'Donnell of Saint Anthony's, Allston (author of the satirical poem on O'Connell's red hat), and Father George Patterson, pastor of two of the largest parishes in South Boston, were less visible but still active in the opposition movement. Outside Massachusetts, Bishop Harkins of Providence suffered his defeat in silence, but Louis Walsh, who had his own reasons to oppose O'Connell after inheriting his questionable financial legacy as bishop of Portland, became the point man in the war against the cardinal. The ringleader of the group was Father John Mullen, ousted by O'Connell as rector of the Boston cathedral. Mullen's reciprocal dislike and distrust for his new superior was both undisguised and unlimited.

The hostility of these men toward their spiritual shepherd may not have been particularly edifying in religious terms, but it was deeply felt. Wary of O'Connell from his arrival, their rancor grew with time. Their genuine affection for Williams made them wince every time they heard the cardinal proclaim the glorious improvements he had effected since the older prelate's death. O'Connell passed up few chances "to cast discredit on his Predecessor," Mullen complained privately in 1915, scolding the *Pilot* for "continually harping on the 'wonderful new life,' the 'magnificent reorganization' of the diocese 'these last few years' [i.e., since O'Connell's accession]. . . . There has been much more noise and parade than improvement." When, in a speech that same year, O'Connell implicitly chided Williams for lukewarm support of parochial schools, Mullen observed that the cardinal's own record in that regard was unimpressive. Bishop Walsh concurred. The near-constant allusions to the disorderly administration O'Connell had inherited from Williams were a "slur" that was "both unjust in itself, and highly offensive to those who loved him." Walsh needed a new word to express his contempt, deciding that O'Connell's principal characteristic was not so much megalomania as "megalophonia."[2]

Mullen and Walsh thought they knew why O'Connell was so persistent in drawing invidious comparisons with his predecessor: it was because he recognized that most churchmen had liked Williams better. The bishops of New England wanted nothing to do with O'Connell, Mullen told Archbishop John Ireland, "except when officially obliged to do so." The "extraordinary and even unique absence of all friendly relations" in clerical Boston derived from what Walsh identified as the cardinal's "taunting and flaunting style." O'Connell knew "the high esteem and reverence in which the last Archbishop is held," Mullen concluded, and he knew just as surely that he himself would never enjoy such esteem.[3] Since the best defense was a good offense, O'Connell inflated his own accomplishments as a way of demonstrating that, even if he lacked the affection of his men, he nonetheless deserved their respect and compliance.

Beyond his combative personal style, O'Connell's opponents found him wanting in other ways. Most tellingly, they perceived in him a lack of true religious feeling. One priest told the apostolic delegate that O'Connell's grand public persona was setting a bad example. An "awful worldliness . . . has crept into the sanctuary here," the cleric reported, condemning the cardinal's "scandalous parade of wealth, . . . his arrogant manners, his strange and unecclesiastical method of living." Even worse were the evidences that O'Connell had little interest in the liturgical and devotional duties at the heart of a genuinely devout priestly life. Father Mullen claimed that the cardinal neither said daily mass nor recited the prayers of the breviary. What is more, when O'Connell presided at mass, he rushed through it as quickly as he could and "did not pronounce the words." Midnight mass on Christmas Eve 1914 was over in half an hour, according to a report, and such speed was common whenever O'Connell was in charge. A solemn high mass on the feast of the Immaculate Conception in 1920 should have lasted an hour and a half by Mullen's reckoning; a layman reported that the ceremony had begun at 9 o'clock in the morning and that he was back out on the sidewalk, waiting for a streetcar, at quarter to ten. O'Connell later complained that bad knees made it painful for him to genuflect or to stand for long periods, and he counseled a fellow bishop against extended rites: "usually everyone is bored to death and exhausted," he said.[4] Opinions of that kind were, for his enemies, but one more indication that Rome had made a disastrous choice in sending him to Boston.

The tenacious opposition facing O'Connell was widely known in clerical circles, which like any closed group had its own sources of rumor and gossip. The correspondents of Archbishop Ireland, slowly sinking into history but still the patron saint of the Bostonian's opponents, kept the aging Americanist apprised of their combat with the "red star" of New England. Rectory chatter in other dioceses often turned to the same topic. "There are a few things seething up Boston way," a Manhattan priest told Patrick Hayes, the future archbishop of New York, in 1917. "His Eminence is trading punches with his good men who are willing and eager for the fray. Someone ought to 'can' him before he drives the priests into open rebellion."[5] The tension within clerical Boston built steadily, needing only a particular event to release it into open warfare.

The crisis came quickly enough when a private scandal, threatening always to break out into public view, unfolded close to the cardinal. The tangled events were set in motion by Monsignor James P. E. O'Connell, the cardinal's nephew and the chancellor of the archdiocese. Beginning in 1913, the young priest led an increasingly curious life, and in 1920 he abruptly resigned his office and disappeared. There followed a widening circle of scandal, with the archbishop of Boston standing at its center. O'Connell sought to control the damage, but at every turn his troubles seemed only to intensify. His opponents eagerly pounced on him, fired by the notion that they could indeed "can" him. They were ultimately unable to do so, but their efforts to destroy him and his resistance occupied a decade at the heart of his tenure as archbishop. Once the storm subsided, he was a very different man.

* * *

James Percival Edward O'Connell was born at one of the family's homes in Lowell on April 29, 1884, and baptized the next day at Sacred Heart church. His unusual middle name he acquired from his godfather, a friend of the family, and he added the Edward at confirmation. His father was the future cardinal's older brother Matthew, a bricklayer by trade, and James was one of twin boys born to him and his wife, the former Bridget Byrne. The other baby was christened William Henry in honor of his young uncle, then in Rome, where he would be ordained the following month. The family's joy was cut short in the late summer when baby William died.[6] The "might-have-beens" of the infant's death are intriguing. Had the young namesake lived, might not he have been the one destined for a career in the priesthood, rather than his brother? Irish families cherished the thought that a son might be ordained, and with the death of his twin brother at the age of only four months, that responsibility devolved, however unwillingly, upon James. No other siblings were born, and the boy grew up with a career that seemed predetermined for him.

After a primary education in the public schools of Lowell, the boy was sent briefly to Holy Angels College, a high school or "minor" seminary in Buffalo. In the fall of 1900 he enrolled in the American College, Rome, to which his uncle had by now returned as rector. The older O'Connell left that post for Portland the next spring, but Jim stayed behind for another two years. He failed to return for the beginning of classes in the fall of 1903, however, perhaps at the suggestion of the college's officials, and he transferred instead to the Grand Seminaire in Montreal.[7] This put him closer to his uncle's diocese in Maine, and the new bishop began to look on his nephew as a special protégé. He wrote the seminarian regularly, expressing satisfaction that "you are getting along so well in your work." He arranged for the rector of the Montreal school to look after the lad and even to advance him money on the credit of the Portland diocese. His uncle's support was useful, but the blessing was mixed. A few years before, O'Connell had remarked to his sister Julia on the frequently baneful effect of family connections. "Perhaps if I had an uncle I would never be anything," he had written in 1899. "I think after studying the question all over that uncles do more harm than good—young people ought to be taught to depend on themselves. They are all the better for it in the end."[8] To his sorrow, the bishop failed to heed his own advice.

Seminarians were ordained to different clerical ranks short of the priesthood itself at the end of each year of study, and James O'Connell followed the prescribed route. In September 1905 he was ordained a subdeacon by his uncle in the Portland cathedral, and then he changed seminaries again, enrolling for a year in the prestigious Canisianum at Innsbruck, Austria, run by the Jesuits. There he added German to the French and Italian in which he was already fluent, and he seemed "careful [in] observance of the discipline of the house." At the same time, he was somewhat "impatient," and the rector worried that "he spends money impulsively." His studies completed, the young man returned to America, where his uncle, by now coadjutor archbishop of Boston, ordained him to the priesthood in September 1906. He was just over twenty-two years old, technically too young for ordination (the canonical age was twenty-four), and the ceremony took place privately in Lowell, as Archbishop Williams noted without comment in his journal.[9] Instead of a parish assignment, the new priest was given a post as secretary to his uncle. The two shared the townhouse on Boston's Union Park that was the coadjutor's residence, and they appeared together at all the older man's ceremonial functions. When O'Connell succeeded Williams in August 1907, James O'Connell continued as his secretary, already well along on his priestly career without ever having set foot in a rectory or encountering ordinary Catholic believers in the confessional or at the altar rail.

From the beginning of O'Connell's regime, the nephew-secretary played the part of general adviser, factotum, and indispensable man. "I have a general impression that His Grace cannot spare you for more than an hour at a time," one observer commented. He held his secretary's title until February 1912, when he was promoted to the even more central position of chancellor of the archdiocese, competent to superintend all matters, spiritual and temporal. He was, in effect, his uncle's prime minister. In December 1914, as a reward for what a Boston newspaper called "his brilliant and consistent work," the pope gave him the rank of monsignor, surely one of the youngest men—he was only thirty—in American Catholic history to receive such an honor. Monsignor O'Connell maintained a low public profile, even on great occasions. "I am not anxious to be conspicuous," he wrote while planning the celebration for his uncle's return from Rome after his elevation to the cardinalate, preferring a less visible place to a seat at the head table.[10] Those in the know, however, appreciated his true importance.

Behind the scenes, James O'Connell was a man of enormous power. Virtually no aspect of diocesan affairs escaped his scrutiny, especially in managing the church's money. He personally kept the chancery office's account books, toting up bank balances in his own hand and shuttling assets in and out of various accounts. He monitored the insurance on parish property, overseeing policy renewals and sending out statements to local pastors. He managed the sizable portfolio of investments of the archdiocesan corporation, objecting whenever taxes were deducted from dividends because of the church's tax exemption. Later, he hectored the administrators of Prohibition over the availability of altar wine, and he pestered officials at the post office when they planned to close the branch office handiest to the chancery. He served as treasurer of the *Pilot*, drawing an additional salary in that capacity and arranging the newspaper's accounting system so as to minimize the possibility of an outside audit: that "would not be a pleasant matter," he told his uncle.[11] Of his interior, spiritual life little evidence survives, but in looking after the practical affairs of the archdiocese he showed a genuine aptitude and ability.

The monsignor was tireless in scrutinizing the affairs of the diocesan clergy, and he took special delight in exercising authority over pastors who were older and more experienced than he. He reported any infractions of official regulations: Father Mullen, who was eighteen years older than the chancellor, was violating the procedures governing parish insurance, James O'Connell noted, and Father Doody, twenty-four years his senior, had left a ten-dollar obligation to the chancery unpaid for more than a year. The chancellor could sometimes be a friend to the younger clergy—he argued unsuccessfully for an increase in their base salary in 1919—but he could also treat them with the same imperious manner he adopted with his elders. The young and ambitious Father Francis Spellman was a favorite target. Newly ordained, Spellman (the future cardinal archbishop of New York) in 1918 assumed direction of something called the Catholic Literature Campaign, an effort to boost subscriptions to the *Pilot*. When the campaign's accounts seemed out of balance by fifty cents, James O'Connell wrote him almost daily for two weeks, seeking a satisfactory explanation. Spellman was not appropriately deferential, and the chancellor warned him "not to allow yourself to get any false conception of your own importance. . . . One of your recent letters to me savored of arrogance, a quality which ill befits a subordinate."[12] Priests who had never liked the archbishop were even more unhappy with the officious young alter ego.

Throughout his six years as secretary and eight years as chancellor, Monsignor James's relations with his uncle were of the closest kind. The two spent virtually every waking moment more or less together: they lived and worked in the combined residence and chancery office in the Back Bay. Just as he managed official business, so the young chancellor managed personal affairs for the cardinal. He oversaw the purchase of an income-producing apartment house in 1915 and the establishment of trust funds for various family members. He also looked after the affairs of his own branch of the clan. In 1916 he acquired title to a second apartment house and a single-family home in Brookline, in the latter of which he installed his parents. These several parcels of real estate, all held in the nephew's own name, were valued two years later at just under $100,000, a respectable sum at the dawn of the Roaring Twenties.[13] The O'Connells of immigrant Lowell were now the O'Connells of a much more fashionable suburb, and Monsignor James was the agent and the beneficiary of that improvement.

Many signs of affection passed between the cardinal and the younger cleric, frequently taking the form of "Italianisms," which their mutual fluency could sustain as a knowing form of private communication. Whenever the uncle was away from Boston, James would sign his letters "Giacomo," and the cardinal would usually begin his replies "Carissimo Giacomo." James would sometimes exaggerate this usage deliberately, perhaps in a tone of self-mockery at the elaborate formulae of official church documents, closing one letter to the vacationing cardinal: "Di nuovi tanti saluti a tutti i tre, ed infiniti rispeti a V[ostra] E[minenza]."[14] These private jokes underlined their affinity, emphasizing their shared experiences by resorting to a language and a manner of address meant for their ears alone.

Monsignor O'Connell threw himself wholeheartedly into all the tasks assigned to him, expressing satisfaction with his work. "For whatever little I have . . . done to fulfill the office you have entrusted to me, and to discharge the duties with which you have honored me," James wrote his uncle expansively, "you have seemed [sic] fit to exalt me to the skies. . . . I can only say," he continued in a false prophecy, "that I shall go on to the end of my days thanking you in thought, word and deed, principally by leaving no stone unturned whereby I may make your path lightsome and easy, and your burdens light." Taking a brief vacation in the summer of 1911, while the cardinal himself was in Europe, James praised the benefits of such a rest, foremost of which was that "it will fit me for another five years of any arduous labor, such as nervous little morsels like myself need to keep them healthy."[15]

Notwithstanding the protests of his love for the cardinal's service, the years of responsibility were draining, and James's jocular reference to his "nervous" condition may have had a clinical dimension. He later claimed to have suffered three nervous breakdowns during this time, however loosely that term may have been defined in the popular psychology of the age: one in 1907; another, "which nearly resulted fatally," in 1909; and a third in 1914. He was deeply sensitive over his position and anxious to belie the presumption, so plausible on the face of it, that he owed his authority to nepotism. On one occasion he sternly corrected a pastor who had offhandedly used the phrase "you and your uncle" while writing on parish business. "The term 'Uncle' or anything approaching it or meaning the same has never once passed my lips," he retorted, a tacit warning to the priest never to say it again. He also showed signs of chafing under his burdens. "I am indispensable only inasmuch as he believes so," James complained to the archdiocesan attorney in 1915, expressing the hope that O'Connell would rely more on others. "He and I would be much better off," the chancellor continued, "and the work would run less risk of suffering in an emergency. However," he concluded ruefully, "this is something that I cannot arrange."[16] Despite his brave front, James O'Connell remained uncomfortable in his position—perhaps because of his relative youth, but more likely because of lingering doubts about the validity of his vocation to the priesthood.

That he lacked a sincere commitment to his calling is evident from his highly irregular personal life in the years after his appointment as chancellor in February 1912. Sometime that spring, while in New York, he met a woman named Frankie Johnson Wort, the wife of a Newark, New Jersey, ear doctor, and an instant infatuation began. Mrs. Wort left her husband and moved to South Dakota to establish residence and thus take advantage of the state's liberal divorce laws. She was granted her divorce from Doctor Wort on April 8, 1913, whereupon she immediately boarded a train headed east; James O'Connell had already taken to the rails, heading west. They met in Crown Point, Indiana (just outside Chicago), and were married by a justice of the peace on April 9. They were both twenty-eight years old. Frankie entered the marriage knowing fully who and what her husband was: he never concealed it from her, and he used his real name and usual signature on the marriage license.[17]

The couple returned to the east coast, where they set up a home in New York City, and James O'Connell began the practice of commuting between New York and Boston, spending a few days each week in each city. For seven and a half years, he lived a bizarre and schizophrenic existence, switching back and forth between two entirely different lives. In Boston he played the part of a priest as if nothing had happened. Technically, of course, his "attempted marriage" (the quaint phrase of the canon law) not only deprived him of his clerical status, but it also automatically subjected him to excommunication from the church altogether. Nonetheless, he continued to serve as chancellor of the archdiocese, and he participated in the normal round of devotional functions, saying mass and performing other priestly duties. His appointment to the rank of monsignor came a year and a half after his marriage. To those who knew him in that life, it seemed natural to expect that, like his uncle, he too would someday be named a bishop. Such a model priest, and one so young, surely had a promising career ahead of him.

At the same time, he was an entirely distinct person in New York, where he and his wife had adopted the surname Roe. They moved twice into successively better homes in Manhattan, the last "a white private dwelling in one of the most exclusive and expensive neighborhoods of the city" at 102 East 36th Street, which they purchased in May 1916 for $32,000. Mrs. Roe's mother, Lillian Johnson, lived with them; no children were ever born of the marriage. They lived comfortably, with house servants and vacations on Long Island. In the summer of 1913, they sailed to Europe for a delayed honeymoon, declaring $1,600 worth of purchases after returning on the later-famous S.S. *Lusitania*. Mr. Roe speculated in real estate, almost certainly with money that Monsignor O'Connell was embezzling from the church. The need to support his life in New York gave him the motive for such a crime just as surely as his access to the large sums in Boston gave him the opportunity. Father Mullen later claimed that an unnamed Boston banker estimated the pilfering at three-quarters of a million dollars. Father Doody thought that sizable kick-backs from the insurance company handling archdiocesan accounts also found their way into Mr. Roe's deep pockets.[18]

The split personality was striking, but the young man had already demonstrated a capacity to divide what most people cannot.

"Forget, if you can, that there is anybody in America that you know. It is the only way that you can entirely enjoy your freedom," he told his vacationing uncle in 1911. "Leave your Boston self in a dark corner." Now, James O'Connell had his own "Boston self," his own "dark corner," his own "freedom," and the psychic toll was inevitably serious. He lived in an age when the abandonment of the Catholic priesthood by anyone was seen as a tragic, virtually unthinkable, defection.[19] That he chose such a course bespeaks the intensity of his rejection of the only career that had apparently ever been open to him and his striking back at the family pressures that had forced him into it. He was playing a dangerous game, for exposure meant disaster. If the allegations of embezzlement could be proved, he faced jail. Still, his decision was enthusiastically embraced. Even the pseudonym he used in New York—Roe—was significant. It was a traditional name for denoting legal anonymity, but it was also an intricate bilingual pun on his real identity. The Gaelic root for the name O'Connell signified a deer, and a great stag appeared on the family coat of arms. The choice of the name Roe, with its parallel English meaning (as in "roebuck"), showed the deliberate construction of a new life out of elements of his old one.

For several years, James O'Connell successfully disguised his life in New York City. Although his Boston enemies began to unravel the mystery around 1916, he held on to his position as chancellor until the end of 1920. More to the point, however, is the question of what the cardinal knew of the matter. Was he merely an innocent victim of deception, or did he participate in it? Knowing or even suspecting such a scandal involving any priest demanded a swift investigation: not to do so would be a serious sin of omission. He was, after all, responsible for the spiritual welfare of his flock. What would be the effect on them and their souls if they were, for example, to receive the sacraments from such a priest? What about the prospect for "giving scandal," always a serious offense in church law? With the case involving one so close to him, however, the cardinal's culpability for failure to act would be that much greater. James O'Connell was his righthand man, his closest associate. Did the weekly absences from Boston not even arouse his curiosity? What explanation for them that the chancellor could offer in 1913 would still be plausible in 1920? As late as September of that year, O'Connell was reassuring an official at the Vatican of the young man's *"absolute innocence"* and saying of himself: "Never in my life have I known such a thing."[20] The evidence in the case suggests another conclusion.

* * *

Complicating O'Connell's role in the matter of his nephew was the problem of another errant priest, Father David J. Toomey. Born in New York but raised in Cambridge, Toomey was a seminarian at the American College at the turn of the century, when both O'Connells were there, and he became a fast friend of young James. After ordination, he returned to Boston, assigned as a curate at Holy Cross cathedral. When O'Connell acquired the *Pilot* in 1908, Father Toomey, whose star was in the ascendant because of his friendship with the powerful nephew, was made its editor. In 1912 he was designated personal chaplain to the cardinal, an assignment that included the responsibility for hearing the prelate's confession. In order to carry out these duties successfully, he moved into the official residence on Bay State Road, where he, Monsignor James, and the cardinal himself made for a very interesting household.[21]

The behavior of the two younger members of this group began to attract notice among the diocesan clergy, already predisposed to dislike them. The two never joined their fellow priests for the annual spiritual retreats at the seminary, arranging to perform these exercises privately, something they probably never really did. Word spread, too, that they were the leaders of an informal group of younger priests known as "Il Circolo" ("The Circle"), which developed a reputation for raucous dinner parties. Father Mullen passed along evidence of one of these to the apostolic delegate in 1916. The whole affair had cost more than $500 (about $35 per guest, a staggering sum for the time), and it was highlighted by "enough liquors to float a battleship," including a vintage 1840 Madeira. Handpainted menu cards, "so indecent" that the printer had refused to let his female employees see them, were distributed. Such was "the priestly character of the Chancellor and Doctor Toomey," the ever-watchful Mullen concluded. For those who thought Cardinal O'Connell himself insufficiently religious, evidence of worldly behavior by his immediate advisers was proof that something was rotten at the center of Boston Catholic officialdom. "If the new Archbishop had surrounded himself with a group of worthy priests, he could have overcome to a considerable extent the bad effect" of his appointment, another priest observed. As it was, however, the "relatives and personal friends" closest to him were, "in the judgment of many," unworthy.[22]

One might muster a certain degree of sympathy for James O'Connell, if he was indeed forced into the priesthood by family expectations, but little consideration is due David Toomey. If the young O'Connell went astray amid the temptations of power, Toomey carried the irregular clerical life to an uncontrollable extreme. In March 1913, while the Boston chancellor was waiting for Mrs. Wort's divorce, the editor of the archdiocesan newspaper was carrying on a dalliance with a young woman who sued him for breach of promise to marry, which was still an actionable cause in civil law. Father Toomey enlisted Henry V. Cunningham, the cardinal's attorney, to defend him in the case, which dragged on quietly for nine months. It was finally settled out of court, apparently with a cash payment to the woman to ensure her silence. Undaunted, Toomey joined Mr. and Mrs. Roe on their European honeymoon that summer. He was briefly detained on arrival home for not declaring certain items to customs and because a search of his luggage had turned up several "French postcards," which he described to the agent as "novelties."[23]

Toomey's sexual fires were banked but not extinguished. In the spring of 1914, he visited the Roes in New York and was introduced to a young woman named Florence Marlow, whose father owned a small grocery store in Manhattan. The two fell in love, and they were married by a justice of the peace on June 22 of that year. Unlike Frankie Johnson, who had known what she was doing when she married, Miss Marlow was in the dark about her spouse, who used the alias "Fossa." Like Monsignor O'Connell, he chose to pun on his real identity: "fossa" was an Italian word that meant, among other things, "tomb," a play on "Toomey." Florence Marlow Fossa was a practicing Catholic, however, and she was troubled that her wedding had not been performed in church. Accordingly, she and her husband had the marriage validated later that summer by a priest: Mr. Fossa, who claimed not to be a Catholic, was even baptized (that is, rebaptized) for the occasion, an event that Father Toomey knew to be unnecessary and perhaps blasphemous. Like James O'Connell, Fossa/Toomey led a double life, telling his wife that he was a secret service agent and commuting weekly between New York and Boston for the next four years.[24]

As time went by, Florence Fossa began to suspect that some-thing was just not right with her husband because, as she said, "his visits to our home became more or less infrequent." Accordingly, she followed him to Boston and discovered not only that he was a priest but also that he was occasionally living in Cambridge with yet another woman, his secretary at the *Pilot*. Bursting in on them one Saturday night in October 1918, she caused a sufficiently tempestu-ous scene so that the police had to be called to restore order. Before the case could appear in court, however, Mrs. Fossa was summoned to an interview with Cardinal O'Connell.

According to her sworn statement, made the following spring, the cardinal had arranged for the disturbing the peace charges to be dropped. In return, he urged her not to press a civil case against her priest-husband. O'Connell questioned her closely about both Toomey and his nephew "so as to understand it thoroughly" and, for her part, she told him "all about our relations and also all about the Chancellor," whose identity she had known from the outset. At one point, she asked the cardinal bluntly why he kept James O'Connell, whom she referred to as "that dirty skunk," as chancellor. "For the sake of his mother and father," O'Connell answered forlornly, thereby acknowledging (as Father Mullen would later point out) that he already knew of the young man's transgression. The cardinal closed the interview by promising to meet with her again, and he left her with Henry Cunningham, the lawyer, to arrange for a payment of $7,500 "in order to purchase my silence." In fact, O'Connell did not meet with her again, but within the week he called in a number of parish priests to quiz them on what they knew of Toomey's carrying-on. Those who admitted to having heard gossip about it were enjoined to keep quiet. The cardinal pointedly did not ask about his nephew's circumstances, and none of them was brave enough to offer him any information unbidden.[25]

Toomey's house of cards now collapsed entirely. He was auto-matically excommunicated because of his marriage, and he was quietly removed as editor of the *Pilot*, though a book he had written on the Catholic doctrine of the sacraments was advertised in its pages for another several weeks. Word of his dismissal and disgrace never appeared in the local secular newspapers, still deferential enough of O'Connell's authority to kill an embarrassing story about one so close to him. Indeed, how much the local newspapers actually knew of all this cannot now be determined. The news spread like wildfire among the clergy, however, providing the cardinal's enemies with their first taste of blood. The unfortunate Father Toomey left Boston for New York, though his sordid story may ultimately have had a happy ending. A Boston newspaperwoman named Dorothy Wayman wrote long afterward that Archbishop Richard Cushing, O'Connell's successor, "discovered" an old and sick Toomey in the 1950s. The prelate installed him in an archdiocesan hospital for the terminally ill and reconciled him to the church before his death.[26]

* * *

The exposure of Father Toomey moved the struggle of Cardinal O'Connell and his enemies to a higher and much more serious plane. Father Mullen had recognized that his own preoccupation with the case could be dismissed: he was something of a crank who had never gotten along with his superior. Now, however, those in authority had to pay attention. The cardinal's apparent collusion with the straying priests raised serious questions. As leader of the archdiocese, he had the responsibility to punish such behavior, but instead he had tolerated and permitted it. He may even have been an accomplice: had the archdiocesan attorney involved himself in Toomey's problems, for example, without the cardinal's knowledge or approval? His apparent laxity demanded investigation by his superiors and possibly action against him.

What is more, his troubles were deepening, as the chancellor's dam of secrecy began to leak in several different places. By December 1918, more gory details of Il Circolo had emerged, and a cab driver was produced who had delivered the two priests and their wives to the cardinal's residence when he was not there. The rumor was abroad that James O'Connell and Frankie Johnson Roe had even slept in the cardinal's own bed. Mullen and his friends speculated that O'Connell had known of his nephew's marriage from the beginning; another story had it that he learned of the New York lives of Roe and Fossa in 1915. Father Doody reported that O'Connell had confronted his nephew with what he knew and ordered him to resign. "You go to hell," James shouted back, according to the priest's informants; "I'll leave when I damn please"—a taunt he could back up, Mullen concluded, because "the Chancellor has so much of the Cardinal's money."[27] By the spring of 1919 the apostolic delegate, the highest official of the church in America, had enough information to begin his own investigation.

Archbishop Giovanni Bonzano had been the delegate, the pope's eyes and ears in the United States, since 1912. Generally aligned with the Roman faction that secured the election of Pope Benedict XV in 1914, he was on the other side of the ideological spectrum from Cardinal Merry del Val and the members of the old Pius X circle with which O'Connell was identified. This may have disposed him to distrust the Bostonian in any event, but even so Bonzano had to do something: the potential for embarrassment if O'Connell's problems became publicly known was too great to be ignored. Carefully and precisely, he assembled as much information as he could, even taking the occasion of a trip to New York in March 1919 to meet personally with Florence Fossa and to take her sworn deposition.

In resolving the case of the cardinal's nephew, however, one critical piece of evidence was missing: the proof that Mr. Roe of New York City and Monsignor O'Connell of Boston were one and the same man. The matter was not a simple one. As a result of his deliberately low visibility, few photographs of the monsignor existed, though Bonzano eventually did secure one, together with a studio portrait of Mr. Roe. To prove the dual identity, the delegate contacted the chancery office of the New York achdiocese and asked for assistance. Accordingly, Monsignor John Dunn, New York's chancellor, hired a private detective named Talley who went to work in March 1919. Using several different operatives, Talley staked out the house at 102 East 36th Street, and before long the quarry appeared. Mr. Roe arrived on Friday, April 11, and spent the night. On Saturday morning he and Mrs. Roe went walking, stopping to buy some things in "one of the high priced shops in the district." They took a deliberately circuitous route home, and Roe, apparently suspicious that he was being followed, kept glancing over his shoulder.[28]

The detectives' cover was blown when both the hunters and the hunted returned to the house on 36th Street. Mr. and Mrs. Roe went inside, but Talley's men were confronted by gumshoes from another detective agency, apparently hired by Roe to watch whoever was watching him. A shoving match ensued in the middle of the street, and both sets of spooks were dragged off to the local station house. Roe's men were warned off, but not before they let their employer know that he was indeed being tailed. For the remainder of that day and all of the next (which was Palm Sunday), he remained inside.

Talley was a dogged fellow, and he next assigned some new and more discreet men to take up the case. On Monday night, Mr. and Mrs. Roe emerged, elegantly attired, to attend a performance of "Carmen," featuring the legendary duo of Caruso and Farrar, at the Metropolitan Opera. On Tuesday evening they pursued a more popular entertainment, a performance of a play called "Up in Mabel's Room," described by Dunn as "a lascivious production." On Wednesday afternoon, Roe appeared, suitcase in hand, walked to Grand Central Station, and boarded the three o'clock train for Boston. Taking a private compartment, he did not come out for dinner. When the train pulled in at Boston, the young man emerged, having exchanged his business clothes for a black suit and Roman collar. He was met at the train by a layman who drove him to the chancery office on Granby Street. About ten minutes later, he and his driver, later identified as a lawyer named Garo, came back out and drove to a restaurant in the city's North End, "a notorious place frequented by Black-handers and Italian criminals," Dunn editorialized. A Boston undercover man, hired by Talley's agency, entered the restaurant soon afterward and was introduced to the mysterious traveler, who was identified as James O'Connell.

The noose was beginning to tighten. That Sunday, which was Easter, the cardinal got word that information about his nephew was beginning to circulate among the laity. Following mass at the cathedral that morning, O'Connell was visited in the sacristy by Joseph C. Pelletier, who was the district attorney of Suffolk County. A prominent Catholic layman, Pelletier was a national officer of the Knights of Columbus and would soon be made a Knight of Saint Gregory, a prestigious honor—there were only a few hundred in the world—conferred by Pope Benedict XV at O'Connell's recommendation. Perhaps drawing on reports he had received from his legal counterpart in New York, Pelletier (who later claimed to have had a similar conversation with O'Connell three years before) gingerly told the cardinal of charges that had come his way about young James, "touching his moral reputation." O'Connell dismissed the stories as "a conspiracy to ruin the young man," Pelletier later deposed, but he also questioned the layman closely, and the district attorney was "obliged to repeat the above serious facts several times."[29]

Pelletier was hardly the most reliable informant. A hero to the local Catholic community, he nonetheless had a somewhat unsavory reputation. His conduct in office was controversial enough to result in his impeachment, removal, and disbarment in 1922 after a politically charged trial. He was reputed to be a master of the so-called badger game—the practice of luring respectable older men, usually wealthy Yankees, into compromising positions with young ladies and then soliciting blackmail to keep the incidents out of the courts and the newspapers.[30] Precisely what game Pelletier was playing in approaching the cardinal that Easter morning is unclear: perhaps he thought that he simply had on his line the biggest fish of his career. At the very least, O'Connell left the interview knowing that his own and his nephew's troubles were worsening by the day. Unfortunately, he had no clearer idea of what to do than to continue to sit tight, hoping the whole business would go away.

Archbishop Bonzano did not have to rely entirely on the likes of Pelletier; he already had the more incriminating evidence turned up by the detectives. Still, he had not risen so high in the world of intrigue that was the Vatican diplomatic corps without a certain degree of caution. As a result he sought to introduce a "control" on the case, a means for corroborating the accusations of O'Connell's enemies, whether in Boston or the New York chancery. He accomplished this by seeking the opinion of a universally respected observer, a priest named James Anthony Walsh. Originally a Boston curate and later director of the archdiocese's office for supporting foreign missionary endeavors, Walsh had founded the Maryknoll order of priests, a group devoted to sending American missionaries to faraway lands, especially in the Orient. His ties to the Boston church were still strong, and the nature of his self-sacrificing work made him both a reliable and an entirely credible source.

The missionary responded to the delegate's request for information in June of 1919: things were every bit as bad as Mullen and his associates had been saying. Father Walsh had heard too many sad accounts from "earnest priests, speaking of conditions in Boston." The bad impression left by O'Connell's ambitious rise to power had never dissipated, and the clergy "felt helpless against the cleverness that had enabled an American curate [i.e., O'Connell] to boldly push his way . . . into the College of Cardinals." As archbishop, O'Connell had instituted a system of informers, and any "critical remarks reached headquarters through unknown agents." So completely had the well been poisoned, Walsh concluded, that pastors and curates maintained speaking relations with their leader only with difficulty. He suggested no remedy, but he left little doubt that he concurred with Father Mullen, who had already told Bonzano that "there is only one cure, and that is one Rome alone can take" by removing O'Connell as archbishop.[31]

The Washington-based diplomat was slow to come to that final conclusion, but there seemed little other choice. Fathers Mullen and Doody were in hot pursuit of new evidence, fearful that the cardinal and the chancellor would be able to hang on by maintaining a bold public front. New York's Father Dunn speculated that O'Connell had staged an otherwise unnecessary archdiocesan synod the previous spring for the purpose of pretending that everything was normal. In November 1919 the two Boston pastors managed to track down David Toomey in exile, and he provided them with a new and more damaging set of charges. Yes, Toomey said, O'Connell had known of the scandals in his household from the outset. James O'Connell was blackmailing his uncle, however, not only with evidence of financial shenanigans in archdiocesan accounts, but also with "proofs of the Cardinal's sexual affection for *men*."[32]

Few accusations against a Catholic priest, then or later, were more potentially damaging than this one. An all-male, celibate clergy seemed to many a hospitable climate for homosexuality, and the importance of defending themselves against such suspicions made this the most serious charge one priest could make against another. In O'Connell's case, the origin of the accusation, which Mullen said he had heard "often" but refused to believe because it was so "detestable," derived from his long association with a Boston physician named William Aloysius Dunn. Born in 1852, Dunn had graduated from Boston College and the Harvard Medical School before going into private practice in the West End. He and O'Connell probably met during the young curate's service at Saint Joseph's parish thirty years before. Dunn had traveled extensively in Europe, sometimes with O'Connell, and the two had hiked around Lake Como and into Switzerland together in the summer of 1900. A respectable layman, Dunn was made a Knight of Saint Gregory by

Pope Pius X at O'Connell's urging, and he had frequently been a part of the cardinal's entourage.[33] Any stains on Dunn's character could reflect on O'Connell, for theirs had been a close friendship of long standing.

After Dunn's death in March 1918 some of the unusual circumstances of his life began to emerge. The doctor had never married, and when he left the bulk of his sizable estate to a male companion, several nieces and nephews contested the will. It had been drawn up, they claimed, under the "undue influence" of the man, whom they suspected of having been their uncle's lover. They wanted especially to have introduced in court a number of Doctor Dunn's private letters, a prospect that worried Cardinal O'Connell's friends. The cardinal's enemies speculated that the collection contained love letters that had passed between the two, and perhaps other men besides, but they never got the chance to find out. The letters were not admitted in evidence, but were instead turned over to the ever-serviceable Henry Cunningham, who destroyed them, and the case was settled short of trial.[34]

By the beginning of 1919, O'Connell's pursuers were ready to believe anyone with incriminating evidence, even David Toomey. They recognized that he was a hostile witness now that he had been cashiered, but they noted hopefully that his information had been otherwise reliable and that this accusation deserved a hearing. Whatever the precise circumstances of Dunn's private life, however, O'Connell cannot be judged guilty simply by association with him. The charge of homosexuality against Catholic clerics was easy to make but difficult to prove. The psychology of celibacy was at least as complex at the beginning of the twentieth century as it is now, but the inference that in forgoing an actively heterosexual life O'Connell necessarily embraced an actively homosexual one is too broad a leap. Still, by including the charge in their catalog against him, his enemies may have accomplished their larger purpose: to force action by convincing Rome that "the whole atmosphere of religion in Boston is impregnated with hypocrisy" and scandal.[35]

By the spring of 1920 the case against Monsignor James O'Connell and the cardinal neared completion. Both the apostolic delegate and officials in Rome knew the real story. The other bishops of New England had also learned the details, and two of them were deputized by their colleagues to press the case. Fearful that public exposure could not be held off much longer, Fall River's Daniel Feehan and Burlington's Joseph Rice visited Rome at the beginning of April and raised the matter with Benedict XV. "We have the documents," they reported the pope as having said; "we know the facts; we are looking for a remedy, and we will apply it." O'Connell himself visited Rome soon after and had a curt half-hour interview with the pope on May 4. Reportedly, Benedict confronted him with all the accusations, and O'Connell foolishly tried to bluff his way through. He protested that the charges against his nephew were untrue, but the angry pope produced the marriage record from Indiana and other incriminating evidence. The cardinal was seriously embarrassed at having been caught in a lie, but in any case it was already too late. The documents for James O'Connell's dismissal, confirming his excommunication, had already been drawn up, and by the beginning of June 1920, the papal secretary of state informed both Cardinal O'Connell and Archbishop Bonzano that the Boston chancellor had to be removed.[36]

The resilient young man did not go down easily, managing to hold on to his office for another five months. The cardinal was stalling. Mullen and Doody were dismayed to continue receiving official chancery communications signed by Monsignor James throughout the summer, but it soon became clear that the two O'Connells were looking for a way out that would save public appearances. Finally, in November, they hit on a plan. On the eighth of the month, the chancellor wrote a formal letter of resignation, requesting a year's leave of absence "so that I may at last secure a respite from the arduous duties and responsibilities which I have carried constantly for over fourteen years." He even went so far as to request designation as pastor of a parish when he returned from this leave (something that he knew he would never do) and also to ask for a celebret, a canonical document testifying to his good standing as a priest, for use during his time away (something that he knew his uncle could not grant). The letter was all a cover, of course: it was part of an elaborate plan the two men, who had always been careful to document things for the record, had worked out to make his departure look like anything but what it really was. A short announcement of the change at the Boston chancery was inserted in the secular newspapers right after Thanksgiving—the *Herald* ran it at the bottom of page sixteen, surrounded by shipping news, not the usually prominent place given to happier archdiocesan appointments—and the career of James P. E. O'Connell came officially to an end.[37]

* * *

Inevitably, the personal turmoil aroused by his nephew's behavior had larger consequences for Cardinal O'Connell. His failure either to discover or correct the abuses of his priests called into question the advisability of his continued service as archbishop. The immorality at the heart of official Catholic Boston was destined to influence the cardinal's position within the church and to provide an opening for his opponents. Once critical as "Rome's man" in the remaking of the American hierarchy, he now risked loss of the influence he had so carefully cultivated for more than twenty years. The possibility that he would actually be removed, probably by being "kicked upstairs" to a fine-sounding but powerless position in Rome, became real. He feared that outcome, even as his enemies found it tantalizingly close.

O'Connell was particularly vulnerable at this time because his power in the church had already begun to slip. His chief patron, Pope Pius X, had died unexpectedly in the summer of 1914, leaving the throne of Saint Peter subject to a bitter factional struggle. O'Connell, who had already visited the Vatican once that year, raced across the Atlantic for the election of a new pope. Cardinal Merry del Val, the *éminence grise* of the deceased pontiff, was eager to fend off the forces that had opposed the two of them. Merry was a Spaniard, however, and knew that he himself could almost surely not be elected, so he settled instead on an Italian cardinal who headed the Holy Office, the latter-day successor of the Inquisition. If O'Connell could make it in time for the conclave, the first one in which he was entitled to sit, he would be the American anchor to this voting bloc. Custom dictated a very short interval between the death of the old pope and the election of a new one, however, and that worked against O'Connell. The ship carrying him and Cardinal Gibbons docked at Naples one hour after the election of Giacomo Della Chiesa as Pope Benedict XV was announced to the public. Merry del Val was brusquely removed as secretary of state, and his faction went into permanent decline. O'Connell had put all his eggs in that basket, and he now found himself very much on the outs with the men who controlled the church. "What marvelous changes in

Rome!" John Ireland crowed to Portland's Louis Walsh. "I am overjoyed. . . . I feel that the reign of William [i.e., O'Connell] is cut short and for good. Are you sorry?"[38]

"Not sorry" barely describes the sentiment of Bishop Walsh, who now took over leadership of the opposition to the archbishop of Boston. In September 1920, Walsh prepared a letter to Benedict, formally requesting the cardinal's removal. It was a drastic step, he acknowledged, but the idea had received the nearly unanimous endorsement of the bishops of New England: the leaders of the dioceses in Connecticut, Rhode Island, and Vermont, together with the other bishops in Massachusetts, all signed their names to Walsh's letter. Bishop George Guertin of Manchester, O'Connell's only friend among his colleagues, was alone in demurring, and that was understandable, Walsh said, because he was "afraid of his own shadow"—or, perhaps more precisely, afraid of the shadow cast on Manchester from Boston.[39]

The fiery bishop of Portland was not content with letter-writing, however, and in April 1921 he staged a dramatic personal confrontation. The bishops of New England convened formally every other year and, as luck would have it, a gathering (which O'Connell would probably have preferred to avoid) had already been scheduled. Meeting at the Boston chancery office on April 21, Walsh and his allies brought the scandal into the open. Following the routine business of the meeting, Walsh rose ceremoniously in his place, turned toward O'Connell, and launched a denunciation of "the scandalous conditions in the Curia of Boston during several years." The facts about James O'Connell, Toomey, and the cardinal himself were widely known, he declared, even to laymen. His assertions were confirmed by the others. Bishop John Nilan of Hartford said that the scandals were "common subjects of discussion," an opinion repeated by Daniel Feehan of Fall River. Burlington's Joseph Rice was outraged that O'Connell had "long condoned the crime" of his nephew, and Nilan fixed the blame squarely: "No one finds a way to absolve Your Eminence from responsibility," he said.[40]

O'Connell could muster only a weak rebuttal. He denied any knowledge of what was going on, saying that he had attributed rumors about his nephew to "jealousy and enmity." Feehan cited "certain persons [presumably Pelletier, Florence Marlow Fossa, and perhaps even Toomey himself] and proofs to the contrary," but the cardinal "would not admit their worth." When the bishops declared their intention to lay the matter before Benedict XV, O'Connell "became incensed at the mention of the Holy Father's name, and ordered it left out of the discussion." That "could not be done," Feehan snapped back. O'Connell seemed "abjectly afraid" during the whole scene, concluded the coadjutor bishop of Providence, William Hickey, who was about to succeed O'Connell's ailing and absent nemesis, Matthew Harkins; "his denials did not bear any resemblance to those of an innocent man." Rice "called upon the Ordinary of Boston to resign his see and to place himself at the disposal of the Holy Father," a suggestion O'Connell naturally rejected. The meeting broke up in acrimony, with Walsh warning that he would "take these matters up with a view to reparation" and punishment from "the proper authorities."

The threat was no idle one, and within a matter of days Walsh was on a ship bound for Rome. He met with Benedict on May 9 and later reported that the pope listened to him attentively, asked many questions, and promised to find the right solution. During a second audience on May 19, Walsh presented evidence, including a deposition from Pelletier, that O'Connell had been warned about his nephew as early as 1916. The pope responded that the situation was "very serious and very sad" and that he knew now that removing O'Connell was "the only effective remedy." Rather than try to oust the cardinal through any formal proceeding, Benedict said, he would offer the Bostonian a position in Rome that would allow him at least to preserve his public reputation.[41] When Walsh left the Eternal City in mid-July, he was convinced that his goal was within reach.

Benedict had specified only one condition before he would act. A substantial number of other American bishops, not just those from New England, would have to demonstrate their disapproval of O'Connell. Back home, Walsh thought he had the perfect opportunity to prove this point: the regular annual meeting of the American hierarchy at the Catholic University in Washington, scheduled for the middle of September 1921. Cardinal Gibbons, the de facto primate who had traditionally chaired these gatherings, had died the previous spring, and O'Connell, now the senior American cardinal, was expected to preside. The pope said that if there were a spontaneous reaction against O'Connell's assuming the chair by at least one quarter of those in attendance, he would take it as a vote of no confidence and remove O'Connell from Boston. Since the meetings were closed to the public, there was no risk of open embarrassment, and Walsh readily agreed to this test. Conveniently forgetting the pope's condition that the protest be spontaneous, he wrote to like-minded bishops around the country, urging a walkout.[42]

Despite Walsh's confident hopes, there was little support for such drastic action among his brother bishops. No evidence survives as to how many he found to agree to his plan, but the number willing to force the issue was so small that nothing unusual happened when O'Connell opened the meeting in Washington; not even the New England delegation walked out. The idea was "childish," Bishop Paul Heffron of Winona, Minnesota, said, fearing that "if the plan were carried out, the Catholic Church would have one of the most sensational scandals of its history." Heffron had already warned O'Connell that something was up, and the new first-among-equals of the American hierarchy thanked his informant, whom he did not otherwise know, for revealing the plots of his enemies. He left their "despicable chicanery" to God, O'Connell said, hoping for the exaction of a suitable "punishment due their treachery."[43]

Even Archbishop Bonzano, so zealous in his pursuit of the case of the wayward chancellor, was cooling off. Walsh was probably exaggerating the extent of the opposition to the cardinal, he told Rome. Bonzano was also angry that Walsh had attempted to engineer the protest, rather than relying on the spontaneity the pope had demanded. He scolded William Russell, the bishop of Charleston, South Carolina, a Walsh accomplice who was rabid enough in his hatred of O'Connell to call him "this perjured Cardinal" and a "degenerate"—code words that indicated how widely the story of O'Connell's attempt to bluff Benedict XV and the suggestions of homosexuality had spread. Russell calmed down, withdrawing his threat to go public with what he knew, but Bonzano concluded that further prosecution of the case was too risky. Time was pushing the affairs of James O'Connell farther into the past; since the church had thusfar avoided any negative publicity, the delegate thought, why reopen the wound? Perhaps realizing he had passed an important test, O'Connell was quick to praise his own role at the bishops' meeting. He told Bonzano ostentatiously that the participants found it "the most expeditious and orderly meeting at which they had ever assisted," a backhanded insult to the dead Gibbons.[44]

Throughout, O'Connell was not without allies and defenders. Among the Boston diocesan clergy, his troubles were by this time generally known, and from a few of them he received words of encouragement. "You have the deepest sympathy of many of us," wrote Monsignor Edward Moriarty, pastor of Saint Thomas Aquinas parish, Jamaica Plain. Advising O'Connell to ignore "the hounds and skunks masquerading under their religious garb," Moriarty urged reliance on "your old sublime courage" as the surest way through the crisis. From Rome, too, came messages of condolence. Merry del Val commiserated over his friend's "recent trials" and expressed the "hope that what you have had to bear may not have affected you too deeply." O'Connell thanked him for the moral support, condemning the present "intrigue" and longing for "the wonderful days of Pio X," when the two of them had been riding high.[45]

O'Connell was chastened by his troubles, but he did not leave his fate entirely in the hands of others. He began a vigorous counteroffensive, not answering the accusations against him but following Moriarty's advice to "do mighty things" to show that he was undiminished by the crisis. The *Pilot* swung into action and eventually ran a three-month series of front page stories on how the work of the archdiocese had "surpassed the fondest hopes of Catholics" since O'Connell's accession. Bishop Walsh later cursed the effectiveness of this *"bluff record* of the Pilot." It had "done its work," he lamented, "and of course it is hard if not impossible to counteract it."[46]

More practically, O'Connell relied on an agent in Rome as he had in the past. This time it was not Francis MacNutt but an Augustinian priest named Charles M. Driscoll, from whom the cardinal got regular reports on the comings and goings of his enemies, planning his own strategy accordingly. At Driscoll's urging, he immediately doubled the Peter's Pence contribution from Boston: previously running at just under $30,000, the 1921 offering to the pope jumped to $60,000 and remained there for the rest of the decade. He reasserted himself in other ways. He took Merry del Val's suggestion and distributed to several cardinals in the curia copies of the then-seven volumes of his collected sermons. (The set would eventually run to eleven volumes.) These constituted "proof of your labours," Merry told him. "This is a tangible [sign] that will serve a purpose to your advantage and it will be understood." He played up to powerful officials who might defend him or, if left unmollified, might seriously hurt him. He translated and published a book of meditations on Christ's passion written by Cardinal Gaetano DeLai, secretary of the Vatican's consistorial congregation, the office that would oversee any canonical action to remove him as archbishop. Above all, he maintained a brave front, telling a Roman acquaintance that "I thank all my good friends in Rome and beg their prayers. It is the only thing I beg."[47]

O'Connell was also lucky. Both he and his enemies waited to see what action, if any, the pope would take, but in January 1922 Benedict abruptly died with nothing resolved. Again, O'Connell dashed to Rome, resolved not to miss this second opportunity to restore his friends to power, but once more he was disappointed. Though the conclave extended to seven ballots, O'Connell could not get there in time, arriving in Rome on February 6 to be greeted by the news that Achille Ratti, the tough-minded archbishop of Milan, had been elected, taking the name Pius XI. Still, the cloud had a silver lining. The new pontiff was unlikely to restore O'Connell, Merry del Val, and their circle to positions of authority, but his accession also meant that Walsh and company had to begin all over again their efforts to have the Bostonian deposed. Pius and his advisers "will go no further than they are obliged to go," Father Mullen summarized for Walsh's benefit. "They are not anxious to burn their fingers, especially when they have [n]o immediate interest in the case." Others concurred. "If you are to do anything effective you must do your work directly with Rome, and do it strongly," Baltimore's new archbishop, Michael J. Curley, counseled Walsh. "There is only one way to handle the question. . . . It must be done by a figurative bomb shell thrown into the heart of the Eternal City."[48]

Walsh was quite prepared to throw his bomb, but throughout 1922 and 1923 the assault on O'Connell was thrown off track by Walsh's concurrent efforts on behalf of the National Catholic Welfare Conference (NCWC). Originally formed to coordinate American Catholic efforts in support of World War I, the NCWC had become a permanent structure for collective action among the American bishops. It was unprecedented in canon law, however, which at the time made no provision for national organizations of bishops. O'Connell opposed the whole idea, thinking the NCWC an infringement on the authority of individual bishops and finding it dangerously radical in promoting social welfare programs. The product of a typically devious "Sulpician intrigue," he told Cardinal DeLai, it was a hotbed of "Democracy, Presbyterianism, and Congregationalism," loaded words designed to frighten. Walsh was a staunch backer of the NCWC, and when O'Connell and Cardinal Dennis Dougherty of Philadelphia sought to have the Vatican suppress the organization, the Portland bishop was temporarily put on the defensive. Rome condemned the NCWC at the beginning of 1922, and Walsh and his cohorts spent the better part of the next year rescinding the denunciation and restoring both the conference and themselves to good graces. Walsh continued to plot strategy against the man he now called simply "the Boston Dictator," but his efforts were repeatedly derailed. Archbishop Pietro Fumasoni-Biondi had replaced Bonzano as apostolic delegate at the beginning of 1923, and he was presumably among those unwilling to "burn his fingers." Later that year, Walsh, who had become obsessed by his struggle with O'Connell, was hospitalized for exhaustion.[49] By the beginning of 1924, however, the bishop of Portland had recovered his strength, and he was resolved to make one last attempt.

Acting still with the support of the other New England bishops, Walsh set sail for Rome in February 1924. He traveled alone but expected to meet Bishops Rice and Feehan on arrival. A Puritan at heart, Walsh was scandalized by what he saw of Jazz Age America aboard ship, noting the "unholy show" of young men and women who smoked cigarettes and danced the "tango and fox trot and Devil's hold," but he landed none the worse for wear at the end of the month. En route, he had time to reflect on his motives. Asserting his desire to promote "the dignity and vitality of the Holy See," he spoke of the importance of Rome's "creating a sound Episcopate in each country" (in this case, by unseating O'Connell) and then "letting such Episcopate govern" (in this case, by supporting the NCWC). In Rome he met his fellow New Englanders, who had already seen the pope and prepared him for what their champion would say. He also called on various cardinals in the curia, seeking their support.[50]

Walsh got his chance for frank talk with the pope on Monday, February 25. After morning mass he proceeded to the Vatican, where he chatted amiably with the guards, who seemed most interested in quizzing this American on what was to them the very curious subject of Prohibition. Ushered into the formidable presence of Pius XI, Walsh began by reporting on the state of affairs in the Portland diocese, but he quickly got around to the subject at hand. He described the questionable circumstances under which O'Connell had left Portland in 1906—"the books, funds etc." He emphasized "the absolute lack of confidence" in O'Connell, the "scandal for which he is held responsible by everybody," and the "danger of volcanic eruption." The pope listened closely, asked a number of questions, and himself proposed the idea of bringing O'Connell to Rome as a way of burying him alive. The meeting ended with the pope's recommendation that Walsh talk to Cardinal DeLai and with a promise to meet with him again. Barely disguising his glee as he left, Walsh concluded that it was "a most delightful audience, apart from the sadness of [the] subject."[51]

If Walsh presented the case for the prosecution, O'Connell soon got the chance to offer a defense. New England weather was always "very disagreeable" at that time of the year and "nothing of importance happens" then, he had told the apostolic delegate a little too casually, and so he had been off leading a pilgrimage to the Holy Land. His sense of timing undiminished by the years, O'Connell's return trip conveniently landed him in Rome three days after Walsh's interview with the pope. O'Connell got audiences of his own, once on March 1 and again on March 8. No record of their proceedings survives, but the cardinal took the occasion to show that he was still firmly in control. He presented a check for a whopping $88,000 to support foreign missionary work and called on various powerful officials. He knew that Walsh was in Rome, but to no one's surprise the two did not meet.[52]

In the meanwhile, Walsh was also making the rounds and, despite his early optimism, he began to see his anticipated victory slipping away. The "*Pilot* hot air," which apparently showed that religion was thriving in Boston, made it difficult for him to argue that the archdiocese was in chaos. Cardinal DeLai acknowledged that O'Connell was a problem but did not like the idea of transferring him to Rome. Cardinal Gasparri, the papal secretary of state and a longtime O'Connell adversary, was disposed toward that plan but refused to take the lead. When Walsh met DeLai a second time, the cardinal noted the absence of a groundswell from America against

O'Connell, and Walsh concluded that this old ally of Merry del Val and O'Connell's other antimodernist friends was "the real obstacle."[53]

Walsh's last chance came on March 12, when he met for one final time with Pius XI. Taking a page from his enemy's book (a pale one by comparison), he first presented his Peter's Pence check for almost $17,000, "a big sum in Lire," he noted hopefully. When it came time to discuss the crucial question, however, he was disappointed. "I could see that Card. DeLai had been at work," he noted, adding that he "argued and explained," but to no avail. The pope was distressed at the formation of an anti-O'Connell "party," and his opinion was "very strong" that "*prudence* and *silence*" were necessary to allow the whole business, now more than three years old, to blow over. Walsh was "phased" by the pope's sudden reluctance, and he left the audience dejected. He remained in Rome for another two weeks, trying vainly to breathe life back into his cause. Unsuccessful at that, he sailed for home in April, and in the middle of May he died in Portland, defeated and exhausted at the age of sixty-six.[54] With him died the hopes of O'Connell's enemies. In a show of priestly brotherhood, the cardinal traveled to Portland, where he presided solemnly at Walsh's funeral on May 16, no doubt smiling to himself as his adversary's coffin was sealed into a vault in the cathedral crypt. O'Connell had survived the great crisis of his career.

* * *

The enduring marvel about the turmoil at the heart of Cardinal O'Connell's tenure in Boston was that it happened at all. In the world of American Catholicism of 1920, the tangled story of James O'Connell and the maneuverings of the cardinal's enemies were a truth stranger than any fiction. Churchmen simply did not behave this way. Bright, capable priests like Monsignor O'Connell seldom abandoned the priesthood for any reason, let alone to marry secretly. Influential archbishops like William O'Connell, so committed to enunciating ethical standards for their church and for society at large, tolerated no moral nonsense in their domains. Bishops like Louis Walsh from small, backwater dioceses did not take on cardinals of international renown, exultantly gossiping about them and seeking both to remove them from power and to humiliate them in the process. One diocesan chancellor did not hire private detectives to follow another diocesan chancellor around. To be sure, there had been examples of impropriety in high ecclesiastical places in the past, but those were tales of Borgias and Medicis in sixteenth-century Italy, not of O'Connells and Walshs in twentieth-century America.

Not even the strangeness of the circumstances, however, absolves the participants in this drama from responsibility, beginning with Cardinal O'Connell himself. Though it is impossible to say exactly when the cardinal first learned of the immoralilty in his own inner circle, there can be no question that he knew of it long before he took any action—or, rather, before action was forced on him. If Joseph Pelletier was telling the truth, he had known something was wrong by April 1919; he had possibly known three years before that. Florence Marlow Fossa had told O'Connell about the scandal to his face in October 1918, two full years before his nephew's resignation. If David Toomey was telling the truth—perhaps a remote possibility— the cardinal had known much earlier, maybe even at the time of the Toomey breach of promise troubles in 1913, the summer after James O'Connell's marriage. Whether or not the cardinal knew for certain, did he not have some responsibility to inquire about the strange circumstances in his official family? In civil law, the term for O'Connell's reluctance to investigate would have been misprision: knowing of the existence of a serious offense and doing nothing either to stop or expose it. In canon law, the consequences of deliberately covering up a serious sin, especially a sin in which the cardinal himself might share some culpability, were dreadful. Such eternal consequences might hold no terror for a worldly man, but a cardinal archbishop might well be expected to fear them.

In the face of those sanctions, what explains O'Connell's failure to act? He may have been motivated, as he told Florence Fossa, by a concern for the young man's parents and, indeed, for the honor of the entire family. He and the rest of the clan had a great deal invested in James O'Connell: the young man was to be a leader in the next generation of this newly "respectable and respected" family. The cardinal may also have feared, as David Toomey maintained, that his nephew's removal would bring about his own downfall as well. An audit of archdiocesan accounts might reveal behavior similar to the "very unusual" bookkeeping practices of Portland twenty years before; an investigation of the charges of homosexuality would be damaging whether they were ultimately proved or not. O'Connell was trapped. At every turn, he tried to avoid the complex scandal, but ignoring his problems made them worse rather than better. By the time the cancer was finally removed, the entire body was in jeopardy.

If the cardinal's actions were less than honorable, the actions of his opponents were but little better. Walsh, Mullen, and their cohorts maintained that they were prompted only by concern for the well-being of the church, that they wanted to remove O'Connell before the scandal became public and did real damage to Catholicism in America. Baser motives were also at work. These men had never accepted O'Connell's victory in the struggle for the Boston succession in 1906. Now, more than a decade later, they thought they saw a way to win the prize that had eluded them then. They relished the thought of taking revenge on this man whom they had never liked or trusted. They embraced the opportunity to denigrate his reputation, just as he had denigrated Archbishop Williams, in whose administration they had been closer to the center of things and for whom they felt enduring affection. O'Connell's own clumsy management of the crisis made their task that much easier. Who else but a desperate man would, as the cardinal had done with Benedict XV, look the pope straight in the eye and lie to him? Here was an opportunity O'Connell's enemies could not resist.

How these scandals escaped wider public exposure remains a mystery. The cardinal's detractors claimed that the problems of official Catholic Boston were common knowledge, even among laymen, and there is no reason to doubt that at least some prominent Catholics knew or suspected that something was amiss. Why did no newspaper look into the rumors which, if proved true, would be a guaranteed blockbuster? In the modern era, accustomed as it is to tough, sensational, investigative reporting, avoidance of such a story would be unthinkable. At the beginning of the twentieth century, however, the canons of journalistic behavior were very different, and public figures were accorded a deference that seems naive today. In the decade after O'Connell's troubles, for example, news photographers would tacitly agree not to show a president of the United States walking with his crutches, and news conferences would be informal, off-the-record affairs. Cardinal O'Connell's "kept reporter" at the Boston Globe (jealous of its circulation, which it boasted of as the largest in New England) served as a useful conduit to the ink-stained brotherhood. The press was not so sure of itself that it dared take on so potent a figure as the leader of Boston's one million Catholics.

Unanswered questions about the scandal remain, but its consequences for Cardinal O'Connell were very real. He was neither turned out of office nor embarrassed in public, but he was a very different man after the turmoil than he had been before. Prior to it, he was accustomed to being the principal actor in everything he did, not the man who was acted upon by others; now the roles were reversed. Already declining in influence in Rome, and apparently unable to reassert himself because it was so hard for him to get to papal conclaves on time, his slide continued unabated. In 1925, the apostolic delegate conducted a formal visitation of all the dioceses of New England, investigating for himself the animosity that marked internal church affairs.[55] No restrictions on O'Connell came from that inspection, but the occasion served as a reminder that his superiors were watching him more closely than before.

More pointedly, O'Connell lost the ability to secure the appointment of bishops favorable to him, a significant measure of influence within the church. To replace the dead Louis Walsh in Portland, for example, the cardinal wanted one of his most faithful aides, Monsignor Michael Splaine. The designation went instead to John Gregory Murray, an auxiliary to Hartford's John Nilan, Walsh's fellow conspirator. Even the cardinal's own auxiliaries were forced on him. In 1932 the ambitious Francis Spellman, who had survived James O'Connell's scolding and was now well-connected with powerful new forces in the Vatican, was made auxiliary bishop of Boston against O'Connell's wishes. The cardinal could barely contain his anger, tersely sending the new bishop a congratulatory wire that read: "Welcome home. Confirmations begin Monday October tenth. You are expected to be ready." He perceived the fine French hand of his old adversaries in these appointments, attributing them to a plot by "the Sulpicians and their favorites."[56] The cardinal could rail against his enemies and his fate, but he was powerless to change either. He probably did not appreciate the irony that, just as he had been imposed on Archbishop Williams, others were now being imposed on him. Rome might not remove him from office, but it was not about to let him control the future of Catholicism in New England.

O'Connell's role in the American hierarchy was similarly diminished. The public at large remained unaware, but he had still been embarrassed in front of his colleagues. Seniority and his cardinal's hat may have given him claim to the title of leader of the hierarchy, but he retained none of the substance of that position. "Many of us older bishops who know him," Cincinnati's Archbishop John McNicholas told a correspondent, "do not believe him; we do not trust him; we consider him a most dangerous Prelate."[57] Real leadership passed to other hands, especially midwestern bishops, through the agency of the NCWC. Once, O'Connell had seemed capable of dominating church life in America for a generation. Instead, his troubles had left him on the outside looking in, ostensibly the "dean" of the American Catholic hierarchy but curiously unwelcome in it. In time he stopped attending their meetings altogether.

At home, too, the scandals surrounding O'Connell had a chastening effect. Diocesan affairs, which had formerly turned around the wastrel chancellor, continued to run on their own momentum, but they had lost much of their vigor. Routine business was handled well enough, but the clergy learned that they could resist their leader with impunity. There was, James Walsh of Maryknoll concluded, "a positive fear, on the part of the Archbishop, of any one who opposes him. He is known not to be brave, and his boldness is so easily repulsed that even curates do not hesitate to speak their minds plainly when confronted by him."[58] O'Connell's early years as archbishop had been marked by vigor, but the later years came to be characterized by maintenance of the status quo, with much of the energy dissipated in the struggle to survive.

Only time cured O'Connell's ills. One by one, his enemies died off: Father Doody followed Bishop Walsh in death during the summer of 1924, and Father Mullen did likewise three years later. Bishops Feehan and Rice died in the 1930s. The cardinal's own formidable longevity served him well. James O'Connell moved permanently to New York, where he and Frankie continued to live happily under the name Roe. So far as is known, he and his uncle never met again after the fall of 1920. No inquiry was ever made to determine just where his money had come from, and Mr. Roe became a respected man in the community, eventually serving as secretary of the board of trade in Manhattan. He wrote an occasional letter on business or politics to the editor of the *New York Times*, but he stayed out of the public eye. Beyond his real estate holdings in the metropolis, he also acquired a summer home in Lenox, Massachusetts, a small town in the western Berkshire hills, and it was there that he died of heart disease on November 29, 1948. He was buried at Kensico Cemetery, Valhalla, New York, survived only by his widow, who joined him there in her family's plot after her own death in April 1969.[59]

The crisis of O'Connell's life passed, and he survived it, but it had a lasting effect. It broke his hitherto unbroken string of successes and put him on the defensive. For the first time in his career, he was unable to shape his own destiny, forced to respond to circumstances controlled by others. He had reached the peak of his authority and power, and if his enemies had not been able, as they had hoped, to cast him down from that height, they had at least guaranteed that he would go no higher. With his survival assured in 1924 on Louis Walsh's death and Pius XI's refusal to act, O'Connell had another twenty years to live. They would be years of increasing isolation and eventual irrelevance in the only world in which he had ever hoped to succeed.

9

THE LONG TWILIGHT:
MANAGING THE ARCHDIOCESE, 1924–1944

FOR HIS LAST TWENTY YEARS, O'Connell lived in a prolonged twilight. Unwelcome and distrusted elsewhere in the church, he concentrated the energies that remained to him on local matters. He devoted himself to diocesan business even as that work became less demanding. He had been a bishop for a quarter of a century, and there was little new about his job that could surprise him. The administrative style he had more than once identified as "our system" ran according to its own internal momentum, with a succession of younger priests taking over the duties of the departed nephew. The machinery kept running, but the pioneering work had been done. Church administration was simply a matter of more of the same.

Despite James O'Connell's systematic embezzlement, the Boston archdiocese remained a basically healthy institution throughout the second half of the cardinal's tenure. The Catholic population grew from an estimated 850,000 in 1907 to about 1.1 million at O'Connell's death in 1944. New parishes were created to serve those people: after an initial burst of enthusiasm early in the century, the pace of parish formation slowed but held even. (See Figure 2.) Increasing numbers of well-off Catholics could support church endeavors, though it was still the high volume of small contributions from ordinary believers, many of whom sacrificed like the scriptural widow, that ensured solvency. "The magnitude of the charitable work of the Archdiocese," the *Pilot* had proclaimed in 1924, was matched only by the "constructive . . . accomplishment along educational lines" and "a vigorous and healthy spiritual life." The usual tone of self-promotion does not minimize the achievement: even during the economic retrenchment and uncertainty of the 1930s, the archdiocese retained a stable institutional presence.[1]

208

Figure 2

New Parishes Created by O'Connell, 1907–1944
(Source: *Official Catholic Directory*)

	1907–1910	1911–1915	1916–1920	1921–1925	1926–1930	1931–1935	1936–1940	1941–1944
New Parishes	30	18	13	16	16	17	18	0
Total Parishes (last year of date span)	225	243	256	272	288	305	323	323
% Increase	15.3	8.0	5.3	6.2	5.8	5.9	5.9	0

At the center of things, O'Connell's own financial security as well as his reputation for shrewd management had been secured by his inheritance of a fortune from the Keith family. He had first met Benjamin Franklin Keith, the owner of vaudeville theaters that were, O'Connell said, "distinguished for their excellent reputation for decent amusement," in the American circle of Rome in the 1890s. Mrs. Keith was a Catholic and, although her husband was not, together they supported many church causes. Their only son, Paul, who was generally indifferent about religion but nominally a Catholic, shared this interest, and when he died in October 1918 with no heirs, he made an unusual disposition of his parents' money. After making gifts to some old family retainers, he bequeathed "the rest, residue and remainder" to "William O'Connell of Boston, Massachusetts, a Cardinal of the Holy Roman Church, and to the President and Fellows of Harvard College, a Massachusetts corporation."[2] Apparently deliberately, the will omitted any reference to O'Connell's legal status as archbishop, in which capacity he was every bit as much "a Massachusetts corporation" as Harvard. Instead, the money was to be his personally, and the immigrant's son from Lowell stood on the verge of becoming a millionaire.

The clipped legal language of the bequest obscured its real value, for the "residue" of the Keith estate amounted by the time the will was finally probated in 1922 to more than $5.1 million. Much of it consisted of real estate, and after dividing it with Harvard, O'Connell took title to properties in Marblehead, Swampscott, and Lowell, as well as income-producing buildings in Pittsburgh, Jersey City, and New York. The cardinal's Manhattan holdings were especially lucrative: one was a building of offices and stores on Fifth Avenue in lower Harlem, and the other was a similar property in the heart of the Tin Pan Alley neighborhood at Broadway and 28th Street. In early 1924, these two buildings alone were producing almost $8,000 per month in rentals. The cardinal's office managed these with its usual attention to detail, gradually selling them off before the real estate market collapsed in the depression.[3]

Sale of the buildings was just the beginning of the Keith estate's true worth. Realizing just under $3 million, O'Connell made some benefactions directly to church causes, but most of the money he invested in stocks, bonds, and other securities that constituted a blue-chipper's dream. Railroad, oil and gas, public utility, and heavy industrial stocks predominated, and despite the problems of Wall Street they produced a healthy return: in 1931, for example, they brought in more than $41,000 in dividends, and even in 1937 the figure remained high at $38,000. The cardinal eventually sold off his holdings with the help of another nephew, Joseph O'Connell, an officer of the Shawmut Bank in Boston who had none of his cousin's moral peculiarities but all of his financial skill. The fortune was handled expertly, converting it from real estate to investments to ready cash, its value increasing at every stage.[4]

Management for management's sake was not the purpose of the bequest, of course, and Paul Keith's will had specified that O'Connell use the money "for such charitable purposes as he may deem best, in memory of my mother, Mary Catherine Keith." This the cardinal did with a vengeance. Saint John's Seminary received $300,000 outright; the Clergy Fund Society (the archdiocesan health insurance system for priests) got $100,000; and the American College, Boston College, and the Catholic University got $50,000 each. Living as he did in the great age of Catholic monumentalism, O'Connell also used the money to erect new buildings. A high school for boys and another for girls, known respectively as Keith Academy and Keith Hall, were opened in Lowell. A high school for the Holy Cross cathedral parish, a chapel for Saint Elizabeth's Hospital, and a gymnasium for the Working Boys Home also came from the Keith bequest. Back at the seminary, O'Connell rebuilt a dormitory damaged by fire, renaming it Saint William's Hall in honor of his own patron saint, together with a new chancery office and a palatial official residence, into which he moved in 1927. The cardinal liked to think of these structures as constituting a "little Rome," with church-related buildings crowning every Boston hilltop, and when he closed the books on the Keith money he thanked the family for "giving back to God what, in His Providence, He had given to them."[5]

In managing the Keith money and in overseeing the rest of archdiocesan business, O'Connell followed the same procedures on which he had always relied. If the forms of activity were familiar by this time, however, so too were the limitations on the cardinal's authority. To the end, O'Connell relied on close scrutiny of all aspects of church life, but he was no more successful than he had previously been at imposing his undisputed will within his domain.

Severe limitations on his powers remained, and he had to continue to balance the localized forces that governed life in a church that still resembled a feudal kingdom as much as a modern corporation.

* * *

The affairs of archdiocesan parishes continued to occupy much of the cardinal's attention. Close examination of accounts, detailed if not very imaginative, remained the hallmark of "our system." One priest was informed that his total receipts for a particular year added up to $173,043.20, not the $173,042.80 he had reported, a difference of 40 cents. Others were reprimanded for failing to secure permission to expend sums greater than $100, though there was seldom any penalty for transgressing this rule. Control of information was still the basis for all decisions. When Father Hugh F. Blunt, who had succeeded the crusty John O'Brien as pastor of Sacred Heart, Cambridge, wrote in May 1924, asking to spend $950 to repair his church's roof, the cardinal's staff checked the latest report. The diocesan chancellor penciled on Blunt's letter, "Balance on hand $38,741.28; Debt $10,000," and then passed it along to O'Connell, who wrote a simple "OK" on it; the work went ahead.[6] The administrative routine itself governed the determination of policy, a routine founded on management tools no more sophisticated than the adding machine.

As usual, fear of debt was paramount. Parishes with outstanding notes, even mortgages secured by real property, were watched closely. The parish of Our Lady of Perpetual Help in Boston's Roxbury neighborhood, popularly known as the "Mission Church," bothered O'Connell because, he complained, it had a debt "at least five times greater than that of any other Parish." The cardinal wanted the rector to reduce this amount "as speedily as you can," and he was only partially mollified when the priest explained that much of the debt came from a "paper" transfer to the church by the Redemptorist priests who staffed it and who expected no repayment. The parish was large and thriving, evoking a strong sense of loyalty from its parishioners and lending its name to the entire district of the city ("Mission Hill") around it. The place was in little danger of going under, but O'Connell was still worried. He could not actively redirect its finances, though he did assert himself in little things: in 1931 he refused the rector's request to install two tennis courts for the parish's overflowing high school on the grounds of alleged insolvency.[7]

From a distance, O'Connell also monitored the spiritual activities of his parishes. He was troubled by the debt at Mission Church, but he nevertheless approved enthusiastically its services for deaf Catholics in the late 1930s, a program that included ceremonies conducted in sign language. In general, though, he was wary of liturgical innovations, thinking they would "inevitably be subject to many abuses." He frowned on offering mass in the afternoon—the canonical requirement of the era that worshippers fast from midnight the night before if they wanted to receive communion presented practical problems here—and he refused a pastor's request to teach all the children in his parish, boys and girls, those portions of the mass usually recited only by the altar boys.[8] The cumulative effect of these constantly sought and granted (or denied) permissions was to make the cardinal seem to be the center of diocesan affairs, the sole reference point for local church life.

In more substantial matters, however, O'Connell was not always so successful. Contemporary church law made each parish a benefice, originally a medieval legal construct that vested in the priests a great deal of autonomy. The pastor took in all the financial offerings of his people and paid the expenses of his church, including the salaries of the curates; whatever was left was his to dispose of as he wished. Some used the money to advance the fortunes of their families, but most reinvested their surpluses in new parish buildings or endowments for charitable and educational works. Since diocesan priests took no vow of poverty, control of the money gave local clergymen an independence they did not willingly surrender. Hedged in by this system—which remained in place in the Boston church until 1952—O'Connell had to tolerate a significant degree of local initiative, even as he continued to speak the language of centralized administration. The rector of the Mission Church could ignore the cardinal's finger-wagging about the parish debt because, beyond persuasion and reprimands, O'Connell had no effective recourse if a subordinate chose simply to ignore him. The cardinal could ban new tennis courts, but he could not control more important matters.

Few priests understood this dynamic better than the diminutive Monsignor Richard Neagle, who presided over the huge suburban preserve that was Immaculate Conception parish, Malden, from 1896 until his death in 1943. A former archdiocesan chancellor under Williams, Neagle knew that his name had been on the *terna* to succeed the old archbishop, and he also knew that O'Connell's had not. This gave him all the self-assurance of a powerful feudal baron. He built a parish high school in 1931, paid for it entirely out of his own accounts, and privately engaged the Xaverian brothers, a teaching order, to run it. When O'Connell stumbled across a newspaper story about the new school (it was the first he had heard of the project) and demanded an explanation, Neagle was unfazed. "As they [that is, the Xaverians] are already in the diocese I assumed your approval," he responded in a deliberately casual way, "but it is no harm to ask it formally."[9] O'Connell acquiesced, not even bothering to point out to this over-mighty subject the technical transgression of established procedures.

Neagle probably enjoyed tweaking his archbishop in this way, but he was far from unique in being able to get what he wanted, even in the face of O'Connell's opposition. Some priests found passive-aggressive ways around the cardinal. Father John Harrigan, pastor of Saint Ambrose's parish in the heart of the heavily Catholic Dorchester district of Boston, wrote O'Connell in 1928, alleging that the people of his parish were clamoring that he build a new rectory. When the cardinal found the architectural plans for the house too elaborate and suggested a more modest dwelling, Harrigan responded by biding his time. About a year later, he wrote again, this time submitting plans for a rectory precisely one foot smaller in each of its dimensions and saving only $3,000 on a total cost of more than $70,000. These plans were approved in full, and Harrigan came away with substantially what he had wanted all along. Ecclesiastical theory may have made the bishop supreme in his diocese: "according to that wonderful system that runs through the whole Church," O'Connell had said in 1909, the bishop was "entirely responsible" for everything, fixing rules that underlings obeyed with "coordination and subordination."[10] In reality, O'Connell had to accommodate himself to those who were technically subordinate to him. Faced with a pastor inclined to resist him, O'Connell would usually back away from confrontation.

He did regulate lesser aspects of clerical life, if only to demonstrate, as he had said on assuming the coadjutorship, that priests were the church's army and he was the general. Overlooking his own proclivities for travel, he discouraged trips abroad by his men, saying that "constant roaming about the world" had a "bad effect on the Parish." Applying another standard from which he exempted himself, he was suspicious of priests who maintained vacation homes at the seashore. In at least one case, he assigned a young curate to a parish with instructions to keep an eye on the pastor, who seemed a little too fond of spending his summers at the beach. He actively discouraged the ownership of automobiles by his priests, thinking them an unnecessary extravagance. One cleric in a rural town far from Boston was told he could have a car, provided that he not "give too much publicity to the granting of this permission" among his priestly colleagues.[11] The cardinal's authority in such cases was genuine enough, but by focusing on such relatively minor matters it also threw into sharper relief what he could not do in controlling the lives and activities of his clergy.

The limitations on O'Connell's authority were evident when he encountered a priest who was prepared to stand up to him. Such a man was Joseph V. Tracy, pastor of Saint Columbkille's, Brighton. A native of Ireland, Tracy had earned a national scholarly reputation during his days on the faculty of Saint John's Seminary before assuming the Brighton pastorate in 1907. The priest's Sulpician associations from his seminary days made him a suspicious person in O'Connell's regime, and the two men often played a cat-and-mouse game. In 1915 Tracy objected to the opening of a public chapel connected with a monastery that was within Saint Columbkille's boundaries, fearing that it was "stealing" his parishioners for Sunday mass and thus reducing the parish's revenue. O'Connell deliberately avoided answering Tracy's protests, but he abandoned his plan to turn the chapel into a separate parish that would permanently divide Tracy's benefice. A more serious confrontation came in 1923. In a stormy interview, O'Connell accused Tracy of "Sulpician intrigue," a code-phrase for collusion with his enemies, but the charge brought a sharp retort from the priest. Tracy figuratively embraced his former colleagues, saying that the Sulpicians were "part and parcel of whatever good there may be in me" and insisting that his conduct had always been honorable.[12] O'Connell and Tracy stared each other down, and neither the allegedly all-powerful general nor the supposedly docile foot soldier blinked.

The consequences of this confrontation were mild. Barely two weeks later, Tracy asked permission to take out a mortgage to build a convent for the nuns who staffed his rapidly expanding grammar school. O'Connell refused, claiming that the parish debt was too high. Undaunted, the pastor went to work, and within a few months he had in hand 70 percent of the proposed building's cost. When he applied again for a mortgage, he secured the cardinal's permission and perhaps even his grudging admiration. In the next decade, O'Connell arranged for Tracy to be honored with elevation to the rank of monsignor.[13] Tracy was temporarily delayed by crossing his superior, but by holding to his position he was ultimately successful. On the face of things, the cardinal was the more potent figure, but in fact his power was circumscribed: he could berate the priest and make his life difficult. In the end, however, O'Connell had to tolerate and find a way of living with him.

Not even in extreme cases could O'Connell exercise what one historian later saw as "swift and total" mastery or unilateral "thought control" over his subjects.[14] The involved history of Father John Chmielinski, pastor of Our Lady of Czestochowa, South Boston, illustrates the cardinal's limitations. The "dean" of the Polish clergy in the Boston area, Chmielinski had recurring difficulties in managing the practical affairs of his parish. The church debt mounted in spite of O'Connell's admonitions, and as early as 1916 the cardinal's office was receiving regular demands from creditors. Worse, Chmielinski had been holding money in trust for several parishioners, including his own housekeeper, promising to pay them back at a rate of 4 percent; in reality he was able to repay neither principal nor interest. Parish accounts were hopelessly confused, and an investigation eventually turned up three different sets of record books, each more confused than the one before. Whatever his other abilities—he built an impressive physical plant for his parish and superintended Polish mission chapels in the West End and in faraway Ipswich—the priest was in over his head in matters of finance.

O'Connell maintained a not entirely laudable patience with Chmielinski for almost twenty years. His repeated scoldings fell on deaf ears. Finally, in 1930, the cardinal delegated two local Irish pastors to bring some order out of the chaos. The recalcitrant Pole refused to cooperate, leading 'O'Connell to make his threats explicit: Chmielinski had ten days to straighten matters out or he would be summarily dismissed as pastor. Unintimidated, the priest blamed all his troubles on the cardinal's "unfriendly attitude," and he even dared O'Connell to act: any attempt to remove him from his benefice, he said, would have to proceed through "canonical channels," a signal that he would fight the move. O'Connell hesitated, twice drawing up the documents necessary to dismiss Chmielinski but twice pulling back from executing them, all the while hoping that his exhortations would be sufficient. He even paid some of the overdue parish bills himself, insisting hollowly that these payments be carried on the parish books as debts owed the archdiocese. Not until the spring of 1935, two full decades after the trouble had started (by which time the parish indebtedness had climbed to an astounding $106,000), was Chmielinski relieved of his responsibilities. Even at that, he was allowed to keep his title of pastor, with another priest appointed as administrator of the parish to oversee its affairs.

Ironically, O'Connell may have been poorly served by the very administrative system he had created. His control of the flow of information often substituted for effective control of the diocese itself. Over the entire period of Chmielinski's troubles, the cardinal was fully informed about the negotiations among the pastor, his parishioners, his creditors, and archdiocesan officials. As usual, O'Connell wanted "to take complete cognizance" of church affairs, but that knowledge did not necessarily lead to anything. All the knowledge in the world could not overcome the caution—and perhaps even cowardice—at the heart of the cardinal's personality, particularly after the collapse of his own credibility that resulted from the troubles with his absconding nephew. The Maryknoll priest James A. Walsh had hit the mark when called upon to explain O'Connell to the apostolic delegate in 1919. The cardinal, Walsh said, had "a positive fear . . . of any one who opposes him. He is known not to be brave, and his boldness is so easily repulsed that even curates do not hesitate to speak their minds plainly when confronted by him."[15] If "even curates" could get their way with the supposedly all-powerful cardinal, how much more easily could independent-minded and financially autonomous pastors resist him.

The archdiocese was something other than the smooth, efficient monolith O'Connell liked to think it.

* * *

Like any other group of people, the diocesan clergy of Boston embodied virtually every human type, from exemplary to eccentric, and in overseeing their affairs O'Connell had to be prepared for many different challenges. While he was watching the Chmielinski drama unfold, he was also getting complaints from lay people about Father Daniel Sheerin, pastor of Saint Joseph's parish in Belmont, a high-toned suburb. The crotchety priest chased children away from the communion rail if they dared to show up at a Sunday mass other than the one he had designated for youngsters. He refused to provide the required baptismal certificates to children receiving their first communion at a nearby private Catholic school rather than in the parish. No more than with Chmielinski, however, was O'Connell moved to swift action, contenting himself with repeated scoldings about the "numerous flagrant breaches of discipline" and "tyrannical action."[16] Several years passed before the difficult priest was removed from Belmont, only to be reassigned to a parish in the equally fashionable town of Hingham.

Complaints from unhappy parishioners also came in concerning Father John T. Creagh, pastor of Saint Aidan's, Brookline, but more telling were the objections of Creagh's own curates. The pastor's behavior toward the junior priests assigned him was nothing short of bizarre, leading one of them to assert that he would need the skill of Dickens to describe rectory life. Creagh was arbitrary and grumpy, and the presence of his sister as housekeeper and a fierce bull terrier named "Major" (each of whom was, apparently, a force to be reckoned with) only made a bad situation worse. One curate after another begged for a transfer after only a short stay, but O'Connell did not venture to move against the apparently crazy pastor. Instead, the cardinal sent Creagh a priest who had been a practicing psychiatrist before entering the seminary.[17]

Reporting regularly to the chancery office, the priest-psychiatrist confirmed that Saint Aidan's was indeed as badly off as the cardinal had been told. The pastor was completely unable "to work in Christian harmony and unity with his fellow priests," and he took special delight in pitting the curates and the people of the parish against one another. For all the trouble he caused, however, Creagh knew better than anyone else how limited the cardinal's options were. In younger days a distinguished canon lawyer who had taught at the Catholic University in Washington, Creagh had written the definitive statement on the rights of the holder of a parish benefice, including effective tenure. If Chmielinski could threaten a fight through "canonical channels," Creagh could be expected to do the same; if the cardinal attempted to remove the man, he was likely to get a long struggle in which there was no guarantee of success. O'Connell was sympathetic toward the younger priests he had necessarily to place in the pastor's path, but the most he could do was to transfer them to more stable places after they had served a period of trial in Brookline. The benefice system put too many obstacles in O'Connell's way, blocking any swift action, even in cases where he may have been more inclined than usual toward boldness.[18] Unaffected, Creagh continued to terrorize Saint Aidan's until his death in 1951.

The cardinal was not without resources, however, in attempting to conform archdiocesan parishes and personnel to his will. His most useful weapons were those that combined the prevailing ideology of a centralized, hierarchical church with his own success at creating an imposing, apparently all-knowing public persona. In many cases he was able to triumph over local centers of power merely by pressing his case, a form of what would later be called "winning through intimidation." When the circumstances were right, he could get around the inherent difficulties of the benefice system by deliberately ignoring them. Once in 1922 and again in 1923, for example, he took advantage of the death of two pastors—one in Lowell, the other in Medford—and swept in to claim funds from the parish treasuries in the absence of an incumbent pastor, to whom the money would otherwise have belonged. The small sums in question (a combined total of not even $500) were less important to him than an assertion that, when a parochial benefice fell vacant, its privileges and revenues devolved upon the archbishop.[19]

Occasionally, he won even larger victories. Scrutiny of annual reports in the late 1920s identified All Saints parish, Roxbury, as a place worth watching. For many years, the pastor, Father Mark J. Sullivan, had been accumulating money in this small, inner-city parish with a view toward building a grammar school. By 1931 the changing demographics of the neighborhood (an increase first of

Jews and then of non-Catholic blacks) had made a school unlikely and unnecessary, and the priest was left with an unusually large surplus of $100,000. O'Connell's chancellor called Sullivan in and flattered him shamelessly: wouldn't he like a transfer to a nicer, suburban parish? No, Sullivan replied, he was happy where he was. Then the chancellor came to the point, as the priest afterward recorded. "The Cardinal knew I could not build a School as the Parish was poor and fast running down," Sullivan noted in a memorandum of record. "It was the Cardinals [sic] wish that I should hand over to him the money." Against some future eventuality, Sullivan managed to get permission to keep $10,000 for the parish, and when he returned home he had a second thought and decided to keep $25,000. This was acceptable to the chancery, and he withdrew $75,000 from his account in the form of a check payable to the "Roman Catholic Archbishop of Boston." As the chancellor had directed, Sullivan carefully left off the phrase "Corporation Sole," a specification that would have destined the money to O'Connell's official rather than his personal capacity.[20]

O'Connell won his battle with Father Sullivan because, for whatever reason, the priest went along with the cardinal's requisition. One can imagine the curt, negative reply the chancellor's demand would have received from a Father Neagle, a Father Tracy, or even a Father Chmielinski. Sullivan was beaten because he allowed himself to be—perhaps because he knew that he could not put his surplus to its original purpose, perhaps because he was overwhelmed by O'Connell and hoped that the cardinal would do the right thing by supporting some other worthy cause with the money. The case was an unusual one, but it nonetheless delineated the circumstance that Father James Walsh had already identified. If, like Tracy or Chmielinski, a pastor held his ground and refused to yield, O'Connell would give up on any attempt to assert his authority. If, like Sullivan, a pastor was intimidated by the central authority figure, O'Connell would press his advantage.

O'Connell understood the constraints of the benefice system so well because he simultaneously shared its privileges. Throughout most of his tenure, the cardinal retained for himself the position of pastor at two large and well-to-do churches, the Cathedral of the Holy Cross and Saint Cecilia's in Boston's Back Bay. A resident priest was given the title of administrator of each parish, but the legal role of pastor was reserved for O'Connell, giving him direct control over the substantial revenues of the two churches. This unusual arrangement was very beneficial. The cathedral parish was a big one, and the steady pace of financial support from its people made it highly lucrative. As pastor, O'Connell received the annual Christmas collection (never less than $4,000), the Easter collection (about half that), and all the "stole fees" (offerings from families in connection with baptisms, weddings, and other services), in addition to the normal pastor's annual salary of $1,000. Saint Cecilia's was even more profitable. Revenues consistently outran parish expenses by a factor approaching three to one, and the treasury constituted a reserve account from which O'Connell could draw up to $40,000 on demand.[21] The cardinal's personal access to these funds underscored the already prosperous state of diocesan finances, though it did nothing to lessen his old habits of mixing personal and official business.

His relationship to these two churches was not merely predatory, and he did take an interest in their affairs. In every diocese, the cathedral is in a special way the bishop's church, and it was there that O'Connell appeared on all great ceremonial occasions. He presided there for the wedding of Governor James Curley's daughter in 1935, though he drew the line at the politician's plans for turning the event into a great political spectacle. He also encouraged special devotions at the cathedral, including novenas, holy hours, and the veneration of a relic of the true cross. At Saint Cecilia's, where many of the rising class of Catholic business and professional people worshipped, he encouraged a high liturgical style, complete with a semiprofessional choir, and he relaxed somewhat the usual discouragement of marriages between Catholics and non-Catholics. He likewise returned to these churches some of the money he took from them, providing college scholarships to deserving parish youth and other direct charity.[22] The structure of church organization in O'Connell's era could sometimes work against him, but it could also work for him. With careful maneuvering he could live within constraints he could not change by force of will alone.

* * *

O'Connell's supervision of the affairs of the women religious of Boston in his later years displayed many of these same dynamics. He could generally secure small, immediate aims in particular cases, but the notion that he completely dominated the work of religious sisters is false. Given their subordinate position in the church of that era—a position they themselves did not challenge—nuns usually possessed neither the ability nor the will to resist the cardinal, but they were not passive agents. When they decided that his plans were not in their best interests, they found ways to deflect him. As with the clergy, O'Connell had to negotiate and compromise.

On the surface, his scrutiny of the sisters and the institutions they managed was as keen-eyed as that given to the other divisions of his "army." The Sisters of Saint Joseph, for example, the principal teaching order which staffed most of the archdiocese's parochial schools, had to provide O'Connell's office with monthly accountings of their funds. The religious community stood in civil law as a separate corporation in which neither the cardinal nor his representative had any standing, but the nuns still cooperated with him in promoting the work of the church. Like most other diocesan agencies, the sisters' convents and schools maintained a healthy solvency throughout this period, though life was never easy for them: many sisters had to take on additional work, such as after-school art and music lessons, to help their orders make ends meet.[23]

Nor was O'Connell reluctant to remind nuns of their religious duties. Like most bishops before him and since, he expected that women, both professed and lay, would play a limited, essentially passive role in church affairs. "He spoke very strongly on the necessity of obedience in the most insignificant things," one somewhat skeptical sister had noted of an O'Connell talk in 1907. "Always do as you are told," he had a priest say for him on another occasion. "If you think it wrong, appeal after having obeyed." He could be deliberately unpredictable with nuns as a means of demonstrating his own authority and catching them off guard. The superior of one convent received a telephone call from the chancery on a Saturday evening, telling her that the cardinal would appear the following Tuesday morning to dedicate a new wing that had been under construction for several years and that outside observers (family members, benefactors, former students) would be barred from the ceremony. "Imagine the confusion caused by the short notice!" the convent's chronicler wrote.[24]

In all respects, communities of sisters were watched as closely as parishes, and they needed the same permissions to spend money or expand their activities. Any sign of apparent extravagance was sure to bring intervention. In 1928 O'Connell discovered that the Daughters of Charity who staffed the Carney Hospital in South Boston provided a nearby house to the priest who was chaplain to both them and the patients. The offending clergyman was swiftly transferred to the far-off town of Holliston, and the sisters were directed to offer his replacement "modest quarters in some part of the Hospital, not certainly a separate house." An officer of the Sisters of Saint Joseph defended her convent's electrical fixtures—"too elaborate," O'Connell had said—by explaining that "thro' the kindness of a friend" she had been able "to get the better kind for less than she would pay for poorer ones."[25] Like the diocesan priests, Boston's sisters were always potential targets for O'Connell's well-developed eye for detail.

Similar, too, was the complex character of the cardinal's relations with his underlings. Although O'Connell could be stern, the sisters did not hesitate to stand up for themselves. The way in which the Daughters of Charity had blocked his attempt in 1908 to muscle his way onto the boards of directors of their hospitals demonstrated that even otherwise demure and obedient nuns were not without resources. In the same way, the superior of the Academy of the Assumption, a private high school in Wellesley, met O'Connell's refusal of permission for a new mortgage with a creative financing plan that involved broad lay support; her project went ahead after a delay of only six months. More seriously, the Sisters of Saint Joseph headed off his plan to have them open a retreat house, a ministry sufficiently far removed from their traditional teaching duties to arouse their considerable opposition. "I want the Sisters to do all kinds of work," one of them quoted him as saying; "some of them don't want to do anything but teach." His wish was not their command, however, and they forced him to back away by reacting to his suggestion with uniform coolness.[26] The "good sisters"—the deliberately patronizing phrase by which hierarchs often referred to nuns—may not have shared in the full counsels of power in the church, but they were neither fools nor incompetents. They did not abandon their own plans and objectives just because their spiritual father told them to.

As with his priests, O'Connell was occasionally reduced to petty sniping with sisters. He reduced the number of sisters from one convent who would be allowed to attend the funeral of a nun from another convent, and in 1924 he angrily abolished the practice of sending out notices requesting prayers on the death of a sister. Funerals should "not be impressive, but simple," he said; "a Religious is a Religious in life and death, and simplicity is the note of the Religious life." As he had done in Maine, he also restricted the ability of sisters to visit their families, thinking in particular that spending a night at home compromised the separation from the world that religious life was then thought to require.[27]

O'Connell's arbitrariness could also turn to more important matters, but even then the sisters were able to outflank him. Renewed scrutiny over the diocesan seminary in 1927—a campaign spurred largely by the move into his new residence on the seminary grounds—led him to write the superior of the Sisters of Notre Dame, who ran Emmanuel College in Boston. He abruptly withdrew the services of several seminary professors who did double duty on the college's faculty. The superior necessarily accepted this disruption, which came in the middle of an academic term, but she reminded him at the same time that the priests in question taught courses that were "among the most important in the College." She asked that other diocesan priests be assigned as replacements, and her request was readily granted. Turning the occasion to advantage, she also secured permission to send several sisters for advanced degrees at nearby non-Catholic universities, including the Massachusetts Institute of Technology. This was a long-sought goal that was part of her plan to get Emmanuel fully accredited and eventually freed from all association with the archdiocese.[28]

Open disputes between O'Connell and women religious were rarer than disputes with his clergy, but when they occurred the results were not always victories for the central authority. The most serious incident was a protracted feud with the Sisters of Saint Joseph in 1934. The community had the right to elect its own superior, and it had always done so, though on one occasion O'Connell had invited himself to the election and may even have helped count the ballots. Faced with the retirement of their leader in 1934, the sisters began the normal procedure for choosing a successor, but before they got very far O'Connell intervened. He chose a sister himself and designated her "coadjutor with the right of succession," an action without foundation in canon law. This brought loud protests from the nuns, who persuaded the apostolic delegate to investigate, an action that both angered and embarrassed the cardinal. O'Connell minimized the problem, blaming the turmoil on "the agitation of a few rather emotional nuns," but he was thwarted nonetheless. The delegate ordered a proper election, which rejected O'Connell's choice in favor of another sister. The well was sufficiently poisoned that he even had to replace his longtime aide, Monsignor Michael Splaine, as chaplain to the sisters, whose confidence he had entirely lost.[29]

The sisters had stood up to him, and in so doing they prevented what they took to be an unwarranted extension of his power. Not even the explicit wish of the cardinal was sufficient to sweep away their independence and to replace it with a world populated by docile automatons. "I have no other purpose in life save to please and to serve you," Monsignor Splaine had told the cardinal on one occasion.[30] In the Boston Catholicism of the early twentieth century, Splaine's servility was the exception rather than the rule.

* * *

As O'Connell's long twilight deepened during the last two decades of his life, both the authority he possessed and the limitations on it became clear. His regime sometimes had an appearance of the authoritarian clarity often attributed to American Catholic bishops of his age. Just before O'Connell's death, his official historians praised him for establishing the proper relationship of the whole diocese to "the direction of the constituted authorities: the Archbishop, in the first place, and, above him, the Holy Father." Expressing the cardinal's hopes as much as his reality, they echoed his own praise for "the Church's wonderful organization," which responded completely to his single-minded direction.[31]

Form is not substance, however; appearance is not reality. A whole range of structural factors stood in the way of O'Connell's efforts to impose a monolithic, dictatorial regime. Catholicism in Boston was too varied to be so easily controlled from the center. The persistent localism of his early years was undiminished, and Boston's Catholics continued to be a diverse lot. They had minds of their own, plans and desires apart from those they shared with him. They had their own individual and collective sense of religious mission and of the work they were about. When their interests came into conflict with his, they could and did resist him. In O'Connell's church central authority was always acknowledged, but it was not always deferred to.

Still, the very image of the all-powerful archbishop had its usefulness. For O'Connell and his flock one of the principal virtues of Catholicism was its certainty, the unhesitating way with which it resolved the problems of doubt and authority. "We are so SURE," a midwestern Catholic woman had written approvingly to the Jesuit magazine, *America*, in 1927; Catholics were a "people who are so certain and set apart."[32] Other denominations lacked that happy conviction, a gift that seemed all the more necessary in a world turned upside down by war and social change. The supposed authority of O'Connell in the Boston church, where everything ran with clockwork precision and the archbishop had the last word on every subject, supported this certitude. Just as the cardinal's easy movement among the non-Catholic elite symbolized that Catholics were now a people of substance, so the notion that he was a leader of limitless capacity symbolized the assurance that came from entrusting matters of religion to the divinely ordained "constituted authorities."

In this way O'Connell's subjects could still recognize and accept him as their leader even when they went against his wishes. He could not always control their thoughts and their actions, but they still looked to him for direction. He embodied their "certain and set apart" church; he represented it and spoke for it. Theirs was a Catholicism that was, in the words of the ancient formula, both militant and triumphant, and they looked to him to symbolize those characteristics. It is to that symbolism that we must finally turn if we are to understand him.

10

MILITANT AND TRIUMPHANT:
MORALISM AND SELF-ASSERTION IN
O'CONNELL'S CATHOLICISM

"THANK GOD WHO GAVE US YOU," Daniel Coakley exclaimed to Cardinal O'Connell in the winter of 1917. Coakley, later called "the knave of Boston" for a political career that embraced bribery, extortion, and disbarment, was no less devout a Catholic for his rascally public life. Nor did his legal problems affect his understanding of social conditions in early twentieth-century Boston. Responding to an editorial in the *Pilot* which had criticized social-climbing "nice Catholics" who abandoned their heritage, Coakley praised O'Connell for giving his people firm guidance. The cardinal had checked "the kow-towing of our own" that was "from a layman's point of view our present chief handicap." Instead, "your militant stand has made kow-towing unpopular," Coakley said. "Your splendid work is infusing into the younger set . . . a pride and a glory in religion. . . . May God give you health and strength to keep up his fight." Heartened by the devout scoundrel's letter, O'Connell found "renewed courage to continue the battle—for it is nothing else. . . . If even [a] few remain steadfast and faithful we shall soon compel peace terms."[1]

As Coakley had accurately perceived, the Catholicism William Henry O'Connell both defined and came to embody was nothing if not militant. O'Connell's was a mental world of "battle" among contending moral and religious forces, and his goal was to win that battle, to "compel peace" on his own terms. In turning a martial bearing toward their surroundings, the Catholics of O'Connell's church had to be prepared for the "storm and trial" he had predicted at his installation. Faint hearts need not apply: "Fierce is the fight/For God and the right," went the lyrics of the "Holy Name Hymn" O'Connell had composed. "When I hear those words sung," he told a group of laymen in 1929, "my heart is thrilled with the thought that I was allowed to send that message out to the Catholic world."[2]

As bearer of this militant message, O'Connell reminded Catholics that they need no longer be apologetic for their religion. They had a duty to assert themselves, especially in what Coakley had called "mixed company." The right which the cardinal had claimed to press the church's position in political questions applied equally in other areas. The high state of culture to which immigrant Catholics could lay claim gave them a natural superiority over declining, unchurched Protestants. Supremely self-confident, O'Connell never doubted that there was a clearly identifiable Catholic position on everything or that he himself could and should state that position with "manly firmness." The modern world was too often uncertain and out of control, and it needed "firm, intellectual and high moral leadership," a Boston newspaper argued in 1932; O'Connell, "strong and impressive," provided just that. He was "a veritable Christian Rock of Gibraltar," another journal said, in a "transient age of muddled thinking and uncertain values."[3]

If his church was militant, however, it likewise embodied the other part of the traditional couplet: it was triumphant. The words had originally been used to distinguish believers on earth (called "the church militant" by the theological textbooks) from the saints in heaven ("the church triumphant"), but a more literal meaning was also apt. The very self-assurance of a militant Catholicism would, O'Connell thought, guarantee its success. The vigor with which he enunciated Catholicism's message made his church essential in a distracted, seemingly irreligious world. The unrelenting antiworldliness and antimodernism of traditional Catholic belief would certainly win out; by being so rigorously countercultural, Catholicism would save culture. In politics, the triumph was already under way: "the city where a century ago he [i.e., the immigrant Catholic] came unwanted he has made his own," O'Connell proclaimed in his 1908 centennial sermon. Despite the slowness of genuine social change, the final victory seemed palpably close. One priest identified the cardinal as "the providential leader of [his] people . . . from out of their remarkably promising youth into their glorious maturity." No lionizing of him was too much. Another suggested erecting "a heroic bronze statue of Your Eminence . . . on Copley Square Green, . . . a massive figure standing, facing Eastward."

Such a monument would "exalt and exult." O'Connell demurely rejected this proposal, but he still rejoiced in his famous epigram: Catholics had not only arrived, they remained. The cardinal was the prophet of this triumph, which would bring "a full realization" of the "proper destiny" of the Catholic church in America.[4]

O'Connell may not have been entirely successful either as an administrator or as an influential figure within the hierarchy. In those aspects of his career, limitation rather than triumph was the hallmark. Still, he retained what a journalist had correctly identified as "impact" because he never lost his skill at public drama, at creating a symbolic role for himself in personifying the church of his age. The years of fending off his ecclesiastical enemies and the priests and nuns disposed to go their own way had not diminished his capacity to arrange a successful and telling spectacle. He could still keep himself in the public eye as the apparently inevitable emblem for his church. Appropriately enough for a Catholic prelate, he knew the emotional power of liturgy, of dramatization and ceremony. The troubles of his reign notwithstanding, he lost few opportunities to assert the Catholic sense of being "so certain and set apart."

* * *

O'Connell's later years offered a succession of occasions for him to present himself as the paragon of this militant and triumphant Catholicism. He was in the public eye to the very end, his celebrity undiminished by the scandal and opposition that had reduced his impact in internal church affairs to virtually nothing. Every anniversary was transformed into a public event in which he and his church were made to seem synonymous.

In May 1926, for example, he observed his twenty-fifth year as a bishop. A round of masses and receptions was arranged, each fully covered by the local and national press; during one of them he was tendered the Grand Cross of the Crown of Italy, a sign of the coming rapprochement between the Vatican and the Italian government. With an eye toward history, the cardinal issued a thin autobiographical volume of *Reminiscences of Twenty-Five Years*, containing character sketches of famous people he had known or, perhaps more to the point, who had known him. Encouraging the celebration of his personality, he also issued a collection of "Aphorisms of His Eminence." Some of these had explicitly religious content—"A bishop is shepherd of even the black sheep"—but most expressed a simple, if sometimes peculiar, folk wisdom—"A flying fish is soon back in the water."[5] O'Connell was making himself the touchstone for local Catholics: like Chairman Mao in another place and time, he even provided them with a handy set of proverbs for study and reflection.

Five years later, in the spring of 1931, another personal achievement became a public event. This time it was the fiftieth anniversary of O'Connell's graduation from Boston College, and the school spared no flourish, rhetorical or otherwise, for the man who justly claimed to be its most distinguished living alumnus. Fearing that a mere honorary doctorate might be too common for him, the Jesuits of his alma mater concocted a new distinction and proclaimed the cardinal a "Patron of the Liberal Arts." The citation read at commencement honored him as "an ecclesiastical statesman," and it noted the "halo on halo encircling his reverend brow," enumerating his supposed accomplishments as a scholar, author, orator, musician, and administrator. So shameless was the glorification that one graduating senior remarked tartly that the newspaper accounts of the day's proceedings could only be headlined: "Cardinal's Buttocks Bandaged after Inspiring Ceremony."[6]

It was the golden jubilee in 1934 of O'Connell's priestly ordination, however, that provided the apotheosis. A full weekend of events began on Friday, June 8, with a high mass featuring a letter of greeting from Pope Pius XI, together with nine expressions of loyalty, each delivered in a different language representing every ethnic group in the archdiocese. Saturday was "children's day," with 25,000 parochial school pupils gathering at Boston College to honor their cardinal. On Sunday, June 10, a "civic ceremony" packed Fenway Park, normally the home of the city's American League baseball team, as public officials high and low praised O'Connell at length. A "national celebration" in Washington followed that November, complete with written congratulations from President Roosevelt and the governors of the forty-eight states. For the occasion a Boston priest issued a digested version of the cardinal's multivolume speeches, expressing a belief in "the definitive quality of Cardinal O'Connell's messages" and the hope that his edition would instill in readers "the longing to pursue further the study of Cardinal O'Connell."[7]

The phrase is startling, perhaps even idolatrous. The priest wanted to encourage not the study of the Bible or the catechism, not papal teaching or even Saint Thomas Aquinas. Rather, it was "the study of Cardinal O'Connell" that was necessary because he was "definitive." The cult of personality around the man was completed with the concurrent release of O'Connell's second and more extensive autobiography, his *Recollections of Seventy Years*, praised by no less an authority than the *New York Times* for "great forthrightness" and its "vivid and vigorous pen." To have stood so firmly for what he believed was, another priest commented, "in the America of our day . . . to be a personality, which the Cardinal most especially is. . . . It is impossible to be unaffected by him."[8]

Allowing for the exaggeration common during such celebrations, O'Connell's stature derived in some measure simply from his having lived as long as he had. By the early 1930s he had outlasted friend and foe alike. Cardinal DeLai, the man who had saved him from dismissal, died in 1928, and his longtime friend Merry del Val died two years later. Bishop Louis Walsh went to his reward in 1924, and O'Connell's local antagonist, Father John Mullen, did the same in 1927. O'Connell began to shed some of his always-substantial frame, but his health remained generally good into his eighth decade. He suffered from the occasional cold and a mild form of diabetes; failing sight in one eye was checked by cataract surgery in 1937, but disease left him otherwise untouched.

Venerable old age alone, however, could not account for his persistence as a symbol and spokesman for his church. Even in his advancing years, he maintained a schedule and a visibility that commanded attention. He was still the man whom the public, Catholic and non-Catholic alike, thought of when they thought of a Catholic leader. He still went about his duties in an inexorably public way, and the populace was by now well trained to expect that the head of Boston's Catholic church would be seen prominently as he fulfilled the demands of his office. Religious ceremonies of all kinds (confirmations, dedications, ordinations, parish anniversaries) combined with civic events (visiting dignitaries, support for worthwhile public causes) to keep him always in the public eye.

As he had been in earlier days, he remained an ardent traveler. Between 1920 and 1940 he traveled outside the United States, often for months at a time, at least once in every year except 1921, the time of his maximum vulnerability after James O'Connell's ouster. His itineraries took him to Rome eight times in that period, including a

1939 trip for the only papal election that he managed to make on time. His globe-trotting also included a vacation in England in 1923, a pilgrimage to the Holy Land the following year, and an appearance at a eucharistic congress in Dublin in 1932. The percentage of his time spent away from home was lower in Boston than it had been in Portland: he was absent for at least 81 (19 percent) of the 428 months of his tenure as archbishop. (His absentee rate in Portland had been 24 percent.) The comings and goings meant that several times each year "Gangplank Bill" would appear, surrounded by reporters and well-wishers who were either sending him off or welcoming him home. These "photo opportunities" gave him the chance to comment on current events, thereby reinforcing his role as the preeminent Catholic spokesman.

Sometimes his travels raised eyebrows and in 1931 O'Connell found himself defending his annual January-through-March vacation in the Bahamas to the apostolic delegate. Critics complained that a churchman should not be vacationing in the tropics while his flock suffered the ravages of a depression-era economy, but O'Connell justified the habit on personal and religious grounds. He had acquired a decaying property in the islands, he said, and had renovated it as a winter home. "Instead of a castle in Bermuda," as some people thought it, O'Connell wrote defensively, "the story ought to be entitled a 'shack in Nassau.'" Yes, the house let him escape the harsh New England winter, but he was also supporting a group of missionary nuns there; he would eventually donate the property, known as the Hermitage, to the local bishop. When the delegate expressed satisfaction with this explanation of "the Romance of the Shack," O'Connell observed that "I am sure the archives of the Delegation have plenty of other Romances," probably a reference to the fat dossier about himself. "I only wish I could rest my eyes on them," he concluded wistfully.[9]

Foreign travel reinforced O'Connell's plausibility as a cosmopolitan and an expert on international affairs, and in commenting on such matters he consistently articulated an aggressively Catholic position. Whenever and wherever the church was under attack, he was quick to defend it. The continuing revolution in Mexico, overtly anticlerical in its attempts to redistribute church land to the peasants, caused him special concern throughout the 1920s. Lurid tales of priests assassinated and nuns violated were circulating widely in the

United States, and the cardinal joined the chorus in decrying "Mexico's bloody altars." In the next decade, O'Connell and most other American Catholics would support Francisco Franco and his fascist forces in the Spanish Civil War, affirming that "El Caudillo" was "fighting for Christian civilization."[10]

Understandably, it was Ireland that interested O'Connell most, as the island of his parents emerged from colonialism into nationhood in the years following the First World War. "Ireland's cause is the cause of freedom everywhere," he wrote encouragingly to a rally supporting independence. Irish leaders touring America were eager to be seen with him, and at various times he received John Redmond, longtime head of the Home Rule party, and Eamon De Valera, an alumnus of the Easter uprising of 1916 who would eventually become president of the Irish republic. He presided at a memorial mass for the Lord Mayor of Cork, Terence McSwiney, who died after a long political hunger strike. Most visibly of all, O'Connell delivered a speech entitled "Ireland: One and Indivisible" before 12,000 Irish American firebrands in New York's Madison Square Garden in December 1918. "There is no legitimate length, no limit within Christian law, to which I and every prelate and priest of America should not be glad and happy to go," the cardinal told the cheering audience, "when the cry of the long-suffering children of the Gael comes to us."[11]

This rousing speech served several purposes and, as usual with Irish politics, had several layers of meaning. It certainly helped cement O'Connell's position as the leading Irish Catholic churchman in America. Coming only a month after the armistice that ended the Great War, it also signaled that he and other bishops were ready to take the brakes off American agitation on the Irish question, suspended for the sake of solidarity during the conflict. That prospect troubled Woodrow Wilson, who took a dour, Presbyterian view of Catholics under the best of circumstances, and his advisers, who feared that O'Connell might jeopardize Irish-American, Democratic support for the League of Nations. Wilson took the threat seriously enough to write a deliberately cordial letter to Cardinal Gibbons, hoping to head off hierarchical attacks on his pet project.[12]

At the same time, O'Connell's appearance in New York was significant in the realm of ecclesiastical politics. The archbishop's seat there was vacant at the time, Cardinal John Farley having died the previous September. A rumor was then making the rounds that O'Connell would be transferred from Boston to the larger, even more visible diocese. He never commented on this possibility, though he seems to have been genuinely interested; he wrote an overanxious letter to the papal secretary of state describing the kind of leader Catholic New York needed, a description that had a familiar ring to it. Patrick Hayes, New York's auxiliary bishop and the likely local candidate for the job, chafed at having to welcome a rival, and he even attempted to disinvite O'Connell after the arrangements had been made. Other New Yorkers were similarly wary: Monsignor John Dunn, the archdiocesan chancellor who would a few months later be hiring detectives to tail his Boston counterpart, pronounced himself "much disappointed in the address" at the rally. O'Connell's "presence [was] impressive as an elephant is impressive, but beyond that there is nothing to be said." Only intense lobbying by the planning committee secured O'Connell's appearance at Madison Square Garden, and the event ultimately turned out happily for all concerned: the Irish nationalists got their endorsement from the hierarchy; O'Connell got the public glory for speaking out; and Hayes was made archbishop of New York two months later.[13]

O'Connell was smart enough to balance public harangues about Ireland with private diplomacy. Only a month before the Madison Square Garden speech he transmitted a personal message to the British embassy in Washington, warning (in the ambassador's paraphrase) that "as [the] principle of self-determination of peoples has been recognized by all, England could not refuse it to Ireland." The ambassador was impressed, explaining to the Foreign Office at home that O'Connell was the "dominating figure among Irish Americans and his influence is recognised." The cardinal would continue to speak out on the subject, but he also sent word to the British government that it could take what he said with a grain of salt. He "desires to hold out the olive branch," the embassy concluded. "He desires it to be understood . . . that he wishes no ill to England and that he is forced to use vigorous language in order to retain control of the forces he is attempting to lead."[14] The clever maneuvering indicated that O'Connell had a sophisticated understanding of his role as a public man. As the influential, "dominating figure" he was, there were certain things he had to say if he were to "retain control of the forces he is attempting to lead." That did not preclude the possibility that his private opinions might be more tractable.

More often, events closer to home brought forth O'Connell's vigorous articulation of "the true Catholic standpoint." In particular, he permitted no slight of his church to pass without correction. Whether in the form of the "gratuitous insult" he thought the 1917 anti-aid amendment to be, or the snide implications of "holier-than-thou" Protestants seeking to steal Catholic immigrants, he was always swift in rebuttal. "His Catholicism has always been militant," one mildly hostile journalist observed. "Few attacks, direct or implied, on his faith or his Church has he permitted to pass unchallenged. He has struck back, not deftly [or] politely, but with hammering blows." A biographer concurred, praising O'Connell for the "courage to state the Church's doctrine on many a question . . . where this was not done, at least so frequently and confidently, before."[15]

Not even unconscious slurs could pass. In early 1918 he reacted sharply to an "objectionable" reference to the pope in a publication of the American Red Cross. The humanitarian organization's magazine had published a poem by the aging Rudyard Kipling which seemed to lump Benedict XV with other "swithering neutrals" uninterested in supporting civilization by fighting the kaiser. O'Connell protested the poem to the New England director of the Red Cross, and when the man's private apology seemed tepid, O'Connell went public. He could understand Kipling's use of the phrase, the cardinal said, since this was not the first time that the poet's "abnormality has led him to prostitute a noble gift to a base purpose." Finding "such stuff in a Red Cross magazine" was more disturbing. Though further apologies finally pacified the matter, the war offered other examples of perceived covert anti-Catholicism, including a proposal to conserve food by declaring meatless Tuesdays. O'Connell objected. Catholics would go without meat twice each week because of traditional Friday abstinence, thus requiring more of a sacrifice from them than their fellow citizens. "It seems the same old story," he complained to Cardinal Gibbons; "the plans seem to be to get as much from us as possible, to give nothing in return." The division of the world into "us" and "them" was by this time instinctual, and O'Connell's flock praised him for being, as his official historians phrased it, "absolutely fearless when there is a question of principle or the interests of the Church."[16]

* * *

Catholic sensitivity turned to self-assertion under O'Connell's leadership, a transition most clearly evident when the cardinal took on the powerful institutions of the local Yankee elite. He used his formidable persona to make the Catholic presence felt in areas where it had been unaccustomed to operating, infusing what "Darlin' Dan" Coakley had called "a pride and a glory in religion." A writer planning a book on changes in Boston during the previous century, for instance, was told by the cardinal's office that his plan to include a photograph of O'Connell was not enough. A full biography was needed, one that did not slight "in any haphazard way or give a meagre description of so great a moral force." Similarly, the cardinal tried to be helpful when the director of the city's staid Museum of Fine Arts sought assistance in broadening its membership. "I have an idea in mind," the cardinal proposed coyly, "which I honestly— though of course not in any personal sense—feel would do a great deal towards attracting Catholics to the Museum." The idea was to hang a likeness of O'Connell himself, thereby including his image among society portraits by John Singer Sargent and James Whistler. The director politely wiggled off this hook, settling instead for free advertising in the *Pilot*. His demurrer did nothing, however, to diminish O'Connell's desire to make sure that Brahmin Boston knew Catholics were a force to be reckoned with.[17]

In dealing with another of the city's venerable institutions, the Boston Public Library, O'Connell adopted a similarly aggressive stance. In 1916 he approved the library's plan to include a pastor from Jamaica Plain on its board of trustees, but he also gave the priest explicit instructions. Another trustee was "reported to be continually taking a stand opposed to everything Catholic," the priest was informed; "it will be your duty, therefore, to keep a close watch over him." Here as elsewhere, the cardinal wanted a kind of enlightened self-interest: "while you are a Trustee, it will always be your duty to be fair and . . . this includes fairness to Catholics and their interests."[18]

In 1932 O'Connell got the chance to put this policy into effect himself when his old nemesis, Mayor Curley, appointed him to what was by then a "Catholic seat" on the library's board. O'Connell took these duties seriously, attending the fortnightly trustee meetings and even serving a term as the board's chairman. More critical to his plans for Catholic self-assertion, he also saw to it that the library and all its branches were well supplied with books promoting "fairness to Catholics and their interests," beginning of course with a complete set of his own writings. He resigned as a trustee after only four years, but the pattern had already been set: through constantly watchful involvement in the wider world, a world formerly dominated by non-Catholics, his church would secure and defend its rightful place. "We have passed the day, and passed forever, when we quietly stole unnoticed to our humble little chapel and were grateful for being ignored," he had written as a younger man. Now, the church's voice "must be heard and felt."[19]

O'Connell's attitude toward the quintessential establishment institution, Harvard University, was more ambiguous. The presence of Catholics there was a welcome enough sign, but the lure of acceptance was counterbalanced with hesitation. O'Connell remembered a time at the turn of the century when Catholics were unwelcome at America's oldest university: in the 1890s graduates of Jesuit schools like Boston College and Holy Cross were required to take remedial courses before enrolling in Harvard's professional schools. He knew of experiences like that of the young Joseph P. Kennedy (class of 1912), who was passed over for membership in Harvard's exclusive clubs because of his religion. Slights of this kind galled O'Connell and he resolved to keep an eye on the place. He never quite got over the idea that Harvard was "unreligious," advising the Belgian cardinal Desiré Mercier (who received an honorary degree in 1919 for his heroism during World War I) to block one of his seminary professors from accepting a position in the philosophy department there. "Participation in the teaching of Harvard would certainly be the occasion of *much more harm* than good," O'Connell warned.[20]

He sometimes enjoyed good personal relations with individuals at Harvard, but he could also bite. He wrote a scathing, anonymous review of the autobiography of Harvard's treasurer (and a leader of Boston society), Charles Francis Adams, Jr., in 1916, calling it "a dreary story of utter failure." O'Connell remained deeply suspicious of the school, and he worried over whether Catholics should have anything to do with it. In 1930, he commissioned Father Augustine

Hickey, who was the pastor of Saint Paul's parish, Cambridge, and the longtime superintendent of the archdiocesan school system, to investigate. The results were not encouraging. Harvard was "utterly indifferent to religion and maintains an attitude by which religious faith and religious principles are utterly ignored," Hickey said. The history department was "fairly sympathetic" to Catholic achievement in the Middle Ages, but in other disciplines the faculty was hopeless. The philosophy department treated "every school [of thought] except Scholasticism," though the damage was minimal since so few students of any religion studied philosophy. Confirming the cardinal's worst fears, Hickey concluded that Catholic students with a solid grounding in their faith might survive Harvard, but weaker Catholics, particularly the offspring of mixed marriages with Protestants, would be "confirmed in their indifference and laxity."[21]

Father Hickey had reaffirmed what O'Connell feared all along. Central for both of them was the conviction that, because Harvard lacked the true faith, it lacked a true purpose. The university had "just missed the real thing," O'Connell had said at the dedication of Saint Paul's in October 1924; "they have missed the way because they have cut off the light" which came from the Roman church. Harvard had "a certain usefulness," he said with studied condescension, and it did "without doubt a very large amount of good in a civic way." It was the Catholic church, however, not the famous school, that possessed "the whole truth, the real truth, the fundamental truth."[22] Even the symbolism of the contrast made this clear: Saint Paul's, which was located just outside the Harvard Yard, was built with a campanile that towered over the university's low brick buildings. The cardinal himself accepted an honorary degree from Harvard in 1937, an honor long delayed by the often mutual hostility.

O'Connell's concern for Catholics at Harvard was not merely that they would lose their faith. He was also worried that they would lose their docility and deference to church authority. He approved of higher education for young Catholics—though he thought it best accomplished in Catholic schools—just as he was eager to promote other forms of advancement. Producing Catholic leaders for society at large was an important goal, but it had to be achieved carefully, especially since it now seemed within reach. "To lead one must first learn to obey," he warned: to obey the laws of God as set forth by His church. The realization that Catholics were now "making it" meant that even greater diligence was needed, lest in the midst of newfound prosperity they lose touch with the source of their strength, that "great principle of Catholic life—obedience."[23] Success was a mixed blessing.

O'Connell's militant Catholicism was fueled by a fear that, as Catholics put the world of their immigrant parents behind them, they put loyalty to their church at risk. He fretted about "a certain coterie of Catholics" who were "influenced more by [secular] Social Service ideals than by Catholic zeal" in supporting charitable programs. Coakley had put his finger on the problem by identifying what amounted to Catholic fifth-columnists, "those who have gotten a few dollars together" and desired "to be classed as 'a bit different from the rest'." Catholics like that were too readily impressed by their own progress, O'Connell thought, and they had to be reminded not to let success go to their heads. "My dear girls, do not sell your birthright," he told the graduates of Emmanuel College in 1927. "Do not let your heads be turned by money. . . . Money can do nothing for you but spoil you."[24]

Safely out of poverty himself, O'Connell could afford to romanticize it. "Some Catholics had much better remained poor," he told the men of the Saint Vincent de Paul Society in 1926: "much better for their own lives, for their prospects of Heaven, for their own characters." Advancement too often brought spiritual decay, leading otherwise sensible children of the faith into "the silliest kind of vanity." Some in the rising Catholic middle class were too ready to mimic their Protestant neighbors, failing in their duty to pass on solid religious values to the next generation. Addressing the Guild of the Infant Saviour, a group of wealthy Catholic women who supported archdiocesan charities, the cardinal mocked such social pretensions as finishing schools for girls. "Oh, yes, it is a Finishing School," he said sarcastically; "it finishes the child and sends her on her way to foolish snobbery, removing her from the good influences of her Catholic associates." In 1923 he had made the same point to the Boston College alumni association, itself a group of Catholics on the way up. "Far from being so eager, as some deluded people imagine we are," that Catholics rise in society, he said in a sermon on the "true" Christian life, "I, for my part, can frankly say . . . that I feel no such desire." The loss of "obedience to Holy Mother Church" was too great a risk.[25]

As usual, O'Connell exempted himself and his own family from the strictures he enjoined on others. He had given his brother Edward a job as superintendent of a large Catholic cemetery in the suburbs, and he paid for the education of Edward's daughters at the finest Catholic colleges, Emmanuel in Boston and Manhattanville in New York. Still, he thought himself immune from temptation. Success would not go to his head. Wealth, houses at the shore, and world travel were risky for other second-generation immigrants, but not for him. Money would spoil other Catholics, but it would leave him unaffected. He could "accept the friendship of the men who ruled society, created its opinions, and took its praise or blame with Jovian unconcern."[26] That characterization belonged to a local novelist, describing a character modeled on O'Connell, but it applied to the real man as much as to the fictional one. Concern was appropriate for lesser men, but "Jovian unconcern" was rightfully his.

The best Catholics were thus not achievers according to the criteria of this world. Rather, another set of standards applied, standards which the cardinal thought himself uniquely qualified to set. The truly successful were those who, almost in spite of success, remained loyal to a rigorous Catholic outlook, an outlook most clearly defined by a particular moral vision. It was this moral vision, designedly opposed to so much that seemed characteristic of the modern world, that came to exemplify the Catholicism of O'Connell and his generation.

* * *

The boundary line between religion and morality is a thin one; believers, particularly in America, have tended to the opinion that religious faith is genuine only to the extent that it is reflected in an upright life. The "purgative way" of nineteenth-century immigrant spirituality, of which Cardinal O'Connell was a product, emphasized asceticism and self-control as the heart of the Christian life.[27] That the cardinal should have expended so much effort in articulating a code of morality is thus understandable. Beyond that, however, he seems to have blurred the distinction between religion and morality, obscuring in the process his own personal religious sensibilities. What, in fact, did he believe?

Like many Catholics of his time, clerical and lay, O'Connell took for granted the basic spiritual assumptions in a way that seems alien to a more skeptical generation. His religion operated within a fixed world in which the terms of discussion were not open to debate. The need to personalize belief or to decide whether one actually believed was absent. His real faith was in the institutional church: it was the authentic transmitter of religion, the means of salvation. The church was, after all, guaranteed infallibility by a divinely appointed leader and a teaching hierarchy of which he himself was a part. He did not doubt the sureness of that institution, but even so the absence of overtly religious content in his writings is conspicuous.

His sermons, compiled regularly into little red volumes that were distributed to rectories around the archdiocese, focused more on church-related subjects rather than on spiritual ones. The nature of the priesthood, the role of nuns, support for foreign missions and charitable causes were more common themes than the nature of God, the lordship of Jesus, or the example of the saints. He some-times treated such distinctively Catholic subjects as devotion to the Virgin, the doctrines of purgatory and the Eucharist, and the newly created feast of Christ the King. His preaching on these topics was largely formulaic, however, more an echo of papal pronouncements than a statement of personal conviction. His 1926 collection of aphorisms was even more remarkable for its lack of religious content. In the 109 proverbs, God is mentioned only twice, the saints three times, and sin and hell twice; prayer, faith, and Christian love get one reference each.[28]

This-worldly morality rather than other-worldly religion pre-occupied the cardinal, and it was in morality that the firmness and rigor of his Catholicism were most clearly expressed. The Puritan may well have passed, but Catholics were ready to take up where the old religion had left off in guarding public morals. "Although he might take exceptions to the remark," one reporter wrote approv-ingly in 1936, "it is obvious that Cardinal O'Connell stands . . . [for] Catholic puritanism." Propriety was always important, even in little things. As early as his tenure in Portland he had forbidden parish baseball and football teams to bear the designation "Holy Name" on their jerseys, saying that "this is no honor to the Holy Name what-ever, and is rather a disgrace to it and everything Catholic." In later years he remained alert to unseemliness. Pastors were instructed to "avoid the words Whist and Dance" when advertising such events "and to call the party merely a Reunion. . . . No mention should be made of card playing," and wheels of chance at charity bazaars were "to be covered when His Eminence is present."[29]

As time went on, broader questions of public morality concerned him, including the "indecent" books, plays, and motion pictures that O'Connell saw flooding the market. Here was a clear-cut example of militant Catholicism taking the place of a supposedly declining Protestantism as the defender of society and its values. Boston's Yankee elite had organized a Watch and Ward Society in the 1870s to keep an eye on drama and literature, closing objectionable productions and banning offending books. O'Connell's conviction that Yankee power was in retreat across the board led him to the conclusion that he and his church had to fill the void. In fact, the Watch and Ward Society, headed by the indomitable Godfrey Lowell Cabot (whose family, the famous ditty asserted, spoke "only to God"), remained active throughout O'Connell's tenure, raiding the burlesque houses that clustered in the city's Scollay Square district.[30] Notwithstanding the society's efforts, O'Connell's belief that Catholics had to assume larger societal responsibilities gave those crusades a distinctly Catholic character. "Banned in Boston" had not implied Catholic action before O'Connell; with him, the phrase acquired new religious meaning.

"Immoral literature . . . gluts the bookshelves," the cardinal complained, presenting "dangers of corruption to the growing generation." He was himself a man of more classical taste in books. He answered a newspaper's inquiry about the ten titles he would choose if stranded on a desert island with selections that included Horace, Saint Augustine, and Dante; the most risqué item on the list was the Arabian Nights. Modern authors did not measure up. "It is about time someone called his bluff," O'Connell wrote the polemical English apologist Hilaire Belloc, after Belloc had denounced H. G. Wells, "and especially someone like yourself who makes jellyfish out of his pompous nonsense. More power to you!" Similarly, he approved the public denunciation made by his associate, Monsignor Michael Splaine, of George Bernard Shaw, "a writer of works that are most offensive." Elsewhere in Catholic America, Shaw might pass without comment, Splaine said, but not in Boston: "Boston is orthodox, and not only orthodox but honest and fearless. That is why Boston has succeeded."[31]

The theater too brought the cardinal's "honest and fearless" disapproval. He joined other community leaders in 1923 in protesting a production of Richard Strauss's opera *Salome* in the interest of maintaining "decent moral standards." He was always deeply suspicious of the burgeoning film industry, even though his friend, the ambitious Joe Kennedy, was dabbling in it and carrying on a romantic affair with one of its goddesses, Gloria Swanson. O'Connell supported formation of a national Legion of Decency that policed movies for their morally objectionable content. He also lost few opportunities to denounce the "unutterably filthy plots and their unspeakably brazen presentation" which presented "the most subtle and most menacing of present dangers." Unsuspecting and easily influenced Catholics—especially women, he thought—were duped into accepting movie stars "as models, foolishly and slavishly aping their dress and their mannerisms," all to bad effect. "Everyone knows what Hollywood is," he said; "it is the scandal of the world."[32]

The fear that women were particularly susceptible to bad example led O'Connell's antimodernism into what was, even for his own time, an old-fashioned suspicion of "sinister feminism." Women were "becoming masculine," he feared, "and the men are becoming effeminate," a strong statement for a man who had been accused of homosexuality. He demanded modesty in dress, and he warned women against approaching the communion rail with "face painted and lips incarnadined." He was absolutely inflexible on such matters, and his young nieces always scurried to remove their makeup when they saw "Uncle Cardinal's" car pulling up to their house for a surprise visit. They risked his disapproval if he found them wearing anything that resembled "the kind of dress that many years ago would have been hissed off the stage as indecent."[33] Such sentiments cannot be judged against the opinions of a later period, but even at that they represent an extreme position. That they were a significant part of the Catholic critique of a changing world, however, demonstrates how comprehensive that critique was, both for the cardinal himself and for his people.

Other forms of popular amusement presented similar hidden dangers. The cardinal opposed Sunday baseball until 1928 because "the noise made in rooting" seemed a form of sabbath-breaking, and he worried generally about the public celebration of athletics. The nun in charge of Regis College, a women's school in the suburban town of Weston, received a sharp rebuke in 1931 when a newspaper ran a photograph of two students playing softball. "It does not become a student of a Girls' Catholic College to have the pictures of such games appear in the daily newspapers," O'Connell's secretary wrote. "His Eminence . . . hopes he will never see such a picture again." This offense was probably greater in the cardinal's eyes because the athletes were girls rather than boys, but Catholic propriety extended to both genders. Until a late date, O'Connell remained suspicious of the Boy Scouts because they seemed inclined toward "nature worship" and too preoccupied with "naiads and dryads."[34]

O'Connell's most widely publicized venture into the supposed immorality of public entertainment was his attack in 1932 on crooners and crooning. Addressing the men of the Holy Name Society (a popular parish organization, dedicated to stamping out swearing through devotion to the name of Jesus), the cardinal lashed out against this "degenerate form of singing," this "bleating and whining, with disgusting words which may prove a sexual influence." He feared the impact of "this immoral slush" on young people, and he denounced it as "a sensuous, luxurious sort of paganism." Newspapers around the country picked up the story, and most of them editorialized in support of the cardinal. Several of the best known crooners, including Rudy Vallee, Bing Crosby, and Russ Columbo, even took to the airwaves to deny that they were the kind of singers O'Connell had been talking about.[35]

The cardinal could claim expertise in this because he was something of a musician himself. He was reasonably accomplished at the piano, once engaging in a good-humored keyboard "duel" with the journalist William Allen White when they were passengers together on a cruise ship: the two challenged each other to play and sing a succession of songs to the delight of onlookers. O'Connell composed a number of hymns, eventually compiled into a *Holy Cross Hymnal*, which was used throughout the archdiocese. The lyrics presented a characteristically martial image. "An army of youth, flying the banners of truth," went the words to his hymn for the Catholic Youth Organization, "we are fighting for Christ the Lord." He had very clear opinions on what constituted good music, refusing permission for concerts on the carillon at the church of Our Lady of Good Voyage, Gloucester, if they included anything inappropriate: "no love songs or drinking songs or music of that order," he wrote across the pastor's request for approval of the program. O'Connell had legitimate standing to comment on popular musical taste, but even if he were unmusical his opinion of the crooners would still have been widely reported and approved.[36]

* * *

To modern sensibilities, O'Connell's moralism may seem quaint. To make fun of it, however, is to miss its significance. He was stating his views with such force and clarity because he saw these little things as part of a larger, more important whole. The modern world was in decline, he thought, and it was up to him and his church to reverse that trend. "Not so very long ago life was simpler," he told a group of lay women in 1925, "and it was better for everybody." Now, with other institutions collapsing, Catholicism had the duty to uphold standards under attack everywhere else. "Whither is the world going?" he asked. "When you stop for a minute and think of your own life amid the atmosphere of to-day, you begin to wonder. Jazz, dances, card-playing, one continuous whirl of so-called pleasure" presented constant dangers.[37]

The only antidote was the unflinching faith and certainty that the Catholic church offered. The church alone held fast to established values and traditional understandings: the divinely controlled nature of the universe; the centrality of formal religion; the reality of the spiritual world and the responsibility of humans not to reach into the realm of God; the docile acceptance of authority. In an age of questioning, while other denominations might abandon those fixed points of reference, Catholicism would remain firm. It would "oppose a bulwark against the disintegrating and destructive tendencies that are running riot." The church alone would defend "objective reality, . . . an immutable code of morals," and belief in "God's fatherly governance of the world."[38] In church-related matters, O'Connell had long since defined himself as the upholder of centralized, Roman authority. Articulating a clear code of behavior for his people, one that derived from that very authority, was simply a logical extension of his understanding of the role the church was supposed to play. Moralism and self-assertion at home were as inevitable for him as *Romanità* in the church universal.

Jazz, card-playing, and movie stars were not the only destructive aspects of modern life that needed the opposing bulwark of the church. More substantial matters were also at stake. Skepticism had muddied the intellectual waters, and modern science was spinning out of control. The desire to combat those trends led O'Connell into scornful denunciations of anything that smacked of modernism. When scholars and even some Protestant ministers (including William Lawrence, the Episcopal bishop of Massachusetts) questioned the historical validity of the virgin birth, for example, O'Connell retorted that to refuse to accept the doctrine was "to reject the whole scheme of Christianity." Though he never expressed a public opinion on the famous "monkey trial" in Tennessee in 1925—a proceeding in which the long-dead Charles Darwin seemed as much on trial as the young instructor who taught his theories—O'Connell did wonder aloud about "the grotesque gullibility of so-called scientists" who mounted an exhibit on human evolution. That "hodge-podge of miscellaneous bones, originally strangers to each other," he said, deserved no respect. Like his contemporaries among American evangelical Protestants, O'Connell found in the reassertion of traditional religion a remedy for modern ills. By almost any standard, a Roman Catholic prelate like O'Connell and a fundamentalist like William Jennings Bryan (the prosecuting attorney in the Tennesee case) seemed poles apart. In fact, they shared a broad common ground in combating the disintegration of standards with a firm sense of "objective reality" and "an immutable code of morals."[39]

O'Connell's opposition to the modern outlook was most sharply drawn in relation to what became two of its characteristic features: psychoanalysis and relativity. In O'Connell's view, Freud was not merely wrong; he was positively dangerous. Father Hickey had warned that Harvard's psychology department relied on the "indefiniteness" of Freud, who rejected "the nature of the human soul" in favor of the uncontrollable subconscious. Freud's program was "not a cure but a disease," a sorry example of "the sex madness that has taken hold of the modern world." Psychoanalysis was "a bad imitation of the confessional," the *Pilot* editorialized, a "repulsive method of dealing with mental abnormalities" and a "debasing cult that has claimed so many converts among the so called intelligentsia." The growth of psychology was regression, not progress: better to use "the confessional which Christ instituted to minister to our moral diseases" than the "repulsive method of . . . Sigmund Freud, a Jewish physician of Vienna in the early 90s."[40]

Faring little better was Albert Einstein, the target of a sustained attack by O'Connell in 1929. The cardinal was tapping into a larger stream of American Catholic anti-intellectualism, mocking "petty, befogged professors, . . . who have set up some new standard to attract attention to themselves." Taking the occasion of a departure for Rome, O'Connell expressed particular doubts about the German mathematician, "with his relativity and his utterly befogged notions about space and time." He doubted that anyone, including Einstein himself, really understood what relativity was all about, but O'Connell knew enough to conclude that its effects were pernicious. "Without perceiving the drift, innocent students are led away into a realm of speculative thought, the sole basis of which, so far as I can see, is to produce universal doubt about God and His creation." Speculation about time, space, and cosmology was nothing but "a cloak beneath which lies the ghastly apparition of atheism." Speculation of any kind was unnecessary in the cardinal's universe. "Faith settles . . . our problems. Faith clears away the mists," he said. "Truth is so simple, so clear, so substantial, so solid, so eternal!" Einstein was unimpressed by O'Connell's comments—the newspapers reported that they "left him cold"—but his response to them demonstrated two things nonetheless: first, the Catholic church vigorously opposed the new trends in science and philosophy; and second, when Cardinal O'Connell spoke, even such a man as Albert Einstein had to pay attention.[41]

Never very far beneath the surface of O'Connell's militant Catholicism was the presumption that Freud and Einstein shared a disability: they were Jewish. Anti-Semitism was common among American Catholics and if the cardinal never publicly voiced such sentiments, he was not immune to the anti-Jewish bias that thrived among his people. He might never be caught making uncharitable remarks himself, but his newspaper could identify the father of psychoanalysis as "a Jewish physician," and its readers would get the message. O'Connell made a few public overtures to the Jewish community. He corresponded cordially with several local rabbis, and he received a flood of favorable mail when he invited Jewish representatives to share the platform during his jubilee celebration at Fenway Park in 1934. His expressed "sympathy with the Jews in their aspirations for liberty" was interpreted as support for the establishment of a Zionist homeland, and suspicions about the treatment of Jews in Nazi Germany seem to have occurred to him sooner than to many other American religious and political leaders. Beyond that, however, Catholic-Jewish relations in Boston remained tense. The city persisted in its support of Detroit's increasingly anti-Semitic Father Coughlin in spite of O'Connell's denunciations of him, and roving gangs of Irish toughs beat up Jewish youths who ventured onto the wrong streets in the changing neighborhoods of Roxbury and Mattapan.[42] Like other groups recently emerged from discrimination, Boston's Catholics were not always understanding of those who found it difficult to get along in the dominant culture.

Notwithstanding this bitter underside of O'Connell's definition of resurgent Catholicism, his attack on modern culture was broadly based. His critique was intended to be more than a narrowly religious one, and it was given that wider interpretation by Catholic and non-Catholic alike. When he addressed any subject, O'Connell's clerical biographer observed in 1926, he commanded attention because he spoke "so firmly, so clearly, and so eloquently." Even the descendants of the Puritans appreciated the cardinal's efforts. "Your influence, Sir," a Yankee investment banker told him in the late 1930s, "has always been patriotic, honorable and clean in thought, expression, purpose and action. It has helped vastly in improving the situation within our Commonwealth." Journalists agreed that his impact had been consistent and firm: "those who did not agree with him at every turn," one writer said after his death, "were forced to admit that he never left any doubt as to where he stood." To be "such a steady and steadying figure in the community while the nation is in a state of flux," the solidly Republican *Boston Herald* commented, was a welcome contribution. To have someone who was unafraid to hold on to "fundamentals" was a service beyond religion, one that extended to society as a whole.[43]

What is more, O'Connell presumed that the very militance of the church's position would be the cause of its eventual triumph. As his hymn for the Holy Name Society had predicted, "the fight for God and the right" would be fierce, and it would be long. The difficulty of the strife, however, contained the promise of assured victory. "We shall conquer in the Holy Name," the hymn concluded, appending the cry: "Victory is ours!"[44]

The assertive church was the last bastion against modern disorder, and that was its glory. "It is to your credit and honor, my dear men," the cardinal told one group, "that in these days of weakening faith you hold your heads erect and your souls in . . . perfect conviction." That conviction gave to modern American Catholicism a potency other denominations, less committed he thought, lacked. "Look around you," he cried in 1930. "Catholics go to church. We simply cannot supply them with churches enough. But how about the rest of the population? With churches near their doors, some of them do not go near the church." The reason was "perfectly obvious." Other denominations lacked the certainty of faith that Catholicism retained.[45] Other denominations dallied with questionable modern attitudes and refused to hold the line on traditional values. Protestants in particular, lacking "the true light," were probably predisposed to failure in any event. O'Connell's image of the decline of Protestantism and the reassertion of Catholicism offered the proof of what he had told Daniel Coakley years before: if Catholics remained firm in their warfare with the modern world, they would assuredly "compel peace terms."

Changes in the moral and public dynamics of Boston in particular and America in general were not really so dramatic as O'Connell supposed, but it mattered little. There was much exaggeration in the cardinal's perception of the shift going on around him. His characterization of the transition from one epoch to another was overstated. Catholics were indeed advancing to new positions in politics and the world of affairs, but a Catholic "golden age" was nowhere apparent. The descendants of the Puritans had not passed from the scene altogether, as he thought or hoped, and they still exercised a decisive economic and social power. Rapidly advancing secularism, whether a result of the intellectual trends O'Connell decried or not, was in the end irresistible and would transform public and private life within decades of the cardinal's death.

Still, in the world that O'Connell constructed for himself and his people, Catholic self-assertion would inevitably bring the desired results. "We must be alert, as true soldiers of the Faith," he told the Holy Name men. "Be strong. Fear no one." His advice was full of confidence, for alertness would transform struggle into success. God always "rewards those who have been true and faithful," the cardinal said, and the reward was "triumph."[46] There was already evidence enough, from political life and elsewhere, to make that prediction plausible. In a very real way for O'Connell's Catholics, thinking success and wishing for it hard enough were almost sufficient to make it happen. The cardinal himself had seemed to triumph over adversity, both inside and outside the church, by relying on the "*vigor in arduis*" that adorned his episcopal crest. By adopting that same stance, he hoped, his people would achieve a like triumph.

EPILOGUE:
WILLIAM O'CONNELL AND AMERICAN
CATHOLICISM

WHEN THE END FINALLY CAME for Cardinal O'Connell, it came quickly. His pace had slowed, with fewer trips and only occasional surprise visits to parishes and religious institutions. His eyesight failed, and he became for all practical purposes blind and noticeably old. In the spring of 1944, he simply began to give out, much as his predecessor had. In April he was confined to his residence, and there he suffered a cerebral hemorrhage, a crisis soon complicated by pneumonia. For several days he wandered in and out of consciousness while officials and his nieces and nephews gathered to pray over him. Even while unconscious, witnesses reported, he waved at the air with his right hand, unknowingly imparting his blessing as he had done habitually for years. At quarter to six on the afternoon of Saturday, April 22, 1944, he died quietly in his own bed at the age of eighty-four.[1]

The funeral was every bit as grand as one might have expected. Dressed in a simple black "house cassock," he remained at the residence in Brighton over the weekend for a private wake for the personal and official family. On Monday afternoon, prepared now in impressive ceremonial robes—purple slippers and gloves, episcopal ring on his right hand, a white silk miter on his head, the large red cardinal's hat with thirty trailing tassels at his feet—the body was transferred to the Cathedral of the Holy Cross, where it lay in state through Thursday. A quarter of a million people filed past to see him. Messages of condolence streamed in from all over the world, and flags were lowered to half staff. On Friday morning, April 28, Archbishop Amleto Cicognani, the apostolic delegate, presided at the funeral mass, and Richard J. Cushing, the auxiliary bishop of

Boston who would formally be designated O'Connell's successor that fall, pronounced the eulogy. Afterwards, the casket was returned to Brighton in a twenty-car cortege and escorted to a small chapel built for this purpose fifteen years before on a rise overlooking Saint John's Seminary. A pair of stone lions and two carved angels guarded the approach to the tomb. The body was lowered into the ground, and the doors of glass and wrought iron closed behind it. O'Connell's era was over.[2]

In the decade between the celebration of his golden jubilee in 1934 and his death in 1944, many changes had overtaken him. Newspapers began to describe him as "venerable"—a term of respect, to be sure, but also one that marked him as a man of the last generation rather than the current one. "He sticks to his guns," one reporter said, not unsympathetically, "the guns of an elder and more serious age, in the face of a wide and general laxity. . . . He is less popular than respected." The cardinal even adopted this imagery himself, telling students at Boston College how as a lad he had risen early every day and, after the train ride from Lowell, walked to the school, "often with snow up to my knees."[3] It was the classic story an old man tells a younger generation he thinks unappreciative of the struggles of the past and too apt to take for granted its own ease and privilege.

The world he knew was disappearing. He was the sole survivor among his siblings now, and his fellow churchmen were dying off as well: Cardinals Hayes of New York and Mundelein of Chicago, both appointed to office well after O'Connell, were dead by the late 1930s. Even new accomplishments were tinged with the sense that they came too late. In 1939, for example, O'Connell finally participated in the election of a new pope, having missed his chances in 1914 and 1922. Pius XI died in February while O'Connell was spending one of his last vacations at "the shack in Nassau." Knowing that the opportunity would never come again, the cardinal sailed to New York and boarded another ship for Rome, arriving with great ceremony on the morning the conclave opened. One of the shortest elections in history then chose the aristocratic Cardinal Eugenio Pacelli as Pope Pius XII, a man with his own connections in America. The choice portended the rise of O'Connell's hated subordinate, Bishop Francis Spellman, soon to be promoted to the archbishopric of New York. From that position Spellman would assume the position of kingmaker in the American church, a role the older prelate had coveted but never acquired.[4] O'Connell had at last helped select a pope, but the personalities and issues he had struggled with in the days of Pius X and Merry del Val were long gone. By the time he exercised this power, the loftiest and most exclusive responsibility of a cardinal, it no longer meant anything: events had passed him by.

Also signaling his decline was the rise of a new generation of leadership in Catholic Boston. The turnover of younger priests, begun with the departure of Father Toomey and his nephew, continued. Father Jeremiah Minihan, only thirty years old, became secretary to the cardinal in 1933, and the brilliant John Wright joined the inner circle in 1940 at thirty-one. In 1938 Father Edward Murray became the "boy rector" of the seminary at thirty-three. Most promising of all was Richard Cushing, a son of South Boston who had made a name for himself as director of the archdiocesan office that raised money for foreign missions. A prodigious fundraiser and a man whose talent for public relations matched that of O'Connell himself, Cushing succeeded to the position of Boston's auxiliary bishop and heir apparent when Spellman left for New York in the spring of 1939.[5]

In Cushing, Boston Catholicism found its man for the future. At home with a group of rising politicians, including a promising young war hero named Kennedy, and able to tap new sources of wealth both inside and outside the Catholic middle class, Cushing represented a new generation that was comfortable with a more modern outlook. Stylistically, he and O'Connell were a stark contrast. The older man was uniformly stiff and imposing, always maintaining a dignified bearing: he was, in fact, virtually never photographed smiling, preferring instead to peer out from narrowed eyes that could only be described as cold and harsh. Cushing, by contrast, had an easy grin, and he was breezy and approachable. The newspapers loved to run photographs of cuddly little children kissing his bishop's ring to the delight of all. The gesture itself was familiar, but for O'Connell ring-kissing had been solemn, still the ritual of docility and obeisance it had originally been. With Cushing, it was an act of affection, accompanied perhaps by some embarrassment that such an aristocratic practice survived in a democratic country. Approachability was evident in other ways. A surviving motion picture of a 1942 parish May festival shows Bishop Cushing, attired in plain clerical suit and sporty straw boater, mugging for the camera and taking his turn in a baseball throwing contest.[6] O'Connell, who had viewed sporting events with some suspicion, may well have wondered about this potential successor who could throw a fastball with the same arm he raised in blessing.

Cushing's style was partly natural and partly contrived so as to distinguish himself from O'Connell. Possessed of a remarkable speaking voice that rocked back and forth before rising to dramatic, nasal climaxes, Cushing was folksy where O'Connell had been formal. The younger prelate constructed a persona he thought more appropriate to a generation of successful, "remaining" Catholics and their children. Though he had been born into solidly middle-class respectability, Cushing portrayed himself as the product of noble, log-cabin poverty. This image, so different from O'Connell's sometime attempts to link himself to the ancient kings of Ireland, seemed more appropriate for a Catholic populace that had achieved enough success to indulge the luxury of romanticizing past hardships.[7] Cushing was prepared to take the church into an era O'Connell could perhaps foresee but never reach, including the honor of invoking the deity at the inauguration of a Catholic president in 1961.

Despite the new world emerging as he went to his grave, O'Connell had nonetheless had a substantial impact on American Catholicism. He had set out the path down which Cushing and others would go. The intervening years have placed a gulf between that era and our own, and the Catholic church of today seems very different from the one he knew. The outward signs of change are so apparent. Elaborate ceremonial has been largely reduced, and the vernacular has replaced Latin as the language of worship. Priests and nuns routinely wear secular clothing instead of distinctive religious garb. Many of them leave the religious life altogether to marry and raise families without the stigma that accompanied the cardinal's nephew. Lay people on the whole wear their Catholicism more lightly than their parents and grandparents did, preferring other, nonreligious sources of identity. From the perspective of the present, O'Connell and his church seem longer ago than merely half a century.

Still, for American Catholics in the early twentieth century, who were emerging from the uncertainties of immigration and economic hard times, O'Connell defined the way they looked at themselves and the world around them. He helped transform their preoccupation with discrimination, both real and perceived, from the whine of self-pity into the confidence of self-assertion. "Our time has come," his implicit message ran. "We are not only as good as everyone else, particularly those who once looked down on us; we are probably better." O'Connell's official biographer had been right to characterize his tenure as a passage from youth to maturity. It was a period of transition from ghetto Catholicism, fearful of nativist hostility, to public Catholicism, eager to compete on equal terms in American society and to succeed. From the days when job listings in the newspapers could specify "no Irish need apply"—"Irish" in this sense meaning by extension other Catholic ethnics as well— O'Connell had unapologetically advanced his people toward the notion that they could apply anywhere, succeed anywhere.

He had come to represent the church in a singularly American sort of way, through concern over public image. His ecclesiastical critics may have choked on the "limelight and big advertising" that always surrounded him, but they benefited from it in spite of themselves. Experimenting with a wider public role from his earliest days, O'Connell quickly perfected it and used it to good advantage. In the process he established a new style and a new set of expectations for American Catholic leaders. Whether in the realm of secular politics or the definition of community standards in even the smallest details of public morality, Catholic bishops after O'Connell would no longer be reluctant to speak. They were expected to have opinions about everything, and the public had to take notice of what they said. Their views might be controversial; they would be accused of trying to impose one moral vision on a pluralistic society. Still, whether they were discussing birth control, abortion, nuclear warfare, or the national economy, American Catholic churchmen commanded attention and provoked debate. Even when faced with criticism, Catholic prelates would no longer doubt that they were significant players in the public drama, and it was O'Connell who helped give them that certitude.

To say this is not to overlook the limitations that accompanied O'Connell's successes. The reality behind the public image too frequently diverged from his clear, correct, and consciously edifying image of respect and respectability. His supposed reorganization of church affairs and his vaunted administrative abilities were more

imagined than real. Despite his brave rhetoric, he had to accept the
limitations on his influence and the persistently local nature of his
church. Whether facing powerful pastors or resourceful nuns, he
clung to a belief in himself as the potent savior of his church from
chaos and disaster. In his mind, the lines of authority were clear: they
proceeded directly from God to the pope, from the pope to himself,
and from himself to everyone else. The real dynamics in the church
were more complicated, but in the end the gap between image and
reality may not have mattered. Indeed, the very survival of the myth
demonstrated how much he and his people sought the assurance of
clarity and unambiguous authority in an uncertain world.

Nor should an appreciation of O'Connell's success in setting a
tone for American Catholicism dismiss his personal failings. For all
his force of moral expression to the public at large, he was a man who
excused immorality in himself and those around him. Too ready to
exempt himself from the ethical standards he articulated publicly, he
was crippled throughout his career by a split personality that
accepted too wide a gap between what he said and what he did.
Hypocrisy is a part of every human personality; none of us is as good
as we think we are, pretend we are, or hope to be. In O'Connell's
case, however, the dissembling crossed the line of acceptability.
Skimming money from the diocese of Portland was somehow excus-
able, as if the purpose for which he intended to use it—simply
because it was *his* purpose—justified the means of acquiring it. The
ideology of authority was out of control, and since the church vested
so much authority in him, he did not need to be accountable. He
tolerated his nephew because exposure would derail the rest of his
program, a program whose value he took so for granted that nothing
could be permitted to stand in its way. O'Connell was too successful
in creating and recreating his own outward personality and he lost
the ability to distinguish his creation from the real core of it.

The public at large never saw this underside, and they were left
with the image of the assertive churchman who at once heralded the
dawning of a new day and helped speed its arrival. Like him, they
were ready to believe that a new age, a distinctively Catholic age,
was dawning for the United States. The militant and triumphant
church that O'Connell defined would set a tone for public life, they
thought, and unbroken success would be its characteristic. In reality,
O'Connell's era was an end rather than a beginning, the culmination

of an old world rather than the opening of a new one. Catholics would indeed grasp the brass ring of acceptance when "one of their own" moved into the White House, but the modern world O'Connell had sought to hold off would prove too strong. Not even so well-defined an outlook as his could resist it. Radical change would come to Catholicism as well. Two decades after his death, the church would abandon its self-description as a "mystical body," directed always by its head, and define itself instead as "the people of God." That was a more democratic image in which the lines of power were blurred and autocrats had at least to speak the language of participation.

In his own times and on his own terms, O'Connell represented a standard of leadership in church and society that was aggressive and self-confident, an embodiment of the certainty he found at the heart of Catholicism. Even if that standard is one that is, for the most part, no longer accepted, he must nonetheless be acknowledged as one who helped fix it firmly in the public mind. He set the terms of discussion at a crucial time and, in many ways, gave subsequent generations something to react against. Once a key figure in defining American Catholicism, he has perhaps become a negative definition—what the church is not, rather than what it is—for a more recent Catholicism that is less sure and set apart. In the ongoing processes of history, that is still something.

ABBREVIATIONS

AABa   Archives, Archdiocese of Baltimore
AABo   Archives, Archdiocese of Boston
AANY   Archives, Archdiocese of New York
AASF   Archives, Archdiocese of San Francisco
ADB   Archives, Diocese of Burlington
ADFR   Archives, Diocese of Fall River
ADPo   Archives, Diocese of Portland
ADPr   Archives, Diocese of Providence
ADUSA   Apostolic Delegate, U.S.A.
APF   Archives, Sacred Congregation de Propaganda Fide, Rome
ASSJ   Archives, Sisters of Saint Joseph, Boston
ASV   Archivio Segreto Vaticano, Rome
CCB   Catholic Charitable Bureau, Boston
JIP   John Ireland Papers (Microfilm Edition: Minnesota Historical Society; originals in Catholic Historical Society of Saint Paul)
SAB   Sulpician Archives, Baltimore
SJS   Saint John's Seminary, Brighton

Catholic Boston   *Catholic Boston: Studies in Religion and Community, 1870–1970.* Ed. Robert E. Sullivan and James M. O'Toole. Boston: Archdiocese of Boston, 1985.

CHR   *Catholic Historical Review*

HAB   Robert H. Lord, et al. *History of the Archdiocese of Boston in the Various Stages of Its Development, 1604–1943.* 3 vols. Boston: Pilot Publishing Company, 1944.

O'Leary, "Cardinal O'Connell"   Robert A. O'Leary. "William Henry O'Connell: A Social and Intellectual Biography." Ph.D. dissertation: Tufts University, 1980.

Pilot   *Boston Pilot*

Recollections   William Cardinal O'Connell. *Recollections of Seventy Years.* Boston: Houghton Mifflin, 1934.

258

S&A

Sermons and Addresses of His Eminence, William Cardinal O'Connell. 11 vols. Boston: Pilot Publishing Company, 1911–1938.

Wayman, *Cardinal O'Connell*

Dorothy G. Wayman. *Cardinal O'Connell of Boston: A Biography of William Henry O'Connell, 1859–1944.* New York: Farrar, Straus and Young, 1955.

NOTES

INTRODUCTION

1. *S&A*, 11:175; Peter K. Guilday, *The Life and Times of John England, First Bishop of Charleston, 1786–1842* (New York: The America Press, 1927).

2. O'Connell to Guilday, October 28, 1927, AABa O–299.

3. Quoted in Owen Chadwick, *Catholicism and History: The Opening of the Vatican Archives* (Cambridge: Cambridge University Press, 1978), 98.

4. *Pilot*, October 3, 1947; O'Connell to Coakley, February 19, 1917, O'Connell Papers, AABo 3:12.

5. Henry Morton Robinson, *The Cardinal* (New York: Simon and Schuster, 1950), 409. For a further discussion of these themes, see James M. O'Toole, "The Name That Stood for Rome: William O'Connell and the Modern Episcopal Style," *Patterns of Episcopal Leadership*, ed. Gerald P. Fogarty (New York: Macmillan, 1989), 171–184.

1. THE PATH TO POWER: O'CONNELL'S EARLY LIFE AND CAREER, 1859–1901

1. On the definition of the Immaculate Conception and its importance, see J. Derek Holmes, *The Triumph of the Holy See: A Short History of the Papacy in the Nineteenth Century* (London: Burns and Oates, 1978), 141–142, and Gerald A. McCool, *Catholic Theology in the Nineteenth Century: The Quest for a Unitary Method* (New York: Seabury Press, 1977), 129–135. For the less than completely enthusiastic American response to the dogma, see James Hennesey, "A Prelude to Vatican I: American Bishops and the Definition of the Immaculate Conception," *Theological Studies* 25 (1964): 409–419.

2. Baptismal register, Saint Peter's, Lowell, AABo, entry of December 8, 1859. The baby's godparents were his oldest brother, John, and his mother's sister, Sarah Fay. Over the years, there has been some confusion about O'Connell's precise birth date. The records in the Lowell city clerk's office indicate that the baby was born on December 22, and this error is repeated in the vital records for Lowell now held by the Archives of the Commonwealth of Massachusetts, Boston. Such mistakes and delays in recording were quite common, however, and there is no reason to question the accuracy of the earlier entry in the parish records.

3. Somewhat conflicting accounts of the Irish origins and status of the O'Connell and Farrelly families are given in *HAB*, 3:441–444, and Wayman, *Cardinal O'Connell*, 3–5. *HAB* (3:443) even claims a relationship to Daniel

O'Connell, "the Liberator," which seems entirely without foundation. No complete genealogy of the O'Connell family has ever been undertaken.

4. The conditions in Cavan immediately before and during the Famine are meticulously described in Kevin O'Neill, *Family and Farm in Pre-Famine Ireland: The Parish of Killashandra* (Madison: University of Wisconsin Press, 1984), esp. 23–25. O'Neill's study is based on an analysis of a district located about twenty miles north-west of the area where the O'Connells lived. See also Kerby A. Miller, *Emigrants and Exiles: Ireland and the Irish Exodus to North America* (New York: Oxford University Press, 1985), 576 (Table 5) and 370; the quotation is ibid., 290.

5. Again, accounts of the family's emigration differ slightly. See Wayman, *Cardinal O'Connell*, 5–6, for the most plausible version. Cardinal O'Connell himself later indulged in some perhaps forgivable romanticizing of the story, including the assertion that, while in New York, his father had helped build the Erie Canal, a project he only missed by about twenty years; *Recollections*, 2.

6. See the descriptions and analyses by A. Gibbs Mitchell, Jr., in his very helpful "Irish Family Patterns in Nineteenth-Century Ireland and Lowell, Massachusetts" (Ph.D. diss.: Boston University, 1976), iv–vi, 195, 289, 306–308, and 337–340. See also Brian C. Mitchell, "'They Do Not Differ Greatly': The Pattern of Community Development Among the Irish in Late Nineteenth-Century Lowell, Massachusetts," *From Paddy to Studs: Irish-American Communities in the Turn of the Century Era, 1880 to 1920*, ed. Timothy J. Meagher (New York: Greenwood, 1986), 53–73, and Brian C. Mitchell, *The Paddy Camps: The Irish of Lowell, 1821–1861* (Urbana: University of Illinois Press, 1988).

7. The occupations and residences of the O'Connells have been traced in the Lowell city directories (titles and imprints vary), 1865–1881. On John O'Connell, Jr., see *Massachusetts Soldiers, Sailors, and Marines in the Civil War* (Brookline, Mass.: Riverdale Press, 1935), 8:509, and *Boston Globe*, August 22, 1932. In his memoirs, O'Connell tells a very stylized story of working in a spinning mill for a single day; *Recollections*, 36–39. The story, which has been repeated elsewhere, cannot be independently verified, and it lacks a true ring.

8. Joseph B. Fuller, "At the Very Center of Things: The Catholic Secular Clergy in the Redirection of Catholic Boston" (Honors thesis: Harvard College, 1979), 69–90; *Recollections*, 47. On the increase in religious practice among the Irish, see Emmet Larkin, "The Devotional Revolution in Ireland, 1850–1875," *American Historical Review* 77 (1972): 625–652.

9. See Christopher J. Kauffman, *Tradition and Transformation in Catholic Culture: The Priests of Saint Sulpice in the United States from 1791 to the Present* (New York: Macmillan, 1988) for a history of the Sulpicians; O'Connell's experiences at Saint Charles's are described 229–230. See also *Golden Jubilee of Saint Charles' College, Near Ellicott City, Maryland, 1848–1898* (Baltimore: John Murphy, 1898), 76–79, and *A Complete List of the Students Entered at Saint Charles' College, Ellicott City, Maryland, Since the Opening, October 31st, 1848* (New York: Press of the Mission of the Immaculate Virgin, 1897). A useful general account of the training of Catholic priests is provided in Joseph M. White, *The Diocesan Seminary in the United States: A History from the 1780s to the Present* (Notre Dame, Ind.: University of Notre Dame Press, 1989).

10. *Recollections*, 50. Manuscript recollections of Father Arsene Vuibert, January 5, 1919, SAB, RG9, Box 6. Wayman, *Cardinal O'Connell*, 15–16, hints at the boy's general unhappiness. See also John E. Sexton, *Cardinal O'Connell: A Biographical Sketch* (Boston: Pilot Publishing Co., 1926), 9–10, and *Recollections*, 71. The letters ostensibly written by O'Connell during this period and published later as *Letters of His Eminence William Cardinal O'Connell* (Cambridge, Mass.: Riverside Press, 1915), are wholly unreliable and cannot be used, as previous historians have unfortunately done, as authentic descriptions of these early years; see the discussion of these letters below, chapter 4.

11. On the foundation and early history of the school, see David R. Dunigan, *A History of Boston College* (Milwaukee: Bruce, 1957); see also Charles F. Donovan, "Student Enrollment at Boston College in the Nineteenth Century," *Occasional Papers on the History of Boston College*, January 1984.

12. *Recollections*, 71–72; *Catalogue of the Officers and Students of Boston College for the Academic Year 1878–1879* (Boston: Duffy, Cashman & Co., 1879), 9–10.

13. *Catalogue of the Officers and Students of Boston College for the Academic Year 1879–1880* (Boston: Duffy, Cashman, & Co., 1880), 10–11, 21, 31; *Catalogue of the Officers and Students of Boston College for the Academic Year 1880–1881* (Boston: Duffy, Cashman, & Co., 1881), 11, 21, 23, 29, 31; *Current Biography: Who's News and Why, 1941* (New York: H. W. Wilson Co., 1941), 624. Unfortunately, no early photographs of O'Connell in sartorial and hirsute splendor survive.

14. The origins and early years of the college are traced in the opening chapters of Robert F. McNamara's fine study, *The American College in Rome, 1855–1955* (Rochester, N.Y.: The Christopher Press, 1956); on the college's enrollment, see the list of students in Henry A. Brann, *History of the American College of the Roman Catholic Church of the United States, Rome, Italy* (New York: Benziger Brothers, 1910), 547–570. O'Connell's description of his journey to Rome is in *Recollections*, 81–109. Wayman, *Cardinal O'Connell*, 19–23, presents a stylized, somewhat romantic, and probably not overly accurate account of O'Connell's application and acceptance to the Roman seminary.

15. *Recollections*, 132; James Hennesey, *American Catholics: A History of the Roman Catholic Community in the United States* (New York: Oxford University Press), 166–167.

16. *Recollections*, 123–131.

17. On student life, see McNamara, *American College*, 94–105, and Brann, *History of the American College*, 197–234.

18. *Recollections*, 134–137. Here again, O'Connell's published *Letters* from this period cannot be considered authentic.

19. *Recollections*, 137–139. It was not uncommon for ordained graduates to continue their studies temporarily, so his enrollment does not necessarily imply an intent to obtain the graduate degree.

20. Episcopal Register, AABo, December 12 and 23, 1884. Though the appointment was effective earlier, Williams let O'Connell remain at home in Lowell for the holiday itself; Wayman, *Cardinal O'Connell*, 43.

21. Baptismal and marriage registers, 1885–1886, Saint Joseph's, Medford, AABo. In his two years O'Connell officiated at eighty-three of the ninety-five

baptisms and twenty of the twenty-six marriages. On the confirmation, see Episcopal Register, AABo, October 25, 1885. The size of this class was a little high in relation to that of the parish, but it is inflated because confirmation was not administered every year. O'Connell's description of his life in Medford is in *Recollections*, 142–145. A good recent history of the town is Carl Seaburg and Alan Seaburg, *Medford on the Mystic* (Medford: Medford Historical Society, 1980); see especially 21, 44–46, 132–133. The classic study of the growth of towns like Medford is Sam Bass Warner, Jr., *Streetcar Suburbs: The Process of Growth in Boston, 1870–1900* (Cambridge, Mass.: Harvard University Press, 1962).

22. *Americans in Process: A Settlement Study*, ed. Robert A. Woods (New York: Arno Reprints Edition, 1970; originally published 1903), 38–39, 41, 95, 190–223, 136; *Twenty-Third Annual Report of the Bureau of the Statistics of Labor, March 1893*, Public Document No. 15 (Boston: Wright and Potter, 1893), 120, 122, 125, 172–173. For O'Connell's appointment to the West End, see Episcopal Register, AABo, October 7, November 3, and November 11, 1886. See also O'Connell's description of the parish in *Recollections*, 145.

23. This occupational analysis is based on a sample of 173 (19.28 percent) of the 892 marriages performed in the parish between 1887 and 1895; Marriage Registers, Saint Joseph's, Boston, AABo.

24. Parish activities are described in the *Pilot*, December 11 and 25, 1886; January 1, 22, 29, February 26, March 12, and April 2, 1887. On the concern for drinking and crime in the West End, see Perry R. Duis, *The Saloon: Public Drinking in Chicago and Boston, 1880–1920* (Urbana: University of Illinois Press, 1983), 118–119, 236.

25. *Pilot*, January 29, March 12, and April 2, 1887; March 3 and July 7, 1888; June 22, 1889; March 15, 1890; and March 4, 1893. See also Episcopal Register, AABo, April 30, 1890, May 18, 1892, and May 30, 1895, and the history of the parish, *History of Saint Joseph's Church* (Boston: Privately printed, no date but probably 1903), 35–37. The standard work on parish missions is Jay P. Dolan, *Catholic Revivalism: The American Experience, 1830–1900* (Notre Dame, Ind.: University of Notre Dame Press, 1978). Less comprehensive but still useful is Ann Taves, *The Household of Faith: Roman Catholic Devotions in Mid-Nineteenth Century America* (Notre Dame, Ind.: University of Notre Dame Press, 1986).

26. *Recollections*, 147. The analysis of O'Connell's sacramental activity is based on a tabulation of all the baptisms and marriages in the parish, recorded in Baptismal and Marriage Registers, 1887–1895, AABo. The daily routine of the parish clergy in this period is described in Robert E. Sullivan, "Beneficial Relations: Toward a Social History of the Diocesan Priests of Boston, 1875–1944," *Catholic Boston*, 235–237.

27. *Pilot*, July 18, 1891, October 22, 1892, and March 25, 1893.

28. Ibid., March 19, March 26, and December 24, 1892; March 10, 1894; October 26 and November 9, 1895.

29. The turmoil at the college during this period is described in McNamara, *American College*, 260–336. The most detailed study of the controversial rector is Gerald P. Fogarty, *The Vatican and the Americanist Crisis: Denis J. O'Connell, American Agent in Rome, 1885–1903* (Rome: Universita Gregoriana Editrice, 1974).

A useful study of the Americanist vision and program is Thomas E. Wangler, "American Catholic Expansionism, 1886–1894," *Harvard Theological Review* 75 (1982): 369–393; see also Hennesey, *American Catholics*, 202–203. The ultramontane faction in America was led by New York's Archbishop Corrigan, for whom see R. Emmett Curran, *Michael Augustine Corrigan and the Shaping of Conservative Catholicism in America, 1878–1902* (New York: Arno Press, 1978). On the rise of ultramontanism in the European church and its reassertion of papal authority, see Alec R. Vidler, *The Church in an Age of Revolution, 1789 to the Present Day* (New York: Penguin, 1971), 68–78 and 150–156. On the apostolic delegation, see Robert J. Wister, "The Establishment of the Apostolic Delegation in the United States of America: The Satolli Mission, 1892–1896" (Ph.D. diss.: Pontifical Gregorian University, 1980). See also Wister's article, "The Establishment of the Apostolic Delegation in Washington: The Pastoral and Political Motivations," *U.S. Catholic Historian* 3 (1983): 115–128.

30. The formal minutes of this meeting are contained in a letter of Gibbons to Ledochowski, October 3, 1895, APF 153/1895, N.S. 55:155–157. A more lively and frank account of the discussions is contained in Corrigan to Brandi, October 6, 1895, ibid., 159–159 verso. Corrigan's correspondent was Salvatore Brandi, S.J., editor of the powerful conservative newspaper, *Civiltà Cattolica*.

31. HAB, 3:461. The assertion that it was Gibbons who suggested O'Connell is repeated in McNamara, *American College*, 337. The belief that it was in fact Williams who put his name forward is supported by Corrigan to Brandi, October 6, 1895, APF 153/1895, N.S. 55:159. The rumor about O'Connell's campaigning for the job is told in the *Boston Journal*, December 30, 1903. Archbishop Robert Seton, son of the prominent American convert and future saint, Elizabeth Seton, recorded the same story in his memoirs, written about 1910, saying that Gibbons himself had told him that O'Connell had visited Baltimore to ask for the job; see Seton's manuscript memoirs, 1 (1910): 49 verso, New York Historical Society, New York, New York.

32. Corrigan to Brandi, October 6, 1895, APF 153/1895, N.S. 55:159; Corrigan to Ledochowski, November 5, 1895, ibid., 177 verso; McDonnell to Mazzella, October 4, 1895, ibid., 162 verso; Satolli to Ledochowski, October 4, 1895, ibid., 153–154. Satolli's assertion that he did not particularly know O'Connell at this time is at sharp variance with later assertions that the two had remained close over the intervening years and that it was the powerful Italian who engineered the promotion for his former pupil; see Wayman, *Cardinal O'Connell*, 70–71. Propaganda's decision is recorded in APF 153/1895, N.S. 55:170–176. For O'Connell's notification and acceptance of the appointment, see O'Connell to Gibbons, December 7, 1895, AABa 94–E–4.

33. This analysis was first suggested in McNamara, *American College*, 338. On Corrigan's preference for O'Connell, see Corrigan to Brandi, October 6, 1895, APF 153/1895, N.S. 55:159.

34. *Recollections*, 165, 165–166, 178–179.

35. Brann, *American College*, 204, 205, 216, 225–227, and 497–505. O'Connell to Gibbons, February 14, 1896, AABa 94–H–9; O'Connell to Corrigan, March 26, 1896, Corrigan Papers, G–12 (microfilm roll 18), AANY.

36. O'Connell to Corrigan, February 15, 1896, Corrigan Papers, G–12 (microfilm roll 18), AANY; *Recollections*, 168; O'Connell to Gibbons, March 15, 1896, AABa 94–K–3; McQuaid to O'Connell, September 16, 1897, O'Connell Papers, ADPo. Archbishop Williams encouraged the young priest in a similar vein; see Williams to O'Connell, January 3, 1897, ibid.

37. O'Connell to Gibbons, June 9, 1898, AABa 96–J–4; this letter is probably misdated and should be 1897. On general conditions at the college, compare the two financial reports, one for the six-month period (July–December 1895) immediately before O'Connell's arrival and the other for his last full year (1900), ibid., 94–B–C and 98–N–8, respectively. See also O'Connell to Gibbons, May 2, 1898, ibid., 96–G–1; O'Connell to Gibbons, January 25, 1901, ibid., 98–P–10; and O'Connell to Ledochowski, no date but probably November 1899, APF 153/1899, N.S. 149:863–864.

38. O'Connell to Corrigan, November 11, 1898, Corrigan Papers, G–21 (microfilm roll 20), AANY; O'Connell to Gibbons, November 11, 1898, AABa 96–T–1. On the acquisition of the new villa, see also *Recollections*, 200–201, and McNamara, *American College*, 357–363.

39. *A Papal Chamberlain: The Personal Chronicle of Francis Augustus MacNutt*, ed. John J. Donovan (London: Longmans, Green and Co., 1936), 75.

40. *Recollections*, 181; Wayman, *Cardinal O'Connell*, 83–84. There is no modern critical biography of Merry, but for the outlines of his life see the excessively pious Marie Cecilia Buehrle, *Rafael Cardinal Merry del Val* (Milwaukee: Bruce, 1957). Perhaps the truest portrait of this controversial churchman is the brief description of the fictional character based on him in the prologue to Willa Cather's *Death Comes for the Archbishop*.

41. Ella B. Edes, quoted in Gerald P. Fogarty, *The Vatican and the American Hierarchy from 1870 to 1965* (Wilmington, Del.: Michael Glazier, 1985; originally published Stuttgart, 1982), 196; *Recollections*, 160, 161.

42. Henry James, *William Wetmore Story and His Friends* (Boston: Houghton Mifflin, 1903), 2:206–207. For studies of the American expatriate community, see Van Wyck Brooks, *The Dream of Arcadia: American Writers and Artists in Italy, 1760–1915* (New York: Dutton, 1958) and Ernest Earnest, *Expatriates and Patriots: American Artists, Scholars, and Writers in Europe* (Durham, N.C.: Duke University Press, 1968).

43. *Recollections*, 181–193, 209; McNamara, *American College*, 349–352. On O'Connell's arranging audiences and otherwise entertaining visiting Americans, see O'Connell to Corrigan, May 1, 1896, Corrigan Papers, G–12 (microfilm roll 18), AANY. See also MacNutt's description of the American colony and the papal court in *Papal Chamberlain*, 74–75 and 213. On O'Connell's promotion of MacNutt, see O'Connell to Gibbons, November 11, 1898, AABa 96–T–1. Other activities of the Roman circle are described in O'Connell to Julia O'Connell, April 22 and October 3, 1900, O'Connell Papers, ADPo. On Dunn's later unsavory reputation, see below, chapter 8.

44. On the nieces and nephews, see O'Connell to Julia O'Connell, November 15, 1897, and January 30, 1899, as well as O'Connell to "My dear Sister" (probably also Julia), June 13, 1900, O'Connell Papers, ADPo. On the general concern for

finances and rental of the property, see O'Connell to Julia O'Connell, February 19, 1898, and March 8, 1901, ibid.

45. O'Connell to "Dear Brother," March 26, 1896, ibid. See also O'Connell to Julia O'Connell, January 30, 1899, ibid. On his search for mass intentions, see O'Connell to Corrigan, April 8, 1899, and Corrigan to O'Connell, April 20, 1899, Corrigan Papers, G–21 and G–16 (microfilm rolls 20 and 18, respectively), AANY.

2. DRY RUN: O'CONNELL AS BISHOP OF PORTLAND, 1901–1906

1. The outlines of Healy's career are described in Albert S. Foley, *Bishop Healy: Beloved Outcaste* (New York: Farrar, Straus and Young, 1954), a work that is now old but still useful.

2. Statistics for the Portland diocese are taken from the *Catholic Directory, Almanac, and Clergy List, 1901* (Milwaukee: Wiltzius, 1901), 456–460. The status of the Portland diocese is also described in a report to Rome made by Healy in 1898; APF 153/1898, N.S. 145:348–361. The total population of Maine was reported in the 1900 census as 694,466; see *Historical Statistics of the United States* (Washington D.C.: Government Printing Office, 1957), 12–13 (tables A123–180).

3. Ethnic turmoil is discussed in some detail in Foley, *Bishop Healy*, 153–168, and William Lucey, *The Catholic Church in Maine* (Francestown, N.H.: Marshall Jones, 1957), 224–225.

4. On Healy's death and the early steps in this procedure, see O'Brien to Ledochowski, August 14, 1900, APF 153/1901, N.S. 215:250–252. The delegate's remark is in Martinelli to O'Brien, August 7, 1900, ADUSA, IV:41, ASV.

5. The two *ternae*, dated August 27 and August 28, 1900, were submitted by Williams to Ledochowski and are in APF 153/1901, N.S. 215:253–257. See also Williams's Episcopal Register, AABo, August 17, 1900, and O'Brien to Williams, August 15, 1900, Williams Papers, AABo, 4:8.

6. Martinelli to Ledochowski, October 5, 1900, APF 153/1901, N.S. 215:261–262.

7. Trudel et al. to Propaganda, October 8, 1900, ibid., 263–266. See also Charland to Propaganda, October 19, 1900, ibid., 267–270, and Dupont to Propaganda, November 9, 1900, ibid., 273–274. Precise figures on the relative size of the French and Irish portions of Maine's Catholic population are difficult to determine. In his 1898 report to Rome, Healy had calculated almost 27,000 Irish Catholics in English-speaking parishes, 20,000 in French-speaking parishes, and 45,000 in "mixed" parishes; see APF 153/1898, N.S. 145:348–361. Wallace's withdrawal, precisely on the grounds that he did not speak French and was too old (fifty-six) to learn, is in Wallace to Martinelli, October 14, 1900, ADUSA, IV:41, ASV.

8. Trudel et al. to Propaganda, October 15, 1900, and December 30, 1900, APF 153/1901, N.S. 215:271–272 and 303–304, respectively; Genereux to Propaganda, November 3, 1900, ibid., 278–279. Trudel's abortive payoff is discussed in Martinelli to Trudel, February 18, 1901, ADUSA, IV:41, ASV; see also Wallace et al. to Martinelli, February 8, 1901, ibid. The French endorsement of O'Brien had been hinted at in earlier communications with Archbishop Williams; see Trudel and Dupont to Williams, October 15, 1900, Williams Papers, AABo 5:30.

9. The letter from the laity, dated February 7, 1901, APF 153/1901, N.S. 215:317–324, appears to have been written with the same typewriter used by the pastors in their earlier communications with Rome. See also *Recollections*, 216, and Lucey, *Catholic Church in Maine*, 272.

10. Harkins to Martinelli, February 26, 1901; Michaud to Martinelli, March 4, 1901; Belleau to Martinelli, January 18, 1901; and McSweeney to Martinelli, February 9, 1901: all in ADUSA, IV:41, ASV.

11. *Recollections*, 211. On the possibility that O'Connell's appointment was the "reward of discretion," see McNamara, *American College*, 368. On the speculation that Satolli was O'Connell's principal backer, see James Gaffey, "The Changing of the Guard: The Rise of Cardinal O'Connell of Boston," *CHR* 59 (1973): 227–228. The actual appointment and the announcement of it are in APF 153/1901, N.S. 215:365–369; Ledochowski to Martinelli, May 29, 1901, ADUSA, IV:41, ASV; and Episcopal Register, AABo, May 7, 1901.

12. Sayre to O'Connell, July 26, 1901, O'Connell Papers, ADPo; Edes to Corrigan, January 6, 1900, and May 17, 1901, quoted in Fogarty, *Vatican and the American Hierarchy*, 196; see also Corrigan to O'Connell, April 26, 1901, Corrigan Papers, G–16, AANY; *Recollections*, 212.

13. O'Connell to Ledochowski, December 28, 1901, quoted in Gaffey, "Changing of the Guard," 228. The full text of O'Connell's sermon is given in the *Pilot*, July 13, 1901. Throughout the sermon, he consistently referred to himself in the first person plural ("we" and "our"), a grandiloquent construction usually reserved for monarchs and the pope himself.

14. *Portland Eastern Argus*, October 21, 1901; *Recollections*, 218. On the free railroad passes, see O'Connell to Cram, August 26, 1902, and Evans to O'Connell, December 28, 1903, O'Connell Papers, ADPo.

15. O'Connell to "M," undated, O'Connell Papers, AABo 1:8. This is one of the so-called spurious letters, written long afterwards but in the present tense, prepared for publication but never printed. Despite this curious character, it may be treated as a kind of memoir, though not as a contemporary statement. Wherever these letters have been used, their dates are placed in quotation marks to indicate their misleading character. See the discussion of these letters in chapter 4.

16. *Bangor Commercial*, August 23, 1901; *Portland Eastern Argus*, October 21, 1901; *Bangor News*, July 5, 1901.

17. For earlier discussions of O'Connell's public style, see Lucey, *Catholic Church in Maine*, 275; O'Leary, "Cardinal O'Connell," 62–63; Wayman, *Cardinal O'Connell*, 103, 102, 95.

18. O'Connell to Putnam, March 23, 1903, Chancery Letterbooks, ADPo; O'Connell to Weeks, September 24, 1903, ibid.; Flagg to O'Connell, August 21, 1902, O'Connell Papers, ADPo; O'Connell to Flagg, August 25, 1902, Chancery Letterbooks, ADPo; *Portland Express*, August 27, 1902; O'Connell to "X," "September 10, 1901," O'Connell Papers, AABo 1:8. The last item is one of O'Connell's spurious letters, composed long after the date it bears.

19. Yates to O'Connell, March 5, 1904, O'Connell Papers, ADPo; O'Connell to Yates, March 7, 1904, Chancery Letterbooks, ADPo; Codman to O'Connell, August 19 and 26, 1903, O'Connell Papers, ADPo; O'Connell to Codman, August

22, 1903, Chancery Letterbooks, ADPo; Goodwin to O'Connell, June 9, 1902, O'Connell Papers, ADPo; O'Connell to Goodwin, June 11, 1902, Chancery Letterbooks, ADPo; O'Connell to O'Brien, July 11, 1901, ibid., *Bangor Commercial,* August 16, 1902; *Portland Telegram,* June 7, 1903.

20. O'Connell to Begin, September 14, 1901, O'Connell Papers, ADPo; undated fragment and O'Connell to "M," "August 21, 1901," O'Connell Papers, AABo 1:8; *Recollections,* 221. The two letters cited from AABo, though purporting to be contemporary with his Portland tenure were in fact written at least ten years after it and must, therefore, be treated, like the *Recollections,* as memoirs. The motto was not a quotation from Scripture, as the usual practice demanded, but a demure editing of the more assertive O'Connell family motto, *"Victor in Arduis."*

21. Collins to O'Brien, July 8, 1901, Chancery Letterbooks, ADPo; O'Brien to Collins, July 13, 1901, Parish Files (Immaculate Conception Cathedral), ADPo; O'Connell to Wallace, March 28 and May 23, 1903, and January 11, 1904, Chancery Letterbooks, ADPo; O'Connell to Williams, October 20, 1903, Williams Papers, AABo 4:11.

22. Michael J. Guignard, *La Foi, La Langue, La Culture: The Franco-Americans of Biddeford, Maine* (Biddeford: Privately printed, 1982), 103–104. On the problems of French Catholics generally, see Jay P. Dolan, *The American Catholic Experience: A History from Colonial Times to the Present* (Garden City, N.Y.: Doubleday, 1985), 178–180. The tensions, culminating in the so-called "corporation sole crisis" of 1909, are described in Gerard J. Brault, *The French-Canadian Heritage in New England* (Hanover, N.H.: University Press of New England, 1986), 68–73. See also Michael J. Guignard, "Maine's Corporation Sole Controversy," *Maine Historical Society Newsletter* 12 (1973): 111–126, and Kenneth B. Woodbury, Jr., "An Incident between the French Canadians and the Irish in the Diocese of Maine in 1906," *New England Quarterly* 40 (1967): 260–269.

23. O'Connell to Lacroix, August 6, 1901, Chancery Letterbooks, ADPo. For other examples of his concern with parish loans and indebtedness, see O'Connell to Bergeron, July 25, 1901, and O'Connell to Reilly, October 31, 1902, ibid.

24. O'Connell to Etenaud, August 23 and October 10, 1901, ibid.; O'Connell to Dupont, May 4, 1902, and O'Connell to Kealy, September 13, 1901, ibid.

25. O'Connell to Laflamme, March 24, 1903, ibid.; Baraldi to O'Connell, October 27, 1902, O'Connell Papers, ADPo, and O'Connell to Baraldi, October 31, 1902, Chancery Letterbooks, ADPo; O'Connell to Charland, October 18, 1902, Parish Files (Saint Francis de Sales's, Waterville), ADPo; O'Connor to Collins, October 30, 1904, Parish Files (Saint Benedict's, Benedicta), ADPo.

26. *S&A,* 2:361.

27. *Catholic Directory, 1901,* 460; *Catholic Directory, 1906,* 527; O'Connell to Ferrier, October 19 and 25, 1901, Chancery Letterbooks, ADPo; O'Connell to all pastors, August 21, 1905, O'Connell Papers, ADPo.

28. O'Connell to Lacroix, June 6, 1902, Chancery Letterbooks, ADPo; O'Connell to all pastors, February 1, 1904, O'Connell Papers, ADPo; O'Connell to "Julian," undated, O'Connell Papers, AABo 1:8; O'Connell to Falconio, February 10, 1904, O'Connell Papers, ADPo.

29. *Catholic Directory, 1901,* 460; *Catholic Directory, 1906,* 527.

30. O'Connell to Vose, November 23 and 29, 1901; April 27, 1903; November 27, 1903; and February 12, 1906; Chancery Letterbooks, ADPo; Vose to O'Connell, November 26, 1901, and November 30, 1903, Parish Files, ADPo. Vose was the grandfather of the Most Reverend Thomas Vose Daily, who was later chancellor and administrator of the archdiocese of Boston and bishop of Brooklyn.

31. O'Connell to Harrington, September 16, 1901, and March 24, 1902, Chancery Letterbooks, ADPo; O'Connell to Burque, November 28, 1902, ibid.; O'Connell to Michaud and Nadeau, November 28, 1902, ibid.

32. On the affairs of the Catholic Indians, see O'Connell to Ahern, Walsh, and Trudel, all July 18, 1901, ADPo, and Trudel to Collins, July 22, 1901, Parish Files (Saint Joseph's, Oldtown), ADPo. For O'Connell's interest in European immigrants, see his pastoral letter, "Ad Clerum," May 31, 1903, S&A, 2:281–289.

33. O'Connell to Charland, October 15, 1901, February 12, 1902, and October 31, 1903; O'Connell to Friel, March 25, 1902; Collins to Kealy, July 8, 1905; O'Connell to Charland, July 31, 1905; all in Chancery Letterbooks, ADPo. See also Charland to O'Connell, January 27, 1902, and the other correspondence on this case in Parish Files (Saint Francis de Sales's, Waterville), ADPo.

34. O'Connell to Marsan, July 27, 1901, Chancery Letterbooks, ADPo; Collins to five priests, October 12, 1903, ibid.; O'Connell to all pastors in Aroostook County, May 18, 1903, O'Connell Papers, ADPo; O'Connell to Dupont, October 27, 1904, Chancery Letterbooks, ADPo.

35. O'Connell to Lecoq, March 24, 1902; O'Connell to Beaven, July 4, 1902; O'Connell to Clary, February 24, 1902; O'Connell to Hamakers, August 3, 1903; all in Chancery Letterbooks, ADPo; O'Connell to O'Connor, August 13, 1901, and O'Connell to Kenny, August 1, 1902, ibid.

36. Catholic Directory, 1901, 456, 460; see also Healy's ad limina report for 1898, APF 153/1898, N.S. 145:348–361.

37. O'Connell to pastors, August 14, 1902, Chancery Letterbooks, ADPo; O'Connell to Mother Teresa, August 1, 1901, ibid.; O'Connell to Dupont, September 26, 1903, and O'Connell to Superior, Grey Nuns, Quebec, April 4, 1903, ibid.

38. O'Connell to Directress, Healy Asylum, March 5, 1903, ibid.; O'Connell to Superior, Hospital of Our Lady of Lourdes, March 4, 1903, ibid.

39. See "Financial Statement of R[oman] C[atholic] B[ishop] of Portland, Sept. 17, 1906," ADPo. O'Connell to Forest, March 12, 1903, Chancery Letterbooks, ADPo.

40. Collins to Maher, December 5 and 10, 1903, Chancery Letterbooks, ADPo; Collins to Libby and Chapman, July 22, 1905, and Collins to McDonald, July 12, 1905, O'Connell Papers, ADPo; O'Connell to Linehan, September 22, 1904, Chancery Letterbooks, ADPo.

41. O'Connell to Sweron and O'Connell to Burque, both October 16, 1901, Chancery Letterbooks, ADPo; O'Connell to LaRiviere, August 22, 1901, and O'Connell to Clary, August 23, 1901, ibid. McCarthy to O'Connell, May 29, 1905, Parish Files (Saint Mary's, Houlton), ADPo, explains the difficulty pastors had in increasing these collections.

42. O'Connell to Sweron, August 30, 1901, Chancery Letterbooks, ADPo; circular letter, June 8, 1902, O'Connell Papers, ADPo; circular letter, June 22,

1903, ibid.; circular letter, July 25, 1904, and Falconio to O'Connell, October 22, 1903, ibid.

43. The following narrative of the diocese's financial condition is taken from Walsh's "Financial Statement of the R. C. B. of Portland, Sept. 17, 1906," ADPo. This single volume, unpaginated, is written entirely in Walsh's hand. Though dated from the time of his arrival in Portland, the statement seems from internal evidence to have been written in June 1910, by which time most of the problems Walsh notes had been fully explored and corrected. On the various modes of church legal structure, see Patrick J. Dignan, A History of the Legal Incorporation of Catholic Church Property in the United States, 1784–1932 (New York: P. J. Kenedy and Sons, 1935); Portland is discussed 238–240 and 251–252. See also Chester J. Bartlett, The Tenure of Parochial Property in the United States of America (Washington, D.C.: Catholic University of America, 1926), 77–81, and Thomas F. Donovan, The Status of the Church in American Civil Law and Canon Law (Washington, D.C.: Catholic University of America, 1966), 94–96.

44. Walsh, "Financial Statement," ADPo. O'Connell's letter, though noted by Walsh, does not survive, either in ADPo or AABo.

45. Bangor Commercial, August 16, 1902.

46. O'Connell served as bishop of Portland for fifty-five months, and he was away from Maine for thirteen of them, an absentee rate of 23.63 percent.

3. AMBITION: THE CAMPAIGN FOR BOSTON, 1904–1907

1. Despite his long tenure, Williams is one of the "forgotten men" of American Catholic history, and he has no decent biography. He is treated, not always sympathetically, in HAB 3:3–437; see especially pages 416–437 for a discussion of his last years. There is an unpublished "Life of Archbishop Williams" in AABo that provides a more detailed and more personal narrative of his career. This massive work (almost 800 typed pages) was written shortly after his death by a Carmelite nun, Mother Augustine of the Mother of God, who in lay life had been Eulalia Tuckerman. The daughter of Boston businessman Samuel Tuckerman, who had converted to Catholicism under the instruction of the young Father Williams, Mother Augustine had known the archbishop from her childhood and had access in preparing her biography to many Williams letters which do not now survive. The work is marred by a hagiographic, uncritical tone, but it is nonetheless the fullest exposition of the prelate's life and career.

2. Hale to Falconio, May 7, 1904, and Murphy to Falconio, May 3, 1904, both ADUSA, IV:73/1, ASV. On the changes in Boston in this era, see Thomas H. O'Connor, Bibles, Brahmins, and Bosses: A Short History of Boston (Boston: Boston Public Library, 1984), 119–134. On the early career of Fitzgerald and his significance for the local Catholic community, see Doris Kearns Goodwin, The Fitzgeralds and the Kennedys (New York: Simon & Schuster, 1987), 69–76 and 92–129.

3. The literature on Americanism is vast and that on modernism less so but still growing. For a useful summary of the impact of these controversies in America see Hennesey, American Catholics, 196–203 and 216–217.

4. *Bangor Commercial*, August 16, 1902; *Boston Journal*, October 4, 1903; *Boston Herald*, October 9, 1903.

5. Margaret M. Reher, "Pope Leo XIII and 'Americanism,'" *Theological Studies* 34 (1973): 679–689; see also Reher's "The Church and the Kingdom of God in America: The Ecclesiology of the Americanists" (Ph.D. diss.: Fordham University, 1972); Gibbons to Ireland, June 20, 1901, JIP, microfilm roll 8, frames 128–130. On Ireland, see Marvin R. O'Connell, *John Ireland and the American Catholic Church* (Saint Paul: Minnesota Historical Society, 1988).

6. O'Connell to Falconio, May 25, 1903, Chancery Letterbooks, ADPo; O'Connell to Falconio, July 29, 1903, ibid. On the death of Leo, O'Connell also wrote to Merry del Val: "As I feel sure of your sincere and deep interest in all that concerns his [i.e., Leo's] memory, I have thought it proper thus to bring to your knowledge that the Diocese of Portland is not lacking in this solemn duty"; O'Connell to Merry del Val, July 29, 1903, ibid. For O'Connell's refusal to comment on speculations about his future, see his correspondence with Lockney (December 1903) and Ruffin (September 1904), O'Connell Papers, ADPo.

7. O'Connell to Merry del Val, February 16, 1904, Secretary of State Files 1904 (Rub. 280, Prot. 4150), ASV; Ireland to Harkins, July 16, 1904, SAB, RG9, Box 6.

8. MacNutt to O'Connell, "Befana [i.e., Epiphany] 1902," O'Connell Papers, ADPo. MacNutt described his activities in a surprisingly frank autobiography, *A Papal Chamberlain*. O'Connell later remembered him as a man with "an extremely brilliant mind, very witty and at times somewhat cynical"; *Recollections*, 191.

9. MacNutt to O'Connell, [June 1903] and May 5, [1904], O'Connell Papers, ADPo; O'Connell to Farley, June 14, 1904, Farley Papers I–7 (microfilm roll 2), AANY; see also MacNutt to Farley, June 19, 1904, ibid., and O'Connell to Corrigan, March 21, 1902, Corrigan Papers, G–27 (microfilm roll 21), ibid. O'Connell had also discussed MacNutt's advancement with Cardinal Gibbons; see O'Connell to Gibbons, June 15, 1904, AABa 101–K–5.

10. O'Connell to Fitzgerald, November 4, 1902, and October 1, 1904, Chancery Letterbooks, ADPo; O'Connell to Boulger, February 1, 1904, ibid.; O'Connell to Maher, March 9, 1903, ibid.

11. *Recollections*, 224–226. The records in the Secretariat of State (1903/Rub. 76666, ASV) in the Vatican Archives relating to the Manila appointment are still closed and unavailable for research, but the files of the American apostolic delegation contain most of the relevent documents; see especially Rampolla to Falconio, April 17, 1903, ADUSA, IV:61, ASV.

12. O'Connell to Rampolla, April 20, 1903, copy in ADUSA, IV:61, ASV; the documents concerning the eventual appointment to Manila of Father Jeremiah Harty are in ADUSA IV:61, ASV; MacNutt to O'Connell, undated but perhaps June 1903, O'Connell Papers, ADPo.

13. Williams to Gotti, September 16, 1903, Williams Papers, AABo 2:20; Gotti to Williams, October 17, 1904, ibid., 4:45. On Williams's earlier consideration of this step, see also Matthew Harkins Diary, April 15, 1903, ADPr.

14. Harkins Diary, November 23 and December 2, 1903, ADPr. Williams's communication with the delegate is cited in Gaffey, "Changing of the Guard," 229. On Harkins's earlier career, see *HAB*, 3:213, 241, and 273.

15. Episcopal Register, AABo, April 4 and 7, 1904; "Minutes of the meeting of the suffragan bishops of the Province of Boston," SAB RG9, Box 6; Harkins Diary, April 7, 1907, ADPr. O'Connell's Italian version of the minutes was even more emphatic about his nonparticipation, saying that he "ne parlo ne voto" (neither spoke nor voted). The recorded votes confirm that he did not participate in the selection: in every ballot there was one blank; Falconio to Williams, April 16, 1904, Williams Papers, AABo 2:1.

16. O'Connell's assessment of candidates (undated but probably April 1904) is filed with a letter of Walsh to Bonzano, June 5, 1914, ADUSA, IV:73/2, ASV. There is also a copy in SAB RG9, Box 6.

17. O'Connell to Merry del Val, April 17, 1904, quoted in Gaffey, "Changing of the Guard," 230. On the attempt to meet with the delegate, see O'Connell to Falconio, May 23, 1904, and Falconio to O'Connell, May 26, 1904, ADUSA, IV:73/1, ASV.

18. Supple to Falconio, April 9, 1904, and Cummins to Falconio, April 18, 1904, both ADUSA, IV:73/1, ASV. Other letters supporting O'Connell dated April–May 1904, are ibid. See also Supple to Gotti, April 26, 1904, Secretary of State Files 1904 (Rub. 280, Prot. 5323), ibid.

19. Murphy to Falconio, May 3, 1904; Power to Falconio, April 19, 1904; Daly to Falconio, April 27, 1904; all ADUSA, IV:73/1, ASV.

20. Hale to Falconio, May 7, 1904, ibid. The reference to "Doctor" O'Connell was not entirely out of place, since bishops were awarded the title of "Doctor of Divinity" whether they had actually earned the academic degree or not.

21. The letters endorsing Harkins, dated between April 18 and 29, 1904, are ibid.; Williams to Falconio, April 20, 1904, ibid. See also Supple to Gotti, April 17, 1904, ibid.

22. Cummings to O'Connell, and O'Connell to Cummings, both February 17, 1904, O'Connell Papers, AABo 4:5; Collins et al. to Falconio, April 23, 1904, ADUSA, IV:73/1, ASV. There is also a copy of this statement in Correspondence Files with Other Dioceses (Portland), AABo.

23. For Catholic reactions to the war see Hennesey, *American Catholics*, 204–205, and Dorothy Dohen, *Nationalism and American Catholicism* (New York: Sheed & Ward, 1967), 116–121. Healy to O'Connell, April 12, 1898, O'Connell Papers, AABo 5:12; O'Connell to Julia O'Connell, May 27, 1898, O'Connell Papers, ADPo; Merry del Val to O'Connell, April 22, 1898, ibid.

24. Though Denis's letters to William do not survive, the course of their exchange may be followed in William's letters to Denis, February 17, February 23, and March 14, 1904, all in Chancery Letterbooks, ADPo; the quotation is from the letter of February 23. Even Dorothy Wayman, respectful as always of members of the hierarchy, found sufficient evidence to convict Denis of complicity; see her *Cardinal O'Connell*, 109–111. On the future coolness between the two men see, for example, William O'Connell to Gibbons, November 17, 1908, AABa 106–L–12.

25. Gaffey, "Changing of the Guard," 232.

26. *Boston Herald*, March 12, 1905; MacNutt, *Papal Chamberlain*, 279. As usual, O'Connell traveled to Rome with a small entourage, including two priests from Boston and three former parishioners from Saint Joseph's, Boston; see O'Connell to Manager, White Star Line, November 4, 1904, Chancery Letterbooks, ADPo.

27. *Recollections*, 232.

28. Otis Cary, *A History of Christianity in Japan: Roman Catholic, Greek Orthodox, and Protestant Missions* (Rutland, Vt.: Charles E. Tuttle, 1976), 1:366–367; Richard H. Drummond, *A History of Christianity in Japan* (Grand Rapids, Mich.: Eerdmans, 1971), 308, 311–312. O'Connell's description of the mission is in *Recollections*, 232–250; Wayman's account is in *Cardinal O'Connell*, 118–129.

29. Igino Cardinale, *La Sainte-Seige et la Diplomatie: Aperçu Historique, Juridique et Pratique de la Diplomatie Pontificale* (Paris; DesClees, 1962), 143; Robert A. Graham, *Vatican Diplomacy: A Study of Church and State on the International Plane* (Princeton: Princeton University Press, 1959), 96, 337; *Recollections*, 247, 249–250; O'Connell to "X," "December 5, 1905," O'Connell Papers, AABo 2:4.

30. Stang to Riordan, January 22, 1906, quoted in Gaffey, "Changing of the Guard," 235. The letters to Rome are cited ibid., 233 n. 22 and 235 n. 36.

31. Father Charles Collins Diary, January 12, 13, 14, 15, 18, 19. and 22, 1906, AABo. This diary is incorrectly attributed in the *Guide to the Archives of the Archdiocese of Boston* (New York: Garland, 1982), 94, to James P. E. O'Connell.

32. Collins Diary, January 22 and February 1, 1906, AABo; for the pope's approval of the choice, see Veccia to Falconio, February 6, 1906, ADUSA, IV:73/2, ASV. See also *Recollections*, 263.

33. Harkins Diary, March 10, 1906, ADPr; Stang to Falconio, February 17, 1906, ADUSA, IV:73/2, ASV; Gibbons to O'Connell, March 21, 1906, O'Connell Papers, AABo 5:6. See also O'Connell's reply to Gibbons, March 24, 1906, AABa 103–F–10. Though he was disappointed, Williams wrote swiftly to Propaganda, accepting the choice; Williams to Gotti, February 21, 1906, cited in Gaffey, "Changing of the Guard," 237 n. 34.

34. Stang to Falconio, February 10 and 13, 1906, ADUSA, IV:73/2, ASV; Riordan to Stang, March 5, 1906, Stang Papers, ADFR, copy in AASF; Stang to Riordan, February 27, 1906, Riordan Papers, AASF. Beavan's comment is quoted in Harkins Diary, March 15, 1906, ADPr. The protest letter, dated June 5, 1906, is in ADUSA, IV:73/2, ASV; there is also a copy in the Archives of the Archdiocese of Hartford; Harkins to Ireland, December 6, 1906, JIP, microfilm roll 10, frames 563–564.

35. These quotations and those that follow are taken from O'Connell's "Address to the Clergy on Assuming the Coadjutorship," *S&A*, 3:9–17.

36. The activities of O'Connell's coadjutorship are outlined in *HAB* 3:494–498.

37. For discussions of the content of Americanism, see Thomas T. McAvoy, *The Great Crisis in American Catholic History* (Chicago: H. Regnery, 1957); Robert D. Cross, *The Emergence of Liberal Catholicism in America* (Cambridge, Mass.: Harvard University Press, 1958); and Fogarty, *Vatican and the Americanist Crisis*.

38. Norman P. Tanner, ed., *Decrees of the Ecumenical Councils* (London: Sheed & Ward, 1990), 813–814; "Longinqua Oceani," *The Papal Encyclicals, 1878–1903,* ed. Claudia Carlen (Raleigh, N.C.: McGrath, 1981), 2:364–365.

39. For the career and ideological significance of Archbishop Corrigan, see Curran, *Corrigan and the Shaping of Conservative Catholicism.*

4. *VIGOR IN ARDUIS:* THE MAKING OF A NEW EPISCOPAL STYLE, 1907–1915

1. Williams's last days are touchingly described in *HAB,* 3:420–424; the quotation is at page 422. See also Mother Augustine, "Life of Archbishop Williams," AABo, 716–752.

2. *S&A,* 3:70, 68, 63, 71. In later years, O'Connell (perhaps contemplating the prospect that he might see Williams in the next world) mellowed in his opinion of his predecessor; see his *A Tribute of Affectionate Memory to Most Rev. John J. Williams* (Boston: Privately printed, 1940); *Recollections,* 266.

3. *Pilot,* October 5, 1907. O'Connell's schedule has been reconstructed with the aid of the scrapbooks of newspaper clippings, covering his entire tenure, which are preserved in the Saint John's Seminary Library, Brighton, Massachusetts.

4. Clippings scrapbooks, 1907–1920, Saint John's Seminary Library.

5. Maher to O'Connell, October 26, 1908, O'Connell Papers, AABo 7:4. The pastoral letters and other speeches are faithfully reproduced in *S&A.* The Kennedy wedding is described in Goodwin, *Fitzgeralds and Kennedys,* 259. Goodwin describes the similar press treatment accorded Mayor "Honey Fitz," the other engaging public personality of the day; ibid., 116, 122.

6. On the development of the newspaper business generally in this era, see Frank Luther Mott, *American Journalism: A History, 1690–1960* (New York: Macmillan, 1962), 546–560 and 577–592; his discussion of Boston papers is 559–560 and 661–662. See also Herbert A. Kenny, *Newspaper Row: Journalism in the Pre-Television Era* (Chester, Conn.: Globe Pequot Press, 1987), 55. On the use of Cunningham, see J. P. E. O'Connell to Cunningham, December 10, 1915, Institution Files, AABo 9:13. On Flynn, see Sullivan to Bouve, March 27, 1913, Chancery Central Subject File M–1754, ibid., and Mullen to Bonzano, March 22, May 22, and June 26, 1920, ADUSA, IX (Boston): 95/2, ASV. On the *Globe's* ready compliance with his wishes, see Louis M. Lyons, *Newspaper Story: One Hundred Years of the Boston Globe* (Cambridge, Mass.: Belknap Press, 1971), 289.

7. Francis R. Walsh, "The Boston *Pilot*: A Newspaper for the Irish Immigrant, 1829–1908" (Ph.D. diss.: Boston University, 1968).

8. *Recollections,* 294. The acquisition of the paper is described in detail in the court decision *James T. Murphy v. Pilot Publishing Company* (Suffolk Superior Court #54184), a copy of which is in *Pilot* Files, AABo 1:5. After his work was completed, Murphy had sued the newspaper, claiming that he had not received the compensation due him, and the court awarded a nominal amount. On the question of whether it was legal to sell the paper in churches, see Brett to O'Connell, September 29, 1909, and O'Connell to Brett, October 2, 1909, Institution Files, ADBo, 12:22; Hausser to Hayes, September 26, 1909, and J. P. E. O'Connell to Splaine, October 5,

1909, *Pilot* Files, AABo, 1:8. See also O'Connell to priests, September 14, 1908, Chancery Circulars, AABo 2:17.

9. Auditor's reports, December 8, 1909, March 23, 1911, and March 25, 1912, *Pilot* Files, AABo 1:5–6. For the hounding of pastors, see, for example, Haberlin to Butler, December 4, 1916, and Butler to O'Connell, December 29, 1916, Parish Files, AABo, 70:9; the less favorable view of the paper is in Doody to Haberlin, December 16, 1916, ibid., 35:2. The records of the Catholic Literature Campaign are in *Pilot* Files, AABo 9:15–20 and 10:1–7.

10. *Boston Journal*, December 20, 1903. The "quantitative values" of the turn-of -the -century era, in which bigger always meant better and weight and solidity had both literal and figurative meanings, is remarked on in Robert H. Wiebe, *The Search for Order, 1877–1920* (London: Macmillan, 1967), 41–43.

11. *Boston American*, February 2, 1913.

12. O'Connell to Tracy, April 10, 1908, Parish Files, AABo 10:7. O'Connell's rejection of joint billing with Curtis Guild did not result from any hostility between the two men, who were in fact personally close. Guild addressed the archbishop as "My dear William," a familiarity O'Connell reciprocated. On this subject see O'Toole, "'That Fabulous Churchman,'" 37.

13. O'Brien to O'Connell, October 17, 19, and 24, 1907, Parish Files, AABo 33:15; Perkins to O'Connell, February 9 and July 9, 1909, Institution Files, AABo 1:1; Chancery Account Book ("Bank Accounts, 1908–1916"), AABo, 911.

14. *Boston Journal*, July 11, 1908; *Boston Evening Transcript*, November 7, 1908; Fitzgerald to O'Connell, May 2, 1911, and O'Connell to Fitzgerald, May 3, 1911, Parish Files, AABo 1:1. On O'Connell's summer place in Gloucester, see Joseph E. Garland, *Boston's North Shore: Being an Account of Life among the Noteworthy, Fashionable, Wealthy, Eccentric and Ordinary, 1823–1890* (Boston: Little, Brown, 1978), 335.

15. *New York American*, November 13, 1908; *Boston Post*, March 29, 1910. On his election to The Country Club, see Sheehan to J. P. E. O'Connell, March 26, 1910, O'Connell Papers, AABo 14:5; the correspondence regarding the other clubs is ibid., 14:5–6. On O'Connell's friendship with Mrs. Gardner, see *New York Evening Journal*, February 15, 1908, *Washington Post*, February 17, 1908, and Louise H. Tharp, *Mrs. Jack: A Biography of Isabella Stewart Gardner* (Boston: Little, Brown, 1965), 140, 275.

16. On the 1911 European trip see O'Connell to J. P. E. O'Connell, June 9 and August 20, 1911, and J. P. E. O'Connell to O'Connell, June 14, 1911, O'Connell Papers ("Uncataloged"), AABo. The objections to the nickname, a title that endures today in the oral tradition of Catholic Boston, were related to me by O'Connell's nieces, Anna O'Connell Downing and Josephine O'Connell Kirk, during my interview with them at Osterville, Massachusetts, on July 6, 1984. This nickname also had a darker aspect, implying a "walk-the-plank" approach to anyone who crossed him.

17. On the emotional and symbolic significance of public figures, see Orrin E. Klapp, *Symbolic Leaders: Public Dramas and Public Men* (Chicago: Aldine, 1964), esp. 211–249 ("vehicle for identification," p. 43), Murray Edelman, *The Symbolic Uses of Politics* (Urbana: University of Illinois Press, 1964), and Kathleen Dalton, "Why

America Loved Teddy Roosevelt; Or Charisma Is in the Eyes of the Beholders,"
Psychohistory Review 8 (1979): 16–26. Jack Alexander, "The Cardinal and Cold
Roast Boston," *Saturday Evening Post*, October 4, 1941, 116.

18. *S&A*, 3:137, 120.

19. O'Reilly to O'Connell, May 18, July 23, and August 1, 1908; J. P. E.
O'Connell to O'Reilly, July 1908, all in O'Connell Papers, AABo 8:9; see also
Maher to O'Connell, October 26, 1908, ibid., 7:4.

20. O'Connell to Gibbons, January 2, 1911, AABa 109–A–2; O'Connell to
Gibbons, June 20, 1918, ibid., 122–J–2.

21. Hayes to O'Connell, March 28, 1919, O'Connell Papers, AABo 5:11;
Ireland to Gibbons, November 17, 1917, SAB, RG9, Box 6; Harkins to Beavan,
December 12, 1910, Beavan Papers, Archives, Diocese of Springfield.

22. The text of the encyclical, *Pascendi dominici gregis*, dated September 8,
1907, is in *The Papal Encyclicals*, ed. Claudia Carlen, 3:71–98; the quotation is at 89.
On the impact of Pius's letter in the United States, see Michael V. Gannon, "Before
and After Modernism: The Intellectual Isolation of the American Priest," in *The
Catholic Priest in the United States: Historical Investigations*, ed. John Tracy Ellis
(Collegeville, Minn.: Saint John's University Press, 1971), 337.–340. O'Connell's
pastoral letter is in *S&A*, 3:72–87; the quotations are at pp. 73 and 82. See also
O'Connell to Harkins, December 6, 1907, Correspondence Files with Other
Dioceses (Providence), AABo.

23. On the musical commission, see *Boston Record*, May 13, 1908. See also
Merry del Val to O'Connell, February 16, 1911, O'Connell Papers, AABo 7:9, and
Merry del Val to O'Connell, December 26, 1909, ibid., 7:8. The Theodore
Roosevelt affair was a convoluted one, absorbing a great deal of energy on all sides;
see the correspondence about it, ibid.

24. O'Connell to Merry del Val, August 9, 1910, and Merry del Val to
O'Connell, August 23, 1910, O'Connell Papers, AABo 7:8. The Spanish problem is
described briefly in Carlo Falconi, *The Popes in the Twentieth Century: From Pius X to
John XXIII*, trans. Murial Grindrod (London: Weidenfeld and Nicolson, 1967),
75–76.

25. *Boston Record*, December 24, 1908; *New York Times*, March 28, 1909;
Lowell Sun, June 9, 1909.

26. See the letters between O'Connell and Merry del Val, dated January 14
and 27, 1909; December 1909; February 16 and March 2, 1911; March 12, 1912; and
April 13, 1918; all in O'Connell Papers, AABo 7:8–9. The cardinal secretary's interest in the Trastevere orphanage is described in Buehrle, *Merry del Val*, 33–35
and 181–188.

27. Collections and Donations Account Book, 1892–1904, AABo;
Collections and Donations Account Book, 1905–1907, ibid. Boston's contribution
was about $8,500 in 1903 and nearly $14,000 (more than 10 percent of the total
from the entire country) in 1907. The figure of $80,000 for all American giving is in
Edward R. Kantowicz, *Corporation Sole: Cardinal Mundelein and Chicago Catholicism*
(Notre Dame, Ind.: University of Notre Dame Press), 42. The instruction that
priests take up the offering is in O'Connell to pastors, February 1908, Chancery
Circulars, AABo 2:17.

28. Chancery Account Book, 1908–1916, AABo; O'Connell to pastors, March 1910, Chancery Circulars, AABo, 2:18; O'Connell to Merry del Val, April 4, 1911, and February 26, 1910, O'Connell Papers, AABo, 7:9 and 7:8. The account books indicate that O'Connell was equally willing to deduct from the actual collection in the interests of achieving a round number. In 1911, the returns from the parishes brought in $22,310.17, but an even $20,000 was sent to Rome, the remainder kept in Boston. In 1915, the difference was even more exaggerated: $39,023.46 came in from Boston's Catholics but only $30,000 went to Rome.

29. *Boston Journal*, May 22, 1911.

30. Merry del Val to O'Connell, October 18, 1911, O'Connell Papers, AABo 7:9.

31. Cary to O'Connell, November 3, 1911, ibid., 3:9; Prendergast to Pius X (copy), October 31, 1911, ibid., 9:3; Kelley to O'Connell, October 31, 1911, ibid., 6:2; Sister M. Romualda to O'Connell, December 16, 1921, Institution Files, AABo, 8:18.

32. Walsh to Ireland, December 8, 1911, JIP, roll 11, frames 604–607; Harkins to Ireland, October 30, 1911, ibid., frames 595–596; MacNutt to O'Connell, November 1, 1911, O'Connell Papers, AABo 7:2. For Gibbons's reaction, see Gaffey, "Changing of the Guard," 242. On Ireland's prospects for the red hat, see O'Connell, *John Ireland and the American Catholic Church*, esp. 492–498.

33. *Recollections*, 310, 311; *S&A*, 3:430–431.

34. The events of the consistory are described in detail in *Recollections*, 312–314, Wayman, *Cardinal O'Connell*, 151–155, and *HAB*, 3:555–557. Each cardinal received the "title" to a church in Rome as a means of maintaining the ancient tradition that they surrounded the pope literally and figuratively as his closest advisers. Cardinals enjoyed no practical jurisdiction over these titular churches, though they were expected to contribute to their upkeep. Other details of the trip were provided in the author's interview with Anna Downing and Josephine Kirk, July 6, 1984.

35. J. P. E. O'Connell to O'Connell, December 4 and 22, 1911, O'Connell Papers ("Uncataloged"), AABo. Whereas archbishops were addressed as "Your Grace" or "Your Excellency," cardinals were entitled to the grander "Your Eminence." The donations in support of San Clemente are described in *Recollections*, 315–316, Wayman, *Cardinal O'Connell*, 168, and *HAB*, 3:560–562, 565. The family name of "Uncle Cardinal" was made known in author's interview with Anna Downing and Josephine Kirk, July 6, 1984.

36. *Recollections*, 313.

37. *HAB*, 3:558–561. The dispute over the regiment is in *Boston Post*, January 9, 1912. *Boston Evening Transcript*, March 16, 1912, describes the controversy over the dinner. The paper also reported that Foss had originally been placed second until a telephone call from O'Connell's office to the planning committee had demanded that position for the cardinal. Foss was eventually pacified by a visit from the former diocesan chancellor and close O'Connell aide, Father Michael J. Splaine. See ibid. and *Boston Traveler*, March 21, 1912.

38. A copy of "The Charge of the Gold Brigade," which was given a dramatic reading at a meeting of Boston's Clover Club, is in the Walsh Papers, ADPo; O'Donnell, "How History Is Made, 1912," ibid.

39. *S&A*, 10:102, 103. On the contemporary understanding of the nature of Catholic Holy Orders, see Sullivan, "Beneficial Relations," *Catholic Boston*, 217–219.

40. Carr to Burke, October 20, 1931, Chancery Central Subject File M–1963, AABo. The other great self-creating personage of this era was O'Connell's political analog, Theodore Roosevelt, who invented and publicized a childhood and early career in the interests of his electoral and foreign-policy goals; see John Milton Cooper, Jr., *The Warrior and the Priest: Woodrow Wilson and Theodore Roosevelt* (Cambridge, Mass.: Belknap Press, 1983), 5–14.

41. *Letters of His Eminence William Cardinal O'Connell, Archbishop of Boston*, vol. 1: *From College Days, 1876, to Bishop of Portland, 1901* (Cambridge, Mass.: Riverside Press, 1915).

42. I have discussed the spurious nature of these letters in "'That Fabulous Churchman,'" 39–40. See also John Tracy Ellis, *Catholic Bishops: A Memoir* (Wilmington, Del.: Michael Glazier, 1983), 75. Subsequent volumes of the series of letters never appeared, at least in part because their suspect nature was widely known.

43. O'Connell to Merry del Val, November 21, 1923, O'Connell Papers, AABo 7:10.

44. *Recollections*, 268.

5. "THE MAXIMUM OF EFFICIENCY": ADMINISTRATIVE MYTH AND REALITY, 1907–1920

1. *Catholic Directory*, 1907, 47.

2. The assignments of all these priests may be traced in the Priests Correspondence Files, AABo. For Mullen, see William Wolkovich-Valkavičius, "Cardinal and Cleric: O'Connell and Mullen in Conflict," *Historical Journal of Massachusetts* 13 (1985): 129–139. For the significance of O'Connell's position as rector of the cathedral, see Sullivan, "Beneficial Relations," *Catholic Boston*, 228.

3. O'Connell to priests, November 22, 1907, January 12, 1911, and March 2, 1912, Chancery Circulars, AABo 2:16, 3:1, and 3:2, respectively; *HAB*, 3:525; *Constitutiones Dioecesos Bostoniensis* (Boston: Pilot Publishing Company, 1910).

4. Krasnickas to Sullivan, November 13, 1915, Parish Files, AABo 32:15; *Recollections*, 301.

5. On the development of American business as a whole at this time, see Alfred D. Chandler, Jr., *The Visible Hand: The Managerial Revolution in American Business* (Cambridge, Mass.: Belknap Press, 1977), and JoAnne Yates, *Control through Communication: The Rise of System in American Management* (Baltimore: Johns Hopkins University Press, 1989). On the conservatism of church administration, see James Gollin, *Worldly Goods: The Wealth and Power of the American Catholic Church, the Vatican, and the Men Who Control the Money* (New York: Random House, 1971), 167, 172, and 190–191.

6. Leo XIII quoted in Alexander, "Cardinal and Cold Roast Boston," 116; "Cardinal O'Connell, His House, and His Long Daily Routine," *Boston Herald*, June 2, 1912.

7. *Recollections*, 271, 270.

8. Alexander, "Cardinal and Cold Roast Boston," 116; *HAB*, 3:501; Donna Merwick, *Boston Priests, 1848–1910: A Study of Social and Intellectual Change* (Cambridge, Mass.: Harvard University Press, 1973), 177, 178. On the development of the image of Catholic bishops as shrewd businessmen, see James M. O'Toole, "The Role of Bishops in American Catholic History: Myth and Reality in the Case of Cardinal William O'Connell," CHR 77 (1991): 595–615.

9. *HAB* 3:57–63; *Catholic Directory*, 1907, 47; O'Connell to Havey, November 14, 1907, and O'Connell to Chapon, December 5, 1907, Saint John Seminary Files, AABo 1:2. "Notes by Father Havey," August 15, 1935, SAB, RG9, Box 6; *Recollections*, 287.

10. Havey, "Brief Notes on Archbishop O'Connell and Sulpicians at Brighton Seminary," no date but probably 1910, SAB, RG9, Box 6; Dyer, "Notes on conversation with Father Price," April 30, 1911, ibid.; *Recollections*, 285. The Sulpicians were also under siege elsewhere, accused of doctrinal irregularities and modernism; see Kauffman, *Tradition and Transformation in Catholic Culture*, 199–223.

11. There are two accounts of the fateful meeting, different in some details but in agreement on substance, from which this narrative is constructed. They are Havey's "Visit of V. Rev. Fr. H. P. Garriguet to His Grace the M. Rev. W. H. O'Connell, D.D.," October 4, 1910, SAB, RG9, Box 6; and "Agreement reached by R. C. Abp. of Boston & Sup. Gen. of Sulpicians," September 29, 1910, Saint John Seminary Files, AABo 1:12. See also Kauffman, *Tradition and Transformation*, 229–238.

12. O'Connell to Garriguet, October 21, 1910, SAB, RG9, Box 6; Peterson to O'Connell, October 27 and December 28, 1910, Saint John Seminary Files, AABo 1:13; *Pilot*, May 20, 1911. The story of the Sulpician ouster is told with refreshing candor in John E. Sexton and Arthur J. Riley's official *History of Saint John's Seminary, Brighton* (Boston: Archdiocese of Boston, 1945), 140–143. See also White, *Diocesan Seminary in the United States*, 261–262.

13. Merwick, *Boston Priests*, 177; O'Connell to priests, November 22, 1907, Chancery Circulars, AABo 2:16. The development of charitable institutions in the Williams era is described in *HAB*, 3:358–382, and in Susan S. Walton, "To Preserve the Faith: Catholic Charities in Boston, 1870–1930," *Catholic Boston*, 67–119. See also Peter C. Holleran, *Boston's Wayward Children: Social Services for Homeless Children, 1830–1930* (Rutherford, N.J.: Fairleigh Dickinson University Press, 1989).

14. Collections and Donations Account Book, 1892–1904, AABo; annual reports on charities collection, 1909–1917, Chancery Circulars, AABo., 3:1, 5–8.

15. *Recollections*, 273–274; O'Connell to Redican, December 6, 1907, Institution Files, AABo 13:20; copy of mortgage document, February 1909, ibid., 14:1; "Letter read to pastors on Retreat, Fri., July 30, 1909," ibid.

16. Annual reports, 1900–1905, Institution Files, AABo 3a:1; the auditor's reports for 1911 and 1914, ibid., 1:13, describe the home's status in those years and also provide comparative retrospective data for the end of the Williams episcopate. The home's investments, consisting mainly of railroad securities, municipal bonds, and blue chip stocks such as AT&T, are described in Bruen to O'Connell, January 24, 1910, ibid., 1:11.

17. Annual report, 1907, ibid., 7:5; *Recollections*, 277; "Opinion of Judge Joseph D. Fallon concerning 'House of the Angel Guardian,'" February 8, 1908, Institution Files, AABo 7:5; O'Connell to Fallon, February 20, 1908, and O'Connell to Brother Jude, January 29, 1909, ibid.; Sullivan to Brother Jude, November 2, 1914, and Brother Jude to Sullivan, November 3, 1914, ibid.

18. Reports of the corporation, April 30, 1894, February 10, 1902, and December 16, 1904, Saint Elizabeth's Hospital Corporation Records, 1872–1904, AABo; see also the valuation of landholdings, September 10, 1907, Hospital Files, AABo 1:1. On the increase in patients and services see "Report for Years 1911 & 1912," ibid., 1:2. The purchase and sale agreement for the Brighton property is ibid., 1:1. The fund-raising campaign is described in Scanlan, "Full and Final Report on Campaign in Behalf of the New Saint Elizabeth's Hospital," March 25, 1914, ibid., 1:4; see also *HAB*, 3:575–578.

19. Annual reports, 1910 and 1911, Hospital Files, AABo 8:2; O'Connell to Kelley, October 24, 1911, ibid.; O'Connell to Ronan, February 15, 1910, ibid.; annual reports, 1912 and 1919, ibid., 8:3. The 1919 report indicates that, in the period between 1914 and 1919, Saint Margaret's income exceeded that of Saint Mary's by a factor ranging between four and six to one. The newer institution was plainly the economic salvation of the older one. On the Ronan brothers and the hospital, see *HAB*, 3:535.

20. Sullivan to O'Connell, December 7, 1908, and O'Connell to Sullivan, December 9, 1908, Hospital Files, AABo 6:1; Haberlin to Properzi, January 31, 1919, Parish Files, AABo 70:15.

21. *HAB*, 3:501; *Recollections*, 282.

22. Sister Gonzaga to O'Connell, January 15, 1908, Hospital Files, AABo 6:1; Sister Raphael to O'Connell, January 21, 1908, ibid., 12:1.

23. Sullivan to Anderson, February 27, 1909, ibid., 6:1; see also Sullivan to Anderson, December 31, 1908, ibid.

24. Hanselman to O'Connell, June 5, 1912; Sullivan to Gasson, March 12 and April 9, 1912; Sullivan to Gasson, October 16, 1912; O'Connell to Devlin, February 11, 1920; all in Institution Files, ibid., 12:23.

25. On Gasson's tenure, see Dunigan, *History of Boston College*, 180–205.

26. O'Connell to Gasson, June 14, 1910, Institution Files, AABo 12:22.

27. Ibid. Gasson's dreams were only partially fulfilled. A graduate school of arts and sciences opened in 1926 and a law school was started in 1929; Boston College has never had a medical school.

28. Gasson to O'Connell, December 19, 1910, ibid.; Haberlin to Lyons, May 11, 1918, ibid., 12:24.

29. *HAB*, 3:501.

30. The contemporary theology of the priesthood is discussed in Sullivan, "Beneficial Relations," *Catholic Boston*, 217–218.

31. On O'Brien's career and the *Sacred Heart Review*, see Stephanie Lang Martin, "A Guide to the Records of Sacred Heart Parish, East Cambridge" (M.A. thesis: University of Massachusetts–Boston, 1980), esp. 5–24. See also *HAB*, 3:398, and Merwick, *Boston Priests*, 98, 107. For an example of the priest's temper, even

directed against the mild and easygoing Williams, see O'Brien to Williams, February 19 and 22, 1889, Williams Papers, AABo 4:7.

32. O'Brien to O'Connell, October 17, October 26, December 12, and December 15, 1907, Parish Files, AABo 33:15.

33. O'Brien to O'Connell, April 21, 1908, ibid., 33:16; O'Brien to O'Connell, November 1 and November 8, 1911, O'Connell Papers, AABo 8:1; O'Connell to O'Brien, November 2, 1911, ibid.; J. P. E. O'Connell to Tampieri, March 13, 1913, Chancery Central Subject File M–1693, AABo; O'Connell to O'Brien, February 27, 1915, Parish Files, AABo 33:17; Cunningham to Haberlin, May 5, 1919, Chancery Central Subject File M–1693, AABo; Higgins to Haberlin, October 1, 1917, Wills Correspondence ("O'Brien"), ibid.

34. *Recollections*, 270.

6. RENDERING TO CAESAR: O'CONNELL AND THE POLITICIANS

1. The events of the centennial celebration are described in William F. Kenney, *Centennial of the See of Boston* (Boston: J. K. Waters, 1909). O'Connell's sermon is in *S&A*, 3:121–139.

2. The political transition of this period is described in Alan Barbrook, *God Save the Commonwealth: An Electoral History of Massachusetts* (Amherst: University of Massachusetts Press, 1973), 15–33, and Dale Baum, "The Massachusetts Voter: Party Loyalty in the Gilded Age, 1872–1896," in *Massachusetts in the Gilded Age: Selected Essays*, ed. Jack Tager and John W. Ifkovic (Amherst: University of Massachusetts Press, l985), 37–66.

3. On the interplay of religion and politics see William V. Shannon, *The American Irish* (New York: Macmillan, 1963), 64–67, and Murray B. Levin, *The Compleat Politician: Political Strategy in Massachusetts* (Indianapolis: Bobbs-Merrill, 1962), 17–18.

4. Alexander, "Cardinal and Cold Roast Boston," *Saturday Evening Post*, October 4, 1941, 116. On the political attitudes and problems of Boston's earlier bishops, see Thomas H. O'Connor, *Fitzpatrick's Boston, 1846–1866: John Bernard Fitzpatrick, Third Bishop of Boston* (Boston: Northeastern University Press, 1984), esp. 96–98.

5. For Curley see Joseph F. Dineen, *The Purple Shamrock: The Honorable James Michael Curley of Boston* (New York: Norton, 1949) and James M. Curley, *I'd Do It Again: A Record of All My Uproarious Years* (Englewood Cliffs, N.J.: Prentice-Hall, 1957). Fitzgerald has finally acquired adequate treatment after years of neglect in Goodwin, *Fitzgeralds and Kennedys*. For Lomasney see A. D. Van Nostrand, "The Lomasney Legend," *New England Quarterly* 21 (1948): 435–458, and John D. Buenker, "The Mahatma and Progressive Reform: Martin Lomasney as Lawmaker," ibid., 44 (1971): 397–419. Walsh badly needs a modern biography, but see Dorothy G. Wayman, *David I. Walsh: Citizen-Patriot* (Milwaukee: Bruce, 1952).

6. The aphorism that "politics is local" has been attributed to the future Speaker of the U.S. House of Representatives Thomas P. O'Neill so often that, even

if he never actually said it, he might just as well have. For the structure of local politics at this time, see Edgar Litt, *The Political Cultures of Massachusetts* (Cambridge, Mass.: M.I.T. Press, 1965), Richard M. Abrams, *Conservatism in a Progressive Era: Massachusetts Politics, 1900–1912* (Cambridge, Mass.: Harvard University Press, 1964), and J. Joseph Huthmacher, *Massachusetts People and Politics, 1919–1933* (Cambridge, Mass.: Harvard University Press, 1959).

7. Curley, *I'd Do It Again*, 302, 289, 113.

8. *Boston Post*, November 2, 1937. The story of this maneuver still lives in the oral tradition of Boston politics, and it is narrated in several sources, including Wayman, *Cardinal O'Connell*, 226–227.

9. O'Connell to Curley, undated (1916), O'Connell Papers, AABo 4:7; Edwin O'Connor, *The Last Hurrah* (Boston: Little Brown, 1956), 365, 366.

10. Van Nostrand, "Lomasney Legend," 450; O'Leary, "Cardinal O'Connell," 158–160; Goodwin, *Fitzgeralds and Kennedys*, 142–173. Fitzgerald's attribution of credit to O'Connell for advice in the proper Catholic training of his children, especially the girls, is in Fitzgerald to O'Connell, October 20, 1939, O'Connell Papers, AABo 5:3.

11. O'Connell to Walsh, March 2, 1914, O'Connell Papers, AABo 11:4; on O'Connell's private reservations about Walsh's support for the initiative and referendum, see O'Connell to Taft, ibid., 10:14.

12. O'Connor, *The Last Hurrah*, 66; O'Hara to O'Connell, no date but December 1934, Chancery Central Subject File M–855, AABo.

13. Guild to O'Connell, January 31, 1907, O'Connell Papers, AABo 5:8. See also the correspondence with Fuller (ibid., 5:3) and Taft (ibid., 10:14).

14. "Many A Parishioner of Roslindale" to O'Connell, November 4, 1928, Parish Files, AABo, 19:6. The writer had originally signed her name, which was "Mary A." something; thinking better of full disclosure, she erased her last name, substituted the word "Parishioner," and converted the "Mary" to "Many."

15. *S&A*, 3:120, 138.

16. See, for example, Haberlin to Scanlan, February 18, 1920, and Scanlan to Haberlin, February 20, 1920, CCB Files, AABo 1:17. The vigor with which Dorothy Wayman (*Cardinal O'Connell*, 223) denies that O'Connell was called "Number One" is probably the best proof that he indeed was. Wayman is correct, however, in pointing out that his other nickname was "Number Eighty," taken from the high-prestige low-number license plate on his automobile, a distinction he has bequeathed to his successors to the present day.

17. James J. Kenneally, "Catholicism and Woman Suffrage in Massachusetts," *CHR* 53 (1967): 43–57.

18. Ibid. On O'Connell's marginal role in the strike, see Francis Russell, *A City in Terror: 1919, The Boston Police Strike* (New York: Viking, 1975), 188.

19. On the convention generally, see John A. Hague, "The Massachusetts Constitutional Convention, 1917–1919," *New England Quarterly* 27 (1954): 147–167. The anti-aid measure has become article forty-six of the amendments to the state's constitution.

20. See, for example, *Pilot*, April 28, 1917.

21. Ibid., October 13, 1917. On the blocking of aid to the Carney Hospital, see O'Connell to Anderson, February 21, 1908, CCB Files, AABo 1:2. Preventing state financial assistance to the hospital may have been an attempt to keep its finances on the edge of uncertainty, thereby abetting O'Connell's efforts (described above, chapter 5) to secure more direct personal control over it.

22. S&A, 5: 271, 275, 267; Pilot, November 10, 1917.

23. The question of child labor is treated broadly in Francis L. Broderick, Right Reverend New Dealer: John A. Ryan (New York: Macmillan, 1963), 156–159. On the fight over the amendment in Massachusetts, see Richard B. Sherman, "The Rejection of the Child Labor Amendment," Mid-America 45 (1963): 3–17.

24. Huthmacher, People and Politics, 70–71, 296.

25. O'Connell to Proctor, December 15, 1924, Chancery Central Subject File M–28/24, AABo. This letter was written after the amendment was defeated, but it contains the cardinal's fullest statement of his case against it. O'Connell probably also feared that passage of the child labor amendment might prepare the way for creation of a federal department of education, an idea he and other bishops had long feared as a threat to the autonomy of parochial schools; see Douglas J. Slawson, "The Attitudes and Activities of American Catholics Regarding the Proposals to Establish a Federal Department of Education Between World War I and the Great Depression" (Ph.D. diss.: Catholic University of America, 1981).

26. O'Connell to pastors, October 1, 1924, Chancery Circulars, AABo 4:3; All Saints' parish, Roxbury, Pulpit Announcement Books, AABo, November 2, 1924.

27. Pilot, November 8, 1924; O'Connell to Gibbons, October 14, 1924, and Gibbons to O'Connell, October 21, 1924, Chancery Central Subject File M–28/24, AABo. On the tense relationship between Ryan and O'Connell, see Ryan to O'Connell, February 26, 1919, O'Connell Papers, AABo 9:11, and O'Connell to Ryan, undated, Curley Papers O–281–282, AABa. See also Broderick, Right Reverend New Dealer, 156–158. For an understanding of the force of the repeated use of the word "bolshevik" in O'Connell's denouncing of this measure, see Robert K. Murray, Red Scare: A Study of National Hysteria, 1919–1920 (Minneapolis: University of Minnesota Press, 1955).

28. Pilot, November 8, 1924; see also Sherman, "Rejection of the Child Labor Amendment," 3–17.

29. See Mansfield's argument to the court: "In the Matter of the Constitutionality of the Initiative Petition, House Document 2035: Brief for the Opponents" (Boston: Massachusetts Supreme Judicial Court, 1941), 4, 3, 9; a copy of this pamphlet is in AABo. See also Original Papers, House Bill No. 2035, 1941, Archives, Commonwealth of Massachusetts; this collection contains two significant letters of Mansfield to Cook, July 30 and November 5, 1941.

30. Pilot, October 31, 1942.

31. Saint Thomas Aquinas, Jamaica Plain, Pulpit Announcement Books, AABo, October 11 and November 1, 1942; Saint Charles Borromeo, Waltham, ibid., September 27, October 4, 11, 26, and November 1, 1942. See also Immaculate Conception, Everett, ibid., October 11, 1942. The theme that birth control was

"against God's law" returned in 1948, when the subject was again on the state ballot. On the church's effort at that time, when it used the slogan "Birth control is *still* against God's law," see James M. O'Toole, "Prelates and Politicos: Catholics and Politics in Massachusetts, 1900–1970," *Catholic Boston*, 49–56.

32. *S&A*, 9:276; *Recollections*, 160, 162.

33. For general treatments of the controversial priest's career, see Charles J. Tull, *Father Coughlin and the New Deal* (Syracuse: Syracuse University Press, 1965) and Alan Brinkley, *Voices of Protest: Huey Long, Father Coughlin, and the Great Depression* (New York: Knopf, 1982). Curley's description of support for Coughlin in Boston is in Brinkley, p. 206. For Coughlin's brief visit, see *Boston Herald*, August 13, 1935.

34. *S&A*, 11:27, 28. For the later denunciations of Coughlin, see ibid., 11:70–71 and *Boston Herald*, December 7, 1934. For the letters of protest from Coughlin supporters, together with an even larger number of letters supporting O'Connell, see Chancery Central Subject File M–855, AABo.

35. *S&A*, 8:148.

36. The fate of the lottery bill, including the text of O'Connell's statement, may be charted in the *Boston Globe*, May 20–21, 1935. On the earlier opposition to Sunday sports, see *Pilot*, February 19, 1916.

37. *Boston Globe*, May 21, 1935.

38. *S&A*, 7:18, 19. This crucial address had been written for O'Connell by Father Patrick J. Waters, a professor at Saint John's Seminary, Brighton, and a frequent ghostwriter for the cardinal. See the correspondence of May 1919 between O'Connell and Waters, SJS Files, AABo 3:1.

39. O'Connell to Baer, January 28, 1919, O'Connell Papers, AABo 3:3. On the *Pilot's* opposition to a federal education department, see, for example, its editions of September 11, November 13 and 27, 1920.

40. *S&A*, 9:35–39; anonymous correspondent to O'Connell, undated, and Dietz to O'Connell, undated, Chancery Central Subject File M–1052, AABo. See also O'Connell statement to press, November 29, 1933, ibid.

41. On Cushing's political abilities and activities, see O'Toole, "Prelates and Politicos," *Catholic Boston*, 42–65.

7. "THE NEWER CATHOLIC RACES": THE VARIETIES OF ETHNIC CATHOLICISM

1. Scanlan to Haberlin, March 4, 1921, CCB Files, AABo 2:1.

2. *Pilot*, July 23, 1921. On earlier organizational efforts see *Pilot*, November 15, 1913, and March 26, 1921. The activities of the charitable bureau's workers are described in Scanlan to Haberlin, April 18, 1921, CCB Files, AABo 2:2, and CCB annual report, 1921, ibid., 8:11.

3. The standard study of this phenomenon remains Oscar Handlin's *Boston's Immigrants: A Study in Acculturation*, revised and enlarged edition (New York: Atheneum, 1977; orig. pub. 1941). This work is marred by an occasionally odd tone, as the immigrants seem to get blamed for being poor, and its statistical and factual bases have been broadened by more recent studies. Still, it provides a good

introduction to the subject. For the tensions that resulted from immigration in Boston and elsewhere, see Ray Allen Billington, *The Protestant Crusade, 1800–1860* (New York: Macmillan, 1938), and John Higham, *Strangers in the Land: Patterns of American Nativism, 1860–1925* (New York: Atheneum, 1963).

4. For the impact of Irish immigration on the Boston church, see O'Connor, *Fitzpatrick's Boston*, esp. 75–98, and *HAB*, 2:110–140 and 434–466. Merwick, *Boston Priests*, speaks (1–2 and elsewhere) of a population of "Yankee-Catholics" in nineteenth-century Boston, but these conclusions are based on factual errors (she misidentifies the background of several important people, including Archbishop Williams) and a poor understanding of what "Yankees" are. For an overview of Catholic ethnicity elsewhere, see Dolan, *American Catholic Experience*, 127–157, and for particular studies see Jay P. Dolan, *The Immigrant Church: New York's Irish and German Catholics, 1815–1865* (Baltimore: Johns Hopkins University Press, 1975), and Charles Shanabruch, *Chicago's Catholics: The Evolution of an American Identity* (Notre Dame, Ind.: University of Notre Dame Press, 1981).

5. *HAB*, 3:189.

6. O'Connell to Fumasoni-Biondi, January 20, 1928, Chancery Central Subject File M–1000, AABo; *S&A*, 10:59–60.

7. *The John Carroll Papers*, ed. Thomas O'Brien Hanley (Notre Dame, Ind.: University of Notre Dame Press, 1976), 1:441; *Catholic Encyclopedia* (New York: Encyclopedia Press, 1911), s.v. "parish."

8. The extent of the problem of leakage has been debated and studied for many years. See, for example, Gerald J. Schnepp, *Leakage from a Catholic Parish* (Washington, D.C.: Catholic University of America Press, 1942), and the classic Gerald Shaughnessy, *Has the Immigrant Kept the Faith? A Study of Immigration and Catholic Growth in the United States, 1790–1920* (New York: Macmillan, 1925). See also John Simpson, "Ethnic Groups and Church Attendance in the United States and Canada," in *Ethnicity*, ed. Andrew M. Greeley and Gregory Baum (New York: Seabury Press, 1977), 16–22. For the canon law of national parishes, see Charles Augustine, *The Canonical and Civil Status of Catholic Parishes in the United States* (St. Louis: Herder, 1926), esp. 243–245, and Joseph E. Ciesluk, *National Parishes in the United States* (Washington, D.C.: Catholic University of America, 1944).

9. Splaine to J. P. E. O'Connell, October 29, 1909, Parish Files, AABo 47:17. The literature on the theory of ethnicity is vast, but see especially Harold R. Isaacs, "Basic Group Identity: The Idols of the Tribe," *Ethnicity: Theory and Experience*, ed. Nathan Glazer and Daniel P. Moynihan (Cambridge, Mass.: Harvard University Press, 1975), 29–52, and John F. Stack, *International Conflict in an American City: Boston's Irish, Italians, and Jews, 1935–1944* (Westport, Conn.: Greenwood Press, 1979); the quote is from Stack, 12. On the preservation of traditional values by church-reinforced ethnicity, see Robert Anthony Orsi, *The Madonna of 115th Street: Faith and Community in Italian Harlem, 1880–1950* (New Haven: Yale University Press, 1985) and Silvano M. Tomasi, *Piety and Power: The Role of the Italian Parish in the New York Metropolitan Area, 1880–1930* (New York: Center for Migration Studies, 1975).

10. McLeod to O'Connell, June 19, 1917, Parish Files, AABo 4:10; Garka to O'Connell, June 5, 1916, ibid.; Haberlin to Harb, May 28, 1924, ibid., 31:7;

Rocco to O'Connell, September 28, 1927, ibid., 40:1. Throughout this period, Maronite-rite Catholics were identified as "Syrians," though most were ethnically Lebanese.

11. DaSilva to Sullivan, February 10, 1915, and undated chancery memorandum, ibid., 51:13 and 50:3.

12. Wefers to O'Connell, July 22, 1917, and O'Reilly to O'Connell, July 29, 1917, ibid., 45:16.

13. Milanese to J. P. E. O'Connell, November 6, 1915, and Sullivan to Milanese, November 8, 1915, ibid., 45:17; Zmijewski to O'Connell, July 19 and November 3, 1915, ibid., 34:17. The general pattern of ethnicity in Cambridge is described in Robert A. Woods and Albert J. Kennedy, *The Zone of Emergence: Observations of the Lower Middle and Upper Working Class Communities of Boston, 1905-1914*, ed. Sam Bass Warner (Cambridge, Mass.: M.I.T. Press, 1962), 57-115. See also Sullivan to Rainville, June 9, 1915, Parish Files, AABo 69:1, and *HAB*, 3:730-731.

14. Sullivan to Zillinskis, December 30, 1915, Parish Files, AABo 23:11. On the dynamics of parish finances, which frequently motivated such disputes, see Sullivan, "Beneficial Relations," *Catholic Boston*, 227-234.

15. Haberlin to Racette, June 19, 1915, Parish Files, AABo 51:19. On American Catholic attitudes toward the war, see Hennesey, *American Catholics*, 223-226, and Dean R. Esslinger, "American German and Irish Attitudes toward Neutrality, 1914-1917: A Study of Catholic Minorities," *CHR* 53 (1967): 194-216. On Wilson's occasionally grumpy view of Catholics, see Arthur S. Link, *Wilson: Campaigns for Progressivism and Peace, 1916-1917* (Princeton: Princeton University Press, 1965), 130-134.

16. Anonymous to O'Connell, February 4, 1916, Parish Files, AABo 17:5.

17. Lehan to O'Connell, no date but March 1915, ibid., 33:6; see also Sullivan to O'Connell, March 16, 1915, ibid.; Juskaitis to O'Connell, November 5, 1917, ibid., 32:16. On the general phenomenon of hostility between the Irish and other groups, see Stack, *International Conflict*, 29-31.

18. Baxter to Haberlin, October 28, 1922, Parish Files, AABo 72:9; *HAB*, 3:738.

19. "Second Annual Report, League of Catholic Women, May 1, 1912-May 1, 1913," League of Catholic Women Records, AABo 1:4; Stack, *International Conflict*, 29. On the League of Catholic Women generally, see Paula M. Kane, "Boston Catholics and Modern American Culture, 1900-1920" (Ph.D. diss.: Yale University, 1987), 149-159.

20. Unidentified priest, quoted in Orsi, *Madonna of 115th Street*, 56; Denis to Haberlin, February 12, 1917, and Haberlin to Denis, February 14, 1917, Parish Files, AABo 51:1; Adomaneze(?) to O'Connell, November 4, 1911, ibid., 23:11.

21. Sousa to O'Connell, August 15, 1919, ibid., 9:3. The "theology of the streets" phrase comes from Orsi, *Madonna of 115th Street*, 219-231.

22. *Recollections*, 271; Zillinskis to O'Connell, June 22, 1915, and unsigned, undated chancery memo, Parish Files, AABo 23:11. For the problems of a similar organization, the Knights of Lithuania of Saint Joseph's parish, Lowell, see the correspondence ibid., 52:22; see also William Wolkovich-Valkavičius, *Lithuanian*

Fraternalism: Seventy-Five Years of the U.S. Knights of Lithuania (Brooklyn: Knights of Lithuania, 1988).

23. DeBem to Sullivan, February 13, 1915, and Sullivan to DeBem, February 19, 1915, Parish Files, AABo 41:14; *Recollections*, 132.

24. O'Connell to Jusaitis, September 21 and December 10, 1908, Parish Files, AABo 48:13; Sullivan to Zillinskis, October 19, 1915, ibid., 23:11; Haberlin to Virmauskas, August 2, 1919, ibid., 49:1. The nearby diocese of Hartford, Connecticut, was more successful both at recruiting a multi-ethnic clergy and at providing foreign language skills to its English-speaking priests; see Dolores Ann Liptak, *European Immigrants and the Catholic Church in Connecticut, 1870–1920* (New York: Center for Migration Studies, 1987), esp. 60–83.

25. Undated memorandum (ca. November 1918), J. P. E. O'Connell to O'Connell, Parish Files, AABo 34:2; unsigned memo to O'Connell, July 20, 1921, ibid., 34:3. Not only was the Cambridge priest not removed at this time, but he was allowed to remain in charge of his parish until 1950!

26. Terra to O'Connell, July 21, 1922, ibid., 41:16; Haberlin to Toma, July 30, 1919, ibid., 6:17; Haberlin to DiMilla, November 9, 1916, ibid., 5:1. The general problem of wandering ethnic priests is discussed in John P. Marschall, "Diocesan and Religious Clergy: The History of a Relationship, 1789–1969," in *Catholic Priest in the United States: Historical Investigations*, 396–405. On the "export" of priests from Ireland, see Larkin, "Devotional Revolution in Ireland," 652.

27. O'Reilly to O'Connell, June 2, 1908, Parish Files, AABo 47:17; O'Connell to Pimentel, December 8, 1921, ibid., 34:4; Haberlin to DiMilla, September 17, 1923, ibid., 5:6; O'Connell pencil note on DiMilla to Haberlin, February 9, 1926, ibid., 5:8.

28. J. P. E. O'Connell to Cunningham, December 23, 1915, ibid., 63:17; Will & Baumer Co. to O'Connell, April 29, 1912, ibid., 15:6; unsigned memo, December 28, 1923, ibid., 15:6.

29. McGlinchey to Burke, November 22, 1932, ibid., 46:6. See also Hickey and Sullivan to O'Connell, August 25, 1933, ibid., and Hickey and Sullivan to O'Connell, July 3, 1935, ibid., 46:10.

30. Haberlin to O'Reilly, January 18, 1916, ibid., 48:17. For examples of the formulaic rituals of charge and countercharge, see the cases of Holy Rosary, Lawrence (ibid., 46:11), Saint Francis, Lawrence (ibid., 48:17–19), Saint Joseph's, Lowell (ibid., 52:18), and Our Lady of the Cedars of Lebanon, Boston (ibid., 16:9–18).

31. Splaine to J. P. E. O'Connell, October 29, 1909, ibid., 47:17; D'Alfonso to O'Connell, July 16, 1920, ibid., 6:19. The regional factions among Italians are described in detail in William M. DeMarco, *Ethnics and Enclaves: Boston's Italian North End* (Ann Arbor, Mich.: U.M.I. Research Press, 1981), 45–68.

32. Ziaden et al. to O'Connell, August 26, 1926, and Khirallagh to O'Connell, November 6, 1928, Parish Files, AABo 16:10. Similar problems had arisen among Irish immigrants a generation or two earlier. See, for example, Timothy J. Meagher, "Irish, American, Catholic: Irish-American Identity in Worcester, Massachusetts, 1880 to 1920," in Meagher, ed., *From Paddy to Studs* (New York: Greenwood, 1986), 75–92, and Ellen Skerrett, "The Development of

Catholic Identity among Irish Americans in Chicago, 1880 to 1920," ibid., 117–138.

33. Unsigned memorandum to O'Connell, December 12, 1923, Parish Files, AABo 17:7; Jusaitis to O'Connell, October 7, 1915, ibid., 48:17.

34. O'Connell to Bonzano, February 14, 1920, ibid., 46:15. These strikes need a thorough, up-to-date history. Somewhat old but still useful is Donald B. Cole, *Immigrant City: Lawrence, Massachusetts, 1845–1921* (Chapel Hill: University of North Carolina Press, 1963), see especially 177–194.

35. *Pilot*, March 2, 1912; "Roman Catholic Strikers of Lawrence" to O'Connell, May 2, 1919, Parish Files, AABo 49:20.

36. Waters's long, detailed report is contained in his letter to Haberlin, April 12, 1919, SJS Files, AABo, 3:1.

37. *S&A* 7:190. This letter was probably written for O'Connell by Father Waters.

38. The literature on the Sacco-Vanzetti case—polemical, historical, and sometimes both—is large and still growing. The two most complete accounts (which draw different conclusions on the central question of guilt) are Francis Russell, *Tragedy in Dedham: The Story of the Sacco-Vanzetti Case* (New York: McGraw-Hill, 1962) and Roberta Strauss Feuerlicht, *Justice Crucified: The Story of Sacco and Vanzetti* (New York: McGraw-Hill, 1977).

39. Scanlan to Haberlin, May 25, 1921, CCB Files, AABo 2:5. The definitive study of O'Connell's involvement in the entire case is Rosario J. Tosiello's fine "'Requests I Cannot Ignore': A New Perspective on the Role of Cardinal O'Connell in the Sacco-Vanzetti Case," CHR 68 (1982): 46–53.

40. Russell, *Tragedy in Dedham*, 363–365; *Boston Herald*, August 21, 1927. For the pressure on Archbishop Hayes, see Hayes to O'Connell, August 11 and 19, 1927, O'Connell Papers, AABo 5:11, and O'Connell to Hayes, August 15, 1927, Hayes Papers, AANY Q-19 (microfilm roll 6). The visit of the two women to Marblehead is described in Tosiello, "'Requests I Cannot Ignore,'" 46–47, and in Feuerlicht, *Justice Crucified*, 396–398. Feuerlicht maintains that the Sacco-Vanzetti Defense Committee, organized and generally directed by political liberals, was nervous about the overtly religious nature of Luigia's appeal, but that they supported it as a last-ditch effort.

41. Marella to O'Connell, and O'Connell to Marella, both August 10, 1927, Apostolic Delegate Files, AABo. *L'Osservatore Romano*'s coverage of the case is described in Tosiello, "'Requests I Cannot Ignore,'" 51–52.

42. O'Connell to Fuller, August 10, 1927, O'Connell Papers, AABo 5:3. Other correspondence between the two men, 1919–1927, is ibid.

43. Haberlin to Scanlan, January 2, 1917, CCB Files, AABo 1:9; *Pilot*, November 15, 1913, and July 22, 1916. For a general treatment of Protestant prose-lytizing and its impact on Catholic social agenices, see Walton, "To Preserve the Faith," *Catholic Boston*, esp. 67–69 and 89–93. On Episcopal efforts among immigrants, see *The Episcopal Diocese of Massachusetts, 1784–1984: A Mission to Remember, Proclaim, and Fulfill*, ed. Mark J. Duffy (Boston: Episcopal Diocese of Massachusetts, 1984), 19 and 157–159. The sanctuary lamp was viewed as a deliber-

ate deceit to make the Protestant church seem safely Catholic. These lamps remained lit constantly in Catholic churches to symbolize the "real presence" of Christ in the eucharist reserved on the altar. Since Protestants did not believe in the doctrine of the real presence, Catholics thought they had no need for sanctuary lamps.

44. Pimentel to Burke, June 27, 1929, Parish Files, AABo 34:6; Martins to Burke, June 29, 1929, ibid., 41:20; Haberlin to Millet, March 3, 1917, ibid., 37:4; Krasnickas to Haberlin, February 15, 1917, ibid., 32:16.

45. *Pilot*, July 7, 1917, January 5, 1918, and April 12, 1919.

46. Ibid., March 3, 1917, January 5, 1918, and September 9, 1916; *Recollections*, 21.

47. O'Connell to Fumasoni-Biondi, March 7, 1927, Chancery Central Subject File M–1002, AABo. Hennesey, *American Catholics*, 159–162, 193, and Dolan, *American Catholic Experience*, 359–360, treat the subject of blacks and Catholicism generally.

48. Sullivan to Drexel, June 19 and September 28, 1912, Drexel to O'Connell, February 12, 1913, and Haberlin to Drexel, May 31, 1921, Institution Special Correspondence Files, AABo; annual report, Blessed Sacrament Convent, Institution Files, AABo 7:14. O'Connell was interested in special efforts for blacks as early as 1908; see the report of his remarks to a mission to "colored Catholics" in *Boston Post*, March 16, 1908.

49. Mother Mary Charles to Phelan, January 31, 1937, and Drexel to O'Connell, February 12, 1913, Institution Special Correspondence Files, AABo.

50. Haberlin to Sister Mary Emmanuel, February 5, 1919, Institution Files, AABo 7:14; Drexel to O'Connell, May 27, 1921, Institution Special Correspondence Files, AABo.

51. *Pilot*, September 15, 1917.

52. Burke to Fortier, January 7, 1932, Parish Files, AABo 51:6; Committee of Saint Theresa's, Brockton, to O'Connell, May 2, 1939, ibid., 31:10; Haberlin to Gregori, February 5, 1919, ibid., 6:17.

53. Juras to Haberlin, August 10, 1927, ibid., 52:18; Juras to Burke, October 17, 1929, ibid., 49:8; Woods, *Zone of Emergence*, 37. On the greater enthusiasm for parochial schools among non-Irish Catholics, see James W. Sanders, "Catholics and the School Question in Boston: The Cardinal O'Connell Years," *Catholic Boston*, 166–168.

54. Haberlin to Lenzi, December 10 and 12, 1918, Parish Files, AABo 34:8; Haberlin to Liberti, February 20, 1919, ibid., 66:23.

55. Rockwell to O'Connell, April 17, 1919, ibid., 4:1; see also Cohausz to O'Connell, April 28, 1919, and Haberlin to Cohausz, May 1, 1919, ibid.

56. Bonugli to O'Connell, September 19, 1922, ibid., 6:21; Grillo to Haberlin, no date but July 1927, ibid., 51:16. The generational conflicts among Italian Americans are described in Orsi, *Madonna of 115th Street*, 107–149.

57. On Mundelein's aggressive opposition to ethnic splintering in Chicago, see Kantowicz, *Corporation Sole*, 65–83. On Ireland's feuds with ethnic Catholics, especially Germans, see O'Connell, *John Ireland*, 196–199 and 223–226.

58. *Recollections*, 309.

8. SCANDAL AND SURVIVAL: THE CRISIS OF
O'CONNELL'S CAREER, 1915–1925

1. *Boston Globe*, October 29, 1911.

2. Mullen to Bonzano, January 9, 1915, ADUSA, IX (Boston): 95/1, ASV; there are two separate letters of this date, each making the same points. See also Walsh to Bonzano, June 9, 1919, ibid., 94/2, and Walsh to Bonzano, January 13, 1915, ibid., 95/1. On O'Connell's mediocre record on parochial schools, see Sanders, "Catholics and the School Question," *Catholic Boston*, 121–169.

3. Mullen to Ireland, January 5, 1915, JIP, roll #12, frames 442–443; Walsh to Bonzano, January 13, 1915, ADUSA, IX (Boston): 95/1, ASV; Mullen to Bonzano, January 3, 1915, ibid.

4. Anonymous priest (possibly George Patterson) to Bonzano, March 9, 1916, ADUSA, IX (Boston): 55, ASV; Mullen to Bonzano, January 11, 1915, ibid., 95/1; Mullen to Bonzano, February 20, 1920, ibid., 95/2. On the subject of the cardinal's knees and his dislike of ceremony, see O'Connell to Murray, September 21 and October 6, 1925, Correspondence with Other Dioceses (Portland), AABo.

5. Walsh to Ireland, September 29, 1917, JIP, roll #13, frames 341–342; Dunn to Hayes, June 22, 1917, Hayes Papers O–2, AANY (microfilm roll 1).

6. Baptismal register, Sacred Heart parish, Lowell, AABo, entry of April 30, 1884. Baby William's death on August 30, 1884, is noted in Vital Records (Deaths), Archives, Commonwealth of Massachusetts, Boston.

7. McNamara, *American College*, Appendix C, 835. Other biographical details, sometimes contradictory and confusing, are given in *Boston Herald*, February 29, 1912, and *Boston Post*, March 1, 1912.

8. O'Connell to J. P. E. O'Connell, May 26, 1905, Chancery Letterbooks, ADPo; O'Connell to Lelandais, November 12, 1904, ibid.; O'Connell to Julia O'Connell, June 6, 1899, O'Connell Papers, ADPo.

9. Hofmann to O'Connell, March 15 and July 16, 1906, Chancery Central Subject File M–1641, AABo; Rev. Erich Drogsler to author, August 12, 1985, in author's possession; Episcopal Register, AABo, September 8, 1906.

10. Perkins to J. P. E. O'Connell, November 5, 1908, Priests Correspondence Files, AABo; *Boston Journal*, December 10, 1914; J. P. E. O'Connell to Prendergast, January 29, 1912, O'Connell Papers, AABo 9:3. James O'Connell held the rank of "domestic prelate," the middle of the three levels of position that entitled one to be addressed as "monsignor."

11. On his keeping of the accounts and his salary from the *Pilot*, see Chancery Account Book ("Bank Accounts, 1908–1916"), AABo. On his management of the parish insurance, see J. P. E. O'Connell to pastors, undated (but probably July 1912) and March 22, 1913, Chancery Circulars, AABo 3:2 and 3:3. On the overseeing of stock dividends, see Cunningham to J. P. E. O'Connell, November 3, 1913, Chancery Central Subject File M–1712, AABo. His correspondence regarding altar wine, January–June 1920, is ibid., M–424, and his concern over the post office in May 1915 is ibid., M–1712. His worries about an audit of the diocesan newspaper is expressed in "Memorandum for His Eminence," undated but 1918, ibid., M–892; this memo also documents his skillful movement of funds to maximize the return on them.

12. The reports on Mullen and Doody are in undated (but probably June 1919) memoranda of J. P. E. O'Connell to O'Connell, copies of which are in Parish Files, AABo, 35:4 and 44:16. The unsuccessful attempt to raise the salary of curates is in J. P. E. O'Connell to Peterson, March 24, 1919, Archdiocesan Synod (1919) Files, AABo. The harassment of Spellman is documented in the letters between the two men, April 1–13, 1920, *Pilot* Files, AABo 9:18. The letter to Spellman is quoted in Robert I. Gannon, *The Cardinal Spellman Story* (Garden City, N.Y.: Doubleday, 1962), 37.

13. J. P. E. O'Connell to Cunningham, February 19 and 20, 1915, Chancery Central Subject File M–1712, AABo; Town Tax Lists, 1913–1918, Brookline Public Library, Brookline, Massachusetts. Later, James also acquired title to the Brookline home of one of the cardinal's sisters; see *Boston Evening Transcript*, October 2, 1918.

14. J. P. E. O'Connell to O'Connell, March 23, 1911, O'Connell Papers ("Uncataloged"), AABo. The phrase translates: "With renewed good wishes to one and all and infinite respect for Your Eminence." The same portion of the O'Connell Papers collection contains many other examples of these Italianisms.

15. J. P. E. O'Connell to O'Connell, July 19 and November 28, 1911, ibid.

16. J. P. E. O'Connell to Cunningham, September 9, 1915, Priests Correspondence Files, AABo; J. P. E. O'Connell to Lenehan, December 29, 1916, Wills Correspondence ("C"), ibid.

17. Certified copies of the marriage records from the Lake County, Indiana, clerk's office are in ADUSA, IX (Boston): 94/2, ASV. The rest of the narrative of their meeting and marriage is conveyed in a statement prepared by Father John Mullen, November 14, 1920, ibid., 94/3; there is also a copy of this document, filed with a letter of Gillis to Walsh, November 14, 1920, in SAB, RG9, Box 6. The story is further corroborated by a letter of Bishop Louis S. Walsh to Pope Pius XI, January 1924, a copy of which is in the Joseph J. Rice Papers, ADB, Box 4. Long part of the oral tradition among the New England clergy, the story of James O'Connell's marriage is set down in print in Ellis, *Catholic Bishops: A Memoir*, 72–73. Crown Point, Indiana, later gained notoriety as the site of John Dillinger's last jail break.

18. Michael J. Doody, "Memorandum," no date but January 1919, ADUSA, IX (Boston): 94/1, ASV; Detectives' Report ("Rapporto"), included in letter, Dunn to Bonzano, April 20, 1919, ibid., 94/1; Surveyor of Customs, New York, "Hearing in the matter of the declaration and baggage of . . . Mr. and Mrs. James Roe," August 30, 1913, ibid., 94/1; Mullen to Bonzano, March 16, 1916, ibid., 95/1; Mullen to Bonzano, February 14, 1921, ibid., 94/4.

19. J. P. E. O'Connell to O'Connell, June 14, 1911, O'Connell Papers ("Uncataloged"), AABo. The tensions involved in the withdrawal from Catholic holy orders are described in Paul F. Ginnetty's fine study, "Moratorium and Ministry: The Adult Development of Former Roman Catholic Priests" (Ph.D. diss.: City University of New York, 1986).

20. O'Connell to Tampieri, September 30, 1920, Holy Office Files, AABo.

21. *Boston Post*, February 3, 1912; McNamara, *American College*, Appendix C, 844.

22. Mullen to Bonzano, March 16, 1916, ADUSA, IX (Boston): 95/1, ASV; see also Bonzano to Mullen, March 20, 1916, ibid.; Walsh to Bonzano, June 9, 1919, ibid., 94/2. On the meetings of Il Circolo, see Murphy to J. P. E. O'Connell and J. P. E. O'Connell to Murphy, both April 3, 1916, SJS Files, AABo 2:11. On the failure of the two priests to participate in clergy retreats, see J. P. E. O'Connell to Peterson, August 3, 1915, ibid., 2:8.

23. *Leary v. Toomey*, Suffolk County Superior Court, Civil Division, #72110, Suffolk County Courthouse, Boston, Massachusetts. The original papers filed with this case (petitions, statements, etc.) are in the Judicial Archives Division, Archives of the Commonwealth of Massachusetts, Boston. See also Mullen Statement, November 14, 1920, ADUSA, IX (Boston): 94/3, ASV. On Toomey's troubles in reentering the country, see Surveyor of Customs, "Hearing in the matter of . . . Roe," August 30, 1913, ibid., 94/1.

24. Florence Marlow Fossa Deposition, March 20, 1919, ADUSA, IX (Boston): 94/1, ASV. This deposition was signed and sworn to by Mrs. Fossa before Fathers Mullen and Doody and Archbishop Giovanni Bonzano, the apostolic delegate. The record of the church marriage of the Fossas on July 27, 1914, is in the marriage records of Corpus Christi parish, New York, New York.

25. Fossa Deposition, March 20, 1919, ADUSA, IX (Boston): 94/1, ASV. The precise date of her interview with O'Connell is not specified, but it most probably took place sometime in the week after she discovered Toomey and his girlfriend on the night of October 19, 1918. The estimate that Mrs. Fossa was paid $7,500 is in Mullen to Bonzano, March 14, 1919, ibid.; see also Mullen to Bonzano, May 3, 1919, ibid. O'Connell's interrogation of the clergy is described in Mullen to Bonzano, May 15, 1919, ibid., 94/2.

26. See the unpublished (intended for the *Reader's Digest*) memoir of Cushing, dated February 25, 1965, in the Dorothy G. Wayman Papers, Manuscript Division, Library of Congress, Box 8. Wayman wrote O'Connell's biography on commission from Cushing. She knew the full details of both cases, but in keeping with the pious conventions of the time, she made only passing reference to James O'Connell and none at all to David Toomey; see Wayman, *Cardinal O'Connell*, 239–240.

27. Mullen to Bonzano, December 6, 1918, ADUSA, IX (Boston): 93, ASV; Mullen to Bonzano, March 14 and May 3, 1919, ibid., 94/1; Doody Memorandum, January 1919, ibid.; Fossa Deposition, March 20, 1919, ibid.; Doody to Bonzano, April 21, 1920, ibid., 94/3; Mullen to Bonzano, November 21, 1919, ibid.

28. This account, and that which follows, is taken from the Detectives' Report, which is in ADUSA, IX (Boston): 94/3, ASV. The substance of this report was also conveyed piecemeal in a series of letters, Dunn to Bonzano, March 25, April 15, and April 20, 1919, all ibid., 94/1. The two photographs of O'Connell/Roe, together with some informal snapshots of Mr. and Mrs. Roe, are ibid., 94/1.

29. Joseph C. Pelletier notarized deposition, April 21, 1921, SAB, RG9, Box 6. O'Connell's enemies speculated that Pelletier was rewarded with the papal knighthood for agreeing not to press his case against James O'Connell.

30. Pelletier's political and legal troubles are described sympathetically in Christopher J. Kauffman, *Faith and Fraternalism: The History of the Knights of Columbus, 1882–1982* (New York: Harper and Row, 1982), 241–245. A less favorable account, together with a description of his other questionable activities, is outlined in Leon Harris, *Only to God: The Extraordinary Life of Godfrey Lowell Cabot* (New York: Atheneum, 1967), 240–242. The badger game is described in Francis Russell, "The Knave of Boston," *American Heritage* 27(August 1976): 72–80, but its most famous victim remains the fictional Brahmin in John P. Marquand's novel, *The Late George Apley* (Boston: Little Brown, 1937).

31. Walsh to Bonzano, June 9, 1919, ADUSA, IX (Boston): 94/2, ASV; Mullen to Bonzano, March 14, 1919, ibid., 94/1.

32. Mullen to Bonzano, November 21, 1919, ibid., 94/2, describes the interview he and Father Doody had with Toomey in New York on November 18.

33. The outline of Dunn's life is available in his obituary in the *Boston Globe*, March 29, 1918, and in *Brochure of Boston College and the Young Men's Catholic Association* (Boston, 1894), 34. On the hiking trip in northern Italy, see *Recollections*, 209–211. Mullen's remark that he had previously heard about but had discounted the rumors is in Mullen to Bonzano, December 1, 1919, ADUSA, IX (Boston): 95/2, ASV. Ten years earlier, another priest had complained to Rome about Dunn's "private immorality" and O'Connell's association with him; see anonymous priest to Falconio, March 13, 1909, ibid., 55. This letter suggests that it was social climbing rather than sex that attracted O'Connell to Dunn, who was well connected among the Italian nobility.

34. The will and related documents, together with a summary of the legal maneuverings surrounding the case, are in Registry of Probate #181749, Suffolk County Courthouse, Boston, Massachusetts. On the monitoring of the case by O'Connell's friends and associates, see the correspondence of May–June 1918 in Wills Correspondence ("Dunn"), AABo. For guesses as to the contents of the letters, see Mullen to Bonzano, December 17, 1919, ADUSA, IX (Boston): 94/2, ASV, and Mullen to Bonzano, August 22, 1920, ibid., 94/3.

35. Doody to Bonzano, April 21, 1920, ADUSA, IX (Boston): 94/3, ASV; see also Mullen to Bonzano, November 21, 1919, ibid., 94/2. The whole question of homosexuality among the clergy is discussed very sensibly in Kantowicz, *Corporation Sole*, 184–185.

36. On the papal interview with Feehan and Rice, see Walsh to Pius XI, January 1924, Rice Papers, ADB, Box 4. On O'Connell's tense confrontation with the pontiff, see Ellis, *Catholic Bishops*, 72–73. Ellis even provided a genealogy of this story, recounting who had told whom down to the time he heard it. While the details of this version cannot be independently verified, the broad outlines are probably accurate. James O'Connell's excommunication is confirmed in a letter of Gasparri to Bonzano, June 10, 1920, ADUSA, IX (Boston): 94/3, ASV.

37. On the watch by Mullen and Doody to see when the chancellor actually was removed, see their correspondence with Bonzano, July–November 1920, ADUSA, IX (Boston): 94/3–4, ASV. The resignation letter is J. P. E. O'Connell to O'Connell, November 8, 1920, Priests Correspondence Files, AABo; *Boston Herald*, November 30, 1920.

38. The politics of the conclave of 1914 are described in Falconi, *Popes in the Twentieth Century*, 91–110; see also *Recollections*, 337–342, and HAB, 3:579–580. Ireland's letter to Louis Walsh, September 29, 1914, is in SAB, RG9, Box 6.

39. Walsh's letter to Benedict XV is not available in ASV, but the substance of it is described in Walsh's subsequent letter to Pius XI, January 1924, ADB.

40. What transpired at this private meeting, including direct quotations, is recorded in three separate letters addressed to Walsh by other participants, each giving his own version of the confrontation. The accounts corroborate one another in every significant detail. The letters, all in SAB, RG9, Box 6, are: Nilan to Walsh, September 29, 1921; Hickey to Walsh, October 3, 1921; and Feehan to Walsh, undated. See also Walsh to O'Connell, undated, ibid. The narrative in this and the following paragraph is reconstructed from these letters.

41. The only available account of Walsh's meetings with Benedict is in Walsh to Pius XI, January 1924, ADB. Allowing for a certain enthusiasm on Walsh's part, hearing mainly what he wanted to hear and perhaps overinterpreting the pope's remarks, the substance of this account seems accurate. Benedict may have been further antagonized by O'Connell's having lied about the whole affair in their interview of the previous year; see Ellis, *Catholic Bishops*, 72–73.

42. These conditions, given orally to Walsh, were confirmed in a telegram of Pietro Gasparri, Benedict's secretary of state, to Bonzano, the apostolic delegate, in a telegram of August 25, 1921, ADUSA, IX (Boston): 104, ASV; see also Walsh to Bonzano, September 25, 1921, ibid.

43. Heffron to Bonzano, September 25, 1921, ADUSA, IX (Boston): 104, ASV; Heffron to O'Connell, September 26, 1921, and O'Connell to Heffron, October 1, 1921, O'Connell Papers, AABo 5:12.

44. O'Connell to Bonzano, September 27, 1921, American Hierarchy Meeting Files, AABo. On Bonzano's growing hesitancy, see his letters to Gasparri, September 25, 1921, and to Walsh, October 4, 1921, ADUSA, IX (Boston): 104, ASV. See also the correspondence between Russell and Bonzano, March 18–May 8, 1922, ibid. Russell's retreat from his threats resulted both from his own calmer reflection on the matter and from Bonzano's cool vow to remove him summarily as bishop of Charleston if he did anything rash.

45. Moriarty to O'Connell, December 30, 1920, O'Connell Papers, AABo 7:11; Merry del Val to O'Connell, December 10, 1920, and January 15, 1921, ibid., 7:9; O'Connell to Merry del Val, October 1921, ibid., 7:10.

46. *Pilot*, December 1, 1923–February 16, 1924. These articles were being written in the chancery office and sent to the paper for publication; see Haberlin to Driscoll, January 4, 1924, *Pilot* Files, AABo 4:8. See also Walsh Diary, Rome Trip, ADPo, March 11, 1924.

47. On O'Connell's reliance on Father Driscoll, see the correspondence between the two, 1921–1928, O'Connell Papers, AABo, 4:14, and Kevin F. Dwyer, "Charles Mary Driscoll, O.S.A.," *Men of Heart II: Noteworthy Augustinians, Province of Saint Thomas of Villanova*, ed. John E. Rotelle (Villanova, Pa.: Augustinian Press, 1986), 221–244. On the increase in Peter's Pence, see Gasparri to O'Connell, April 24, 1921, July 29, 1927, and July 28, 1928, and O'Connell to Gasparri, October 5, 1923, all in Secretary of State Files, AABo. See also O'Connell to Merry del Val,

December 30, 1922, and Merry del Val to O'Connell, January 16, 1923, O'Connell Papers, AABo 7:10; and O'Connell to Tampieri, September 30, 1920, Holy Office Files, AABo. Finally, see Gaetano Cardinal DeLai, *The Passion of Our Lord*, trans. William Cardinal O'Connell (Boston: Pilot Publishing Company, 1923).

48. On the election of Pius XI, see Falconi, *Popes in the Twentieth Century*, 151–181, *Recollections*, 344–345, and *HAB*, 3:632–633. O'Connell claimed that he and other American cardinals protested missing two successive conclaves, thereby disenfranchising the American church in the selection of the pope, and that this was responsible for lengthening the period between the death of one pontiff and the selection of a new one. On the changed political circumstances for Walsh and his allies in the new regime, see Mullen, "O'Connell: Charges against (summary)," SAB, RG9, Box 6, and Curley to Walsh, October 6, 1922, Curley Papers, W273, AABa.

49. On the NCWC and the long struggle over its status, see Fogarty, *Vatican and the American Hierarchy*, 220–228. See also O'Connell to DeLai, May 10, 1922, copy in Chancery Central Subject File M–103, AABo, and Walsh to Curley, February 5, 1923, Curley Papers W273, AABa.

50. Walsh Diary, Rome Trip, ADPo, February 18–24, 1924. This small travel diary is separate from the normal run of diaries which Walsh kept to record his official duties as bishop of Portland.

51. Ibid., February 25, 1924.

52. O'Connell to Fumasoni-Biondi, December 27, 1923, Apostolic Delegate Files, AABo; other correspondence relating to the pilgrimage is in O'Connell Papers, AABo 16:10–12. See also Borgongini-Duca to O'Connell, March 9, 1924, ibid., 16:11, and *HAB*, 3:649–650.

53. Walsh Roman Diary, ADPo, February 27–28, March 11, 1924. On DeLai, see Falconi, *Popes in the Twentieth Century*, 48–53 and 153–154.

54. Walsh Roman Diary, ADPo, March 12, 1924. See the account of Walsh's funeral, which contains no hint of the hostility between him and O'Connell, in *Portland Press Herald*, May 17, 1924.

55. On the visitation, see Fumasoni-Biondi to O'Connell, April 25, 1925, Apostolic Delegate Files, AABo. ADUSA, IX (Boston), ASV, contains a file on this visitation, but it remains closed and unavailable to research.

56. On Murray's appointment to Portland, see *Boston Traveler*, March 22, 1925. On Spellman's designation as auxiliary, see Gannon, *Cardinal Spellman Story*, 90–93, and O'Connell to Spellman, October 6, 1932, Spellman File, AABo. On the complaint about the Sulpicians, see O'Connell to Cicognani, October 23, 1933, Apostolic Delegate File, AABo.

57. McNicholas to Cicognani, no date but 1935, Apostolic Delegate Files, Archives, Archdiocese of Cincinnati.

58. Walsh to Bonzano, June 9, 1919, ADUSA, IX (Boston): 94/2, ASV.

59. *New York Times*, June 9, 1935, and March 12, 1936. Roe's death certificate is in the Division of Vital Statistics, Commonwealth of Massachusetts, Boston; his obituary, containing no hint of his previous life, is in *New York Times*, December 1, 1948. Frankie Johnson Roe's obituary is ibid., April 22, 1969. Her first husband, Doctor Wort, who married again, had died in 1949; ibid., July 30, 1949.

9. THE LONG TWILIGHT: MANAGING THE
ARCHDIOCESE, 1924–1944

1. *Pilot*, December 22, 1923, and January 12, 1924. These articles were part of O'Connell's publicity campaign to show Rome that, despite the scandal, everything was fine in Catholic Boston. The opening of new parishes can be charted precisely in this period, but the total Catholic population of the Boston archdiocese cannot now be determined. The figures given annually in the *Official Catholic Directory* may vary from one year to another by as much as half a million people. Formal parish censuses were irregular, and since pastors had certain incentives both to inflate and to undercount their people, the officially reported numbers are so unreliable as to be entirely useless.

2. *Recollections*, 205. A printed copy of Keith's will, dated February 26, 1916, is in the International Amusement and Realty Company Records (hereafter IARC), AABo.

3. The final distribution of the assets, which included a cash payment to O'Connell by Harvard of $1,500 to equalize the value, is confirmed by a document signed by the cardinal, Charles Francis Adams (Harvard's treasurer), and the Keith executors, August 1, 1923, IARC, AABo. The same collection contains account books, correspondence, and other materials relating to the management and sale of the properties. Dorothy Wayman, *Cardinal O'Connell*, 190, slightly undervalues O'Connell's inheritance in her frequently confusing account of the whole business.

4. The stock transactions are detailed in the account books in IARC, AABo. On the nature and value of some of these investments, see Thomas R. Navin and Marian V. Sears, "The Rise of a Market for Industrial Securities, 1887–1902," *Business History Review* 29 (1955): 105–138. Joseph O'Connell, son of the cardinal's brother Edward, had a brush with the law in 1932, when he was investigated for pulling archdiocesan money out of a Boston bank only days before it collapsed, allegedly on the basis of inside information; see Chancery Central Subject File M–941, AABo.

5. The construction projects and other benefactions are itemized in the account books, IARC, AABo; *Recollections*, 206. For analysis of the contemporary Catholic fascination with what was often called an "edifice complex," see John Cogley's chapter, "More Stately Mansions," in his *Catholic America* (New York: Dial Press, 1973), 79–115; see also Hennesey, *American Catholics*, 234–235, and Kantowicz, *Corporation Sole*, 36–45.

6. Haberlin to Fitzgerald, July 12, 1922, Parish Files, AABo 39:21; Burke to Cummins, November 28, 1932, ibid., 19:8; correspondence between Blunt and Haberlin, May 26 and 27, 1924, ibid., 33:21.

7. See the correspondence between O'Connell and the rector of Mission church, 1929–1931, ibid., 19:19–20. On the social significance of this parish, see John F. Byrne, *The Glories of Mary in Boston: A Memorial History of the Church of Our Lady of Perpetual Help (Mission Church), Roxbury, Mass., 1871–1921* (Boston: Mission Church Press, 1921).

8. On the services for the deaf at Mission Church, see Conway to O'Connell, March 29, 1937, and Minihan to Conway, March 30, 1937, Parish Files, AABo

19:23. On the opposition to afternoon masses (which did not become common until the rules on the eucharistic fast were changed in the 1950s), see Chaput to Kelleher, August 14, 1929, ibid., 54:13. On the question of broadening participation in the mass, see Kirwin to Burke, January 21, 1930, and Burke to Kirwin, March 21, 1930, ibid., 51:10.

9. See the letters between Neagle and the chancery office, May–November 1931, ibid., 56:24. The canon law of the benefice system is explained in Sullivan, "Beneficial Relations," *Catholic Boston*, 226–230.

10. Harrigan's shrewdness is documented in his correspondence with the chancery office, January 1928–November 1929, Parish Files, AABo 11:24–25; S&A, 3:191.

11. Haberlin to Knapp, December 14, 1926, Deceased Priests Correspondence Files, AABo; Clifford to Burke, February–August 1932, Parish Files, AABo 19:8; Minihan to Murphy, October 18, 1935, ibid., 44:20.

12. For the dispute over the monastery chapel, see the letters between Tracy and O'Connell's office, March 1915–October 1916, Parish Files, AABo 10:7–8. The conflict over the Sulpicians is documented in the letters dated between February 25 and March 1, 1923, ibid., 10:12.

13. See the correspondence relating to the convent, March–July 1923, ibid., 10:12.

14. Merwick, *Boston Priests*, 177, 192. The account that follows is reconstructed from the correspondence of Our Lady of Czestochowa parish, South Boston, 1916–1935, Parish Files, AABo 22:6–19.

15. Walsh to Bonzano, June 9, 1919, ADUSA, IX (Boston): 94/2, ASV. The cardinal's claim to "complete cognizance" is in *Recollections*, 301.

16. Craig to O'Connell, October 3, 1926; Haberlin to Sheerin, October 11, 1926; and Fitzgerald to Burke, April 30, 1931; all in Parish Files, AABo 27:13–14.

17. For complaints about Creagh from the priests in his parish see, for example, Keenan to O'Connell, October 1, 1924, ibid., 31:15; Gough to Minihan, January 1, 1942, and Madden to O'Connell, February 19, 1942, both ibid., 99:1.

18. The evaluation of Creagh is in Kelly to O'Connell, September 16, 1938, ibid., 31:17. For a summary of Creagh's work on the canon law of the benefice system, see his article on the subject in the *Catholic Encyclopedia*, s.v. "benefice." On earlier struggles between bishops and the clergy, see Robert Trisco, "Bishops and Their Priests in the United States," *The Catholic Priest in the United States: Historical Investigations*, ed. John Tracy Ellis (Collegeville, Minn.: Saint John's University Press, 1971), 111–292.

19. Curtin to Haberlin, November 20, 1922, Parish Files, AABo 54:3; Joyce to Haberlin, July 17, 1923, ibid., 59:6.

20. No doubt fearing that such a substantial withdrawal might cause some future pastor to question his probity or common sense, Sullivan left behind, "where it may be found by my successor," a detailed memorandum, dated April 18, 1931, of the entire incident. Originally kept in the parish itself, this memorandum came into the possession of AABo in 1970 when All Saints parish was closed because of insolvency; it is now in Parish Files, AABo 19:13. This was apparently not the first time O'Connell had raided a substantial sum from a parish treasury. On the case of

Saint Leo's, Dorchester, see Doody to Mullen, June 29, 1920, ADUSA, IX (Boston): 94/3, ASV.

21. The files of correspondence between the cathedral parish and the cardinal's office contain regular financial reports and letters transmitting checks; see, for example, "Christmas Collection, 1920," Parish Files, AABo 1:16; Finigan to Haberlin, January 3, 1920, ibid., 1:14; and Finigan to Haberlin, April 21, 1919, ibid., 1:13. On the profitability of Saint Cecilia's, see McGarry to Haberlin, November 18, 1922, ibid., 7:11; McGarry to Haberlin, October 1923, ibid., 7:12; and monthly report, February 1933, ibid., 7:19. Some other bishops followed O'Connell's practice in assuming the pastorate of well-off parishes; see the description of a similar arrangement by the bishop of Manchester, New Hampshire, in Guertin to O'Connell, September 4, 1925, Correspondence with Other Dioceses (Manchester), AABo.

22. On devotions at the cathedral, see Cronin to O'Connell, October 7, 1926, Parish Files, AABo 2:11; O'Conor to Minihan, August 15, 1938, ibid., 3:13; and O'Conor to Minihan, September 3, 1938, ibid., 3:14. On the arrangements for the Curley wedding, see Curley to O'Connell, June 7, 1935, O'Connell Papers, AABo 4:7. On various arrangements at Saint Cecilia's, see Haberlin to McGarry, October 23, 1916, Parish Files, AABo, 7:4.

23. Regular financial reports for the Sisters of Saint Joseph of Boston are contained in Institution Files, AABo 4:14–19. Mary J. Oates has provided a detailed analysis of the financial realities of women's religious communities in her excellent essay, "'The Good Sisters': The Work and Position of Catholic Churchwomen in Boston, 1870–1940," *Catholic Boston*, 171–200. See also Oates's "Organized Voluntarism: The Catholic Sisters in Massachusetts, 1870–1940," *Women in American Religion*, ed. Janet Wilson James (Philadelphia: University of Pennsylvania Press, 1980), 141–169.

24. Sisters of Saint Joseph Motherhouse Annals, ASSJ, April 6, 1907, and June 4, 1921. The "obey-then-appeal" order was contained in the text of a talk given by Father Thomas Magennis, a text O'Connell approved in advance; see Magennis to O'Connell, January 10, 1908, Institution Files, AABo 4:14.

25. Burke to Sister Fidelis, October 15–31, 1928, Institution Files, AABo 6:4; Motherhouse Annals, ASSJ, October 4, 1920.

26. See the correspondence between the chancery and the officers of the Academy of the Assumption, Wellesley, January–December 1920, Institution Files, AABo 16:17. On the question of a retreat house for the Sisters of Saint Joseph, see Motherhouse Annals, ASSJ, June 7, October 22, and October 25, 1921; O'Connell's remark is quoted in the diary of Sister Mary Aloysius, ASSJ, October 15, 1921. On O'Connell's attempt to join the hospital boards, see above, chapter 5.

27. Haberlin to Splaine, June 9, 1922, Institution Files, AABo 4:16; Sister Mary Domitilla to O'Connell, April 5, 1924, with O'Connell's penciled note, ibid., 4:17; Haberlin to Sister Mary Borgia, October 18, 1917, ibid., 4:14.

28. Burke to Sister Mary, December 19, 1927, and Sister Helen Madeleine to O'Connell, December 23, 1927, ibid., 1:6. See also the two separate letters, Sister Mary to O'Connell, both dated December 29, 1927, ibid. The early pattern of the

sisters' navigations around O'Connell is discussed in Mary Friel, "History of Emmanuel College, 1919–1974" (Ph.D. diss.: Boston College, 1979).

29. On this dispute, see Cicognani to O'Connell, June 6 and December 17, 1934, and O'Connell to Cicognani, December 22 and 28, 1934, all in Apostolic Delegate Files, AABo. O'Connell's participation in the earlier election is noted in Motherhouse Annals, ASSJ, July 17, 1920.

30. Splaine to O'Connell, March 1, 1915, Deceased Priests Correspondence Files, AABo.

31. *HAB*, 3:501; *S&A*, 3:191. On the growth and meaning of the image of an all-powerful generation of bishops, see O'Toole, "The Role of Bishops in American Catholic History."

32. McGill to Parsons, October 15, 1927; quoted in William M. Halsey, *The Survival of American Innocence: Catholicism in an Era of Disillusionment, 1920–1940* (Notre Dame, Ind.: University of Notre Dame Press, 1980), 51. See also Hennesey, *American Catholics*, 221–233, for an exploration of this theme.

10. MILITANT AND TRIUMPHANT: MORALISM AND SELF-ASSERTION IN O'CONNELL'S CATHOLICISM

1. Coakley to O'Connell, February 17, 1917, and O'Connell to Coakley, February 19, 1917, O'Connell Papers, AABo 3:12. For an outline of Coakley's colorful life, see Russell, "Knave of Boston," 72–80. Coakley was responding to an editorial in the *Pilot*, February 17, 1917.

2. "Holy Name Hymn," *Holy Cross Hymnal* (Boston: White Smith, 1915); *S&A*, 10:2.

3. *Boston American*, December 8, 1932; *Boston Record*, June 9, 1942.

4. *S&A*, 3:132; Sexton, *Cardinal O'Connell*, 356, 341; Cummins to O'Connell, November 27, 1932, and Burke to Cummins, December 1, 1932, Parish Files, AABo 4:5.

5. The events of the celebration are described in the Boston newspapers of May 16–30, 1926, and in *HAB*, 3:653–655. For the aphorisms, see *Boston Sunday Advertiser*, May 2, 1926, and *Boston Evening Transcript*, May 19, 1926; they are also in *S&A*, 9:59–69. The stuffy Brahmin *Transcript* ran the sayings under the perhaps mocking headline "*Dicta Eminentes*."

6. This story is related in Joseph G. Brennan, *The Education of a Prejudiced Man* (New York: Charles Scribner's Sons, 1977), 39–41. The student wit was John J. Wright, who later became a priest, served as O'Connell's secretary, and was eventually a cardinal himself. An oral tradition among the Jesuits at Boston College maintains that there was opposition to granting O'Connell a formal honorary degree on the grounds that it would devalue the school's currency in that regard, with the "Patron" title invented as a plausible substitute.

7. All the appropriate speeches and letters are reproduced in the commemorative volume, *Golden Jubilee of His Eminence, William Cardinal O'Connell, Archbishop of Boston, 1884–1934* (Cambridge, Mass.: Riverside Press, 1934). See also *Readings from Cardinal O'Connell*, ed. Hugh F. Blunt (New York: Appleton-Century, 1934), v, vii.

8. Sexton, *Cardinal O'Connell*, 347. For the assessment of the *Recollections*, see *New York Times Book Review*, June 24, 1934. The Vatican had expressed some advance concerns about the *Recollections*, fearful that O'Connell might use the book to settle old scores with his ecclesiastical enemies, but he assured the apostolic delegate that he would resist that temptation; see Cicognani to O'Connell, April 19, 1934, and O'Connell to Cicognani, April 23, 1934, O'Connell Papers, AABo 17:21.

9. O'Connell to Fumasoni-Biondi, July 8 and 13, 1931, Apostolic Delegation Files, AABo.

10. For O'Connell statements on Mexico, see, for example, *Pilot*, April 7, 1928, and February 23, 1929; for a general outline of the church's role in the Mexican revolution, see Jean A. Mayer, *The Cristero Rebellion: The Mexican People Between Church and State, 1926–1929* (Cambridge: Cambridge University Press, 1976). O'Connell's statement on Franco is in *New York Times*, March 19, 1938; for a general discussion of the subject, see Donald F. Crosby, "Boston's Catholics and the Spanish Civil War, 1936–1939," *New England Quarterly* 44 (1971): 82–100.

11. The full text of the speech is in *S&A*, 6:190–198; the quotation is at 191. See also O'Connell to Carroll, September 9, 1920, O'Connell Papers, AABo 3:10.

12. Alan J. Ward, *Ireland and Anglo-American Relations, 1899–1921* (London: London School of Economics, 1969), 205; Francis M. Carroll, *American Opinion and the Irish Question, 1910–1923: A Study in Opinion and Policy* (New York: Saint Martin's Press, 1978), 126. O'Connell did not comment on the League until 1922, saying as he emerged from a courtesy call on President Warren Harding that "events have certainly proved our wisdom in not joining the League of Nations"; *Boston Post*, September 26, 1922.

13. The intrigue surrounding the invitation to O'Connell is described in Charles C. Tansill, *America and the Fight for Irish Freedom, 1866–1922* (New York: Devin-Adair, 1957), 277–278, and Patrick McCartan, *With De Valera in America* (Dublin: Fitzpatrick, 1932), 57–58. The coy letter to Rome is O'Connell to Gasparri, undated but January 1919, Secretariat of State Files, AABo. Dunn's less than kind assessment of O'Connell's appearance (he called the Boston cardinal "Czar of all the Russias") is in his letter to Donovan, December 11, 1918, Hayes Papers, O–4, AANY.

14. Barclay to Foreign Office, November 11, 1918, FO 371/3430, Public Record Office, London; Barclay to Balfour, December 12, 1918, FO 115/2398, ibid. On O'Connell's duplicitous game with the British, see also Miller, *Emigrants and Exiles*, 537.

15. Charles J. V. Murphy, "Pope of New England," *Outlook and Independent* 153 (October 23, 1929), 288; Sexton, *Cardinal O'Connell*, 345.

16. *HAB*, 3:763; O'Connell to Gibbons, February 2, 1918, AABa, 120–P–7. The dispute with the Red Cross over Kipling is described in the *Boston Traveler*, March 9, 1918; the dictionary defines "swithering" as meaning "doubting" or "wavering."

17. Haberlin to Barnewell, March 9, 1916, O'Connell Papers, AABo 3:3; O'Connell to Lane, February 22, 1911, and Lane to O'Connell, February 27, 1911, ibid., 6:4.

18. Haberlin to Connolly, May 22, 1916, Parish Files, AABo, 18:1.

19. *Review* 8 (August 8, 1901), 301, quoted in Joseph P. Chinnici, *Living Stones: The History and Structure of Catholic Spiritual Life in the United States* (New York: Macmillan, 1989), 135–136. The correspondence relating to O'Connell's service to the library is in O'Connell Papers, AABo 14:11–15.

20. O'Connell to Mercier, January 4, 1915, O'Connell Papers, AABo 7:6. The professor in question was the internationally renowned philosopher Maurice De Wulf, whose name meant nothing to O'Connell. Assuming that he was a priest, the cardinal thought that Mercier could simply order him not to accept the post. Emma Forbes Cary, doyenne of the Radcliffe Catholic Club, politely set her archbishop straight by explaining that De Wulf (who did indeed join the Harvard faculty for a time) was a layman and could therefore do as he liked; see Cary to O'Connell, January 6, 1915, Chancery Central Subject File M–1770, AABo. On the earlier slights by Harvard against Catholic college graduates, see Merwick, *Boston Priests*, 130–131, and Dunigan, *History of Boston College*, 172–177. Joseph Kennedy's experience at Harvard is described dramatically in Goodwin, *Fitzgeralds and Kennedys*, 208–233.

21. Hickey to O'Connell, May 14, 1930, Parish Files, AABo 35:22. The review, "Confessions of an Adams," is in the *Pilot*, April 1, 1916; for O'Connell's authorship of this review, see Haberlin to Toomey, March 24, 1916, *Pilot* Files, AABo 1:19.

22. *S&A*, 8: 181, 182.

23. *S&A*, 8:137.

24. Haberlin to Scanlan, November 17, 1916, CCB Files, AABo 1:8; Coakley to O'Connell, February 17, 1917, O'Connell Papers, AABo 3:12; *S&A*, 9:174.

25. *S&A*, 9:50, 9:169, and 8:18.

26. Robinson, *The Cardinal*, 514. The cardinal's correspondence with Edward O'Connell and his children is in O'Connell Papers, AABo 12:1–4, and in O'Connell Papers ("Sullivan Collection"), ibid.

27. For an exploration of the "purgative way" of Catholic spirituality, see Chinnici's stimulating *Living Stones*, esp. 52–67.

28. *S&A*, 9:56–69. See ibid., 216–229, for an O'Connell pastoral letter on the Virgin and ibid., 249–261, for an explication of purgatory. For a general survey of the spirituality of this period, see Thomas E. Wangler, "Catholic Religious Life in Boston in the Era of Cardinal O'Connell," *Catholic Boston*, 239–272.

29. Robert Rogers, "This Is Life," *Boston American*, November 27, 1936; O'Connell to Hurley, June 22, 1905, O'Connell Papers, ADPo; Haberlin to Toomey, November 2, 1916, *Pilot* Files, AABo 1:20; Stanley to Haberlin, December 17, 1928, Chancery Central Subject Files M–896, AABo.

30. There is no definitive history of the Watch and Ward Society, but its activities are chronicled in Harris's biography of Cabot, *Only to God*.

31. *S&A*, 9:179; O'Connell to Belloc, October 29, 1926, O'Connell Papers, AABo 3:4; Splaine to Haberlin, October 13, 1916, League of Catholic Women Correspondence, ibid., 1:3. O'Connell's book selections, together with those of several other national celebrities, appeared in the *New York Herald*, February 5, 1923. The occasionally outrageous evangelist Billy Sunday resourcefully included on his list of desert-island reading a book on how to build a radio transmitter, presumably to signal for help in getting off the island. For a general treatment of the censorship

of literature, see Una M. Cadegan, "All Good Books Are Catholic Books: Literature, Censorship, and the Americanization of Catholics, 1920–1960," Ph.D. diss.: University of Pennsylvania, 1987.

32. On *Salome*, see *Boston Evening Transcript*, October 18, 1923. For a typical denunciation of the movies, see *S&A*, 11:118–121. O'Connell's support for the fledgling Legion of Decency is in Chancery Central Subject Files M–940, AABo. Joe Kennedy's involvement with the movies is discussed in Goodwin, *Fitzgeralds and Kennedys*, 369–418; see especially her sensible treatment of the apocryphal story that O'Connell intervened in the Kennedy-Swanson romance, 417–418.

33. *Boston Globe*, March 8, 1920; *New York Times*, March 9, 1920; *S&A*, 10:43; author's interview with Anna Downing and Josephine Kirk, July 6, 1984.

34. For O'Connell's changing views on Sunday sports, see *Boston Post*, October 24, 1919, and *Boston Herald*, February 1, 1928. The rebuke of the Regis softball players is in Burke to Sister Anna Louise, April 16, 1931, Institution Files, AABo 16:22. The suspicion of the Boy Scouts is in *S&A*, 10:22.

35. The denunciation of crooners is in *S&A*, 11:16–22; the largely favorable reaction to it may be seen in the letters and press clippings in O'Connell Papers, AABo 17:16.

36. The piano competition with White is described in *America*, 50 (November 4, 1933): 101. On O'Connell's composition of hymns, see Sullivan to McGarry, August 2, 1916, Parish Files, AABo 7:3. For each hymn, the cardinal would apparently write the words, pick out the simple tune, and then give the sketch to the choir director of one of his churches for elaboration. The question of what music to play on the church bells in Gloucester is discussed in Hart to Haberlin, June 29, 1926, ibid., 41:17, and Haberlin to Hart, May 22, 1928, ibid., 41:19.

37. *S&A*, 9:1, 4.

38. *S&A*, 11:130. The most complete assessment of the Catholic worldview in this era is Halsey, *Survival of American Innocence*; see esp. 138–168. For a study applying this kind of analysis to Boston, see Kane, "Boston Catholics and Modern American Culture, 1900–1920."

39. *New York Times*, March 28, 1924, and February 2, 1926. Unwittingly, O'Connell proved correct in his suspicion of the evolution exhibit, which featured the "Piltdown Man," eventually proved to be a hoax; see J. S. Weiner, *The Piltdown Forgery* (London: Oxford University Press, 1955). On the parallel trends in evangelical Protestantism, see George M. Marsden, *Fundamentalism and American Culture: The Shaping of Twentieth-Century Evangelicalism, 1870–1925* (New York: Oxford University Press, 1980), esp. 153–157 and 204–205.

40. Hickey to O'Connell, May 14, 1930, Parish Files, AABo 35:22; "A Bad Imitation," *Pilot*, April 12, 1924.

41. *New York Times*, April 8 and 9, 1929; see also O'Connell's speech to the Catholic College Clubs of America, *S&A*, 10:25–29. The generally favorable letters O'Connell received after denouncing Einstein are in Chancery Central Subject File M–1022, AABo.

42. See, for example, O'Connell's correspondence, 1941–1943, with the Boston rabbi, Joshua Loth Liebman, O'Connell Papers, AABo 6:12; the cordial

remarks at the Fenway Park celebration are in *Golden Jubilee*, 68. O'Connell's suspicion of the Nazis is apparent in his correspondence with Constantin von Neurath, an old friend from his Roman days who had become Hitler's foreign minister; see O'Connell Papers, AABo 7:13. The cardinal's support for a Jewish state is in *New York American*, December 26, 1918. Catholic-Jewish tension in Boston in this period is described tellingly by Nat Hentoff in his autobiography, *Boston Boy* (New York: Knopf, 1986), esp. 16–17. Hentoff describes escaping one such beating himself by convincing his antagonists that he was Greek and reciting something in the classical language he was learning as a student at the Boston Latin School.

43. Sexton, *Cardinal O'Connell*, 345; Minot to O'Connell, April 27, 1938, O'Connell Papers, AABo 7:11; *Commonweal*, May 5, 1944, 52; *Boston Herald*, June 9, 1934.

44. "Holy Name Hymn," *Holy Cross Hymnal*.

45. *S&A*, 8:235; 10:165.

46. *S&A*, 10:3, 2.

EPILOGUE: WILLIAM O'CONNELL AND AMERICAN CATHOLICISM

1. *Boston Globe*, April 23, 1944; author's interview with Anna Downing and Josephine Kirk, July 6, 1984. O'Connell's last days are also described in Wayman, *Cardinal O'Connell*, 272–275.

2. The events of the funeral are covered extensively in all the Boston newspapers of the week of April 23–29, 1944.

3. *Boston American*, November 27, 1936; *S&A*, 11:151.

4. O'Connell subsequently prepared an account of the adventure of his last dash to Rome for a conclave in the little volume *A Memorable Voyage* (Boston: Privately printed, 1939). For correspondence among his aides, who feared that he might not be able to endure the rigors of the trip, see O'Connell Papers, AABo 17:12. For the impact of Pacelli's election on Spellman, see Gannon, *Cardinal Spellman Story*, 129–151. John Cooney, *The American Pope: The Life and Times of Francis Cardinal Spellman* (New York: Times Books, 1984) is sloppy in its research and biased in its outlook, but it describes generally the rise of Spellman's influence under Pius XII; see especially 72–80.

5. On the role of these younger men in the later years of O'Connell's tenure, see O'Toole, "'That Fabulous Churchman'," 31–32.

6. On the generational shift in local public life, see O'Connor, *Bibles, Brahmins, and Bosses*, 153–172. For a typical photograph of a child kissing Cushing's ring, see *Boston Post*, June 30, 1939. The film of the May festival at Sacred Heart parish, Newton Centre, remarkable for the way it documents popular religious belief and practice, is in AABo.

7. The claims to a noble Irish ancestry for O'Connell are summarized in *HAB*, 3:442–443. There is no adequate biography of Cushing and there may never be; see, however, Joseph Dever, *Cushing of Boston: A Candid Portrait* (Boston: Humphries, 1965) and John Henry Cutler, *Cardinal Cushing of Boston* (New York: Hawthorn Books, 1970).

BIBLIOGRAPHY

Archives and Manuscript Collections

Archives, Archdiocese of Baltimore
    Curley, Michael J., Papers
    Gibbons, James, Papers

Archives, Archdiocese of Boston
    American Hierarchy Meeting Files
    Archdiocesan Synod (1919) Files
    Catholic Charitable Bureau Files
    Chancery Account Books
    Chancery Central Subject Files
    Chancery Circulars
    Charles Collins Diary
    Correspondence with Other Dioceses
    Episcopal Register
    Hospital Files
    Institution Files
    Institution Special Correspondence Files
    International Amusement and Realty Company Records
    League of Catholic Women Records
    O'Connell, William Henry, Papers
    Parish Files
    Parish Sacramental Records
    Parish Special Correspondence Files
    Pilot Files
    Priests Total Abstinence League Records
    Pulpit Announcement Books
    Saint John's Seminary Files
    Society for the Propagation of the Faith Files
    Tuckerman, "Life of Archbishop Williams"
    Vatican Congregations Files
    Williams, John J., Papers
    Wills Correspondence

Archives, Archdiocese of Cincinnati
    Apostolic Delegate Files

Archives, Archdiocese of New York
        Corrigan, Michael A., Papers
        Farley, John, Papers
        Hayes, Patrick J., Papers

Archives, Archdiocese of San Francisco
        Riordan, Patrick, Papers

Archives, Commonwealth of Massachusetts
        Judicial Archives Division
        Original Papers of Legislation
        Vital Records

Archives, Diocese of Burlington
        Rice, Joseph J., Papers

Archives, Diocese of Fall River
        Stang, William, Papers

Archives, Diocese of Portland
        Chancery Letterbooks
        O'Connell, William Henry, Papers
        Parish Files
        Walsh, Louis S., Diaries
        Walsh, Louis S., Papers

Archives, Diocese of Providence
        Harkins, Matthew, Diaries

Archives, Diocese of Springfield
        Beavan, Thomas D., Papers

Archives, Sacred Congregation de Propaganda Fide, Rome
        Rubric #153 (United States of America)

Archives, Sisters of Saint Joseph, Boston
        Motherhouse Annals

Archivio Segreto Vaticano, Rome
        Apostolic Delegate, U.S.A., Files
        Secretary of State Files

Brookline, Massachusetts, Public Library
        Town Tax Lists

John Ireland Papers
    Microfilm Edition, Minnesota Historical Society
    (Originals in Catholic Historical Society of Saint Paul)

Library of Congress, Manuscript Division
    Wayman, Dorothy G., Papers

New York Historical Society
    Seton, Robert, Papers

Public Record Office, London
    Foreign Office Files

Saint John's Seminary Library, Brighton
    O'Connell Clippings Scrapbooks

Suffolk County Registry of Probate, Boston
    Dockets and Case Files

Suffolk County Superior Court, Boston
    Trial Papers, Civil Division

Sulpician Archives Baltimore
    Saint John's Seminary, Brighton, Papers (RG 9, Box 6)

Oral History Interview

Interview with Anna O'Connell Downing and Josephine O'Connell Kirk, July 6, 1984, Osterville, Massachusetts

Books and Articles

Abrams, Richard M. *Conservatism in a Progressive Era: Massachusetts Politics, 1900–1912.* Cambridge, Mass.: Harvard University Press, 1964.
Alexander, Jack. "The Cardinal and Cold Roast Boston." *Saturday Evening Post,* October 4, 1941: 9–11, 112–116.
Augustine, Charles. *The Canonical and Civil Status of Catholic Parishes in the United States.* Saint Louis: Herder, 1926.
Barbrook, Alan. *God Save the Commonwealth: An Electoral History of Massachusetts.* Amherst: University of Massachusetts Press, 1973.
Bartlett, Chester J. *The Tenure of Parochial Property in the United States of America.* Washington, D.C.: Catholic University of America, 1926. Catholic University Canon Law Studies #31.

Billington, Ray Allen. *The Protestant Crusade, 1800–1860*. New York: Macmillan, 1938.

Brann, Henry A. *History of the American College of the Roman Catholic Church of the United States, Rome, Italy*. New York: Benziger Brothers, 1910.

Brault, Gerard J. *The French-Canadian Heritage in New England*. Hanover, N.H.: University Press of New England, 1986.

Brennan, Joseph G. *The Education of a Prejudiced Man*. New York: Charles Scribner's Sons, 1977.

Brinkley, Alan. *Voices of Protest: Huey Long, Father Coughlin, and the Great Depression*. New York: Knopf, 1982.

Brochure of Boston College and the Young Men's Catholic Association. Boston, 1894.

Broderick, Francis L. *Right Reverend New Dealer: John A. Ryan*. New York: Macmillan, 1963.

Brooks, Van Wyck. *The Dream of Arcadia: American Writers and Artists in Italy, 1760–1915*. New York: Dutton, 1958.

Buehrle, Marie Cecilia. *Rafael Cardinal Merry del Val*. Milwaukee: Bruce, 1957.

Buenker, John D. "The Mahatma and Progressive Reform: Martin Lomasney as Lawmaker," *New England Quarterly* 44 (1971): 397–419.

Byrne, John F. *The Glories of Mary in Boston: A Memorial History of the Church of Our Lady of Perpetual Help (Mission Church), Roxbury, Mass., 1871–1921*. Boston: Mission Church Press, 1921.

Cadegan, Una M. "All Good Books Are Catholic Books: Literature, Censorship, and the Americanization of Catholics, 1920–1960." Ph.D. diss.: University of Pennsylvania, 1987.

Cardinale, Igino. *La Saint-Siege et la Diplomatie: Aperçu Historique, Juridique et Pratique de la Diplomatie Pontificale*. Paris: Desclee, 1962.

Carlen, Claudia, ed. *The Papal Encyclicals*. 5 vols. Raleigh: McGrath, 1981.

Carroll, Francis M. *American Opinion and the Irish Question, 1910–1923: A Study in Opinion and Policy*. New York: Saint Martin's Press, 1978.

Carroll, John. *The John Carroll Papers*, ed. Thomas O'Brien Hanley. Notre Dame, Ind.: University of Notre Dame Press, 1976.

Cary, Otis. *A History of Christianity in Japan: Roman Catholic, Greek Orthodox, and Protestant Missions*. Rutland, Ver.: Charles W. Tuttle, 1976.

Catalogue of the Officers and Students of Boston College for the Academic Year 1878–1879. Boston: Duffy, Cushman, 1879.

Catalogue of the Officers and Students of Boston College for the Academic Year 1879–1880. Boston: Duffy, Cushman, 1880.

Catalogue of the Officers and Students of Boston College for the Academic Year 1880–1881. Boston: Duffy, Cushman, 1881.

Catholic Directory. Title and imprint varies.

Catholic Encyclopedia. New York: Encyclopedia Press, 1911.

Chadwick, Owen. *Catholicism and History: The Opening of the Vatican Archives*. Cambridge: Cambridge University Press, 1978.

Chandler, Alfred D., Jr. *The Visible Hand: The Managerial Revolution in American Business*. Cambridge, Mass.: Belknap Presss, 1977.

Chinnici, Joseph P. *Living Stones: The History and Structure of Catholic Spiritual Life in the United States.* New York: Macmillan, 1989.

Ciesluk, Joseph E. *National Parishes in the United States.* Washington, D.C.: Catholic University of America, 1944.

Cogley, John. *Catholic America.* New York: Dial Press, 1973.

Cole, Donald B. *Immigrant City: Lawrence, Massachusetts., 1845–1921.* Chapel Hill: University of North Carolina Press, 1963.

A Complete List of the Students Entered at Saint Charles' College, Ellicott City, Maryland, Since the Opening, October 31st, 1848. New York: Press of the Immaculate Virgin, 1897.

Constitutiones Dioecesos Bostoniensis. Boston: Pilot Publishing Company, 1910.

Cooney, John. *The American Pope: The Life and Times of Francis Cardinal Spellman.* New York: Times Books, 1984.

Cooper, John Milton, Jr. *The Warrior and the Priest: Woodrow Wilson and Theodore Roosevelt.* Cambridge, Mass.: Belknap Press, 1983.

Crosby, Donald F. "Boston's Catholics and the Spanish Civil War, 1936–1939," *New England Quarterly* 44 (1971): 82–100.

Cross, Robert D. *The Emergence of Liberal Catholicism in America.* Cambridge, Mass.: Harvard University Press, 1958.

Curley, James M. *I'd Do It Again: A Record of All My Uproarious Years.* Englewood Cliffs, N.J.: Prentice-Hall, 1957.

Curran, R. Emmett. *Michael Augustine Corrigan and the Shaping of Conservative Catholicism in America, 1878–1902.* New York: Arno Press, 1978.

Current Biography: Who's News and Why, 1941. New York: H. W. Wilson, 1941.

Cutler, John Henry. *Cardinal Cushing of Boston.* New York: Hawthorn Books, 1970.

Dalton, Kathleen. "Why America Loved Teddy Roosevelt; Or, Charisma Is in the Eyes of the Beholders." In *Our Selves/Our Past: Psychological Approaches to American History,* ed. Robert J. Brugger, pp. 269–291. Baltimore: Johns Hopkins University Press, 1981.

DeLai, Gaetano Cardinal. *The Passion of Our Lord,* trans. William Cardinal O'Connell. Boston: Pilot Publishing Company, 1923.

DeMarco, William M. *Ethnics and Enclaves: Boston's Italian North End.* Ann Arbor: U.M.I. Research Press, 1981.

Dever, Joseph. *Cushing of Boston: A Candid Portrait.* Boston: Humphries, 1965.

Dignan, Patrick J. *A History of the Legal Incorporation of Catholic Church Property in the United States, 1784–1932.* New York: P. J. Kenedy and Sons, 1935.

Dineen, Joseph F. *The Purple Shamrock: The Honorable James M. Curley of Boston.* New York: Norton, 1949.

Dohen, Dorothy. *Nationalism and American Catholicism.* New York: Sheed and Ward, 1967.

Dolan, Jay P. *The American Catholic Experience: A History from Colonial Times to the Present.* New York: Doubleday, 1985.

———. *Catholic Revivalism: The American Experience, 1830–1900.* Notre Dame, Ind.: University of Notre Dame Press, 1978.

———. *The Immigrant Church: New York's Irish and German Catholics, 1815–1865.* Baltimore: Johns Hopkins University Press, 1975.

Donovan, Charles F. "Student Enrollment at Boston College in the Nineteenth Century," *Occasional Papers on the History of Boston College.* Chestnut Hill, Mass.: Boston College, 1984.

Donovan, Thomas F. *The Status of the Church in American Civil Law and Canon Law.* Washington, D.C.: Catholic University of America, 1966. Catholic University Canon Law Studies #446.

Drummond, Richard H. *A History of Christianity in Japan.* Grand Rapids, Mich.: Eerdmans, 1971.

Duis, Perry R. *The Saloon: Public Drinking in Chicago and Boston, 1880–1920.* Urbana: University of Illinois Press, 1983.

Dunigan, David R. *A History of Boston College.* Milwaukee: Bruce, 1957.

Dwyer, Kevin F. "Charles Mary Driscoll, O.S.A." In *Men of Heart II: Noteworthy Augustinians, Province of Saint Thomas of Villanova,* ed. John E. Rotelle, pp. 221–244. Villanova, Penn.: Augustinian Press, 1986.

Earnest, Ernest. *Expatriates and Patriots: American Artists, Scholars, and Writers in Europe.* Durham, N.C.: Duke University Press, 1968.

Edelman, Murray. *The Symbolic Uses of Politics.* Urbana: University of Illinois Press, 1964.

Ellis, John Tracy. *Catholic Bishops: A Memoir.* Wilmington, Del.: Michael Glazier, 1983.

The Episcopal Diocese of Massachusetts, 1784–1984: A Mission to Remember, Proclaim, and Fulfill, ed. Mark J. Duffy. Boston: Episcopal Diocese of Massachusetts, 1984.

Esslinger, Dean R. "American German and Irish Attitudes Toward Neutrality, 1914–1917: A Study of Catholic Minorities." *Catholic Historical Review* 53 (1967): 194–216.

Falconi, Carlo. *The Popes in the Twentieth Century: From Pius X to John XXIII,* trans. Muriel Grindrod. London: Weidenfeld and Nicolson, 1967.

Feuerlicht, Roberta Strauss. *Justice Crucified: The Story of Sacco and Vanzetti.* New York: McGraw-Hill, 1977.

Fogarty, Gerald P. *The Vatican and the American Hierarchy from 1870 to 1965.* Wilmington, Del.: Michael Glazier, 1985; orig. pub. Stuttgart, 1982.

―――. *The Vatican and the Americanist Crisis: Denis J. O'Connell, American Agent in Rome, 1885–1903.* Rome: Universita Gregoriana Editrice, 1974.

Foley, Albert S. *Bishop Healy: Beloved Outcaste.* New York: Farrar, Straus and Young, 1954.

Friel, Mary. "History of Emmanuel College, 1919–1974." Ph.D. diss.: Boston College, 1979.

Fuller, Joseph B. "At the Very Center of Things: The Catholic Secular Clergy in the Redirection of Catholic Boston." Honors thesis: Harvard College, 1979.

Gaffey, James. "The Changing of the Guard: The Rise of Cardinal O'Connell of Boston." *Catholic Historical Review* 59 (1973): 225–244.

Gannon, Michael V. "Before and After Modernism: The Intellectual Isolation of the American Priest." In *The Catholic Priest in the United States: Historical Investigations,* ed. John Tracy Ellis, pp. 293–383. Collegeville, Minn.: Saint John's University Press, 1971.

Gannon, Robert I. *The Cardinal Spellman Story.* Garden City, N.Y.: Doubleday, 1962.

Garland, Joseph G. *Boston's North Shore: Being an Account of Life among the Noteworthy, Fashionable, Wealthy, Eccentric and Ordinary, 1823–1890.* Boston: Little Brown, 1978.

Ginnetty, Paul F. "Moratorium and Ministry: The Adult Development of Former Roman Catholic Priests." Ph.D. diss.: City University of New York, 1986.

Glazer, Nathan, and Daniel P. Moynihan, eds. *Ethnicity: Theory and Experience.* Cambridge, Mass.: Harvard University Press, 1975.

Golden Jubilee of His Eminence William Cardinal O'Connell, Archbishop of Boston, 1884–1934. Cambridge, Mass.: Riverside Press, 1934.

Golden Jubilee of Saint Charles' College, Near Ellicott City, Maryland, 1848–1898. Baltimore: John Murphy, 1898.

Gollin, James. *Worldly Goods: The Wealth and Power of the American Catholic Church, the Vatican, and the Men Who Control the Money.* New York: Random House, 1971.

Goodwin, Doris Kearns. *The Fitzgeralds and the Kennedys.* New York: Simon and Schuster, 1987.

Graham, Robert A. *Vatican Diplomacy: A Study of Church and State on the International Plane.* Princeton: Princeton University Press, 1959.

Greeley, Andrew, and Gregory Baum, eds. *Ethnicity.* New York: Seabury Press, 1977.

Guignard, Michael J. *La Foi, La Langue, La Culture: The Franco-Americans of Biddeford, Maine.* Biddeford: Privately printed, 1982.

———. "Maine's Corporation Sole Controversy," *Maine Historical Society Newsletter* 12 (1973): 111–126.

Guilday, Peter K. *The Life and Times of John England, First Bishop of Charleston, 1786–1842.* 2 vols. New York: The America Press, 1927.

Hague, John A. "The Massachusetts Constitutional Convention, 1917–1919," *New England Quarterly* 27 (1954): 147–167.

Halsey, William M. *The Survival of American Innocence: Catholicism in an Era of Disillusionment, 1920–1940.* Notre Dame, Ind.: University of Notre Dame Press, 1980.

Handlin, Oscar. *Boston's Immigrants: A Study in Acculturation.* Revised and enlarged edition. New York: Atheneum, 1977; orig. pub. 1941.

Harris, Leon. *Only to God: The Extraordinary Life of Godfrey Lowell Cabot.* New York: Atheneum, 1967.

Hennesey, James. *American Catholics: A History of the Roman Catholic Community in the United States.* New York: Oxford University Press, 1981.

———. "A Prelude to Vatican I: American Bishops and the Definition of the Immaculate Conception." *Theological Studies* 25 (1964): 409–419.

Hentoff, Nat. *Boston Boy.* New York: Knopf, 1986.

Higham, John. *Strangers in the Land: Patterns of American Nativism, 1860–1925.* New York: Atheneum, 1963.

Historical Statistics of the United States. Washington, D.C.: Government Printing Office, 1960.

History of Saint Joseph's Church [Medford, Mass.]. Boston: Privately printed, 1903.

Holloran, Peter J. *Boston's Wayward Children: Social Services for Homeless Children, 1830–1930.* Rutherford, N.J.: Fairleigh Dickinson University Press, 1989.

Holmes, J. Derek. *The Triumph of the Holy See: A Short History of the Papacy in the Nineteenth Century.* London: Burns and Oates, 1978.

Huthmacher, J. Joseph. *Massachusetts People and Politics, 1919–1933.* Cambridge, Mass.: Harvard University Press, 1959.

James, Henry. *William Wetmore Story and His Friends.* 2 vols. Boston: Houghton Mifflin, 1903.

Kane, Paula M. "Boston Catholics and Modern American Culture, 1900–1920." Ph.D. diss.: Yale University, 1987.

Kantowicz, Edward R. "Cardinal Mundelein of Chicago: A Consolidating Bishop." In *An American Church: Essays on the Americanization of the Catholic Church,* ed. David J. Alvarez, pp. 63–72. Moraga, Calif.: Saint Mary's College of California, 1979.

———. *Corporation Sole: Cardinal Mundelein and Chicago Catholicism.* Notre Dame, Ind.: University of Notre Dame Press, 1983.

Kauffman, Christopher J. *Faith and Fraternalism: The History of the Knights of Columbus, 1882–1982.* New York: Harper and Row, 1982.

———. *Tradition and Transformation in Catholic Culture: The Priests of the Society of Saint Sulpice in the United States from 1791 to the Present.* New York: Macmillan, 1988.

Kenneally, James J. "Catholicism and Woman Suffrage in Massachusetts." *Catholic Historical Review,* 53 (1967): 43–57.

Kenney, William F. *Centennial of the See of Boston.* Boston: J. K. Waters, 1909.

Kenny, Herbert A. *Newspaper Row: Journalism in the Pre-Television Era.* Chester, Conn.: Globe Pequot Press, 1987.

Klapp, Orrin E. *Symbolic Leaders: Public Dramas and Public Men.* Chicago: Aldine, 1964.

Larkin, Emmet. "The Devotional Revolution in Ireland, 1850–1875." *American Historical Review* 77 (1972): 625–652.

Levin, Murray B. *The Compleat Politician: Political Strategy in Massachusetts.* Indianapolis: Bobbs-Merrill, 1962.

Link, Arthur S. *Wilson: Campaigns for Progressivism and Peace.* Princeton: Princeton University Press, 1965.

Liptak, Dolores Ann. *European Immigrants and the Catholic Church in Connecticut, 1870–1920.* New York: Center for Migration Studies, 1987.

Litt, Edgar. *The Political Cultures of Massachusetts.* Cambridge, Mass.: M.I.T. Press, 1965.

Lord, Robert H., John E. Sexton, and Edward T. Harrington. *History of the Archdiocese of Boston in the Various Stages of Its Development, 1604–1943.* 3 vols. Boston: Pilot Publishing Company, 1944.

Lucey, William Leo. *The Catholic Church in Maine.* Francestown, N.H.: Marshall Jones, 1957.

Lyons, Louis M. *Newspaper Story: One Hundred Years of the Boston Globe.* Cambridge, Mass.: Belknap Press, 1971.

McAvoy, Thomas T. *The Great Crisis in American Catholic History, 1895–1900*. Chicago: Regnery, 1957.

McCartan, Patrick. *With De Valera in America*. Dublin: Fitzpatrick, 1932.

McCool, Gerald A. *Catholic Theology in the Nineteenth Century: The Quest for a Unitary Method*. New York: Seabury Press, 1977.

McNamara, Robert F. *The American College in Rome*. Rochester, N.Y.: The Christopher Press, 1956.

MacNutt, Francis A. *A Papal Chamberlain: The Personal Chronicle of Francis Augustus MacNutt*, ed. John J. Donovan. New York: Longmans, Green, and Company, 1936.

Marquand, John P. *The Late George Apley*. Boston: Little Brown, 1937.

Marschall, John P. "Diocesan and Religious Clergy: The History of a Relationship, 1789–1969." In *The Catholic Priest in the United States: Historical Investigations*, ed. John Tracy Ellis, pp. 385–421. Collegeville, Minnesota: Saint John's University Press, 1971.

Marsden, George M. *Fundamentalism and American Culture: The Shaping of Twentieth-Century Evangelicalism, 1870–1925*. New York: Oxford University Press, 1980.

Martin, Stephanie Lang. "A Guide to the Records of Sacred Heart Parish, East Cambridge." M.A. thesis: University of Massachusetts-Boston, 1980.

Massachusetts Soldiers, Sailors, and Marines in the Civil War. Brookline: Riverdale Press, 1935.

Mayer, Jean A. *The Cristero Rebellion: The Mexican People between Church and State, 1926–1929*. Cambridge: Cambridge University Press, 1976.

Meagher, Timothy J. "Irish, American, Catholic: Irish-American Identity in Worcester, Massachusetts, 1880 to 1920." In *From Paddy to Studs: Irish-American Communities in the Turn of the Century Era, 1880 to 1920*, ed. Timothy J. Meagher, pp. 75–92. New York: Greenwood, 1986.

Merwick, Donna. *Boston Priests, 1848–1910: A Study of Social and Intellectual Change*. Cambridge, Mass.: Harvard University Press, 1973.

Miller, Kerby A. *Emigrants and Exiles: Ireland and the Irish Exodus to North America*. New York: Oxford University Press, 1985.

Mitchell, A. Gibbs, Jr. "Irish Family Patterns in Nineteenth-Century Ireland and Lowell, Massachusetts." Ph.D. diss.: Boston University, 1976.

Mitchell, Brian C. *The Paddy Camps: The Irish of Lowell, 1821–1861*. Urbana: University of Illinois Press, 1988.

———. "'They Do Not Differ Greatly': The Pattern of Community Development among the Irish in Late Nineteenth Century Lowell, Massachusetts." In *From Paddy to Studs: Irish-American Communities in the Turn of the Century Era, 1880 to 1920*, ed. Timothy J. Meagher, pp. 53–73. New York: Greenwood, 1986.

Mott, Frank Luther. *American Journalism: A History, 1690–1960*. New York: Macmillan, 1962.

Murphy, Charles J. V. "Pope of New England." *Outlook and Independent* 153 (October 23, 1929): 285–288, 318–319.

Murray, Robert K. *Red Scare: A Study of National Hysteria, 1919–1920.* Minneapolis: University of Minnesota Press, 1955.

Navin, Thomas R., and Marian V. Sears. "The Rise of a Market for Industrial Securities, 1887–1902." *Business History Review* 29 (1955): 105–138.

Oates, Mary J. "'The Good Sisters': The Work and Position of Catholic Churchwomen in Boston, 1870–1940." In *Catholic Boston: Studies in Religion and Community, 1870–1970,* eds. Robert E. Sullivan and James M. O'Toole, pp. 171–200. Boston: Archdiocese of Boston, 1985.

———. "Organized Voluntarism: The Catholic Sisters of Massachusetts, 1870–1940." In *Women in American Religion,* ed. Janet Wilson James, pp. 141–169. Philadelphia: University of Pennsylvania Press, 1980.

O'Connell, Marvin R. *John Ireland and the American Catholic Church.* Saint Paul: Minnesota Historical Society, 1988.

O'Connell, William Henry. *Holy Cross Hymnal.* Boston: White Smith, 1915.

———. *Letters of His Eminence William Cardinal O'Connell, Archbishop of Boston.* Cambridge, Mass.: Riverside Press, 1915.

———. *A Memorable Voyage.* Boston: Privately printed, 1939.

———. *Readings from Cardinal O'Connell,* ed. Hugh F. Blunt. New York: Appleton-Century, 1934.

———. *Recollections of Seventy Years.* Boston: Houghton Mifflin, 1934.

———. *Reminiscences of Twenty-Five Years.* Boston: Pilot Publishing Company, 1926.

———. *Sermons and Addresses of His Eminence, William Cardinal O'Connell.* 11 vols. Boston: Pilot Publishing Company, 1911–1938.

———. *A Tribute of Affectionate Memory to Most Rev. John J. Williams.* Boston: Privately printed, 1940.

O'Connor, Edwin. *The Last Hurrah.* Boston: Little Brown, 1956.

O'Connor, Thomas H. *Bibles, Brahmins, and Bosses: A Short History of Boston.* 2nd edition. Boston: Boston Public Library, 1984.

———. *Fitzpatrick's Boston, 1846–1866: John Bernard Fitzpatrick, Third Bishop of Boston.* Boston: Northeastern University Press, 1984.

O'Leary, Robert A. "William Henry Cardinal O'Connell: A Social and Intellectual Biography." Ph.D. diss.: Tufts University, 1980.

O'Neill, Kevin. *Family and Farm in Pre-Famine Ireland: The Parish of Killashandra.* Madison: University of Wisconsin Press, 1984.

Orsi, Robert Anthony. *The Madonna of 115th Street: Faith and Community in Italian Harlem, 1880–1950.* New Haven: Yale University Press, 1985.

O'Toole, James M. *Guide to the Archives of the Archdiocese of Boston.* New York: Garland, 1982.

———. "The Name That Stood for Rome: William O'Connell and the Modern Episcopal Style." In *Patterns of Episcopal Leadership,* ed. Gerald P. Fogarty, pp. 171–184. New York: Macmillan, 1989.

———. "Prelates and Politicos: Catholics and Politics in Massachusetts, 1900–1970." In *Catholic Boston: Studies in Religion and Community, 1870–1970,* eds. Robert E. Sullivan and James M. O'Toole, pp. 15–65. Boston: Archdiocese of Boston, 1985.

——. "The Role of Bishops in American Catholic History: Myth and Reality in the Case of Cardinal William O'Connell." *Catholic Historical Review* 77 (1991):595–615.

——. "'That Fabulous Churchman': Toward a Biography of Cardinal O'Connell." *Catholic Historical Review* 70 (1984): 28–44.

Reher, Margaret M. "The Church and the Kingdom of God in America: The Ecclesiology of the Americanists." Ph.D. diss.: Fordham University, 1972.

——. "Pope Leo XIII and 'Americanism.'" *Theological Studies* 34 (1973): 679–689.

Robinson, Henry Morton. *The Cardinal.* New York: Simon and Schuster, 1950.

Russell, Francis. *A City in Terror: 1919, The Boston Police Strike.* New York: Viking, 1975.

——. "The Knave of Boston." *American Heritage* 27 (August 1976): 72–80.

——. *Tragedy in Dedham: The Story of the Sacco-Vanzetti Case.* New York: McGraw-Hill, 1962.

Sanders, James W. "Catholics and the School Question in Boston: The Cardinal O'Connell Years." In *Catholic Boston: Studies in Religion and Community, 1870–1970*, eds. Robert E. Sullivan and James M. O'Toole, pp. 121–169. Boston: Archdiocese of Boston, 1985.

Schnepp, Gerald J. *Leakage from a Catholic Parish.* Washington, D.C.: Catholic University of America Press, 1942.

Seaburg, Carl, and Alan Seaburg. *Medford on the Mystic.* Medford, Mass.: Medford Historical Society, 1980.

Sexton, John E. *Cardinal O'Connell: A Biographical Sketch.* Boston: Pilot Publishing Company, 1926.

Sexton, John E., and Arthur J. Riley. *History of Saint John's Seminary, Brighton.* Boston: Archdiocese of Boston, 1945.

Shanabruch, Charles. *Chicago's Catholics: The Evolution of an American Identity.* Notre Dame, Ind.: University of Notre Dame Press, 1981.

Shannon, William V. *The American Irish.* New York: Macmillan, 1963.

Shaughnessy, Gerald. *Has the Immigrant Kept the Faith? A Study of Immigration and Catholic Growth in the United States, 1790–1920.* New York: Macmillan, 1925.

Sherman, Richard B. "The Rejection of the Child Labor Amendment." *Mid-America* 45 (1963): 3–17.

Skerritt, Ellen. "The Development of Catholic Identity Among Irish Americans in Chicago, 1880 to 1920." In *From Paddy to Studs: Irish-American Communities in the Turn of the Century Era, 1880 to 1920*, ed. Timothy J. Meagher, pp. 117–138. New York: Greenwood, 1986.

Slawson, Douglas J. "The Attitudes and Activities of American Catholics Regarding the Proposals to Establish a Federal Department of Education Between World War I and the Great Depression." Ph.D. diss.: Catholic University of America, 1981.

Stack, John F. *International Conflict in an American City: Boston's Irish, Italians, and Jews, 1935–1944.* Westport, Conn.: Greenwood Press, 1979.

Sullivan, Robert E. "Beneficial Relations: Toward a Social History of the Diocesan Priests of Boston, 1875–1944." In *Catholic Boston: Studies in Religion and*

Community, 1870–1970, eds. Robert E. Sullivan and James M. O'Toole, pp. 201–238. Boston: Archdiocese of Boston, 1985.

Tansill, Charles C. *America and the Fight for Irish Freedom, 1866–1922*. New York: Devin-Adair, 1957.

Taves, Ann. *The Household of Faith: Roman Catholic Devotions in Mid-Nineteenth Century America*. Notre Dame, Ind.: University of Notre Dame Press, 1986.

Tharp, Louise Hall. *Mrs. Jack: A Biography of Isabella Stewart Gardner*. Boston: Little Brown, 1965.

Tomasi, Silvano. *Piety and Power: The Role of the Italian Parish in the New York Metropolitan Area, 1880–1930*. New York: Center for Migration Studies, 1975.

Tosiello, Rosario J. "'Requests I Cannot Ignore': A New Perspective on the Role of Cardinal O'Connell in the Sacco-Vanzetti Case." *Catholic Historical Review* 68 (1982): 46–53.

Trisco, Robert. "Bishops and Their Priests in the United States." In *The Catholic Priest in the United States: Historical Investigations*, ed. John Tracy Ellis, pp. 111–292. Collegeville, Minn.: Saint John's University Press, 1971.

Tull, Charles J. *Father Coughlin and the New Deal*. Syracuse: Syracuse University Press, 1965.

Twenty-Third Annual Report of the Bureau of the Statistics of Labor, March 1893. Public Document No. 15. Boston: Wright and Potter, 1893.

Van Nostrand, A. D. "The Lomasney Legend." *New England Quarterly* 21 (1948): 435–458.

Vidler, Alec R. *The Church in an Age of Revolution: 1789 to the Present Day*. New York: Penguin, 1971.

Walsh, Francis R. "The Boston *Pilot*: A Newspaper for the Irish Immigrant, 1829–1908." Ph.D. diss.: Boston University, 1968.

Walton, Susan S. "To Preserve the Faith: Catholic Charities in Boston, 1870–1930." In *Catholic Boston: Studies in Religion and Community, 1870–1970*, eds. Robert E. Sullivan and James M. O'Toole, pp. 67–119. Boston: Archdiocese of Boston, 1985.

Wangler, Thomas E. "American Catholic Expansionism, 1886–1894," *Harvard Theological Review* 75 (1982): 369–393.

———. "Catholic Religious Life in Boston in the Era of Cardinal O'Connell."In *Catholic Boston: Studies in Religion and Community, 1870–1970*, eds. Robert E. Sullivan and James M. O'Toole, pp. 239–272. Boston: Archdiocese of Boston, 1985.

Ward, Alan J. *Ireland and Anglo-American Relations, 1899–1921*. London: London School of Economics, 1969.

Warner, Sam Bass, Jr. *Streetcar Suburbs: The Process of Growth in Boston, 1870–1900*. Cambridge, Mass.: Harvard University Press, 1962.

Wayman, Dorothy G. *Cardinal O'Connell of Boston: A Biography of William Henry O'Connell, 1859–1944*. New York: Farrar, Straus and Young, 1955.

———. *David I. Walsh: Citizen Patriot*. Milwaukee: Bruce, 1952.

Weiner, J. S. *The Piltdown Forgery*. London: Oxford University Press, 1955.

White, Joseph M. *The Diocesan Seminary in the United States: A History from the 1780s to the Present*. Notre Dame, Ind.: University of Notre Dame Press, 1989.

Wiebe, Robert H. *The Search for Order, 1877–1920.* London: Macmillan, 1967.

Wister, Robert J. "The Establishment of the Apostolic Delegation in the United States of America: The Satolli Mission, 1892–1896." Ph.D. diss.: Pontifical Gregorian University, 1980.

———. "The Establishment of the Apostolic Delegation in Washington: The Pastoral and Political Motivations." *U.S. Catholic Historian* 3 (1983): 115–128.

Wolkovich-Valkavičius, William. "Cardinal and Cleric: O'Connell and Mullen in Conflict." *Historical Journal of Massachusetts* 13 (1985): 129–139.

———. *Lithuanian Fraternalism: Seventy-Five Years of the U.S. Knights of Lithuania.* Brooklyn: Knights of Lithuania, 1988.

Woodbury, Kenneth B., Jr. "An Incident Between the French Canadians and the Irish in the Diocese of Maine in 1906." *New England Quarterly* 40 (1967): 260–269.

Woods, Robert A., ed. *Americans in Process: A Settlement Study.* New York: Arno Press, 1970; reprint of 1903 edition.

Woods, Robert A., and Albert J. Kennedy. *The Zone of Emergence: Observations of the Lower Middle and Upper Working Class Communities of Boston, 1905–1914.* Abridged and edited by Sam Bass Warner, Jr. 2nd edition, Cambridge, Mass: M.I.T. Press, 1969.

Yates, JoAnne. *Control through Communication: The Rise of System in American Management.* Baltimore: Johns Hopkins University Press, 1989.

Periodicals and Newspapers

    America
    Bangor Commercial
    Bangor News
    Boston American
    Boston Evening Transcript
    Boston Globe
    Boston Herald
    Boston Journal
    Boston Pilot
    Boston Post
    Boston Record
    Boston Sunday Advertiser
    Boston Traveler
    Commonweal
    Lowell Sun
    New York American
    New York Evening Journal
    New York Herald
    New York Times
    Outlook and Independent
    Portland Eastern Argus
    Portland Express

Portland Press Herald
Portland Telegram
Saturday Evening Post
Washington Post

INDEX